MW01153298

CONTESTS AND SWEEPSTAKES LAW

A Guide Through the Legal Jungle®
Practice Manual

JOY R. BUTLER

SASHAY COMMUNICATIONS

Published by Sashay Communications, LLC
2200 Wilson Boulevard, #102-329, Arlington, VA 22201
www.sashaycommunications.com

ISBN: 978-0-9672940-6-3

Publisher's Cataloging-In-Publication Data (Prepared by The Donohue Group, Inc.)

Butler, Joy R.

Contests and sweepstakes law : a Guide Through the Legal Jungle practice manual / Joy R. Butler.

pages : charts ; cm. -- (Guide through the legal jungle)

Includes bibliographical references and index.

ISBN: 978-0-9672940-6-3

1. Contests--Law and legislation--United States--Handbooks, manuals, etc. I. Title.

KF3992 .B85 2015

344.73099

Book design and layout: Adina Cucicov, Flamingo Designs

Other Books by Joy R. Butler

*The Permission Seeker's Guide Through the Legal Jungle:
Clearing Copyrights, Trademarks and Other Rights for
Entertainment and Media Productions*

*The Cyber Citizen's Guide Through the Legal Jungle:
Internet Law for Your Professional Online Presence*

Summary Table of Contents

Table of Contents

Acknowledgments

Many thanks to Elaine Randall Butler, David J. Friedman, and Khamal Patterson for proofreading and legal editing assistance.

I also thank and acknowledge the attorneys and legal professionals who shared their experiences and insights about contests and sweepstakes. They are C. Christopher Clark, Caleb E. Jay, M. Melisse Lewis, Jeffrey C. Mooradian, Laura Possessky, and Luvie Raines.

Guidelines and Cautions for the Use of This Book

This book is designed to help you identify and resolve legal issues that arise in contests, sweepstakes, and other promotions you organize. There are certain guidelines you should keep in mind as you use this book or any other book on legal issues.

The law is fluid. Industry customs and laws change constantly. Always make sure that you are relying on the most up to date information. Unless otherwise noted, this book covers only principles of United States law. Each principle of law is subject to differing interpretations and may have numerous exceptions. As this book provides a broad overview of the law, it may not cover an interpretation or an exception that applies to your specific legal situation.

The author and the publisher have made their best efforts to ensure that the information presented in this book is as complete and as accurate as possible. However, this book is sold with the understanding that neither the author nor publisher is rendering legal services or advice.

As a result of the above, the author and the publisher cannot assume any responsibility or liability to any person or entity for any loss or damage caused, or alleged to be caused, by the information presented in this book.

PART ONE

Introduction

Part One explains how this book is organized and how it can be of greatest use. Part One includes a detailed checklist which poses a series of questions about your contest and sweepstakes activities and then refers you to subsequent sections of this Guide for more details on the legal issues relevant to your promotion.

Chapters in Part One:

1   Structure of This Guide
2   Checklist of Legal Issues for Contests and Sweepstakes

CHAPTER 1

Structure of This Guide

1.1. Who Should Read This Guide

Contests and sweepstakes are marketing promotions, typically designed to increase sales of a product or service or to increase public awareness of a cause, concept, venture, person, or organization. Fortune 500 companies, small businesses, non-profits, and a variety of other organizations and individuals use contests and sweepstakes on a regular basis. This Guide is for all groups and persons who offer promotions as well as for the attorneys, contest administrators, and other professionals who support promotion sponsors.

The sponsor of a contest or sweepstakes must comply with an assortment of federal and state laws. This Guide provides an overview of the United States federal and state laws that govern contests, sweepstakes, and other prize promotions. This Guide also includes best practice suggestions for maximizing the operational success of promotions while minimizing the risk of legal problems.

1.2. How to Use This Guide

This Guide is not a treatise or an exhaustive treatment of the laws governing promotions. Instead, it is designed to function as a practice manual for attorneys, marketing professionals, and other business people who organize and administer promotions. Readers can use the information in this Guide as a starting point for compliance research for the promotions they organize. This Guide consists of three parts:

Part One. Introduction
Part Two. Overview
Part Three. Summaries of State Laws

Part One, Introduction, provides an overview of how this Guide can be of greatest use. It includes a detailed checklist that helps readers spot legal issues and then refers them to subsequent sections of this Guide for greater explanation.

Part Two, Overview, addresses the basic legal issues one should consider when launching a promotion in the United States and discusses the most common types of promotions. Part Two speaks in general terms so the legal concepts discussed in Part Two may differ in some states.

Part Two is divided into section parts to facilitate cross-referencing. This Guide discusses many federal and state laws that are also often divided into section parts. To avoid confusion and to make the reader aware that a section reference is to a section within this Guide (*i.e.*, the Guide you are now reading), when making a cross-reference to a portion of this Guide, I indicate the cross-reference as "Section # of this Guide" or as "Chapter # of this Guide".

Part Three, Summaries of State Laws, includes a separate summary for each state and for the District of Columbia discussing the laws most relevant to contests and sweepstakes in that state. While there are federal laws relevant to promotions, the bulk of relevant law is state-based law.

This Guide also includes an appendix with states' information presented in table form and a glossary.

1.3. Approach Used by This Guide

The goal of this Guide is to make readers aware of potential promotion risks and the most likely outcomes to legal issues. Unfortunately, there is not always a definitive answer for every contests and sweepstakes legal question. Statutes are sometimes unclear in explaining intent and proper implementation.

I relied on two categories of resources in the writing of this Guide. The first category consists of legal authorities including federal and state statutes, constitutions, court opinions, and regulations, as well as opinions issued by state attorney generals. The second category consists of observations of industry practices and real-life examples.

1.3.1. Caveat Regarding Mix of Gambling and Lottery and Promotion Law

A properly formatted contest or sweepstakes may not be a gambling game or lottery. Hence, basic knowledge of gambling law is important so a sponsor can prevent a legal contest or sweepstakes from unintentionally turning into an illegal lottery or gambling game.

This Guide sometimes addresses legal questions about contests and sweepstakes by using analogous concepts from gambling cases and gambling statutes. This is not always a perfect analogy since some states laws analyze and treat differently a promotion that improperly veers into the gambling realm versus a promotion that improperly veers into the lottery realm.

This Guide discusses gambling only in the context of contests and sweepstakes (*i.e.*, avoidance of gambling). It does not offer an in-depth discussion of gambling law.

1.3.2. Caveat Regarding Value of Best Practice Suggestions

When the law is unclear, I provide possible interpretations and suggestions for best practices. A best practice is a standard technique or procedure that has proven effective for achieving a desired result. Typically, when numerous organizations adopt the same procedure with positive results, the procedure is dubbed a *best practice.*

In the realm of contests and sweepstakes, many best practices have developed because the law is ambiguous, unclear, or silent on what the legal course of action is. That means there are not always court cases, statutory laws, and other legal authorities that sanction a mode of operation that has developed into a best practice.

Hence, while adherence to industry best practices may help to minimize the risk of problems and liability, it is important to understand that employing industry best practices will not always serve as a safe harbor or defense to an action perceived by a regulator as a violation.

1.4. A Note to Legal Professionals about the Citation System Used in This Guide

This Guide aims to be a practice manual and a useful starting point for attorneys and other legal professionals who may require in-depth legal analysis of contests and sweepstakes laws. At the same time, this Guide aims to be accessible and easy to use for non-attorneys who require a more general overview and quick, practical answers to their questions.

To achieve these sometimes competing objectives, I use a modified system of legal citation. This Guide includes legal citations for all the court opinions, statutes, regulations, and other legal authorities discussed. The citation system used is designed to allow legal professionals to locate easily the cited materials without rendering this Guide unreadable for non-attorneys.

While the *Bluebook, Uniform System of Citations* is the citation system on which I rely most heavily, I do stray from exact *Bluebook* format when beneficial to that purpose. The legal citations provided usually do not include complete prior and subsequent case histories.

The citation approach used in Part Two differs from the approach used in Part Three. In Part Two, Overview, when appropriate and able to be done briefly, I include citations in the text of the discussion. I typically use in-text citations when I judge the information to be important to all readers. Otherwise, I include the citations for Part Two, Overview in the endnotes immediately following Part Two. I place the citations as endnotes when I judge the information to be most relevant to legal professionals wishing to conduct further research. In Part Three, State Summaries, the majority of—but now all—case law, statutory, and regulatory citations is included as endnotes at the end of each individual state summary.

CHAPTER 2

Checklist of Legal Issues for Contests and Sweepstakes

The following checklist includes a list of considerations as well as do's and don'ts. By necessity, the discussion within the checklist is cryptic. The checklist refers readers to subsequent sections of this Guide for greater explanation. The checklist is not an exhaustive list of every legal and practical issue that may be relevant to a promotion.

What Type of Promotion Is the Sponsor Offering?

Is the promotion a contest or a sweepstakes? Making this determination is important for structuring the promotion and avoiding offering an illegal lottery or gambling game. (Section 3.2 of this Guide) A lottery combines the three elements of chance, prize, and consideration. With few exceptions, a legal promotion may have only two of these three elements. Sweepstakes have the elements of chance and prize. (Section 3.1.2 of this Guide) Contests have the elements of prize and potentially consideration. (Section 3.1.3 of this Guide)

- **Does the promotion include the element of chance?** The promotion has the element of chance if the sponsor selects a winner randomly. (Section 3.4.1 of this Guide) The opposite of selecting a winner based on chance is selecting a winner based on skill. (Section 3.4.2 of this Guide) A promotion that includes chance typically may not charge any type of entry fee. (Section 3.5 of this Guide) A promotion that has chance and requires no consideration for entry is typically a sweepstakes. (Section 3.1.2 of this Guide)

- **Does the promotion include the elements of both chance and skill in the selection of a winner?** Some promotions include elements of both chance and skill. In such circumstances, the promotion may still qualify as a skill-based contest provided that chance is not the dominant factor or a material element in selection of the winner. (Section 3.4.3 of this Guide) There are best practices for selecting winners in a manner that maximizes a promotion being deemed a skill-based contest. (Section 3.4.2 of this Guide)

- **Does the promotion include the element of consideration?** The promotion has the element of consideration if entrants must pay money or other value in order to participate. Consideration is not limited to money. (Section 3.5.2 of this Guide)

- **Does the promotion include the element of a prize?** Most promotions do offer a prize. However, some creative sponsors with promotions combining chance and consideration may choose to eliminate the prize to avoid categorization as an illegal lottery. (Section 3.3.1 of this Guide) While it is usually obvious whether or not a promotion offers a prize, sometimes a prize takes a less obvious form such as virtual currency, a free play, or publicity. (Section 3.3.2 of this Guide)

Is the promotion a tournament? Examples of tournaments are competitions for poker, chess, and monopoly. If participants must pay any type of entry fee, the sponsor risks the tournament being classified as a gambling game or illegal lottery. (Sections 3.1 and 3.7 of this Guide)

Is the promotion a fantasy sports competition? If participants pay an entry or admission fee and chance plays any role in winning, the sponsor must determine whether these factors make the fantasy sports competition a gambling game. (Section 7.2 of this Guide)

Does the promotion sponsor invite people to submit original content (*e.g.*, best photo, essay, *etc.*)? Promotions accepting original content from entrants raise several potential issues including the following:

- **Is the promotion a contest or a sweepstakes?** Although a promotion for the best original content is typically a contest, such a promotion can also be structured as a sweepstakes—sometimes accidentally. (Section 7.1.1 of this Guide)

• **How does the sponsor intend to use the submissions?** If the sponsor wants to display, post online, publish, or otherwise use the entries, the sponsor needs permission from the entrants for such use. (Sections 7.1.3 and 8.4.1 of this Guide)

• **Do the submissions include creative content or user generated content?** If the sponsor wants to post online, display, or otherwise share the submissions, the sponsor must ensure that the entrants' submissions violate no intellectual property or other laws. (Sections 7.1.3 and 8.4 of this Guide) For some promotions, it may be an appropriate risk-minimizing technique for the sponsor to provide participants with pre-cleared materials (Section 8.6 of this Guide)

• **Are members of the public invited to vote on the submissions?** Using public voting as a method of determining the winner introduces additional complications. (Sections 3.3.1, 5.1, and 7.1.2 of this Guide)

Is the sponsor of the promotion a broadcast station? There are additional rules that radio stations and television stations offering promotions must follow. (Section 7.6 of this Guide)

Is the promotion offered online or via social media? There are a number of additional considerations for online promotions including the following:

• **Does the promotion comply with the social media networks terms of service?** If not, the sponsor risks the social media network shutting down the promotion. (Section 6.2 of this Guide)

• **Does the sponsor use email in conjunction with the promotion?** The email component must comply with the federal anti-spam law, CAN-SPAM, and with other state anti-spam legislation. (Section 6.4 of this Guide)

• **Are children under thirteen allowed to participate in the promotion?** If children participate, the sponsor must comply with the terms of the Children's Online Privacy Protection Act (COPPA) as well as state privacy laws. (Section 6.8 of this Guide)

- **Can the entry method be viewed as the participant's endorsement of the sponsor's company or products?** This is sometimes the result if entry requires "liking" or connecting to the sponsor's social media presence or posting information about the sponsor online. In such circumstances, the Federal Trade Commission's Endorsement and Testimonial Guidelines might require a disclosure. (Section 6.7 of this Guide)

Does the promotion require participants to guess something (*e.g.*, how many beans in the jar, who is behind the curtain, *etc.*)? This type of promotion is generally classified as a sweepstakes since the outcome depends on chance. (Sections 3.1.2 and 3.4.1) As with all sweepstakes, entrants cannot pay consideration to enter. (Section 3.5 of this Guide)

Is it a scratch-off or peel-and-win promotion? This type of promotion is generally classified as a sweepstakes since the outcome depends on chance. (Sections 3.1.2 and 3.4.1) As with all sweepstakes, entrants cannot pay consideration to enter. (Section 3.5 of this Guide)

Does the sponsor want to offer a raffle? Raffles are neither sweepstakes nor contests. In a traditional raffle, the raffle sponsor sells tickets and selects a winning ticket via a random drawing. Raffles have all the elements of a lottery or gambling game. Gambling, with some limited exceptions, is illegal. As one of the exceptions to gambling prohibitions, most states allow non-profit, charitable, and civic organizations to offer raffles for fundraising purposes. (Section 9.2 and Appendix A.4 of this Guide)

Does the sponsor want to offer gambling? Gambling combines consideration, chance, and reward. (Sections 3.7.1 and 3.7.2 of this Guide) Properly structured contests and sweepstakes are not gambling games. Offering gambling games is off-limits to most individuals and businesses. When legal, gambling tends to be highly regulated. As an exception to anti-gambling laws, in most states, non-profit organizations and other civic and charitable organizations are allowed to offer raffles, bingo games, and other gambling games for fundraising purposes. (Section 9.2 and Appendix A.4 and A.5 of this Guide)

How Do Participants Enter the Promotion?

Do participants pay money or other consideration to participate?
Payment or other consideration is permitted for most contests but not for sweepstakes. (Section 3.5 and Appendix A.3 of this Guide) For a promotion requiring payment to enter, in order to avoid being an illegal lottery or other gambling game, the promotion must be a contest in which the sponsor selects the winner based on an objective skill demonstrated by the entrants. (Section 3.1.3 and 3.4 of this Guide) The potential exceptions where payment and chance can legally exist in the same promotion include a promotion with no prize award and a promotion that is actually a raffle operated by a non-profit or charitable organization. (Section 9.2 of this Guide)

Do consumers automatically receive a sweepstakes entry when purchasing the sponsor's product? Contest sponsors may usually charge participants payment or other consideration for entry. Sweepstakes sponsors may not. Hence, if a sweepstakes entry comes automatically with a purchase, the sweepstakes sponsor must provide a free alternative method of entry in order to remove the element of consideration. (Section 3.6 of this Guide) Furthermore, the sweepstakes sponsor may not discriminate between those entrants who receive a chance to play with a purchase and those entrants who receive a chance to play without making a purchase. Both types of sweepstakes entrants must have an equal opportunity to win. This is sometimes referred to as the equal dignity rule. (Section 3.6.3 of this Guide)

Do participants submit original content? See response in this checklist to "Does the promotion sponsor invite people to submit original content (*e.g.*, best photo, essay, *etc.*)?".

Do participants enter through an online social media network? If yes, the sponsor must comply with the social media networks terms of service. Otherwise, the sponsor risks the social media network shutting down the promotion. (Section 6.2 of this Guide) The sponsor should weigh the advantages and disadvantages of offering the promotion on its own website versus a third-party social media network. (Section 6.1 of this Guide)

Winner Selection, Notification, and Validation

Is the winner selected based on a random drawing or other selection process based on chance or luck? In order to avoid being an illegal lottery, participants in a chance-based promotion must not pay money or other consideration to participate. The potential exceptions are if the promotion awards no prize or the promotion is actually a raffle operated by a non-profit or charitable organization (Section 9.2 of this Guide).

Is the potential winner unavailable or uncooperative? Ideally, the promotion rules allow the sponsor to justify the selection of an alternate winner if the initially selected winner is unavailable or uncooperative. (Section 5.2.3 of this Guide)

Are there more sweepstakes winners than the sponsor anticipated? This can happen as the result of a printing error or other mistake. Hopefully, the promotion rules include a Kraft clause that provides the sweepstakes sponsor with an easy-to-implement remedy for such an error. (Section 4.4.7 of this Guide)

What Is the Prize?

Does the sponsor hope to eliminate the prize to avoid an illegal lottery? A lottery combines chance, prize, and consideration, so legal promotions can have only two of these three elements. While most sponsors eliminate either chance or consideration, a few may attempt to eliminate prize. A prize can take various forms. (Section 3.3.2 of this Guide)

Is the prize an expensive item such as a car or a large sum of cash? Sponsors should consider the tax implications on the winner prior to selecting expensive items as prizes. (Sections 5.3.3 and 5.4 of this Guide)

Is the prize a brand-name product? The sponsor can mention the brand name to describe the prize award. The sponsor may want to provide a disclaimer in its advertising and official rules so consumers do not mistakenly believe that the product manufacturer endorses or is affiliated with the promotion. (Section 8.2.2 of this Guide)

Is the prize travel? The sponsor should consider restrictions for travel awarded as a prize. (Section 5.3.4 of this Guide)

If the prize is cash, does the cash include money collected from entrants? The value of a contest prize can not be completely dependent on the amount of money collected from the entrants. In virtually all states, the collection of such a pot for payment to the winning entrant violates state gambling laws. (Section 5.3.1 of this Guide) The common exception is a 50/50 charity raffle which is actually neither a contest nor a sweepstakes but an exception to the anti-gambling laws.

Is the prize a home or other real estate? Offering real estate in a sweepstakes requiring no consideration for participation presents similar tax challenges as offering other expensive sweepstakes prizes. (Section 5.3.3 and 5.4) However, many sponsors with real property to offer want to use the promotion to raise funds—often to pay off debt the sponsor owes on the property. Achieving that objective means charging a monetary entry fee. Hence, the sponsor can achieve the objective only as a skill-based contest or as a non-profit raffle. There are several obstacles to both approaches. (Section 7.3 of this Guide)

What Are the Procedures for Promotion Administration?

Must the sponsor register the promotion? Some states have registration and/or bonding requirements for promotions. The specific requirements often depend upon whether the promotion is a contest or a sweepstakes. (Section 4.1, Appendix A.1, and individual state summaries of this Guide)

Must the sponsor have and publish official rules for the promotion? In some circumstances, yes, a sponsor must have rules and make them publicly available. (Section 4.2 of this Guide) Those circumstances include a promotion in which the sponsor uses direct mail (Section 7.4 of this Guide) or the sponsor is a broadcast station (Section 7.6.1 of this Guide). Otherwise, having published official rules may not be a requirement. Nevertheless, having written promotion rules is always a highly recommended best practice.

Does the sponsor plan to use direct mail? When using direct mail, the sponsor must comply with the federal Deceptive Mail Prevention and Enforcement Act as well as parallel state prize promotion laws. These laws mandate certain disclosures and prohibit certain misleading business practices. (Section 7.4 of this Guide)

Does the sponsor plan to use telemarketing, text messaging, or faxes in conjunction with the promotion? There are restrictions on unsolicited calls to mobile phones, text messages, and faxes. The sponsor must comply with the Telephone Communications Protection Act, the Telemarketing and Consumer Fraud and Abuse Prevention Act, their corresponding regulations, and parallel state laws. (Section 7.5 of this Guide)

Has the sponsor selected a potential winner? The sponsor may want the potential winner to sign certain releases and affidavits prior to confirming the prize award. (Section 5.2.2 of this Guide) Contest and sweepstakes prizes are taxable so there may be tax reporting obligations the sponsor needs to fulfill. (Section 5.4 of this Guide)

Is the promotion a collaboration between for-profit and non-profit organizations or is it advertised as benefitting a charitable cause or organization? State charity collaboration laws might apply. (Section 9.1 of this Guide)

PART TWO

Overview

Part Two addresses the basic legal issues one should consider when launching a promotion in the United States and discusses the most common types of promotions.

Chapters in Part Two:

CHAPTER 3

Deciding on a Contest or a Sweepstakes

3.1. Lottery Versus Sweepstakes Versus Contest

While some people may use the terms interchangeably, there are distinctions among a lottery, a sweepstakes, and a contest.

3.1.1. A Lottery Combines Prize, Consideration, and Chance

A lottery is one form of gambling and, like all forms of gambling, is typically illegal when offered by a person or organization other than the federal or state government. Consideration, chance, and prize are the three elements that combine to form a lottery. I discuss these three elements in great detail throughout this Guide. Here are initial definitions for each of these elements within the context of promotions law:

- Consideration is money or an item of value paid by a person for the opportunity to compete for a prize. In the context of gambling, consideration is sometimes alternatively referred to as a payment, stake, bet, or wager.
- Chance is the process of awarding the prize by a random drawing or other form of random selection. In the context of gambling, the element of chance is sometimes alternatively referred to as luck.
- A prize is something of value awarded to the winning entrant in a lottery, gambling game, contest, or sweepstakes. In the context of gambling, a prize is sometimes alternatively referred to as a reward.

If a sponsor sells (*i.e.*, if the sponsor accepts payment or other form of consideration) opportunities to win a prize where winning the prize is based on chance, the sponsor is offering a promotion with a prize, consideration, and chance, and the sponsor's promotion is actually a lottery. Contests and sweepstakes also have the elements of prize, consideration, and chance. What prevents contests and sweepstakes from being an illegal lottery or illegal gambling game is that a legal contest or a legal sweepstakes has only one or two of these elements—rather than all three.

3.1.2. A Promotion that Awards a Prize Based on Chance Is a Sweepstakes

A sweepstakes is a promotion in which the sponsor awards a prize based on chance or other random selection process. Since a sweepstakes has the elements of prize and chance, to avoid classification of the sweepstakes as an illegal lottery or gambling game, the sponsor must eliminate the element of consideration. As a result, entrants in a legally structured sweepstakes do not pay consideration in order to participate.

3.1.3. A Promotion that Awards a Prize Based on Skill Is a Contest

A contest is a promotion in which the sponsor awards a prize based on a skill demonstrated by the entrants. In a contest, chance does not determine the winner of the prize. While it is possible for a skill-based contest to include some components of chance, chance cannot be a material component or the dominant component determining the contest's outcome. Section 3.4.3 of this Guide includes more discussion on promotions combining both chance and skill.

Since a contest has the element of a prize but not the element of chance, adding consideration places only two of the three lottery elements into the promotion. Hence, the contest sponsor usually has the choice of whether or not to charge entrants a fee or other consideration for participation in the contest. Some contest sponsors charge consideration. Some do not. A few states prohibit or limit the ability of contest sponsors to charge consideration.

3.2. Why Is the Contest/Sweepstakes Distinction Important?

The company or individual offering a simple promotion may question the necessity of knowing whether the promotion is a contest or a sweepstakes. There are a few reasons why the cautious sponsor wants to understand clearly the type of promotion being offered.

3.2.1. Registration, Bonding, and Disclosure Requirements

The federal government and some states have registration, bonding, and/or disclosure requirements for promotions. The specific requirements often depend upon whether the promotion is a contest or a sweepstakes. I discuss many of those requirements in the individual state summaries located in Part Three of this Guide. I also discuss federal and state disclosure requirements mandated for promotions using direct mail or telemarketing in Sections 7.4 and 7.5 of this Guide.

3.2.2. Avoidance of Illegal Lottery

A promoter must identify its promotion as a contest or sweepstakes in order to avoid offering an illegal lottery. Many laws relevant to contests and sweepstakes focus on preventing the promotion from being an illegal lottery. A lottery combines the elements of prize, consideration, and chance. Most states accept the viewpoint that no lottery exists if the promotion lacks one of the three elements of prize, consideration, and chance.

Hence, to avoid classification as an illegal lottery, a promotion operated by an organization or individual may include only two of the three elements of prize, consideration, and chance. The exception is a non-profit or other charitable organization operating a raffle or gambling game under an exception to a state's anti-gambling laws. I discuss these exceptions further in Section 9.2 of this Guide and in the state summaries in Part Three of this Guide.

When offering a sweepstakes, the sponsor eliminates consideration. When offering a contest, the sponsor eliminates chance. Occasionally, there are hybrid promotions in which the sponsor eliminates the prize. To determine which element must be eliminated, it is crucial to know whether the promotion is a contest or a sweepstakes.

3.2.3. Avoidance of Illegal Gambling

A sponsor must identify its promotion as a contest or sweepstakes in order to avoid offering gambling. Each state has its own statutory definition of gambling. One definition describes gambling as the combination of consideration, chance, and reward. These gambling elements are sometimes alternatively expressed as payment, luck, and prize. They are parallel to the consideration, chance, and prize elements comprising a lottery. As briefly discussed in Section 3.7.2 of this Guide, some states require all the elements for a finding of gambling while other states do not require chance or luck for a finding of gambling.

3.3. Does the Promotion Offer a Prize?

People are much more motivated to enter a promotion that offers an opportunity to win a prize. As a result, sponsors typically do not omit the prize from promotions. Instead, sponsors attempt to offer a promotion that eliminates either consideration or chance.

3.3.1. When Offering a Prize Is a Problem

Prizes are permissible in contests and sweepstakes. However, offering a prize in a promotion can become a concern in a few situations:

The Promotion Already Has Consideration and Chance. If the promotion already has both elements of consideration and chance, offering a prize makes the promotion a lottery.

The Promotion Is in Danger of Being Gambling. As discussed in Section 3.7.2 of this Guide, some states deem some games as gambling even if the game has only consideration and a prize with no element of chance (or luck). Hence, if the promotion includes consideration and has a structure leaning towards gambling, offering a prize (a necessary component for a finding of gambling) is problematic.

The Promotion Uses Public Voting to Select Winners. The prize or no-prize question may also become relevant in contests that invite entrants to submit original works and use public voting to select the winning entries. In some circumstances, such a promotion arguably already has both elements of consideration and chance. If that is true, offering a prize makes the promotion a lottery.

Imagine a contest in which the sponsor invites entrants to submit an original video featuring the attributes of the sponsor's product with the best video to be selected based on public voting. As discussed further in Section 7.1.2 of this Guide, public voting places doubt on whether the contest winner wins based on chance or based on skill. Depending on the sponsor's intended use of the winning submissions, the submission itself might qualify as consideration. In such a promotion which at least arguably has both consideration and chance, the sponsor does need to be concerned about the existence of a prize.

3.3.2. What Qualifies as a Prize?

While the existence or absence of chance and consideration in a promotion frequently triggers disagreement, disagreement regarding whether a promotion offers a prize is more uncommon. It is usually obvious whether a promotion offers a prize. However, there are circumstances in which the existence or absence of a prize may be unclear.

Credits or Qualifying Points Might Be a Prize. If winners receive credits or qualifying points that they can trade in for something of value, those credits or qualifying points might qualify as a prize.

For example, participants in an Arkansas poker tournament paid a fifty dollar entrance fee. The tournament sponsor awarded no cash or prizes; however, the top eight tournament performers received qualifying points entitling them to play in an additional series of tournaments. The ultimate winners of the final tournaments received an all-expense paid opportunity to participate in a major poker tournament held outside of Arkansas. Since only some of the tournament competitors received points qualifying them to continue to compete, the Arkansas Attorney General found the qualifying points to be a prize. (Ark. Att'y Gen. Op. No. 2005-034 (March 9, 2005)).

Does Exposure Qualify as a Prize? Some promotions give the winner exposure or publicity. For example, a magazine promoting an essay contest might publish the winning entries. A promotion seeking the entrepreneur with the best business pitch might allow the winning entrepreneur to present her winning pitch at a major industry trade conference. One of my favorite exposure-type prizes is a local or national television news program offering an on-air shout-out to the first person to respond correctly to a trivia question.

If one normally pays for the type of exposure awarded to the winner, such exposure might qualify as a prize. For example, if the winning entrepreneur in the pitch-it contest receives a booth on the exhibit floor of the industry trade conference and the booth is an item that normally requires payment, the booth might be considered a prize.

Virtual Currency or Goods Might Qualify as a Prize. Virtual goods and currency might qualify as a prize. One encounters virtual goods and currency online as part of social networks, online game environments, and other internet communities. Virtual goods are images of objects used to enhance those online communities. A virtual good might or might not have a real-life counterpart. Participants in these online communities might purchase the virtual goods with real currency or with virtual currency. For example, one might purchase a virtual plow for Zynga's social network game, Farmville, using Farmville coins, a currency used within the Farmville game. When participating in Second Life, an online virtual world, one might buy a virtual house using Linden dollars, the currency used within Second Life.

When a sponsor awards virtual currency to winners, that virtual currency qualifies as a prize if recipients can exchange the virtual currency for real money or for something of value. Even if the winner can use the virtual currency only to purchase virtual goods within the origin community, the award of virtual currency might still qualify as something of value and, thus, as a prize. Virtual currency might also qualify as consideration or as a gambling wager if entrants can use the virtual currency to participate in a game or promotion that awards a prize based on chance.

There is increased risk of virtual currency representing a prize if recipients can exchange or use the virtual currency outside the origin community. A social network or game environment can restrict the use of virtual currency outside of the online community through their terms of service and end user license agreements. However, even when there are prohibitions on use outside the origin community, holders of the virtual currency might develop unofficial secondary exchanges not authorized by the social network or game developer.

Research for this Guide uncovered no authority for what impact an unofficial exchange would have on a court's view of whether the social network's virtual currency qualifies as a prize. As a best practice, a social network that offers promotions and wants to avoid such a view should not encourage or facilitate secondary exchanges and should, in fact, take active steps to discourage secondary exchange activity.

Free Plays Might Qualify as a Prize. If a game or promotion awards the opportunity to extend play or for a free chance to play, the free play might qualify as a prize. There is significant variation in the treatment of free plays from state to state.

3.4. Contest Sponsors Select Winners Based on Skill; Not on Chance

Since a promotion may not have all three elements of chance, prize, and consideration, a contest sponsor that charges consideration for entry must select winners based on skill. Selecting a winner based on skill is the opposite of selecting a winner based on chance.

3.4.1. What Qualifies as a Chance-Based Promotion?

Selecting a winner by chance means selecting the winner randomly. In a chance promotion, the participants' actions do not determine the outcome. Instead, circumstances determine the outcome. A participant has little or no control over whether he wins or loses a promotion that employs chance.

The substance of the promotion does not matter. What matters is the selection method. If an organization such as a school sells tickets for participation in a basketball shooting contest and awards a prize by randomly selecting one of those tickets, the school is conducting a chance-based promotion because the winner depends on chance (*i.e.*, random selection). In this case, the promotion is a lottery because consideration and a prize are also present. In contrast, if the school awards a prize to the best shooter, the promotion is a legitimate contest because the outcome of the competition depends on the participants' skill at shooting baskets and not on chance. (Ala. Att'y Gen. Op. No. 89-00168 (Feb. 10, 1989)).

Random Selection or Random Drawing. Random selection is the most obvious form of chance. For example, if the sponsor selects the winner by drawing a name from a hat or a bowl, the sponsor selects the winner by chance.

Guessing. If participants must guess something (*e.g.*, how many beans in the jar, who is behind the curtain, *etc.*), the promotion is generally classified as a chance-based promotion.

Limited Time. Placing a limitation on time to enter or respond can make the promotion a chance-based promotion. Potential examples of such promotions include "first ten to call" or "first fifty to arrive" or "first 100 to respond online".

Prizes Available While Supplies Last. Offering prizes only until supplies last can place some time limitations on responding. This might inject chance into the promotion especially if the amount of the supply does not match reasonable expectations for demand.

Lack of Specific Judging Criteria. Sometimes sponsors trying to structure a contest do not establish objective criteria for awarding the prize and, as a result, inadvertently implement a chance-based promotion. Section 3.4.2 of this Guide outlines guidelines and best practices for selecting winners in a manner that maximizes a promotion being deemed a skill-based contest.

Selection by Public Voting. As discussed in Section 7.1.2 of this Guide, public voting can inject an element of chance into a promotion.

Chance as Part of a Giveaway Promotion. A promotion that awards a prize to everyone who participates or takes a specific action is normally not viewed as incorporating chance. As discussed in Section 7.4.2 of this Guide, this is how many promotional giveaways operate. For example, a car dealer might award a prize or gift to every consumer who test drives one of its vehicles during the month of January. However, a giveaway might still be viewed as having chance if chance determines which of several potential prizes the consumer receives.

3.4.2. What Qualifies as a Skill-Based Promotion?

The opposite to selecting a winner based on chance is selecting the winner based on a skill the participant demonstrates or uses. In a skill-based promotion, winning is based on factors over which the participant has some control and each participant exercises some influence over whether he wins or loses. For example, a skill-based promotion might test the entrants' scope of knowledge, dancing ability, or video production ability.

Some promotions combine chance and skill for determining the winner. As discussed in Section 3.4.3 of this Guide, in those circumstances where the promotion includes elements of both chance and skill, the law evaluates whether chance or skill is the prevailing factor.

Best Practices for Skill-Based Contests. Here are general guidelines and best practices for selecting winners in a manner that maximizes a promotion being deemed a skill-based contest:

Establish Specific Judging Criteria and Share Those Criteria with Entrants. The language used to advertise the promotion should sufficiently inform the participants of the objective criteria used to select the winners. For example, an essay contest might select a winner based on originality of the essay, the entrant's adherence to submission guidelines, and overall appeal of the essay.

A mistake that contest sponsors sometimes make is not having or not announcing the standards for selecting winners. In a worst-case scenario, omitting specific judging criteria can result in a court or state attorney general re-classifying the skill-based promotion as a chance-based promotion. If the promotion also has the element of consideration, the chance re-classification makes the promotion an illegal lottery and/or illegal gambling activity.

Select Qualified Judges and Share the Judges' Qualifications. Contest judges should be qualified to evaluate the submissions on the stated objective criteria. While the sponsor does not necessarily need to identify the judges by name, the better practice is to describe why the selected judges are qualified to judge the particular contest. For example, judges for a humor contest offered by a newspaper included a national social critic who contributed to a popular late night television show, a prize-winning journalist who authored a newspaper humor column and a syndicated comic strip, and a professional stand-up comedian-writer with several television appearance credits.

The level of detail provided in that sample newspaper humor contest is not always necessary. The sponsor might choose to provide less detail if the sponsor wants to preserve more flexibility to appoint an alternative judge in the event one of the original judges becomes unavailable.

If it is clear that the person designated as a judge works with and evaluates material similar to the contest submissions, that person makes a qualified judge. For example, few would disagree that the editors of *Smithsonian Magazine* are qualified to judge the best photographs entered in *Smithsonian Magazine*'s Annual Photo Contest.

Apply the Stated Judging Criteria to Winner Selection. Sponsors must actually use the stated standards to determine the outcome. Not doing so invites entrant complaints of sponsor fraud. It also may result in negative publicity for the sponsor which defeats the positive-image-building purpose of offering a promotional contest.

Do Not Use Chance to Break a Tie. The contest rules should state how the sponsor will break a tie. The contest sponsor cannot settle ties based on chance. For example, if two contestants receive the same score based on the objective criteria, the sponsor can not select the ultimate winner through a random drawing. The ultimate winner needs to be based on criteria that evaluate skill. Section 4.4.5 of this Guide includes sample language for a tie breaker.

3.4.3. Determining whether Chance or Skill Prevails

In some promotions, winning may be based on a combination of skill and chance. In those cases, how does one determine whether the promotion is chance-based or skill-based? The approach is state specific. Most states apply the dominant factor doctrine or the material element test.

In this Section 3.4.3 of the Guide, I describe generally methods of weighing chance against skill for determining whether a promotion is chance-based or skill-based. In the state summaries in Part Three of this Guide, I discuss the approach used by each state.

Dominant Factor Doctrine. Under the dominant factor doctrine, a promotion is a chance-based promotion if chance dominates the selection of the winner, even though skill or judgment may impact winner selection to some degree. Most states have adopted this approach so the dominant factor doctrine is sometimes referred to as the American rule.

Applying the dominant factor doctrine, the Colorado Attorney General concluded that "slot machines are lotteries because chance clearly dominates; blackjack is probably a lottery because chance plays a large part but some skill is necessary; and poker is probably not a lottery because skill plays a larger, perhaps dominant role." (Co. Att'y Gen. Op. No. 93-5 (Apr. 21, 1993)).

Material Element Test. Under the material element test, a promotion is a chance-based promotion if chance is a material element in the selection of a winner—even if chance is not the dominant factor. Since chance need be only material and not dominant, it is easier for a promotion to qualify as a chance-based promotion under the material element test than under the dominant factor doctrine.

Applying the material element test, a New Jersey court held that the game of backgammon is a contest of chance and gambling game under New Jersey law. The court recognized that backgammon does include the component of skill. In a high level backgammon game, the players can influence the outcome by using mathematical and statistical strategies. However, the court also found that backgammon includes a material element of chance. Rolling the dice at the beginning of the game and prior to each player's turn imposes a material element of chance. Therefore, a backgammon tournament that also included an entry fee and monetary prize award was gambling under New Jersey law. (*Boardwalk Regency v. Att'y Gen. of NJ*, 457 A.2d 847 (N.J. Super. Ct. 1982)).

Any Chance Test. Under the any chance test doctrine, a promotion is a chance-based promotion if any element of chance influences the outcome—even if chance is neither a dominant factor nor a material element in determining the winner.

Pure Chance Test. Under the pure chance test, a promotion is a chance-based promotion when the participants' skill has no impact in the determination of the winner. Hence, a promotion requiring only a small amount of skill is not classified as a chance-based promotion. United States courts have consistently rejected the pure chance test.[1]

3.5. Sweepstakes Sponsors Must Not Charge Consideration

A sweepstakes is a promotion awarding prizes based on chance. Since two of the three lottery elements exist in a sweepstakes—chance and prize, a sweepstakes may not incorporate the third lottery element of consideration. Skill-based contests generally do not have this limitation on consideration, although some states do prohibit or restrict the ability of contest sponsors to charge consideration.

3.5.1. Understanding Consideration

Separate Consideration Questions. The concept of consideration injects itself into promotion law in at least two distinct ways. First, there is the question of whether a promotion includes the element of consideration (*i.e.*, do participants pay to compete for the prize), which is one of the three elements required for a lottery. This lottery consideration question, which is the focus of this Section 3.5.1, becomes important when determining whether a contest or a sweepstakes is actually a lottery or gambling game.

In a second context, we refer to consideration when determining whether the promotion rules form a binding contract between promoter and participant. As discussed in Section 4.3.1 of this Guide, every valid contract requires consideration. Sometimes promotion law presents the question of whether a participant's compliance with the promotion rules is sufficient consideration to result in the formation of a binding, enforceable contract between the participant and the sponsor. This contract consideration question becomes important when a participant wants to sue the promoter for breach of contract, or when, alternatively, the promoter wants to sue a participant.

Consideration for Participation in a Promotion. In the context of promotions and a lottery, consideration means that the promotion participant gives something of value or at least inconveniences himself in a manner that benefits the sponsor. The reason the participant gives something of value or inconveniences himself is so he can have an opportunity to win the prize offered in the promotion. In the broader context of gambling, this consideration or payment component may go by the name of bet, wager, or stake.

3.5.2. What Qualifies as Consideration?

While consideration can certainly be money, consideration is not limited to money. Anything that someone values can potentially qualify as consideration. In fact, many states define consideration as *something of value* in their anti-gambling statutes. While most states require that the something of value be something of *marketable* value, a minority of states find consideration simply if the sponsor benefits in some manner from the participant's actions. For example, as discussed in the Michigan state summary in Part Three of this Guide, Michigan case law indicates that there is consideration if the promotion encourages participants to take an action benefiting the promoter that the participant takes only for the purpose of participating in the promotion.

Effort Might Qualify as Consideration. If the participant must expend significant effort to enter the promotion, that effort might qualify as consideration. In contrast, activities that require minimal effort on the part of the promotion participant do not qualify as consideration. Several states identify the following specific activities as not rising to the level of consideration when required of a promotion participant:

- completing an entry form
- returning an entry form by regular mail
- watching television or broadcast program
- completing a survey
- visiting a store
- making a telephone call (as long as the number is not a pay-per-call number)

Section 6.3.1 of this Guide offers a discussion of what qualifies as consideration in an online promotion.

Despite this list of safe activities, the sponsor should be careful not to overreach. If a sponsor requires too much effort for these sanctioned activities, a state might conclude that the sponsor's increased requirements turned the sanctioned activity into a form of consideration. For example, even though requiring a person to watch a single episode of one television program is not consideration, requiring a person to watch every episode in a program's full season might be deemed as sufficient effort to amount to consideration.

Here is a real-life example of effort being deemed as consideration:

Seattle Times Co v. Tielsch, 495 P.2d 1366 (Wash. 1972). There was consideration when contest entrants were required to spend hours following a football forecasting promotion. A Seattle-based newspaper offered the "Guest-Guesser" football forecasting contest. During nine consecutive weeks in the fall, the newspaper included a list of twenty football games to be played during the weekend.

The rules indicated that no purchase was necessary; however, participants did need to obtain a copy of the newspaper. Participants could select their forecasts by completing a form published in the newspaper. Hand-made duplicates of the form were accepted but mechanical duplicates were not.

It was a multiple-round contest that required many hours of a participant's time throughout the entire nine-week promotion period in order to compete for many of the top prizes. Prizes included $1,000 for the contestant who submitted twenty correct predictions in a single qualifying week, $100 for each week's high scorer, and a chance to compete for a trip to the Super Bowl or Rose Bowl for those contestants with the best and second-best scores during the qualifying weeks. Some contestants spent fifteen to twenty hours per week preparing their entries and submitted as many as twenty-five entries per week.

The court concluded that the contest had consideration since participation required so much time of entrants and the sponsor benefited from that expenditure of time.

Participant's Submission of Original Content Might Qualify as Consideration. Sponsors often invite entrants to submit original content. Whether or not the submission qualifies as consideration depends on the type of content the entrant submits, the amount of effort the entrant expends in creating that content, the rights the sponsor will acquire in the content, and the way in which the sponsor will use the content.

If the submission qualifies as consideration and the promotion also includes the element of chance, structuring the promotion as a legal contest or sweepstakes can be a challenge. Structuring promotions to take original or user-generated content is discussed more in Section 7.1.1 of this Guide.

Submission of Entries via Pay-Per-Call Number or Text Messaging Might Qualify as Consideration. A promotion in which participants enter via a pay-per-call number (*e.g.*, a 900 telephone number) or via text message might qualify as a promotion with consideration. Even when there is a free alternative method of entry, sponsors should use caution when establishing sweepstakes with submissions by text messaging or pay-per-call number. Section 3.6 of this Guide includes a discussion of free alternative methods of entry.

A well publicized example of problems created by 900 number and text messaging submission is the call-in giveaways offered as part of the television programs *American Idol, Deal or No Deal, 1 vs 100,* and *The Apprentice.* Each of these four programs is a reality television competition or game show. During each program, at-home viewers competed for a prize by responding to a trivia question or by guessing which televised contestant would make it to the next round. At-home viewers with correct answers were entered into a random drawing for a prize.

Viewers submitted their answers via text messaging or via a designated website. There was no charge for submission by the website other than the fees already paid by the entrant for internet access. However, submission by text messaging generated a ninety-nine cent fee plus standard text messaging fees charged by the entrant's wireless carrier.

Individuals who played these call-in giveaways filed class action lawsuits against the shows' producers. The participants argued that the ninety-nine cent text-messaging fee qualified as consideration which made the promotion an illegal lottery. There was no dispute that the promotion contained the other lottery elements of prize and chance. Finding that viewers who sent in text messages paid only for the privilege of entering the promotions and received nothing of equivalent economic value in return, a California court concluded that the text messaging fee could be consideration. As a result, the court refused to dismiss the case in favor of the shows' producers and allowed the case to go to trial.[2]

The parties did eventually settle the California lawsuit without a trial. A similar lawsuit in Georgia was dismissed in favor of the shows' producers without addressing the validity of the alternative method of entry.[3]

Restricting Entry to Paying Customers Qualifies as Consideration. Typically, if a promotion entry comes automatically with a purchase, the sponsor who wants its promotion to qualify as a sweepstakes must provide a free alternative method of entry in order to remove the element of consideration. Section 3.6 of this Guide includes a discussion of free alternative methods of entry.

In one real-life example, the Tennessee Attorney General indicated that a cash or prize giveaway restricted to purchasers of a calendar sold by an organization would likely be an unlawful lottery because the give-away would have consideration. To transform it into a legal sweepstakes, the organization would need to give persons who had not purchased a calendar an opportunity to win. (Tenn. Att'y Gen. Op. No. 89-71 (May 3, 1989)).

Restricting Entry to Members, Attendees, or Past Customers Might Qualify as Consideration. A promotion open only to paying members, event attendees, or past customers might qualify as a promotion charging consideration. Viewpoints vary among the states.

In one California case, the court found there was no consideration as a result of restricting a promotion to customers as long as being a past customer was the only eligibility requirement, the sponsor did not send out invitations using the customer-only sweepstakes to motivate the recipients to become customers, and the sponsor did not promise a customer-only sweepstakes at the time of purchase. (*Haskell v. Time, Inc.* 965 F. Supp. 1398, 1405-1406 (E.D. Cal. 1997))

In contrast, Arkansas found consideration in a club bingo game that was open only to club members and their guests. Club membership required payment of an admission fee so, according to Arkansas, restricting the bingo game to paying club members functioned as charging consideration for the bingo game. (Ark. Op. Att'y Gen. Op. 99-318 (Dec. 9, 1999)). As another example, a pari-mutuel track located in Oklahoma wanted to operate a promotion in which only those who paid the tracks admission fee could participate. The Oklahoma Attorney General concluded that the track admission fee was consideration for participating in the promotion. (Okla. Att'y Gen. Op. (Feb. 25, 1992))

Best Practices when Restricting Promotion Participation to Customers, Members, and Event Attendees:

- If the promotion is a sweepstakes, do not feature the sweepstakes as a major attraction for the event or as a reward for patronizing the sponsor's company.
- Opt to do the promotion as a skill-based contest. As discussed in Section 3.1.3 of this Guide, skill-based contests may have consideration.
- Offer a free alternative method of entry. Sponsors that want to operate promotions at events to increase attendance can bypass the consideration issue by also offering non-attendees a chance to compete for the prize. This mechanism operates similarly to the alternative methods of entry discussed in Section 3.6 of this Guide. For example, a trade association that wants to offer a drawing from its booth and wants to promote its drawing prior to the trade show might allow non-attendees to enter via the internet during the duration of the trade show.

Requiring Too Much Personal Information for Entry Might Qualify as Consideration. While asking participants to provide basic information or respond to a short survey might not qualify as consideration, requiring too much personal information for entry might qualify as consideration.

Requiring Specialized Software to Access an Online Promotion Might Qualify as Consideration. For an online promotion, requiring specialized software to access an online promotion might qualify as consideration.

Requiring Testing of Product, Making Multiple Trips to a Store, or Listening to a Sales Presentation Might Qualify as Consideration. Some prize notice laws specifically address and regulate any promotions offered as an incentive for consumers to attend a sales presentation or accept a telemarketing call. I discuss state prize notice laws and state telemarketing laws in Sections 7.4.2 and 7.5.2 of this Guide and in the individual state summaries in Part Three of this Guide.

3.6. Free Alternative Method of Entry for Sweepstakes

Most of us have at one time or another purchased a product that came with a sweepstakes-playing opportunity. The product might have been a bottle of soda, a fast-food meal, or a box of cereal. Sweepstakes winning opportunities that come with the purchase of a product are sometimes referred to as an in-package sweepstakes.

So what happens when one gets a sweepstakes-playing opportunity with the purchase of a product? As discussed in Sections 3.1.2 and 3.5 of this Guide, sweepstakes include the elements of prize and chance but may not have the element of consideration without being deemed an illegal lottery. Is the purchase price paid for the product viewed as payment for participation in the sweepstakes so that instead of a legal sweepstakes the promotion is an illegal lottery?

The answer is no, provided that the sweepstakes sponsor properly structures the sweepstakes. Payment for a product that includes a sweepstakes-playing opportunity is permissible as long as the customer pays to obtain the product and not solely for the opportunity to enter the sweepstakes.

Compliance with federal and state laws requires the sweepstakes sponsor to offer an opportunity to play to people who do not purchase the sponsor's product. This offer to non-purchasers is called a free alternative method of entry. It might also be called an alternate means of entry, or be abbreviated as AMOE. An AMOE might take any one of several forms including the following:

- inviting interested people to request a free play opportunity by mail
- inviting interested people to enter via the internet
- distributing free play opportunities at a retail store

3.6.1. Failure of Alternative Method of Entry

Offering an AMOE does not guarantee elimination of improper consideration. If not implemented properly, the free AMOE may be invalid. Actions that invalidate an AMOE include presenting too many barriers to using it and failing to alert participants to its availability.

Real-Life Examples in which the AMOE Failed

Sweepstakes Sponsor Offers Illusory AMOE. A news magazine with a one dollar purchase price contained entries for the Daily Devil, a promotion based on the numbers drawn in the Illinois State Lottery. Although the entry form stated "No Purchase Necessary. Free entry blanks can be obtained at the office of the publisher. No charge or obligation.", there were several obstacles confronting consumers who wanted the AMOE:

- Consumers wanting the AMOE could not request the forms by mail but had to pick them up in person.
- The entry form did not include the publisher's address and the publisher had an unlisted phone number.
- The office of the publisher was the residential apartment address of the news magazine owner and was not staffed.

As a result, the publisher had given away only two or three entry forms at the time the court evaluated the AMOE. Under those circumstances, the Illinois court deemed the AMOE to be illusory and invalid. (*G.A. Carney, Ltd. v. Brzeczek*, 453 N.E.2d 756, 757-758 (Ill. App. Ct. 1983)).

New York Enforcement Action against Tylenol. The manufacturer of Tylenol offered a sweepstakes entitled Survivor All-Stars—Tylenol Push Through the Pain Game. The New York Attorney General brought an enforcement action against the manufacturer for overemphasizing the purchase-based method of playing the sweepstakes and deemphasizing the free AMOE. The print ad copy listed four steps for entering the sweepstakes. "Buy Tylenol" was the first step. The no purchase option appeared in fine print at the bottom of the advertisement.

The attorney general concluded that the prominence of the Buy Tylenol message made the free AMOE less available to customers. The attorney general was also concerned by the fact that eighty-four percent of the sweepstakes participants played via the purchase option. (Press Release, N.Y. Att'y Gen., Tylenol Manufacturer to Amend Sweepstakes Ads (Sept. 10, 2004), http://www.ag.ny.gov/press-release/tylenol-manu-facturer-amend-sweepstakes-ads (last visited Nov. 9, 2014)).

New York Enforcement Action against CVS. For its Trip of a Lifetime Sweepstakes offered throughout its 400 stores in New York, CVS automatically entered consumers into the sweepstakes when the consumer purchased certain products with a CVS ExtraCare card. While there was a free AMOE, the AMOE was available only on the company's website. As part of the settlement of the New York enforcement action, CVS agreed to make free entry forms available in the store, conspicuously post contest rules within participating stores, ensure store staff could direct consumers to no purchase options, and feature no-purchase play options as prominently as purchase play options in sweepstakes advertisements. (Press Release, N.Y. Att'y Gen., CVS to Amend Sweepstakes Promotions (July 8, 2004), http://www.ag.ny.gov/press-release/cvs-amend-sweepstakes-promotions (last visited Nov. 9, 2014)).

3.6.2. Incidental or Non-Existent Product Purchase

For sweepstakes that come with the purchase of a product or in-package sweepstakes, the sweepstakes must be a promotional vehicle to sell the product. The product obtained for payment cannot be incidental or non-existent. The promotion will fail as illegal if the product sale is actually a mechanism to bypass gambling and anti-lottery laws. When evaluating the validity of a sweepstakes, a court considers the substance and not just the form to determine whether the consumer obtained something for value in exchange for his money other than the opportunity to play a game. In-package sweepstakes risk failure when one or more of the following conditions exists:

- Participants' behavior indicates that they do not value the product, but instead only want an opportunity to participate in the promotion.
- The promotion is permanent and ongoing rather than lasting for a finite period of time.
- The promotion involves a gambling device such as a slot machine.

Real-Life Examples in which In-Package Sweepstakes Failed

Sweepstakes at Race Course. In *Barber v. Jefferson County Racing Association*, 960 So. 2d 599, 604–05 (Ala. 2006), *cert. denied,* 551 U.S. 1131 (2007). The owners of a Birmingham-located race course offered a promotion called the Quincy MegaSweeps. Consumers could buy encoded cards that allowed them to use internet service at computers within a cyber café located at the race course. The encoded card also included a predetermined number of MegaSweeps entries. To determine whether they had won in the MegaSweeps, consumers inserted the embedded cards into a MegaSweeps terminal which was designed to look like a slot machine. As an alternative to the card terminals, consumers could determine whether they had won by checking online or calling a toll-free number.

Many of the incidental-product red flags described above existed:

- The race course owners provided more than eleven times as many MegaSweeps sweepstakes readers as internet kiosks.
- Consumers often purchased additional embedded cards even though they still had large quantities of unused internet time.
- MegaSweeps was a permanent, high-stakes game.
- The game used a device that was arguably a gambling device.

These factors along with others convinced the *Barber* court that the consumers' purchase of internet time was incidental to the consumers' purchase of an opportunity to play the MegaSweeps game. In other words, the consumers did not really want the internet time provided on the cards and bought the cards only so they could play the MegaSweeps game. As a result, the MegaSweeps promotion was not a valid sweepstakes and violated Alabama gambling laws.

American Idol Text Messaging. Promotions offered in conjunction with the reality television programs *American Idol, Deal or No Deal, 1 vs 100,* and *The Apprentice* allowed at-home viewers to participate in trivia and other promotions. Viewers entered online or via text messaging. There was no charge for submission by the website. However, submission by text messaging generated a ninety-nine cent fee plus standard text messaging fees charged by the entrant's wireless carrier.

In a series of lawsuits, players argued that the promotion was an illegal lottery. The sponsors countered that while the promotion included a prize and chance, it did not include consideration because there was a free alternative method of entry. A California court refused to dismiss the case finding that the alternative method of entry used by the programs might be defective and, therefore, the promotions might be illegal lotteries.[4]

According to the court, the relevant question was not whether some people could enter for free. Instead, the relevant question was whether anyone did in fact pay for the opportunity to participate. The court stressed that viewers who sent in text messages paid only for the privilege of entering the promotions. The viewers entering via text message received nothing of equivalent economic value in return.

Phone Card Sweepstakes. A series of cases and attorney general opinions in various states in the early 2000's dealt with a promotion in which consumers bought a phone card with one to two minutes of phone time. In addition to the phone time, the card also included either a game card or an opportunity to play a video game offering monetary prizes. The phone card was sometimes priced higher than the cost of phone cards without a promotional component. More significantly, many purchasers did not use the phone time. In almost all of these cases, the court concluded that the sale of the phone card was incidental to the accompanying game of chance and that the game was illegal gambling.[5]

Real-Life Example in which In-Package Sweepstakes Succeeded

Intent of Participant Shows Sweepstakes-Playing Opportunity Is Incidental. The Ohio Attorney General opined that a sweepstakes conducted by a military credit union whereby persons who obtain loans from the credit union are entered into a sweepstakes did not involve consideration and therefore was not illegal gambling. The Ohio Attorney General acknowledged that taking on a loan with the obligation to re-pay it, becoming a member of the credit union, and providing collateral for a loan would be consideration flowing from the participant to the credit union. However, the fact that the participants did not pay the consideration for the purpose of receiving a chance to win prizes convinced the attorney general that receipt of a sweepstakes entry was incidental to securing the loan. (Ohio Att'y Gen. Op. No. 1985-013 (April, 9, 1985)).

3.6.3. Best Practices for Valid Alternative Methods of Entry

Treat All Participants with Equal Dignity. Promotion rules should not discriminate among different categories of participants. This potential danger is most applicable to sweepstakes that have both a purchase-play option and a free alternative method of entry (AMOE). Participants who enter via the free AMOE option must have the same opportunity and odds of winning as the participants who receive an opportunity to play along with the purchase of a product. This concept is the equal dignity rule. It is not a state or federal law. Instead, the concept is written into court opinions. Here are best practices for avoiding violation of the equal dignity rule:

Do Not Offer Separate Sets of Prizes. Offering one set of prizes to those sweepstakes participants who make a purchase and another set of prizes to those participants who use the free AMOE violates the equal dignity rule. It does not matter that the prizes in the sets are identical or have equal value. A court may view the promotion as two completely distinct sweepstakes—one sweepstakes that has a free method of entry and a second sweepstakes that requires a purchase, thus, making the second sweepstakes illegal. (*See e.g.*, Classic *Olds-Cadillac-GMC Truck v. State*, 704 A. 2d 333 (Me. 1997)).

Do Make Accommodations for Participants Submitting Free AMOEs via Regular Postal Mail. If the promotion allows entry by both regular mail and a more immediate method such as the internet, in-store entry, text messaging or phone, people submitting by regular mail or a slower method should have sufficient opportunity to submit.

Do Not Give Paying Participants More Chances to Win. If a paying participant receives a chance to win with each purchase and can make multiple purchases in a day whereas the non-paying participant is restricted to one free play per day, there is no equal dignity between paying and non-paying participants. Similarly, it should not be unduly difficult for the non-paying participant to claim his prize if he does win.

Make AMOE Easily Available. Make sure employees are aware of the free AMOE and can direct inquirers to the free AMOE. If there is an automatic sweepstakes entry upon purchase at a retail store, offer an in-store free play opportunity rather than only a mail-in or internet-based AMOE.

Monitor AMOE. Monitor the disbursement and availability of AMOE mechanisms. Throughout the promotion, verify that a reasonable number of free AMOEs is distributed to consumers.

Do Not Underemphasize AMOE. Clearly and conspicuously disclose in advertisements that no purchase is necessary and that an AMOE is available. Do not overemphasize the purchase-based method or underemphasize the free AMOE. In any advertisement referring to the purchase of a product as a means of entering a sweepstakes, use equally prominent type to refer to the availability of the AMOE.

3.7. Is the Promotion Gambling?

For the most part, in the United States, gambling is illegal. States that do allow gambling tend to regulate it heavily. Gambling is relevant to promotions because the sponsor must structure its contests and sweepstakes so that they do not cross the line into gambling. This Guide discusses gambling only as it relates to contests, sweepstakes, and similar promotions and does not provide an in-depth treatment of the topic of gambling.

3.7.1. What Is Gambling?

Each state offers its own definition of gambling or gaming. One definition of gambling is the risking of money, between two or more persons, on a contest or chance of any kind, where one must lose while the other wins. More colloquial definitions include "playing a game of chance for money" and "wagering money or something of value on an uncertain event with the goal of winning more money".

3.7.2. Gambling Combines Consideration, Chance, and Reward

Another method to express gambling is the combination of the three elements of consideration, chance, and reward. In the context of gambling, these elements might go by other names such as payment, luck, and prize. The consideration or payment component might also be called a bet, wager, or stake. The reader may immediately see how these elements correspond to the three elements that comprise a lottery. Gambling's consideration or payment corresponds to a lottery's consideration, gambling's chance corresponds to a lottery's chance, and gambling's reward corresponds to a lottery's prize.

While every lottery is a form of gambling, the converse is not true. Every gambling game is not a lottery. It is possible for a promotion to escape categorization as an illegal lottery but still be labeled as an illegal gambling game.

States differ in their treatment of a lottery versus the broader category of gambling. Some states have one set of laws for lotteries and a different set of laws for the broader category of gambling. One major distinction is the elements required to establish a lottery versus the elements required to find gambling. With very few exceptions, each state requires a finding of prize, consideration, and chance before categorizing a promotion as a lottery.[6]

For gambling, the same principle is not true across all states for reward, consideration, and chance. Some states will designate a game as gambling even if it does not contain the element of chance.

Chance Is Not Always Required for a Finding of Gambling. There are some state laws that may find gambling even if there is no element of chance or luck. As an example, Arkansas anti-gambling laws prohibit the wagering of anything of value on a game of cards irrespective of whether the card game is one of skill or one of chance. (Ark. Code § 5-66-112 (2013)). That law prompted the Arkansas Attorney General to find a poker tournament to be in violation of the state's anti-gambling laws. At the time of the opinion, there was no Arkansas court case deciding the question of whether poker is a game of chance or a game of skill. The Arkansas Attorney General classified the $50 poker tournament entry fee as a wager paid by tournament participants for the opportunity to win prizes. Therefore, the tournament violated the Arkansas statute prohibiting wagering on card games. According to the Arkansas Attorney General, whether poker was a game of chance or game of skill was irrelevant. (Ark. Att'y Gen. Op. No. 2005-034 (Mar. 9, 2005)).

Consideration Is Required for a Finding of Gambling. A finding of gambling requires consideration. The consideration component of gambling might also be referred to as payment, a bet, a wager, or a stake. It is money or something else of value that the gambler pays in order to play the game. If the participant pays no consideration, the promotion or game is not gambling.

As an example, when responding in an online FAQ to the question "What makes a poker tournament legal or illegal?", the Colorado Attorney General's Office focused on the existence of consideration. Colorado requires consideration, chance, and a prize for a finding of gambling. (Colo. Rev. Stat. § 18-10-102(2) (2014)).

According to the FAQ, it is legal to offer a competition among poker players and award prizes to winners as long as no money is required or solicited from the players. In contrast, requiring any type of fee, buy-in, or other money from the players transforms the legal poker tournament into an illegal gambling activity.[7]

As discussed in Section 3.1.3 of this Guide, contests can charge consideration. Sponsors may wonder how to distinguish between the consideration paid by the participant in a legal contest and the consideration paid by a participant in an illegal gambling scheme. Money a contest entrant pays to participate in a promotion is not the same thing as a gambling consideration, bet or wager. Entry fees are not bets or wagers where

- participants pay them unconditionally for the opportunity to participate in a contest;
- the prize is for an amount that is specified at the start of the promotion and that is guaranteed to be won by one of the contest participants; and
- the sponsor or entity offering the prize has no opportunity to win the prize.

Reward is Required for a Finding of Gambling. The existence of a reward in gambling follows the same analysis discussed in Section 3.3.2 of this Guide for the existence of a prize in a promotion.

3.7.3. Federal Anti-Gambling Laws.

Federal laws that address gambling include the Interstate Wire Act of 1961 (18 USC § 1084 (2014)), the Illegal Gambling Business Act (18 U.S.C. § 1955 (2014)), and the Unlawful Internet Gambling Enforcement Act of 2006 (31 U.S.C. §§ 5361-5367 (2014)). These federal laws do not pre-empt state laws.[8] Instead, they augment state laws and fill in loopholes that state laws may miss. Although these federal laws are likely not applicable to most promoters of traditional contests and sweepstakes, it is helpful to have a general idea of the gambling conduct each law targets.

The Interstate Wire Act of 1961 prohibits using wire communications in interstate or foreign commerce for the purpose of engaging in the business of betting or wagering.[9] In *Vacco v. World Interactive Gaming Corp.*, 714 N.Y.S.2d 844 (N.Y. Sup. Ct. 1999), a New York court concluded that internet transactions as well as telephone communications qualify as wire communications under the Interstate Wire Act. As a result, gambling organizations may not use the internet, the phone, or other wire communications to transmit gambling bets.

The Illegal Gambling Business Act imposes fines and imprisonment on persons that conduct, finance, manage, supervise, direct, or own an illegal gambling business. It targets only gambling activities that produce $2,000 or more in daily gross revenues and exempts those activities with lower daily gross revenues.

The Unlawful Internet Gambling Enforcement Act of 2006 prohibits banks and other financial institutions from implementing financial transactions with internet gambling sites. In essence, this law makes it illegal for gambling sites to accept payments or transfer monetary payments to a player based in the United States.

CHAPTER 4

Administering the Promotion and Preparing Official Rules

4.1. State Registration and Bonding Requirements

Some states have registration and bonding requirements. Appendix A.1 of this Guide includes a summary list of such requirements. Part Three of this Guide includes a detailed state-by-state discussion of such requirements.

4.2. Must a Sponsor Publish Promotion Rules?

There is not one law mandating that every promotion have a set of written official rules and that the sponsor make those rules available to the public. However, promotions that fall into certain categories must have written rules made available to the public:

Federal Law Applicable to Promotions Using Direct Mail. The Deceptive Mail Prevention and Enforcement Act (DMPEA), 39 U.S.C. §3001 *et seq.*, (2014), is a federal act that governs certain promotions distributing written entry materials through the United States Postal Service. A promotion using postal mail is subject to the DMPEA if the promotion is a sweepstakes or a skill-based contest requiring participants to pay, or implying that participants must pay, to enter the contest. The DMPEA does not govern those contests that clearly eliminate the consideration component even if the contest sponsor uses postal mail to distribute entry forms.[10] The DMPEA does not apply to promotions conducted only online since such promotions do not use postal mail.

When applicable, the DMPEA requires sponsors to include written rules as well as other detailed disclosures in their promotion-related postal mailings. I discuss DMPEA requirements in greater detail in Section 7.4.1 of this Guide.

State Law Applicable to Promotions Using Direct Mail. Many states have laws that are parallel to the federal Deceptive Mail Prevention and Enforcement Act (DMPEA). These are state prize promotion laws. The DMPEA does not pre-empt any state laws. For that reason, a state's prize promotion laws may be more stringent or less stringent than the requirements of the DMPEA.

The promotions governed by state prize promotion laws may not match up exactly with the promotions governed by the DMPEA. Some states have very narrow prize promotion laws that are applicable only to prize giveaways requiring attendance at a sales presentation and inapplicable to more traditional sweepstakes and contests. Other states have broad prize promotion laws that apply to all sweepstakes and contests using mail or telephone solicitation. It is often unclear whether the state prize promotion laws are applicable to online-only promotions.

There is a more detailed discussion of state prize promotion law requirements in Section 7.4.2 of this Guide. Also, Part Three of this Guide contains a state-by-state discussion of each state's prize promotion laws, as applicable.

Promotions Offered by FCC Licensees. The Federal Communications Commission (FCC) regulates promotions operated by radio and television broadcast stations. The federal Communications Act and FCC regulations require that radio and television stations disclose the material terms of any promotion by announcing those terms over the air. There is no explicit requirement that the broadcast station provide the public with a written version of the promotion rules. I discuss requirements for promotions sponsored by FCC-licensees in greater detail in Section 7.6 of this Guide.

Raffles. The laws of some states require that sponsors of raffles disclose the raffle terms in writing. As discussed in more detail in Section 9.2 of this Guide, raffles are neither sweepstakes nor contests. Raffles have all the elements to qualify as lotteries or gambling under the laws of most states. However, many states permit non-profit, charitable, and civic organizations to offer raffles for fundraising purposes.

There is a more detailed discussion of raffles in Section 9.2 of this Guide. I also discuss raffles on a state-by-state basis, as applicable, in the state summaries located in Part Three of this Guide.

Other Industry-Specific Requirements. There may also be laws applicable to promotions operated within certain industries that require written promotion rules. Such industries include the alcohol, tobacco, dairy products, gasoline, financial institutions, banking, and insurance industries.

For promotions that do not fall within one of the categories targeted by these laws, there is no requirement to have rules or put them in writing. Many of us have seen online promotions that have no rules or very minimal rules. However, even when there is no legal requirement, it is a best practice and strongly recommended that all sponsors have written rules that they share with entrants.

While protecting consumers is often the main goal of the laws requiring written promotion rules, having and distributing well-written rules also serves as one of the sponsor's best safeguards against legal challenges from dissatisfied promotion participants and from government regulators. Preparing rules gives the sponsor an opportunity to think through the promotion, determine where problem areas exist, and develop procedures and strong language to protect itself from those potential problems.

4.3. Rules as Contract between Sponsor and Participant

Promotion rules serve as the contract between the sponsor and each participant. Legal professionals reading this Guide will be familiar with the concepts of offer, acceptance, and consideration that are requirements for every valid contract. By publishing the rules, the sponsor makes an offer of a contract to potential participants. By performing the requested act required for entry into the promotion, the participant accepts the sponsor's offer and that acceptance completes the formation of a contract between sponsor and participant. If there is a dispute between the sponsor and any participant, the court begins resolution of that dispute by reviewing the contract—which is the promotion rules.

4.3.1. Another Type of Consideration

Readers should not confuse consideration as required for the formation of a contract with the distinct concept of consideration as an element of a lottery or gambling game. While these concepts confusingly use the same term *consideration*, they are in fact distinct.

Consideration for Determination of Lottery or Gambling Game. As discussed in Section 3.1 of this Guide, a promotion may not include all three elements of prize, chance, and consideration. In this context, consideration means the promotion participant pays money or something of value to participate in the promotion. Determining whether a promotion has such consideration is the focus of Section 3.5 of this Guide.

Consideration for Formation of a Contract between Sponsor and Participant. Lawyers are familiar with the term consideration as used in the context of contract law. The benefit a person receives or a person's motivation to enter a contract is what contract law refers to as consideration. In simple terms, consideration for a contract is your reason for entering the contract or what you get out of the contract.

A contract is not valid unless each person entering the contract receives some consideration from the contractual relationship. In this contract formation context, consideration is broader encompassing any benefit to the sponsor or detriment to the participant. That benefit might be one of numerous things such as the payment of money, performance of a service by one contracting party for the other, or a promise to perform (or not perform) an activity in the future. Detriment is any action the participant does not have to perform or would not have performed but for the participant's desire to enter the contract.

While the consideration of contract law shares many similarities with the consideration involved in a promotion or lottery, at least some states distinguish the two. Many courts have said that the consideration required for a finding of gambling is greater than the consideration required for the formation of a contract.[11] The converse statement is also true. The minimal consideration needed for a valid contract to be formed between the sponsor and the participant for contract law terms is not always sufficient to find the element of consideration in a promotional contest.

The consideration-threshold is easily satisfied for the formation of a contract between the sponsor and a participant. Courts hold that the minimal detriment to a participant in a promotional contest is sufficient consideration for a valid contract to be formed between the sponsor and the participant. As an example, a woman who participated in Tropicana Casino's Million Dollar Wheel Promotion provided sufficient consideration to form a contract with Tropicana Casino. There was consideration for a contract because the woman went to the casino, waited in line to spin the wheel, and presented the Tropicana Diamond Club membership card she had previously received from Tropicana in exchange for giving Tropicana her contact information and allowing Tropicana to track her gambling habits. A Pennsylvania court found that all those activities were detriments to the woman that she underwent in exchange for the right to compete for a prize. That detriment was adequate consideration for the woman to form an enforceable contract with Tropicana and allow her to sue Tropicana for breach of contract when Tropicana disputed her winning of a million dollar prize. (*Gottlieb v. Tropicana Hotel*, 109 F. Supp. 2d 324 (E.D.Pa. 2000)).

4.4. Important Provisions for Promotion Rules

This Section 4.4 highlights best practices for promotion rules.

4.4.1. Make Rules Easily Accessible

Consumers interested in the promotion should be able to obtain or access a copy of the rules with ease. A sponsor does not necessarily have to hand the official rules directly to an entrant. If the official rules are easily available, the entrant is responsible for reviewing them.

During a McDonald's *Who Wants to Be a Millionaire* scratch-off game promotion, an entrant filed a federal lawsuit after McDonald's awarded her a low level cash prize when she believed her game card entitled her to the one million dollar grand prize. Relying on the game rules that included mandatory arbitration for the resolution of disputes,

McDonald's filed a motion to compel the entrant to arbitrate. The court agreed with McDonald's and required arbitration for any dispute resolution. The entrant argued that her dispute should not be governed by the official rules because she had not seen or read the rules. The court rejected her argument since McDonald's proved that the official rules had been easily and readily available to her. Participating McDonald's restaurants had posted the official rules conspicuously near the food counter, on the back of in-store tray liners, and near the drive-thru window. In addition, the french fry cartons to which game cards were affixed directed participants to see the official rules for details. It was the entrant's fault for not reviewing the contents of the rules and she could not avoid her participation in the promotion being governed by those official rules. (*James v. McDonald's Corp.*, 417 F.3d 672 (7th Cir. 2005)).

Sponsors offering online contests should also make rules easy to find online with a clearly visible link near the promotion description. In instances where participation is open only to those who like, friend, or link to the sponsor's social networking site, it is a best practice to make the official rules available to everyone. Sponsors should not create a situation in which individuals must like the page or make some other social media connection before the individual can access the official rules.

4.4.2. Specify State Start Time and End Time

The sponsor should specify and adhere to a specific start time and end time for the promotion. For online promotions, the start/end time should include a date as well as a time. If the promotion is open nationwide, sponsors should specify the time zone. Here is an example:

> The promotion start time is October 1, 2016 at 9 a.m. E.T. and the end time is November 1, 2016 midnight E.T. Sponsor's server and computer clock shall serve as the official time-keeping device for the promotion.

If the sponsor reserves rights to modify the rules, as discussed below in Section 4.4.7 of this Guide, the sponsor can arguably extend the deadline of the promotion. Nevertheless, extensions of the end date are risky and sponsors implementing best practices will avoid extending a promotion's end date. The risk increases proportionally with the value of the prize, the number of participants, and the effort required from participants to enter.

There may be no or few complaints if a sponsor extends the deadline for a Write the Best Cartoon Caption Contest when the prize is a $25 gift certificate, there is a low number of entrants at the time of the extension, and writing that caption requires only a few minutes of each entrant's time. The result might be different for the extension of a Make a Video Featuring Our Product Contest when the prize has a significant monetary value and preparation of the video submission requires several hours or days of the entrant's time.

4.4.3. State Who Is Eligible to Enter

There are numerous ways in which a sponsor can legally and might want to restrict eligibility for entry into a promotion.

Restricting Entry to Adults. The sponsor may restrict participation to legal adults. A best practice is to indicate the age requirement as the age of majority within the person's jurisdiction. In that way, the sponsor does not need to be concerned with varying ages of majority across the nation. Here is sample language:

> Contest is open only to individuals who have reached the age of majority in their jurisdiction of residence at the time of entry.

If minors are allowed to participate, the sponsor needs the authorization of the minor's parents or legal guardians in order for the promotion rules and any other documents to serve as binding contracts. Also, as discussed further in Section 6.8 of this Guide, allowing children to participate in an online promotion requires compliance with the Children's Online Privacy Protection Act (COPPA), applicable to children under thirteen, as well as compliance with state privacy laws, some of which apply to all minors under eighteen.

Disqualifying Persons Affiliated with Sponsor. I am not aware of any specific laws that require a sponsor to disqualify affiliated persons from participation in a contest or sweepstakes. In contrast, there are often such legal restrictions prohibiting participation by affiliated persons in raffles, bingo games, and other forms of state-sanctioned charitable gambling.

Nevertheless, to eliminate any appearance of bias or fraud in a contest or sweepstakes, it is a best practice for sponsors to disqualify from participation anyone closely affiliated with the sponsor. Having made such disqualification is a fact in the sponsor's favor in the event a court or government agency reviews the promotion for claims of fraud. Affiliated persons include employees of the sponsor and of any other companies involved in administering the promotion such as advertising agencies. The ineligibility normally extends to the immediate family members of those persons and anyone living in the same residence. Here is sample language disqualifying affiliated persons:

> *Example One.* Employees of Sponsor, its subsidiaries and affiliates, and their immediate family members (spouse, parent, child, sibling and their respective spouses, regardless of where they live) or persons living in the same households of such employees, whether or not related are not eligible to enter or win the promotion.

> *Example Two.* Employees, officers and directors of Sponsor, any prize supplier, and their respective parent companies, subsidiaries and affiliates and their advertising, promotion, and fulfillment agencies are not eligible to enter or win. Immediate family members and household members of such individuals are also not eligible to enter or win. Immediate family members means parents, step-parents, children, step-children, siblings, step-siblings, or spouses. Household members means those people who share the same residence at least three months per year.

Restrict Eligibility by Geographic Region. To avoid international compliance issues, United States sponsors frequently restrict participation to legal residents of the United States. The restriction might or might not extend to territories of the United States. If specific states pose problems for the structure of a particular promotion, the sponsor can make residents of that state ineligible to participate.

There might also be sponsors who want participants from only one or a few states. As in all restrictions and rules, the sponsor must be clear so there is no ambiguity as to geographic-location requirements. Here is some sample language that clearly explains geographic eligibility:

> The Tasty Pastry New Haven Twitter Sweepstakes is open only to permanent legal U.S. residents residing in the state of Connecticut . . . as of the date of their entry.

Here is sample language that does not clearly explain geographic eligibility because the language is too vague:

> The competition is open to people who live or work in Madison, or who grew up in or around the city.

Void Where Prohibited by Law. "Void where prohibited by law" is a standard statement found in promotion rules. While its inclusion does not harm the sponsor, the statement by itself might not be sufficient to insulate the sponsor from liability from a particular state's laws without further action. The sponsor should take steps to avoid encouraging people in restricted states from participating.

Restrict Entrants to Current Customers. While restricting entry to current customers or current members is generally permissible, sweepstakes sponsors must be careful that such restrictions do not introduce consideration. Section 3.5.2 of this Guide includes a discussion on when restricting participation to members, attendees, and customers might qualify as consideration.

Specialized Restrictions and Disqualifications. If there are other eligibility criteria that might be considered subjective, the sponsor should clearly explain what those criteria are and how they will be applied. For example, a humor contest operated by a newspaper was open only to amateur humorists and not to professional humorists. Everyone might not immediately agree on the dividing line between amateur and professional.

The newspaper defined professional humor writers as anyone who earns more than fifty percent of his or her annual income from writing humor, as determined in the newspaper's sole discretion. That definition does make the amateur-professional dividing line more objective; however, it is not a perfect definition. For example, it is unclear if the rule refers to income this year, last year, or a year in the foreseeable future. Also, there are individuals who might earn a substantial annual sum— say $50,000—from writing humor but the $50,000 is less than half of their annual income. A better definition for professional humorist might have been "a professional humor writer is someone who in each of the last two years earned more than $25,000 in income from writing humor".

In making a distinction between amateurs and professionals, a promotion for the best kitchen design restricted eligibility to professionals indicating that "Only professionals, including kitchen dealers, kitchen designers, architects, interior designers and builders/remodelers, are eligible to participate." That is not a clear communication of eligibility. People can disagree on what it means to be a professional kitchen designer.

While there are people who are clearly professional kitchen designers and people who are clearly not professional kitchen designers, there is also a group of people who fall within a gray area between the two. If over the last two years, I have designed my own kitchen and assisted two neighbors with their kitchen designs for nominal pay, am I a professional kitchen designer? What if I previously designed kitchens for customers but have not provided this service for the last five years?

A sponsor's rules should not leave such open questions. A clearer definition for a professional kitchen designer that the contest might have used is "A professional kitchen designer is someone who within the last 18 months preceding entry into this contest has substantially participated in the design of a kitchen (other than his or her own) for a paying customer, as determined in the sponsor's sole discretion."

4.4.4. Explain How to Enter

The sponsor must state the steps an individual must complete in order to participate in the promotion. As discussed in Section 4.3 of this Guide, the participant's completion of the specified actions constitutes the participant's acceptance of the terms offered by the sponsor and forms a valid contract between the sponsor and the participant.

Entry Requirements. If entry requires the participant's creation of original content such as a video, essay, or photograph, the rules should specify word length, subject matter, file size, duration, *etc.* For example, the rules for an essay might specify that the essay must be a minimum of 200 words, a maximum of 1,000 words, written in English, and on the topic of Education. As a best practice, the sponsor can reserve the right to accept entries that contain a slight infraction of one of the submission rules but otherwise comply. For example, such wording allows the sponsor to keep in the contest a stellar video running 62 seconds when the rules specify a 60-second maximum duration.

Here is an example allowing a video contest to keep entries that do not comply fully with a rule requiring that the submitted video contain no third party intellectual property:

> Sponsor reserves the right, in its sole discretion, to remove or blur or to ask the applicable entrant to remove or blur any non-material elements (*e.g.* small logos on clothing, artwork hanging in the background, *etc.*) rather than disqualify an otherwise compliant submission.

Number of Entries. The sponsor should specify the number of times an entrant may enter. For example, can the entrant enter multiple times per day, only one time per day, or only one time during the entire promotion.

Automated Entries. The sponsor should reserve the right to disqualify any entries that are submitted on an automated basis. This is more important for sweepstakes than for contests.

> *Example One.* Use of any automated system to participate is prohibited and will result in disqualification.

> *Example Two.* Entries generated by script, macro or other automated means or by any means which subvert the entry process are void.

Identification of Entrant. The rules should indicate how the entrant is identified. This is important when people might collaborate or a participant in an online promotion enters using an email address shared with someone else. Section 5.2.1 of this Guide delves further into this concept and provides sample language.

4.4.5. Explain How Sponsor Selects Winners

The rules should explain how the sponsor selects the winner.

Winner Selected by Chance. A sweepstakes often selects the winner by random drawing and the rules can contain language as follows:

> On or about June 12, 2016, Sponsor will conduct a random drawing from all eligible entries received. Ten (10) winners will each receive one (1) One Hundred Dollar ($100) gift card.

Winner Selected by Skill. A skill-based contest should specify which criteria the judges use to determine the winner. It is insufficient to indicate simply that the best entry wins. Many people may disagree as to what it means to be the best.

Good Example: All entries in the Best Essay Contest will be judged by a panel of Concord Magazine editors based on the following criteria: originality (25%), creativity (25%), adherence to the rules (25%), and a general sense of the Concord Magazine aesthetic (25%).

Bad Example: Entries will be judged by the editors of the Concord Magazine and Concord Magazine's graphic design staff.

Bad Example: The ABC Company staff will vote on the most creative pinboard entry and announce the winner on June 12, 2016.

Bad Example: Sponsor will choose ten videos from all entries received during the Entry Period to move on to the voting round.

Tie-Breakers. The rules should explain how a tie is broken. As discussed in Section 3.4.2 of this Guide, the sponsor of a skill-based contest should not allow chance to break the tie. A best practice is to use the judging criteria to break the tie.

One common tie-breaking method for contests is to award points based on a point scale such as 0 to 5 for each judging criterion. The entry with the highest cumulative score for all judging criteria awarded by the judges is the winning entry. In the event of a tie, the tie breaker is based upon the highest point score in the first judging criterion, continuing thereafter to each judging criterion in order, as needed, to break the tie.

Here is the language describing the tie-breaking mechanism for a Best Video-Taped Travel Story Contest:

> All entries will be judged based on the following criteria: (a) Originality—30%, (b) On-Camera Presence—30%, (c) Compelling Story—30%, and (d) Ability to Capture the Spirit of the Contest—10%. In the event of a tie, the final winner will be selected based on the highest score for originality, then on-camera presence, and finally compelling story.

Judges Decision Final. The rules should state that the decision of the judges on issues related to winners and all other aspects of the promotion is final. Courts normally respect the judges' final authority on these matters provided that there is no fraud and the sponsor administers the promotion consistently with the stated rules.[12]

> *Example One.* Decisions of the judges are final and binding.

> *Example Two.* By entering, entrants agree (a) to be bound by these Official Rules and (b) that the decisions of the judges are final and binding with respect to all matters relating to the contest.

Resolution of Disputes. The rules should provide a method of resolving disputes. For easier management of participant claims the sponsor might want to provide for binding arbitration and eliminate the right for class actions. To withstand legal scrutiny, the terms of arbitration must be reasonable.

> Entrants hereby agree that any and all disputes arising out of or in connection with this contest or these official rules shall be resolved by arbitration pursuant to this provision and the code of procedures of either the Judicial Arbitration and Mediation Services, Inc. ("JAMS") or the American Arbitration Association ("AAA"), as selected by the entrant.

4.4.6. Identify Prizes and Odds of Winning

It is a best practice to specify the prizes to be awarded along with the retail value of each prize. The sponsor should reserve the right to replace any stated prize with a prize of equal or greater value.

> Sponsor reserves the right, at its sole discretion, to substitute prize (or portion thereof) with one of comparable or greater value.

Sponsors who want additional flexibility in prize offerings sometimes do not describe all prizes. This is not a best practice. While it may not always cause legal concerns, it may cause discontent among participants in the promotion.

4.4.7. Reserve Right to Cancel Promotion or Alter Rules

The sponsor should reserve several rights. If the sponsor does not reserve these rights, the sponsor arguably waives the right to take these actions:

Right to Disqualify Entries and Inappropriate Submissions. The sponsor should have the right to disqualify any submissions that are inappropriate or otherwise non-compliant with the rules. A submission might be found inappropriate due to infringement of another person's intellectual property, obscenity, pornographic material, defamatory statements, hate statements, threats to specific people, groups or organizations; or violation of other applicable laws and regulations. Here is example language from a photography contest:

> The photograph must not, in the sole and unfettered discretion of the Sponsor, contain obscene, provocative, defamatory, sexually explicit, or otherwise objectionable or inappropriate content.

Right to Cancel Promotion. The sponsor should have the right to discontinue the promotion if there is a technical problem, act of nature, or fraud.

Right to Change the Rules Mid-Promotion. To the extent permitted by law, the sponsor should reserve the right to modify the rules. The change in rules might not be effective for entrants who enter prior to the rule change. Some state prize promotion laws explicitly prohibit the sponsor from changing the rules. Hence, it is unclear whether prize promotion laws, when applicable, recognize a sponsor's right to change the rules even if the rules include a right to make those changes.

> Sponsor, in its sole discretion, reserves the right to terminate the contest in the event Sponsor does not receive a minimum of fifty qualified

entries from separate eligible entrants. Furthermore, if for any reason the contest is not capable of running as planned, including infection by computer virus, bugs, fraud, technical failures, or any other causes which corrupt or affect the administration, security, fairness, integrity, or proper conduct of this contest, Sponsor may, in its sole discretion, change these official rules or cancel, terminate, modify, or suspend the contest.

Kraft Clause. The Kraft Clause derives its name from the Ready to Roll Instant-Win Sweepstakes promotion offered by cheese-manufacturer Kraft in 1989. Kraft designed the promotion to have one grand prize of a car worth about $17,000. The odds of winning the grand prize were designed to be about 1 in 15 Million. However, due to a distribution error, almost all the game pieces produced winners. After Kraft declined to award all the winners a grand prize, several participants filed lawsuits against Kraft.

The resulting Kraft clause adopted by subsequent sponsors provides a solution for sweepstakes promotions in which printing or other errors produce more winners than intended. The solution is placing all such winners in a random drawing for the prize.

If due to a printing, production or other error, more prizes are claimed than are intended to be awarded for any prize level per the above, the intended prizes will be awarded in a random drawing from among all verified and validated prize claims received for that prize level. In no event will more than the stated number of prizes be awarded.

4.4.8. Obtain Consents

The sponsor may need permissions to display, distribute, or otherwise use original materials submitted by the entrants. The sponsor may be able to obtain such consents through the official rules. Section 8.4.1 of this Guide contains an in-depth discussion of permissions and consents.

The sponsor may also want to use entrants' name, image, and other personal information for publicity reasons. Here is sample official rule language for publicity consent:

Except where prohibited, participation in the promotion constitutes winner's consent to sponsor's and its agents' use of winner's name, likeness, photograph, voice, opinions and/or hometown and state for promotional purposes in any media, worldwide, without further payment or consideration.

The sponsor may want to obtain a more formal release from winners as part of the winner verification process. Section 5.2.2 of this Guide includes further discussion of such releases.

4.4.9. Disclaim Affiliation with Companies and Products Mentioned

If the promotion mentions brand-name products such as an apple iPod or a stay at the Hilton Hotel as prizes, it is a best practice to mention that the providers of those products or services are not affiliated with the promotion—if that is the case. Here are sample disclaimers:

Example One. One grand prize winner will receive an XYZ Product. XYZ Product is a registered trademark of the XYZ Company. All prizes have been purchased by Sponsor and not provided by the XYZ Company. The award of prizes does not indicate any endorsement, approval or sponsorship of the contest or Sponsor by the XYZ Company.

Example Two. The names of companies, products, and logos have been used for identification purposes only and may be the copyrighted properties and trademarks of their respective owners. The mention of any company, or the inclusion of a product or service as a prize, does not imply any association with or endorsement by such company or the manufacturer or distributor of such product or service and, except as otherwise indicated, no association or endorsement is intended or should be inferred.

Third party social media companies such as Facebook and Twitter that allow the offering of promotions via their platforms often require that the sponsor include a disclaimer that the third party social media site is not affiliated with and does not endorse the promotion.

This contest uses the Facebook platform and Wildfire suite of applications and is not endorsed, sponsored, administrated by, or associated with Facebook or Wildfire.

Sections 6.1 and 6.2 of this Guide offer further discussion about offering promotions through social media networks.

4.4.10. Disclaim Responsibility for Technical Problems or Malfunctions

All sorts of things can go wrong that prevent an interested consumer from submitting a timely entry into a promotion. A relevant internet site can be down. The consumer might misdirect an email or a postal entry. A submission may be lost or delayed in the mail. The sponsor should indicate non-responsibility for any computer or mail delivery malfunctions that impacts a participant's ability to enter.

> Sponsor is not responsible for incomplete, lost, late, post-due, misdirected, copied, transferred, illegible entries or for failure to receive entries due to transmission failures or technical failures of any kind, including, without limitation, malfunctioning of any network, hardware or software, whether originating with sender or Sponsor.

4.4.11. Provide Abbreviated Version of Rules

Putting in all the protections that a sponsor wants can result in a set of rules that are not particularly easy for laypeople to read and understand. While sponsors should always opt to use plain language in their rules, an additional best practice is providing a streamlined, plain-language version of the rules that highlights the most important points and refers readers to the full text of the rules.

The most important terms for abbreviated rules include geographic and age limitations, an alert that other restrictions might apply, the location where consumers can find the complete rules, the fact that no purchase is necessary for sweepstakes, and start date and end dates for the promotion. Of course, the streamlined version must be consistent with the official rules and should not be misleading.

> *Example for Contest.* Open to legal residents of the 50 U.S. & DC, who are of legal age of majority in their jurisdiction of residence. Additional eligibility restrictions apply. Contest starts 12:01am EST 5/1/16 and ends 11:59pm EST 5/30/16. Void where prohibited. Contest sponsor is ABC Company, 123 Main Street, Anywhere, Anystate, 99999. See

Official Rules, which govern, for complete details, available at www.
website.com

Example for Sweepstakes. Sweepstakes begins August 1, 2016. Entries
must be received by 11:59 p.m. (EST) on September 15, 2016. No
purchase or payment necessary to enter or win. Void where prohibited. One winner will receive a cash prize of $5,000. Odds of winning
depend on number of eligible entries received. Sweepstakes open
only to legal residents of 50 United States and District of Columbia
who are 18 or older (or of majority under applicable law). Promotion
subject to Official Rules and additional restrictions on eligibility. Click
here for full details, restrictions, and Official Rules. Sponsor: ABC
Company, 123 Main Street, Anywhere, Anystate, 99999.

When applicable, some state laws might add requirements for what
these abbreviated rules must include. This is particularly true of state
prize promotion and state telemarketing laws, which are discussed in
Sections 7.4.2 and 7.5.2 of this Guide.

4.5. Special Industry Requirements and Restrictions

Promotions within certain industries may be subject to additional laws
and regulations. One such industry discussed in Section 7.6 of this Guide
is the broadcast station industry. Television and radio stations offering
promotions are subject to the federal Communications Act and regulations of the Federal Communications Commission.

Other industries or products that spark special rules for promotions include promotions involving alcohol, tobacco, weapons, motor
fuel, time-shares and financial services. Many of these special rules are
dictated by state law and, therefore, vary by state. This Guide does not
provide extensive detail on these industry and product specific promotion laws and rules. Legal professionals needing additional information
on specific industry requirements, might start with the general anti-
gambling and promotion laws discussed and cited in the state-by-state
summaries of Part Three of this Guide.

CHAPTER 5

Selecting the Winner and Awarding the Prize

5.1. Using Public Voting to Select the Winner

Sponsors running promotions that invite entrants to submit original works often use public voting as a judging criteria for submissions. Public voting gets the public more involved in the promotion, brings more attention to the promotion, and thus, potentially makes the promotion more successful. However, using public voting as a method of determining the winner introduces additional complications.

5.1.1. Does Voting Insert Chance into the Promotion

As discussed further in Section 7.1.2 of this Guide, public voting places doubt on whether the contest winner wins based on chance or based on skill. Although no court opinions have yet addressed this question, one can reasonably argue that public voting introduces the element of chance.

5.1.2. Avoiding Public Relations Nightmares when Using Public Voting

Unless sponsors think carefully and take reasonable steps, they can lose control of promotions with public voting. This includes undesirable content and opportunities for cheating.

Preview User Content. For promotions in which entrants submit original content such as photos or videos, the sponsor should consider previewing entries to verify that submissions are appropriate and do not embarrass the sponsor. The sponsor should include in the rules the right for the sponsor to eliminate any entries the sponsor deems to be inappropriate.

American Apparel's The Next Best Thing. A well-publicized and instructive example of a sponsor's loss of control in a promotion involving public voting involved clothing manufacturer, American Apparel. Perhaps in an attempt to counter some negative publicity for ignoring the needs of average-sized and larger-sized women, American Apparel launched a promotional search for The Next Big Thing. As part of the promotion, plus-size women were invited to submit photographs of themselves. American Apparel invited the public to vote on the photos and planned to give a modeling contract to the entrants with the most favorable votes.

Nancy Upton, a plus-size woman who was offended by language used in the contest and by American Apparel's treatment of plus-size women, entered photographs of herself meant to convey her disdain for the contest. Ms. Upton's photos featured her in outrageous poses eating chicken wings in a pool, lying on a buffet table with an apple in her mouth similar to the position of a pig on a spit, squirting chocolate sauce into her mouth yet missing her mouth, and lounging in a bathtub filled with Ranch dressing.

Ms. Upton received the most votes in the promotion. Nevertheless, American Apparel declined to award a prize to Ms. Upton explaining in an open letter that American Apparel wanted winners who ". . . exemplify the idea of beauty inside and out, and whom [American Apparel] will be proud to have representing our company."[13]

The Next Big Thing Promotion received much publicity. From the perspective of American Apparel, that publicity occurred for all the wrong reasons. Many members of the public criticized American Apparel for not awarding Ms. Upton a prize. The situation received national attention when Ms. Upton told her story on the *Today Show*, CNN, and throughout the blogosphere.

Cheating. Voting may increase opportunities for cheating or rigging the outcome. Cheating includes entrants' using automated voting software, creating fake accounts, and using voting exchanges. Language in the rules to combat vote rigging might include the following:

> Use of script, macro or any other automated system to vote is prohibited and all such votes will be void. Entrants are prohibited from obtaining votes by any fraudulent or inappropriate means, including

offering prizes or other inducements to members of the public, vote farming, or engaging in any other activity that artificially inflates the entrants' votes.

5.1.3. Best Practices for Promotions with Public Voting

Here are some best practices when offering promotions that include public voting:

Encourage Voters to Use Objective Criteria. Encourage voters to view all entries and not just the entries of their friends. Encourage voters to consider certain criteria when casting their vote. Of course, this does not guarantee that public voting will be objective and that voters will do anything other than vote for their friends.

Voting Limits. Limit the number of times a person may vote. Potential limitations include once per day or once during the contest period.

Decrease Impact of Voting. Consider diluting the impact of public voting on the selection of the winner. There are several ways to accomplish this objective:

Multiple Tiers. Make voting a separate tier so that voting takes place only for finalists selected by the contest judges based on objective criteria.

Combination of Public Voting and Objective Criteria. Make public voting only a small component of the winning criteria. Instead of allowing public voting to be the deciding factor in the contest outcome, voting might count for a small percentage in deciding the winner. For example, the winning criteria might be comprised of public voting which counts for ten percent (10%) and the remaining ninety percent would be more objective criteria, decided by a qualified panel of judges, such as originality (30%), aesthetic appeal (30%), and technical proficiency (30%).

Ancillary Part of Promotion. To remove any impact of voting on winning while still keeping the benefits of public involvement, make public voting an ancillary part of the competition for prizes. For example, a panel of judges selects winners of the prizes from the submissions based on objective criteria. In conjunction with the prize competition, the public votes on submissions for an audience choice award. The public voting can be divided into countless categories. For example, for a photograph contest, the public might vote on best caption, most thought-provoking, best slice-of-life, *etc.*

Eliminate Timing of Entry as Chance Component. Structure the contest so that the submission time does not impact an entry's votes. For example, avoid making entries available for viewing and voting on a first-submitted basis. If the sponsor makes entries available for voting in the order received, being one of the first entries elevates an entry's opportunity for being viewed and voted upon. The sponsor might wait to delay displaying the entries until all entries are submitted and shuffle the presentation of entries to voters.

Preview Entries. To avoid a situation in which voters select an entry that is undesirable or embarrassing to the sponsor, the sponsor should preview all entries prior to posting them for voting. The sponsor should also include in the rules the right for the sponsor to eliminate any entries the sponsor deems to be inappropriate.

5.2. Identify, Notify, and Verify the Winner

5.2.1. Who Is the Winner?

It is a best practice to indicate in the rules that only one person can submit each entry. If the rules do allow two of more people to submit a single entry, the rules should indicate that the group of entrants must designate a single person as its contact or spokesperson and that the sponsor will have no liability with respect to disputes within the group concerning sharing of the prize. Here is sample language:

> If any group elects to collaborate on a submission, they are required to designate one (1) person as the agent of the group to enter the contest, to agree to these rules and to accept the prize on behalf of the group. If the group's submission is selected as a finalist, the person designated as the entrant will be deemed to be the winner and awarded the applicable prize. The sponsor is not liable for any disputes between collaborators regarding the contest.

Email addresses are occasionally shared by two or more people. Online promotions that participants may enter via email can potentially generate disputes concerning who the legitimate entrant is. Sponsors can avoid this problem by inserting into the rules a provision stating that the authorized account holder of the email from which the entry is made is the entrant. The rules should also define what it means to be the authorized account holder.

> The authorized account holder is the natural person who is assigned to an email address by an internet service provider, online service provider or other organization (*e.g.*, business, educational institution, etc.) responsible for assigning email addresses for the domain associated with the submitted email address.

5.2.2. Consents and Releases

Sponsors normally want winners to sign releases and other affidavits. Here are the forms that a sponsor might require of winners. Two or more of these releases might be combined into one form. While there is generally no legal mandate that these affidavits be notarized, sponsors often do require notarization.

Eligibility Affidavit. The sponsor might want the winner to provide a signed affidavit confirming that the winner satisfies the eligibility requirements for the promotion.

Publicity Consent. This allows the sponsor to use the winner's name, likeness, and background information in publicity about the sponsor's promotion. Without a publicity consent, a winner might have a privacy or right of publicity claim against a sponsor who uses the winner's name and picture for marketing purposes without consent.[14] There may be some state law limits for this release. For example, Tennessee prohibits sponsors from requiring publicity consents from promotion winner. (Tenn. Code § 47-18-120 (c)(3)(C) (2013)).

Tax Forms. If the value of the prize is over $600, the sponsor must make an informational filing with the IRS (and potentially state tax regulators) and provide the winner with a copy of the filing. To prepare these forms, the sponsor needs the winner's name, address and social security number. To ensure having complete information for the necessary filings, sponsors often require winners to complete and submit a Form W-9, *Request for Taxpayer Identification Number (TIN) and Certification*. Section 5.4 of this Guide includes a discussion of tax implications for promotion winners and sponsors.

Release of Liability. By signing a liability release, the winner absolves the sponsor from responsibility for any harm the winner incurs as a result of receiving the prize. Sponsors offering travel as a prize frequently require liability releases.

Copyright and Other Assignment Documents. If the promotion involves the winner's submission of original works and the rules require the winner to transfer any or all rights in that work to the sponsor, the sponsor should obtain signed assignment documents from the winner. The sponsor may also want consents, releases, and other paperwork showing that the winner has obtained permission for the appearance of any people, trademarks, copyrighted materials, and other proprietary materials in the winner's submission. Sections 8.4.1 and 8.4.2 of this Guide include discussions about obtaining copyright assignments and related rights.

Materials and Permission for Background Check. The sponsor may also want the right to conduct a background check of the winner. This might be prudent when the prize is meeting a high-profile individual such as a former United States president or if the sponsor plans to feature the winner in the sponsor's marketing campaigns.

5.2.3. Alternate Winners

The sponsor should leave itself with options in the event the selected winner cannot be located or in the event the selected winner refuses to complete the necessary paperwork. The sponsor might set a deadline for response and return of the necessary paperwork such as ten business days from the first attempted notification.

A best practice is referring to the winner as a potential winner until the sponsor can verify that the person meets the eligibility requirements and the individual completes and returns any necessary paperwork. The rules should also indicate what happens if the initial person selected as the potential winner is ineligible or unwilling to accept the prize.

Example for Sweepstakes. In the event that a potential winner of any prize is disqualified for any reason, the sponsor will award the prize to an alternate winner by random drawing from among all remaining eligible entries. There will be three (3) alternate drawings after which the prize will remain unawarded.

Example for Contest. The Sponsor will make a maximum of three attempts to contact the eligible winner within ten (10) business days of the end of the contest. If the eligible winner cannot be contacted within three (3) attempts or ten (10) business days (whichever occurs first); then he/she will be disqualified (and will forfeit all rights to the applicable prize) and Sponsor will have the right, in its sole and absolute discretion, to select an alternate winner based on the next highest score.

Example for Contest. Potential winners will be notified on or about February 15, 2016 by telephone, email and/or mail and required to complete a release as well as any additional documents required by Sponsor. The inability of Sponsor to contact a potential winner within a reasonable time period or failure of the potential winner to sign and return all requested documents within ten business days of receipt may result in the potential winner's disqualification. Upon the potential winner's disqualification, Sponsor, it its sole discretion, may award the prize to the entrant with the next highest score.

5.3. Prize Considerations

5.3.1. Limitations on Promotion Prizes

Certain items may be problematic as prizes. These items include alcohol, firearms, certain animals, *etc.* Also, the prize cannot be solely dependent on entry fees paid by participants. This typically places the promotion in violation of state anti-gambling laws.[15] The rationale for the prohibition is that a prize consisting solely of participants' entry fees means that the participants are making a wager with that entry fee and that the promotion is actually gambling.

5.3.2. Delivery of the Prize

If the prize is something heavy such as a car or furniture, the sponsor should consider the cost of delivery of the prize. The sponsor should include in the rules any special accommodations it will need for delivery.

5.3.3. Expensive Prizes

The winner must pay taxes on any winnings worth over $600. If the prize is expensive—such as a car—the winner might not have the cash to pay the tax bill. The sponsor might want to offer the winner the option to choose a cash prize. The cash prize does not need to equal the value of the other prize. The sponsor can also include an amount of cash to go towards paying the winner's tax liability. Here is sample language:

> The Grand-Prize is a 1967 Corvette Stingray Coupe and a 2012 Corvette Grand-Sport Coupe, plus up to forty-five thousand dollars ($45,000) to be applied toward the winner's IRS withholding requirement for federal income taxes (approximate retail value of the Grand-Prize is $247,000); or an alternate cash prize of one-hundred thousand dollars ($100,000 subject to IRS withholding requirements).

Offering a fantasy prize might be a method of giving the winner something he values without triggering a significant tax obligation. A fantasy prize might be meeting a famous person or gaining access to an exhibit before it opens to the general public. Fantasy prizes carry the additional benefit of lowering—or even eliminating—the cost to the sponsor for acquiring the prize to be offered. The Academy of Motion Picture Arts and Sciences used an effective fantasy prize in a video-submission contest targeting aspiring filmmakers. The prize was the opportunity to deliver on-stage an Oscar statue during the 2013 Oscars award program.

5.3.4. Travel as a Prize

When the prize is travel, the sponsor may want to implement one or more of the following best practices:

- Specify which form of transportation the sponsor will provide the winner. For example, indicate whether it will be ground or air transportation and whether the winner is responsible for any portion of the transportation such as transport to the departure airport.
- Leave discretion for the sponsor to decide from which airport (in the winner's surrounding geographic area) the winner departs and to select the hotel accommodations.
- Specify for which additional travel costs the winner is responsible such as certain meals, travel to and from the airport, and incidental hotel expenses.
- Indicate the time frame during which the winner must complete the travel. There might be a specific window if the travel is to attend a designated event such as the Super Bowl or a convention. If there is no event, the sponsor may still want to require completion of the travel within a finite period of time. A reasonable amount of time may be one year from the date of selection of the winner.
- Get a release indicating that the winner will not hold the sponsor responsible in the event the winner suffers an injury during the travel.

5.4. Tax Issues

Winners must pay taxes on prizes won through promotions. (26 U.S.C. § 74(A) (2014)). The winner must report the winnings on income tax filings as part of the winner's gross income. This includes cash winnings as well as any products or services won. The winner pays taxes for products or services based on the products and services' fair market value.

The sponsor's potential tax compliance responsibilities include reporting the income to the IRS, providing the winner with a copy of the IRS information filing, and making tax withholdings. The sponsor's specific responsibilities for each promotion depend on the type of promotion, the amount of the winnings, and whether the winner provides proper identification and a social security number.

The IRS categorizes promotion-related winnings either as other income or as gambling income. If the participant risks money in the promotion, the IRS categorizes such winnings as gambling income. If the participant does not risk money in the promotion, the IRS categorizes such winnings as other income.

Each category carries distinct tax compliance requirements for the sponsor. The amounts provided in the following discussion are the amounts for tax year 2014 and are subject to change. Sponsors seeking to comply with tax withholding and reporting requirements should consult current IRS instructions and regulations.[16] The applicable states may have additional tax withholding and reporting requirements.

Winnings Categorized as Other Income. If a person wins prizes in a promotion in which the person risks no money, the IRS categorizes such prizes as other income. A game show, a sweepstakes[17], or a contest that charges no entry fee results in winners who have placed no money at risk. Their winnings qualify as other income for income tax purposes. For such promotions that do not require payment for entry, the sponsor must report any winnings of $600 or more by filing Form 1099-MISC with the IRS. If the winnings are less than $600, the sponsor has no filing obligations.

Winnings Categorized as Gambling Income. Gambling income comes from lottery, raffles, or bingo games—including those operated by charitable or non-profit organizations. The sponsor must report gambling winnings to the IRS on Form W-2G with a copy to the winner if (a) the amount paid, reduced by the wager, is $600 or more and (b) the payout is at least 300 times the amount of the wager. The threshold is different for poker tournaments, keno, bingo, and slot machines. For bingo, there is no reporting requirement unless bingo winnings (without deducting the wager) are $1,200 or more. In certain situations, the sponsor must withhold, and send to the IRS on the winner's behalf, a portion of the winnings.

Regular Withholdings of Gambling Income. If the fair market value of the gambling winnings is more than $5,000, the sponsor must withhold taxes equal to 25% of the gambling winnings and report this amount to the IRS on Form W-2G. The sponsor must also provide the winner with a copy of the Form W-2G filing.

The IRS refers to this withholding as regular withholding. If the gambling winning is a non-cash item such as a car, the tax amount the sponsor must withhold is computed and paid according to one of the following two methods.

- The winner pays the withholding tax to the sponsor. In this case, the withholding is 25% of the fair market value of the non-cash payment minus the amount of the wager.
- The sponsor pays the withholding tax. If the organization, as part of the prize, pays the taxes required to be withheld, it must pay tax not only on the fair market value of the prize less the wager, but also on the taxes it pays on behalf of the winner. In this case, the withholding is 33.33% of the fair market value of the non-cash payment minus the amount of the wager.

Backup Withholding of Gambling Income. The sponsor must make backup withholding equal to 28% of the gambling winnings if all the following three conditions apply:

- The winner does not furnish a correct taxpayer identification number.
- There is no requirement to make regular withholdings.
- The winnings are at least $600 and at least 300 times the wager (or the winnings are at least $1,200 from bingo or slot machines; $1,500 from keno; or more than $5,000 from a poker tournament).

The sponsor is liable for any tax it fails to withhold correctly. The sponsor should also file Form 945, Annual Return of Withheld Federal Income Tax, to report all its gambling withholdings.

CHAPTER 6

Offering Promotions Online and via Social Media

6.1. Advantages and Disadvantages of Using a Social Media Network

Many businesses incorporate social media into their promotions. A sponsor can offer an online promotion through its own website, through a social media network, or through a combination of both.

A social networking site is an online community of people who share common interests and activities. Most social media networks are web-based and allow users to interact through email, instant messaging, and online forums. People use social networking to expand their business associations and personal networks. There are hundreds of social networking sites. Facebook, Twitter, YouTube, and Pinterest are among the most popular.

A person's participation in a social networking site typically begins by the person becoming a member of and creating an online profile on the social networking site. Basic membership in many of the most popular social networks is free. After creating a profile, the person can invite other people on the social networking site to connect to him. This connection is called by different names on different social networks including friend, fan, and network connection. Just as individual persons create profiles and make connections, many social media networks allow companies to create business profiles and invite persons to connect to them.

For a sweepstakes, sponsors typically ask people to connect with the sponsor on the sponsor's social media account such as Facebook, Twitter, or Pinterest. In return for the connection, the consumer receives an entry for a sweepstakes. Sponsors may also choose to offer their skill-based contests through a social media platform.

6.1.1. Advantages of Social Media Network over Sponsor Website

Reach. The social network may be where the people are. Operating from a social media network may increase engagement for the promotion.

Easy and Low Cost. Setting up a promotion on an existing social media network can be quick, easy, and inexpensive. It can be an attractive option—especially for sponsors that do not have their own website presence or a website that is conducive to an online promotion without editing.

6.1.2. Disadvantages of Social Media Network over Sponsor Website

Some of these disadvantages can be overcome by operating the promotion on the social media network through a third party application.

Ownership of Submitted Content. The social media network may take a license right in content posted to its network. Typically, the license is non-exclusive and the social media network takes the license through language in its terms of use. The social media network taking a license might be an issue for sponsors that want exclusive rights to use entries submitted by promotion participants.

Legal Protections. It is unclear whether a sponsor operating a promotion through a social media network has the full benefits of liability insulation from the Digital Millennium Copyright Act (DMCA) and the Communications Decency Act (CDA). See discussion in Sections 6.6.2, 6.6.3, and 6.6.4 of this Guide.

Data. The sponsor can obtain and collect data—such as an email address and other contact information—from entrants when running the promotion on its own platform or through a third party application. This data collection ability might be restricted or impaired when operating the promotion on a social media platform.

Publication of Rules. Entrants in online promotions sometimes agree to the rules via click-wrap agreement (e.g., checking an "I Agree" box). This click-wrap functionality might not be available for the promotion on a third party social media network.

Control. If the promotion involves public voting, a sponsor offering a promotion on a platform the sponsor controls may have an easier task of implementing the technical best practices for public voting indicated in Section 5.1.3 of this Guide and identifying and resolving any logistical or computer-related problems with the voting mechanism.

Rules of Social Media Network. As discussed in Section 6.2 of this Guide, social media networks have rules or policies for promotions offered through their platforms. Hosting a promotion on a social media network creates another layer of compliance in addition to the federal and state laws with which the sponsor must comply.

6.2. Terms of Service of Social Media Network

Sponsors running promotions on third party social media platforms must comply with any rules the platform issues. Some platforms have very extensive rules governing promotions while other platforms have no specific rules. Rules might come in the form of a specific policy for promotions. Alternatively, applicable rules for a promotion on the platform might be spread across different written policies such as a terms of service, a privacy policy and an advertising policy.

There is also much variation in how rigidly each platform enforces its rules. Some platforms have reputations for being lax in enforcing their promotion rules. However, failure to comply with any rules issued by the platform does put the sponsor at risk of having the platform terminate the promotion and revoking the sponsor's account on the platform.

Here are examples of rules that social media platforms impose on promotions. Social media websites update and change their policies regularly so sponsors should always check the existing rules before launching a new promotion on a specific social media platform.

- The sponsor must have official rules and include a link to the rules from the platform. The platform may also require the sponsor to include links to the sponsor's privacy policy and website terms of use.

- The promotion's rules should include the entrant's release of the social media platform from any liability.
- The sponsor and the entrant must acknowledge that the platform is not sponsoring, endorsing, administering, or associated with the promotion.
- The rules should include a statement or an acknowledgement that any information collected from the participant during the entry process is provided to the sponsor and not to the platform.
- The social network might place limitations on use of the platform functionality for operating the contest. For example, sponsors may be prohibited from using likes, page views, or comments within the platform for automatic entry, for taking public votes, or for the selection of winners.
- If the promotion involves voting, the sponsor must provide its own self-managed method of implementing voting (including dealing with fraud detection).
- Some platforms specify a minimum age for entrants.
- The platform may place restrictions on the sponsor's ability to ask the user to give all rights for, or transfer the ownership of, the entry.
- Some platforms limit how the sponsor may use data collected from entrants. For example, the platform might allow the sponsor to use collected data only for the purpose of administering the promotion and prohibit the sponsor's use of the collected data for marketing purposes.
- Social media platforms frown on promotions that encourage entrants to create multiple accounts or duplicate content. For example, Twitter asks that a sponsor using the network not encourage entrants to tweet the same message repeatedly.

Social media platforms may urge or require sponsors to use a third party application for operation of a promotion on that platform. When using a third-party application, the sponsor needs to consider what indemnification the sponsor must give to third-party application providers and who has responsibility for drafting rules. The advantage of these third party application services is their familiarity with the platform's terms and policies. Using these third-party applications can streamline the sponsor's set-up process and can decrease the risk of running afoul of the platform's rules.

6.3. Online Entries and Submissions

As long as it is a legal contest or sweepstakes and not an illegal lottery or illegal gambling game, there appears to be no prohibition on accepting entries for contests and sweepstakes online or for advertising those promotions online. This is not the case for raffles which are permitted forms of gambling—normally for non-profit and charitable organizations. There may be explicit state prohibitions on selling raffle tickets online. Section 9.2 of this Guide includes further discussion about raffles.

However, rather than having entrants email the sponsor the submission, a better practice is an entry form on the website. Entrants can include their posting and provide the link. The entry page can include a checkbox by which entrants agree to the rules of the promotion.

6.3.1. What Qualifies as Consideration in an Online Promotion?

Section 3.5.2 includes a general discussion of what qualifies as consideration—including a list of activities deemed by many states as requiring minimal effort and, thus, not rising to the level of consideration. There are variations in the types of activities one might require for participation in an online promotion.

There are no definitive legal authorities specifying which types of online activities a sponsor can require from an entrant without the activity being deemed as consideration. However, there is some consensus among professionals that online activities requiring minimal effort and not qualifying as consideration include the following:

- opening an account on a social media network, as long as there is no charge for opening the account
- liking, friending, or otherwise connecting to a sponsor's social media account
- posting a message on the sponsor's social media account
- re-distributing the sponsor's message to the entrant's social media network

- providing names and email addresses of friends as part of a Refer-a-Friend promotion, as long as referring friends is not the sole method of entry (See discussion of Refer-a-Friend promotions in Section 6.5 of this Guide)

Sponsors should note that while requiring these activities of participants might not trigger consideration concerns, they might trigger other concerns. For example, as discussed in Section 6.7 of this Guide, activities requiring a person to post online or distribute information about a sponsor or sponsor product might require a disclosure under the Federal Trade Commission's endorsement and testimonial guidelines. As discussed in Sections 6.4 and 6.5.1 of this Guide, using the wrong methods for encouraging or facilitating a participant's distribution of the sponsor's message via email might violate the federal CAN-SPAM Act or state anti-spamming laws. As discussed in Section 6.2 of this Guide, some social media networks prohibit or limit the incentives sponsors may offer for connecting to the sponsor's social media account.

6.4. CAN-SPAM Compliance for Promotions that Use Email

Sponsors planning to use email as part of their promotion must comply with federal and state anti-spam legislation. Anti-spam legislation regulates commercial email. The federal law designed to combat spam is the Controlling the Assault of Non-Solicited Pornography and Marketing Act of 2003, 15 U.S.C. §§ 7701 to 7713 (2014), or CAN-SPAM for short.

The CAN-SPAM Act does not prohibit sending an initial email. Instead, it requires companies to use honest business practices and to offer an opt-out mechanism when they use email for the primary purpose of advertising a commercial product or service.

Here is a summary of the major requirements for CAN-SPAM compliance:

Use Accurate Header Information. The domain name, email address, and any other information in the from and to sections of the email message must be accurate and correctly identify the person sending the email.

Use Accurate Subject Line. The email subject line cannot mislead the recipient about the contents or subject matter of the message.

Provide Recipients with Opt-Out Option. Each email must contain a clear and conspicuous notice that the message is an advertisement or solicitation and that the recipient can opt out of receiving more commercial email from the sender. The sender must give recipients a reliable method of opting out of receiving additional emails. If a recipient opts out, the sender has ten business days to stop sending email to the recipient's email address. The opt-out mechanism must be functional and able to process opt-out requests for at least thirty days after delivery of the commercial email.

Provide Postal Address. Each email must include a valid physical postal address. There is nothing in the CAN-SPAM Act that prohibits the use of a post office box to fulfill the postal address requirement.

6.5. Refer a Friend Promotions

Some sponsors include a *Refer a Friend* component in their promotions. Other names for the *Refer a Friend* mechanism include *Forward to a Friend* and *Send to a Friend*. With this marketing technique, a company asks promotion entrants and online visitors to provide email addresses of their friends. The company then emails to the friends the company's marketing message or offer. When part of a promotion, the company message is normally an invitation to the friend to enter the company's contest or sweepstakes.

Refer a Friend promotions are legal if handled properly. However, if not handled properly, the sponsor may violate federal CAN-SPAM laws and potentially other anti-commercial solicitation laws.

6.5.1. CAN-SPAM and Refer a Friend Promotions

As explained in Section 6.4 of this Guide, federal anti-spam legislation places several requirements on the sender of a commercial email message. CAN-SPAM defines a sender as the person who initiates a commercial email message and whose product, service, or website is advertised or promoted by the message.

With *Refer a Friend* promotions, it might sometimes be unclear whether the company or the referring friend has the CAN-SPAM obligations. The Federal Trade Commission, the government agency that issues regulations for the CAN-SPAM Act, has strongly suggested that if a company offers an incentive—such as an additional entry in a sweepstakes—to someone for referring a friend, the company is the sender and is responsible for making sure the email sent to the friend is CAN-SPAM compliant.[18]

6.5.2. Best Practices for Refer a Friend Promotions

Best practices for promotions with a *Refer a Friend* mechanism include the following:

Do Not Send Emails to Referred Friends Who Are on the Company's Opt-Out List. If the company implements the email, the company must check the referred friend's email address against its do not mail list. If the email is coming from the referring friend's computer, the company does not have to do a check against its do not mail list.

Do Not Misrepresent the Email as Being from the Referring Friend. The referring friend's name and email address should be in the from line only if the referring friend has complete control over the content of the email. If not, the from line should contain a valid, non-misleading email address or name of the sponsor, administrator, or other entity working on the promotion.

The FTC will take action against *Refer a Friend* misrepresentations. The FTC fined a San Francisco-based internet marketer, Jumpstart Technologies LLC, $900,000 for CAN-SPAM violations for disguising commercial messages as personal messages. As part of its FreeFlixTix Promotion, Jumpstart offered free movie tickets to consumers who provided the names and email addresses of their friends. Jumpstart then sent those friends emails with the consumer's email address in the from line and a personalized subject line such as "Happy New Year," "Movie time. Let's go.," or "Invite." (*U.S. v. Jumpstart Technologies*, Civ. No. 06-cv-02079-MHP (N.D. Cal., Mar. 22, 2006)(consent decree)).

Validate the Referring Friend's Information. The company using the *Refer a Friend* mechanism should require the referring friend to provide his name and email. The company should also verify that the referring person is a real person who has provided a valid email address by querying the email address and using a CAPTCHA check. The company should use the referring friend's name in the subject line of the email and in the body of the email. For example, the subject line might read as follows:

Tom Jones thought this sweepstakes might interest you.

Give the Referred Friend Complete Information. The company should provide the referred friend with complete information as to why he is receiving the message. This step eliminates many potential problems. The body of the message might begin as follows:

Tom Jones has entered our sweepstakes and thought you might also be interested in entering.

Provide Privacy Information. The company should communicate to both the referring friend and the referred friend that the sponsor will not retain and will not use either email address for any other purpose. The sponsor should then adhere to those promises.

Comply with CAN-SPAM. The sponsor should comply with all other CAN-SPAM requirements including providing opt-out procedures and full physical address information. Section 6.4 of this Guide outlines the major CAN-SPAM compliance requirements.

Limit the Number of Referrals. Limiting the number of referrals an individual may send minimizes the risk of a single person submitting an unlimited number of inappropriate referrals.

Provide Other Methods of Entry. Referring a friend should not be the only mechanism for entering a sweepstakes. If it is, providing references of friends might be interpreted as a form of consideration which makes the sweepstakes a lottery. Section 3.5.2 of this Guide contains further discussion on what qualifies as consideration.

6.6. Sharing Entries Online

If the sponsor invites entrants to submit original content, the sponsor often wants to share those submissions with the public. In our digital age, public sharing typically includes making entries available for viewing on the internet. This Section 6.6 of this Guide discusses specific internet-related concerns that arise when posting submissions online. Section 7.1 of this Guide offers a broader discussion of the legal concerns triggered by promotions accepting participants' original creative works.

It does matter at which online location the sponsor posts the entries. If the sponsor posts on its own website or blog, the sponsor has more control of the postings and can benefit fully from the liability protections offered by the Digital Millennium Copyright Act (DMCA) and the Communications Decency Act (CDA). Posting entries on a popular social media network such as Facebook, YouTube, or Pinterest may provide many marketing benefits such as rapid increase in social media followers, increased public engagement, and greater possibility of the promotion going viral (in a good way). However, the legal downside to posting on a third-party network includes less control over the postings and less protection from the DMCA and CDA. There may be compromises that allow the sponsor to use social media networks for advertising the promotion while keeping entries on a site controlled by the sponsor.

6.6.1. Permission from Entrant

As an initial step, the sponsor needs permission from entrants to post their entries online. The sponsor can obtain this permission through its rules. For a more detailed discussion about obtaining permissions from promotion entrants, see Section 8.4.1 of this Guide.

6.6.2. Digital Millennium Copyright Act (DMCA)

In 1998, the United States adopted the Digital Millennium Copyright Act (Pub. L. No. 105-304, 112 Stat. 2860 (1998) (codified in scattered sections of 17 U.S.C. and in 28 U.S.C. § 4001)). The Digital Millennium Copyright Act (DMCA) includes safe harbors that insulate the operators of online sites from claims of copyright infringement for material posted by their customers and online visitors. The DMCA also protects online site operators from claims of copyright infringement for linking to infringing material. If the sponsor allows submissions to be posted on the sponsor's website and those submissions have infringing content, the DMCA can protect the sponsor from copyright infringement liability.

Qualifying for the Safe Harbor. To qualify for the DMCA safe harbor for material posted by others, a sponsor must comply with specific DMCA requirements which include the following:

- Designate an agent to handle claims of copyright infringement, register the name of the agent with the Copyright Office, and post the agent's contact information on the sponsor's website.
- Remove infringing material upon the request of the copyright owner. The request, referred to by the DMCA as a takedown notice, must provide specific information including a description of the copyrighted work and the online location of the infringing material.
- Remove or block access to any posted material that the sponsor discovers infringes someone's copyright—even if the copyright owner has not sent a takedown notice.
- Have no knowledge that infringing material is on the website and gain no financial benefit from the infringing material.
- Adopt a policy of removing or terminating the accounts of individuals who repeatedly infringe copyrighted material and make visitors aware of that policy. This policy could also be stated or referenced in the promotion's official rules.

6.6.3. Communications Decency Act (CDA)

Operators of websites have special protection from defamation actions under the immunity created by Section 230 of the federal Communications Decency Act (CDA), 47 U.S.C. §230 (2014). Section 8.2.5 of this Guide includes a brief discussion of what qualifies as defamation.

If a third party posts a defamatory statement on a website, blog, or community bulletin board, the website operator is not legally responsible. This immunity is available to all interactive computer services, a designation which courts have interpreted broadly to include operators of electronic community bulletin boards, websites, and discussion lists.

Obtaining CDA Protection. The CDA is automatically available to website operators. Unlike the DMCA safe harbor, taking advantage of CDA protections does not require any affirmative actions on the part of the sponsor such as filing an agent designation with the Copyright Office or posting an online notice.

The Website Operator Does Not Receive CDA Immunity for Content It Provides. CDA immunity does not protect the website operator if the website operator functions as the information content provider. An information content provider is someone who is partially or entirely responsible for the creation of the offending content.

For example, if a website owner actively gathers data from external sources and posts the information on its website, the website owner has taken an active role in creating the content and would not be insulated by the CDA if the information is defamatory. The CDA has a good Samaritan provision that allows website operators to remove potentially offending content without danger of being labeled as an information content provider.

6.6.4. Caveats to the DMCA and CDA Protections

Sponsors who want the insulation provided by the DMCA and CDA should be aware of the following caveats:

Protections Might Not Be Available for Material Posted on Third-Party Social Media Networks. The DMCA gives its protection to operators of online sites. The sponsor is not the operator of third-party social networks such as Facebook and Pinterest, so DMCA protections may not be available to the sponsor for such postings. If such DMCA protection is not available, it may be worthwhile to place the material on the sponsor's own website rather than on a social media website.

No DMCA Insulation for Actions by Sponsor. The DMCA offers protection for claims of copyright infringement for material posted by other people. It does not protect the sponsor from claims of copyright infringement generated by material that the sponsor creates or provides.

No CDA Insulation for Actions by Sponsor. CDA insulation is not available for content that the sponsor creates. For example, the CDA did not yield a summary judgment decision in favor of Quiznos during Subway's legal challenge to a Quiznos promotion. As part of the Quiznos-sponsored Quiznos Versus Subway TV Ad Challenge, Quiznos invited entrants to submit videos illustrating why Quiznos is better than Subway. Subway, believing that some of the entries contained false claims about Subway, sued Quiznos. Quiznos offered a CDA defense in an attempt to get a court ruling in its favor without a trial. Its attempt failed.

The court acknowledged that if Quiznos had merely posted the videos submitted by entrants, CDA immunity would apply. However, according to the court, it was also possible that Quiznos had actively contributed to the creation and development of allegedly disparaging representations about Subway, in which case CDA immunity would not be available for Quiznos.

The court recognized that there were facts supporting a conclusion that Quiznos contributed to the representations about Subway. Most significantly, Quiznos had created and posted four sample videos which were designed to shape the contest submissions. As a result, the court left the question of CDA immunity to be decided by a jury.

Quiznos and Subway ultimately reached a settlement agreement without having a trial. (*Doctor's Assoc. v. QIP Holder*, Ruling on Defendant's Partial Motion to Dismiss, No. 3:06-cv-1710-VLB (D. Conn. Apr. 18, 2007))

Subject Matter Limitations. The DMCA's safe harbors apply only to copyright. The DMCA does not provide insulation to claims of defamation, trademark, privacy, trade secret or other intellectual property claims. However, as a risk-minimization method, sponsors might want to allow visitors to notify them of claims other than copyright. While such claims do not fall under the DMCA, reviewing such claims may thwart complaints from visitors who discover violations other than copyright violations on the sponsor's website.

Impact of DMCA Counter Notices. The DMCA offers remedies for the improper removal of material. A person who has content removed pursuant to a takedown notice may submit a counter notice requesting that improperly removed material be reposted. For purposes of promotion entries, the official rules language allowing sponsors to remove any submission for any reason arguably overrides DMCA obligations to repost content upon receipt of a counter notice.

6.7. FTC's Endorsement and Testimonial Guidelines

Sponsors running online promotions need to consider the endorsement and testimonial guidelines of the Federal Trade Commission (FTC). The FTC regulates commercial advertising under Section 5 of the FTC Act, 15 U.S.C. §45 (2014), which prohibits "unfair or deceptive acts or practices in or affecting commerce," including advertising of products and services that misleads consumers. As part of regulating commercial advertising, the FTC maintains a set of guidelines called the Guides Concerning the Use of Endorsements and Testimonials in Advertising. In late 2009, the FTC revised these guidelines to include provisions specifically targeted to new media.

One of the most important principles of the guidelines is the requirement to disclose material connections between the person providing the endorsement and the company being endorsed. The FTC's rationale for the disclosure requirement is that the existence of a material connection impacts the weight consumers will give the endorsement. As a result, anyone receiving compensation for endorsing or recommending products and services is to disclose such compensation.

For example, if a company sends a sample of its product to a blogger with the expectation that the blogger will write and post an online review of the product, the FTC expects the blogger to disclose receipt of the free sample. Disclosures need not be complicated and can be as simple as "ABC Company gave me this product to try."

Initially, there was uncertainty as to whether the guidelines apply to promotions. However, in a 2014 letter regarding a promotion sponsored by shoe manufacturing company Cole Haan, the FTC clarified that the guidelines do apply to promotions.[19] If a sponsor offers a person a sweepstakes or contest entry in exchange for posting favorable informa-tion about the sponsor online or liking or friending the sponsor's social media account, there is a material connection requiring a disclosure. While the FTC expects the person providing the endorsement to provide the disclosure, the FTC also expects the sponsor prompting the endorse-ment through its promotion to inform the participant of the disclosure requirement and monitor the participants' compliance with the disclo-sure requirements.

The Cole Haan situation that sparked the FTC's letter involved Cole Haan's Wandering Sole Contest. As part of the contest, Cole Haan invited contest participants to compile images of Cole Haan shoes onto a Pinterest (a social media network) board and to use the hashtag "#WanderingSole" in the descriptions. The Pinterest boards were acces-sible to the public for viewing on the internet. Cole Haan offered a $1,000 shopping spree for the most creative Pinterest board.

According to the FTC, the contest entrants' Pinterest boards featuring the Cole Haan shoes constituted an endorsement of Cole Haan products and the contest entrants were compensated for that endorsement with the opportunity to win the shopping spree. Hence, there was an incen-tive or material connection between Cole Haan and the contest entrants which should have been disclosed to the public. Failing to disclose that material connection violated Section 5 of the FTC Act. According to the FTC, using the hashtag "#WanderingSole" was not a sufficient disclo-sure. Unfortunately, the FTC did not share in its letter what might have qualified as sufficient disclosure. One can surmise that disclosure of the sponsor and a hashtag such as #contest, #sweep, #ad, or #contestentry might satisfy the FTC disclosure requirements.

Ultimately, the FTC did not take any enforcement action against Cole Haan in part because the FTC had not previously addressed whether the endorsement and testimonial guidelines apply to promotions and Cole Haan subsequently adopted a social media policy that adequately addresses the FTC's concerns.

6.8. Online Promotions for Children

6.8.1. Compliance with Children's Online Privacy Protection Act (COPPA)

If children under thirteen might or do participate in the online promotion, the Children's Online Privacy Protection Act (COPPA), 15 U.S.C. §§ 6501—6506 (2014), applies. The Federal Trade Commission (FTC) issues regulations for COPPA, 16 C.F.R. §312.1 *et seq.*

COPPA requires parental notice and consent before collecting personal information from children under the age of thirteen. Under COPPA, personal information includes name, physical address, email address, image of the child and other information that would make it possible for someone to identify or contact the child.

If COPPA applies, the sponsor must do the following:

- post a privacy policy online,
- provide parental notice and get parental consent before collecting personal information from children,
- allow a parent to review the information collected about the child, and
- delete the child's information upon the parent's request.

Posted Privacy Policy. A website or online service governed by COPPA must include a written privacy policy. There must be a prominent and clearly labeled link to the policy on the home page of the website *and* at each area where the company collects personal information from children. This should include a link at the online location at which children enter the promotion. The policy must include the following information:

- name, address, telephone number, and email address of all operators (or one operator to act as point of contact) collecting and maintaining children's personal information through the website
- description of the type of information collected from children
- indication of whether the operator enables children to make their personal information publicly available
- explanation of how the information is used, and a description of the operator's disclosure practices for such information

- a statement that the parent can review or have deleted the child's personal information and refuse to permit its further collection or use, and an explanation of the procedures for doing so. (16 C.F.R. § 312.4(d) (2013)).

Parental Notice and Consent. Before collecting, using, or disclosing personal information from children, a website must provide parental notice and obtain verifiable consent. The notice must include the following information:

- Statement that the operator has collected the parent's online contact information from the child
- Statement that the parent's consent is required for the collection, use, or disclosure of the child's personal information, and that the operator will not collect, use, or disclose any personal information from the child if the parent does not provide such consent
- Itemization of personal information the operator intends to collect from the child, or how the operator may disclose personal information, should the parent provide consent
- Hyperlink to the operator's privacy policy
- Explanation of how the parent can provide consent
- Statement that if the parent does not provide consent within a reasonable time, the operator will delete the parent's online contact information from its records.[20]

Deletion Upon Request. A parent may revoke consent, refuse to allow an operator to continue using the child's personal information, and direct the operator to delete the information. If a parent revokes consent, the company may terminate any service provided to the child, but only if the company cannot reasonably provide service to the child without access to the information revoked by the parent.

6.8.2. COPPA Exceptions to Prior Parental Consent

Limited exceptions let operators collect certain personal information from a child before obtaining parental consent. (16 C.F.R. § 312.5(c) (2013)). One or both of these exceptions may be available to sponsors that want to open their online promotions to children. These limited exceptions are the one-time contact exception and the multiple-time contact exception. Both exceptions require that the sponsor refrain from using the child's online contact information for any purpose other than the promotion, and that the sponsor ensure the security of the child's information.

One-Time Contact. Properly formatted promotions can rely on the one-time contact exception to prior parental consent. For reliance on this exception, the sole purpose of collecting online contact information from a child must be to respond directly on a one-time basis to a specific request from the child. (16 C.F.R. § 312.5(c)(3) (2013)). The sponsor can not re-use the information to re-contact the child or for any other purpose. Furthermore, the sponsor can not disclose the information and must delete the information from its records promptly after responding to the child's request. If the sponsor expects to contact the child more than one time, the sponsor must comply with the standard COPPA requirements or use the multiple-contact exception if it is available.

A sponsor can use the one-time contact exception if the sponsor collects children's online contact information for entry into a promotion. The sponsor can then contact the child once when the promotion ends to notify the child if the child has won or lost. At that point, the sponsor must delete the child's online contact information.

Collecting Address Information when Relying on the One-Time Contact Exception. When relying on the one-time contact exception, the only information the sponsor may collect about the child is the child's online contact information such as an email address. If the sponsor needs personal information in addition to the child's online contact information— including the child's physical mailing address in order to deliver a prize—COPPA rules for parental direct notice and consent apply.

One suggestion made by the Federal Trade Commission for obtaining the physical mailing address for prize delivery while staying within the one-time contact parameters is to ask the child to provide his parent's online contact information and use that contact information to notify the parent if the child wins the promotion. In the prize notification message to the parent, the sponsor can then ask the parent to provide a home mailing address to ship the prize, or invite the parent to call a telephone number to provide the mailing information.[21]

Multiple-Time Contact. Sponsors can rely on the multiple-time contact exception to the requirement to obtain prior parental consent where the purpose of collecting a child's and a parent's online contact information is to respond directly more than once to the child's specific request, and where such information is not used for any other purpose, disclosed, or combined with any other information collected from the child. Here, the operator must provide parents with notice and the means to opt out of allowing future contact with the child. In this case, the parental notice must include the following:

- Statement that the operator has collected the child's online contact information from the child in order to provide multiple online communications to the child
- Statement that the operator has collected the parent's online contact information from the child in order to notify the parent that the child has registered to receive multiple online communications from the operator
- Statement that the online contact information collected from the child will not be used for any other purpose, disclosed, or combined with any other information collected from the child
- Statement that the parent may refuse to permit further contact with the child and require the deletion of the parent's and child's online contact information, and how the parent can do so
- Statement that if the parent fails to respond to this direct notice, the operator may use the online contact information collected from the child for the purpose stated in the direct notice; and
- Hyperlink to the operator's privacy policy (16 C.F.R. § 312.5(c)(3) (2013)).

6.8.3. Compliance with State Privacy Protections for Children

States are becoming more aggressive in implementing online protections for children. There is a trend for states to extend limitations on collecting personal identification information to all children under eighteen rather than the children under thirteen protected by COPPPA.[22] The FTC has expressed the view that COPPA does not pre-empt state laws that grant privacy protections for children aged thirteen to eighteen.[23]

Of interest to promotion sponsors, these state laws prohibit the operator of a child-directed website or other online platform such as a mobile app from using, disclosing, or compiling children's personally identifiable information for the purpose of marketing or advertising certain products or services to children. Prohibited products include alcohol, tobacco, tobacco alternatives, lotteries, firearms, fireworks, tattoos and piercing, tanning salons, and pornography.

6.9. Other Concerns for Online Promotions

6.9.1. Publishing Rules for Online Promotions

When conducting online promotions on social media or via mobile devices, the sponsor may have limited space in which to provide information. For example, Twitter limits posts to 140 characters and there is limited screen space on mobile devices. When determining placement for the disclosures (link, in-line text, *etc.*), the sponsor should consider the fact that entrants and other interested people might forward the promotional material. If disclosure is through a link, the link might not be part of the text forwarded. One potential solution for providing necessary information in limited space is through the use of a short url. Shortening the uniform resource locator (url, or more colloquially, the website address) is a technique of making a website address substantially shorter in length.

6.9.2. Like-Gating

Some online promotions use like-gating. Through like-gating, companies offer exclusive information, products, and promotion-participating opportunities only to those people who like or otherwise connect to the company's social media account. While it has not been ruled as illegal to require a social media connection (where the connection is at no cost to the entrant) prior to allowing participation in the company's promotion[24], sponsors should not require a social media connection as a prerequisite to seeing the complete promotion rules.

While there have been no court decisions on this point, the Better Business Bureau's National Advertising Division (NAD), a self-regulatory alternative dispute resolution service for advertising disputes, has expressed the opinion that companies should provide a clear and conspicuous explanation of all material terms and conditions of an offer at the outset of the offer and not only after the consumer has made the requisite social media connection with the company. (*In Coastal Contacts, Inc.*, Case # 5387, NAD/CARU Case Reports (October 2011)). Although NAD decisions do not create binding law, the Federal Trade Commission does pay attention to NAD decisions.

6.9.3. Consideration

Requiring a simple activity such as filling out a form for participation is not consideration. More time-intensive activities might be viewed as consideration. In the context of online promotions, requiring an entrant to make multiple visits to the sponsor's website, to search the internet for answers to trivia questions, or to watch an online presentation might be viewed as consideration.

Including consideration is an issue if the sponsor hopes to offer a sweepstakes as opposed to a contest. Section 3.5.2 of this Guide includes a more detailed discussion of required activities that may qualify as consideration.

6.9.4. Privacy Policy

The sponsor may want to have a link in its rules to its privacy policy. In a privacy policy, a website or online service explains to its visitors what information it collects from them, how it will use and secure that information, and whether it will share that information with any third parties.

Federal law does not require a website to post a privacy policy unless the website collects personal information from children. However, trends in state privacy laws are making it more prudent for all websites collecting information from visitors to post a privacy policy. Here are examples of how a sponsor's online privacy policy can be incorporated into promotion rules.

Example One. Please review sponsor's privacy policy at {website link to sponsor's online privacy policy}. By participating in the contest, you agree to all of the terms and conditions of this sponsor's privacy policy.

Example Two. Information submitted in connection with the contest will be treated in accordance with these official rules and sponsor's privacy policy (as may be amended from time to time), currently located at{website link to sponsor's online privacy policy}. In the event of any conflict between these official rules and such privacy policy, the terms and conditions of these official rules shall prevail.

CHAPTER 7

Handling Specific Types of Promotions

7.1. Promotion Inviting Entrants to Submit Original Content

Sponsors frequently offer promotions inviting entrants to submit original content. For example, the requested content might be a photo, essay, novel, or video. The sponsor then judges which entry is the "best". Such promotions raise several issues.

7.1.1. Sweepstakes or Contest?

Although a promotion for the best original content is typically a contest, such a promotion can also be structured as a sweepstakes. Sometimes the sponsor means to structure the promotion as a contest but inadvertently structures it as a sweepstakes or, more disastrously, as an illegal lottery.

As discussed in Section 3.1 of this Guide, promotions have the elements of prize, consideration, and chance. A legal contest or sweepstakes may have no more than two of these elements. If it has all three elements, the promotion is a lottery or a gambling game. Here are additional considerations for these elements as part of a promotion that asks participants to submit original content.

Prize. Most promotions offer a prize. Offering a prize becomes an issue if the promotion already has both elements of consideration and chance. Promotions inviting entrants to submit original content can easily have elements of both consideration and chance. As discussed further in Section 7.1.2 of this Guide, there are sponsors that creatively try to eliminate the element of prize.

Consideration. A participant's submission of original content might qualify as consideration. Whether or not the submission qualifies as consideration depends on the type of content the entrant submits, the amount of effort the entrant expends in creating that content, the rights the sponsor will acquire in the content, and the way in which the sponsor will use the content.

What Type of Content Is Submitted? One can reasonably argue that promotions asking for video or other creative content featuring the sponsor or the sponsor's products qualify as promotions with consideration.

How Much Effort Does Creation of the Submission Require from the Entrant? There may be no consideration if the creation of the content takes minimal effort. For example, if the promotion challenges each entrant to create and post a 140-character original message (*i.e.*, a tweet in the jargon used by Twitter) on the social media platform, Twitter, such effort might be viewed as too minimal to qualify as consideration.

In contrast, entrants can expend substantial effort to write a novel or to create an audio-visual production. Creation of a short essay, a blog posting, or a Facebook entry might fall in between these two extremes of minimal and substantial effort

How Will the Sponsor Use the Submissions? If the sponsor only presents the submissions as a showcase of the entrants' work, that might not be a factor leading to a determination that the submission qualifies as consideration. The analysis is different if the sponsor uses the submission in its regular promotional campaigns, and if the sponsor would have normally paid to obtain such promotional campaign content.

Which Rights Does the Sponsor Obtain in the Submission? If the sponsor takes full ownership of the intellectual property rights in the submission, this is a factor supporting the argument that the submission qualifies as consideration.

Chance. Chance can enter a promotion inviting submissions of original works if the sponsor selects a winning submission without establishing and using objective judging criteria or if the sponsor uses public voting as a basis for selecting the winner.

Turning the promotion into a skill-based contest eliminates the element of chance. Section 3.4.2 of this Guide offers guidelines and best practices for selecting winners in a manner that maximizes a promotion being deemed a skill-based contest.

Public voting raises questions about whether chance or skill determines the selection of the winner. Section 7.1.2 of this Guide contains a discussion regarding the impact of public voting on the element of chance.

7.1.2. Public Voting

Does Voting Insert Chance into the Promotion? A significant uncertainty is the extent to which public voting introduces chance into a promotion. Although no court opinions have yet addressed this question, one can reasonably argue that public voting introduces the element of chance. While some voters might objectively evaluate the merit of the entries, it is unlikely that all voters vote based on the same set of criteria. Many members of the public will vote for a particular entry because they personally know or want to support a specific participant.

Public voting results in a promotion that is not—or at least not entirely—a skill contest in which the participants' demonstration of specific abilities determines whether they win or lose. In essence, entrants in a contest with public voting potentially exercise little influence over whether they win or lose the promotion—a fundamental characteristic of a chance-based promotion. Some might characterize any influence the entrant exercises over winning as the entrant's ability to convince friends, family, and other people he knows to cast a vote for him rather than the entrant's demonstration of skill in the activity being tested by the sponsor.

Eliminating the Prize in order to Avoid Illegal Lottery Classification for Promotion with Public Voting. If voting does qualify as chance and the promotion also includes the element of consideration, legally structuring the promotion presents some challenges. As discussed in Section 3.1 of this Guide, the existence of both chance and consideration means the sponsor must eliminate the element of prize to avoid an illegal lottery. That is not a welcome solution as there is less enthusiasm in competing in a promotion that offers no prize.

One solution adopted by some sponsors for avoiding an illegal lottery situation is offering separate tiers of competition. For the tiers in which participants compete for a prize, qualified judges select winners based on skill and other objective criteria. The tier with public voting offers no prize. Hence, even though this second tier with voting may have consideration as a result of the participant's submission of original content and chance due to the public voting, the absence of a prize prevents this tier from being an illegal lottery. Since there is no prize for the component of the promotion that involves public voting, chance and consideration can co-exist.

Doritos Brand Crash the Super Bowl Ad Contest. For a number of years, Frito-Lay, Inc. has sponsored a Crash the Super Bowl Ad Contest. As part of the promotion, Frito-Lay invites entrants to make a commercial for its product, Dorito brand chips. In the first tier of the competition, a panel of judges review the submissions and select five finalists based on originality and creativity (40%), adherence to creative assignment (30%), and overall appeal (30%). Each of the five finalists receives a cash award of $25,000 and a trip to a private Super Bowl viewing party.

For the second tier, Frito-Lay posts the five finalist videos online for public voting. Public voting results in one grand prize winner. The panel of judges selects a second grand prize winner. The videos of the two grand prize winners are broadcast during the Super Bowl. However, the rules proclaim that there is no monetary value associated with being a grand prize winner and, indeed, the sponsors do not award an additional prize to the grand prize winners. Thus, although this second tier includes public voting which may inject chance into this promotion that already arguably has consideration, Frito-Lay's thinking seems to be that lack of a prize prevents this tier from being an illegal lottery.[25]

The 2006 Star Wars Fan Film Awards. There are a few iterations of this contest inviting fans of the *Star Wars* films to submit a parody or documentary pertaining to the *Star Wars* saga. Various panels of Atom Films and LucasFilm representatives judge the video submissions based on the following criteria: a clear grasp of animation and/or filmmaking as an art form, storytelling ability, character development and character design, voiceover and acting talent, originality, and overall entertainment value.

Films selected as finalists are eligible for Fan Film Awards. The panel of judges uses the same judging criteria to select one winner from the finalists. The judge-selected winner receives $2,000, a trophy, and recognition at that year's Comic-Con International. A winner selected from public voting receives a trophy and the Comic-Con International recognition but not the $2,000. The sponsor's thinking seems to be that the trophy and the recognition are not prizes. Therefore, even if the public voting injects chance and the video submission qualifies as consideration, there is no illegal lottery.

7.1.3. Rights Clearance

If the sponsor wants to display, post online, publish, or otherwise use the entries, the sponsor needs permission from the entrants for such use. The sponsor must consider rights clearance issues and ensure the entrants' work violates no intellectual property or other laws. As discussed in Section 8.6 of this Guide, the sponsor should consider providing participants with pre-cleared materials for promotions accepting original creative works from entrants. Chapter 8 of this Guide includes a discussion of rights clearance issues.

Entertainment Guild Issues for User Provided Commercials. Entertainment guilds are labor unions designed to protect creative people. They negotiate and enforce collective bargaining agreements that establish minimum levels of compensation, benefits, and working conditions for their members. SAG-AFTRA protects performers. SAG-AFTRA collective bargaining agreements may be relevant if the sponsor runs a promotion in which entrants submit commercials advertising the sponsor's goods or services.

The 2013 SAG-AFTRA Commercials Contract runs from April 1, 2013 through May 30, 2016. The SAG-AFTRA contract applies to promotions if the requested entrant submission is a commercial (meaning the submission advertises a product or service) and the sponsor is a SAG-AFTRA signatory or the sponsor uses an agent, such as an advertising company, that is a SAG-AFTRA signatory. The contract allows advertisers to solicit and display via the internet or other new media commercials submitted as part of a promotion without triggering any application of the SAG-AFTRA contract. The entries may be exhibited via the internet/new media during the contest period without triggering application of the payment and other requirements of the SAG-AFTRA contract. If the winning entry is exhibited on any media platform after the expiration of the contest period, the sponsor must pay all performers the rates in the SAG-AFTRA contract and comply with its other terms. Non-winning contest entries must be removed from the internet or new media as soon as the winner is announced or the non-winning entries will also be subject to payment and other SAG-AFTRA terms.

If the sponsor is a signatory to a relevant guild, the sponsor must verify it can obtain clearances with respect to entrant submissions the sponsor wants to use. Here is a sample of such language that might be incorporated into the official rules of a sponsor that is a SAG-AFTRA signatory:

> Each person whose image, likeness and/or voice appears in a finalist video must agree that he/she will execute a standard SAG Commercials Contract; will accept minimum scale compensation and talent residuals; and will be bound by the terms and conditions of such contract, including exclusivity.

7.1.4. Social Media Network

Many promotions accepting submissions of original content are offered through social media which introduces an additional set of challenges for the sponsor. See the discussion of Offering Promotions Online and via Social Media in Chapter 6 of this Guide.

7.1.5. Maintaining Control of the Promotion

As discussed in Section 5.1.2 of this Guide, to avoid a situation in which voters select an entry that is undesirable or embarrassing to the sponsor, the sponsor should preview all entries prior to posting them for voting to determine that submissions are appropriate and do not embarrass the sponsor. The sponsor should also include in the promotion rules the right for the sponsor to eliminate any entries the sponsor deems to be inappropriate.

7.2. Fantasy Sports Competitions

Fantasy sports promotions are games in which participants can simulate the role of an owner or manager of a professional sports team. Other names for this type of promotion include rotisserie, roto, and owner simulation. There are fantasy sports leagues for many sports including football, baseball, basketball, hockey, NASCAR races, soccer, and golf. The simulation game genre has even gone beyond sports and exists for politics, movies, and reality television programs.

In a fantasy sports league, each participant selects a roster of athletes to play on that participant's simulated team. The selected athletes are real people who actually belong to professional sports teams. For example, a baseball fantasy sports league competition might require each partici-pant to select twenty-six players from professional baseball teams for his fantasy sports team. A roster assembled by a fantasy sports team player typically consists of players from several teams. As an example, a fantasy baseball game participant might place on her roster athletes from the New York Yankees, Baltimore Orioles, Washington Nationals, Seattle Mariners, and other baseball teams.

During the fantasy sports game competition, the participant tracks the real-world performance of the athletes on his team. The participant gets points based on the real-life statistical performance of the athletes on his roster. The winner is the fantasy sports league participant with the most points at the end of the promotion.

While games based on sports statistics and probabilities have existed since at least the 1920's, the emergence of the internet transformed and expanded the possibilities for simulation sports games. Instead of having to tabulate and manipulate individual player and team statistics on paper or with a calculator, participants in fantasy sports leagues can rely on internet systems for automatic tabulated statistics. Internet infra-structures for fantasy sports leagues often include expert advice, real-time statistic updates, message boards, and other features. Play via the internet also allows participants from diverse geographic regions to play in the same fantasy sports league.

7.2.1. Are Fantasy Sports Competitions Gambling?

As discussed in Section 3.7.2 of this Guide, gambling includes the elements of consideration, reward, and sometimes chance. Many gambling laws are state specific. Whether or not a fantasy sports league comprises gambling under the laws of a particular state depends upon the structure of the particular fantasy sports game and the gambling laws in that particular state. If the fantasy sports league competition is missing one of the three elements of reward, consideration, and chance, there is a strong argument under many state laws that the fantasy game is not gambling.

However, as noted in Section 3.7.2 of this Guide, unlike an illegal lottery requiring all three elements of reward (referred to as a prize in the lottery context), consideration, and chance, there are a few states that may find gambling even if the game has only reward and consideration and lacks the element of chance. As discussed in Section 3.1 of this Guide, as with most promotions, determining whether the fantasy sports game offers a prize is usually a straight-forward determination. Determining whether the fantasy sports game includes consideration and chance sometimes requires deeper analysis.

Consideration to Participate in Fantasy Sports Leagues. Some fantasy sports providers charge a fee for participation in their fantasy leagues. Others do not. If there is no monetary fee and no other element that might comprise some form of consideration for participating in the fantasy league, one can conclude that there is no consideration serving as the bet, wager, or stake necessary for gambling. Therefore, the fantasy sports competition does not qualify as a gambling game.

Even when participants do pay a fee for fantasy sports league participation, the fee might not be viewed as a consideration, bet, or wager if the fee represents a charge for other legitimate services. A New Jersey court concluded that the operators of several pay-for-play online fantasy sports leagues were not violating any New Jersey anti-gambling laws. The court reached this decision in part because the court viewed the registration fees charged by the operators not as wagers or bets but as payment for the operators' providing information and administrative services that made the games possible. (*Humphrey v. Viacom*, No. 06-2768 (DMC) (D.N.J., June 19, 2007)).

Are Fantasy Sports Promotions Based on Chance or Skill? Fantasy sports games can combine elements of both skill and chance. Skill comes from the fantasy sports participants' use of their knowledge of players, statistics and strategy to pick a winning team. Chance exists because factors that are beyond the fantasy sports participants' control influence the outcome. These external factors include the future performance, injury status, and time at play of athletes on the participants' roster as well as the overall game plan.

In the few states potentially applying the any chance test discussed in Section 3.4.3 of this Guide, those components of chance might be sufficient to push any fantasy sports games charging consideration and awarding prizes into the gambling category. In the remaining majority of states that apply the dominant factor or material element test, whether or not the state classifies a fantasy sports promotion as chance-based or skill-based depends on the promotion's structure. Rules and structural components influencing the skill and chance determination include the following:

Method of Selecting Player Roster. Each fantasy sports league begins with each participant establishing his roster of players. Common roster-building methods are auction, draft, and random allocation. In an auction, each participant bids an amount to have a particular player be on his roster. In a draft, each participant selects one player in each of a series of rounds until each participant's roster is completed. A coin toss or some other method of random selection may determine the order in which participants make their draft picks. Roster building by random allocation might be done via computer program. States would likely view auctions as allowing participants to build rosters based on skill; random allocation as allowing chance to establish the rosters; and drafts as combining skill and chance.

Duration of Fantasy Sports Competition. A fantasy sports league competition might last for the duration of the professional sports league season being simulated. There are also fantasy sports leagues that are perennial as well as leagues that last for multiple seasons.

At the opposite end of the spectrum, there are fantasy sports league competitions as short as one week or even one day. A one-day or one-week competition provides much less opportunity for participants' skill to impact the outcome and may more readily be viewed as a chance-based promotion.

Opportunities to Apply Knowledge and Skill. The greater extent to which participants can trade, cut, and add players, and decide which players start or are benched for each game, the more opportunities participants have to use their knowledge and strategic thinking to influence the outcome of the competition. The more impact participants' knowledge has on the outcome, the easier it is to argue that skill determines the outcome.

7.2.2. Impact of Federal Anti-Gambling Laws on Fantasy Sports Competitions

The fantasy game sponsor should evaluate the applicability of federal anti-gambling laws discussed in Section 3.7.3 of this Guide. It is noteworthy that the Unlawful Internet Gambling and Enforcement Act of 2006, 31 U.S.C. §§ 5361-5367 (UIGEA), creates an exception for fantasy sports leagues.

The UIGEA prohibits unlawful internet gambling defined as transmitting a bet or wager via the internet where the bet or wager violates the gambling laws of any state in which the bet is initiated, received, or otherwise made. The UIGEA specifically excludes from the definition of "bet" or "wager" money paid for participation in a fantasy or simulation sports game as long as the fantasy sports game satisfies the following conditions:

- The sponsor establishes the prizes to be awarded and makes all participants aware of that information prior to the start of the promotion.
- Neither the number of participants nor the amount of fees paid by participants determines the value of the prizes.
- Winning outcomes are determined predominately by accumulated statistical results of the performance of individuals (athletes in the case of sports events) in multiple real-world sporting or other events.
- No winning outcome is based on the score, point-spread, or any performance or performances of any one or more real-world teams.

- No winning outcome is based solely on any single performance of an individual athlete in any single real-world sporting or other event. (31 U.S.C. § 5362(1)(E)(ix) (2014)).

7.2.3. Best Practices for Fantasy Sports Competitions

Here are best practices for sponsors who want their fantasy sports competitions not to be viewed as gambling:

- Consider not charging a fee for entrants to participate in the fantasy sports competition. If the sponsor does charge a fee, the sponsor should provide administrative or informational services in exchange for the fee so that the fee is not viewed as a bet, wager, stake, or consideration.
- Develop a structure in which the participants knowledge of the sport and strategic thinking significantly impact the outcome.
- Avoid establishing fantasy sports leagues in jurisdictions that might apply the any chance test[26] since it is not feasible to eliminate all elements of chance (*i.e.*, future performance of athletes, starting line-up, player injury, *etc.*) from a fantasy sports game.
- Realize that for roster selection methods, auction is preferable to draft and draft is preferable to random selection.
- Consider that a competition that lasts the duration of the sports season is preferable to one that lasts a short period of time such as a day or a week.
- Structure the competition within the framework of the UIGEA carve-out discussed in Section 7.2.2 of this Guide.

7.3. Promotion Awarding Real Estate

7.3.1. Obstacles to Promotions Awarding Real Estate

During the housing bust when the market value of many homes was far less than the dollar amount the home owner owed on the mortgage, the following situation frequently arose. A private home owner wants to sell raffle tickets and award his house to a randomly selected raffle-ticket purchaser. If the homeowner sells a sufficient amount of tickets, the homeowner can transfer the home and walk away from the home with no remaining home-related debts.

Although this promotion might sound like a good solution for both home owners and raffle purchasers, the promotion has several problems. Raffles combine chance, consideration and a prize, and they are, thus, a category of a lottery. The house or real property is the prize, the price of the raffle ticket is the consideration, and the random selection of a winner provides the chance. As discussed in Section 3.1.1 of this Guide, a private individual or organization can not legally operate a lottery. As a result, the scenario described above is not legally permissible for a private person.

In this Section 7.3, I discuss alternative promotion mechanisms that are legal, depending on the state, and that might allow a private individual or organization to achieve the result of awarding real estate through a promotion. The mechanisms include awarding the real estate in a non-profit raffle (discussed in Section 7.3.2 of this Guide); awarding the real estate in a skill-based contest (discussed in Section 7.3.3 of this Guide); and awarding the real estate as part of an in-package sweepstakes (discussed in Section 7.3.4 of this Guide).

7.3.2. Work with an Eligible Organization to Award the Real Estate in a Non-Profit Raffle

One potential legal option for awarding real estate through a promotion is to work with a non-profit or charitable organization. A number of states have exceptions to anti-gambling laws that allow non-profit and other charitable organizations to offer raffles for fundraising purposes. To offer the real estate as a raffle prize, an organization legally qualified to offer raffles must administer the raffle. Even when awarding real estate through a non-profit raffle, state laws may present obstacles that are insurmountable in certain situations.

Laws permitting non-profit raffles vary significantly from state to state. This Section 7.3.2 of this Guide highlights regulations applicable to offering real estate as a non-profit raffle prize. Section 9.2 of this Guide offers a broader, more general discussion of permissible non-profit raffles and gaming.

Charitable exceptions to anti-gambling laws that permit raffles and other forms of non-profit gaming are designed to benefit non-profit organizations and their charitable and civic missions. State regulators do not necessarily want private individuals and for-profit companies to profit from these laws. States sometimes structure their charitable gaming laws to ensure that such groups do not personally profit from charitable gaming.

State Prohibitions and Limitations. Often, the non-profit organization operating the raffle must register as a charity with its state and register the raffle itself with the state or with the town or county in which the raffle takes place. More specifically for real estate, the non-profit might need a special license or other form of state approval prior to offering real estate as a raffle prize, or the raffle might be subject to real-estate related regulations.[27]

Other states prohibit or limit the number of raffles an organization may hold. Some states explicitly prohibit offering real estate as a raffle prize.[28] Other states set a maximum dollar value on raffle prizes which might eliminate the possibility of raffling real estate if the state-imposed maximum is sufficiently low.

Transfer of Real Estate to Non-Profit. When structuring a real estate raffle with a non-profit, the logistics and timing of the real estate transfer can present a problem. For real-estate raffles, state law may dictate when and how the non–profit obtains title to the property. For example, Iowa allows non-profits to raffle only real property that the non-profit acquired as a gift or donation, or real property the non-profit has owned for at least five years. (Iowa Code § 99B.7.1.d(3)(b) (2014)).

Also, a non-profit organization raffling a property to which it does not currently hold title can trigger issues under a state's real estate licensing laws. An individual or organization can legally solicit buyers and make arrangements for the sale or transfer of property it owns. However, a person who arranges the sale or transfer of real property owned by someone else must typically have a real estate license from the state in which the property is located.

For example, the North Carolina Attorney General has suggested that a non-profit organization raffling real property that the non-profit does not own at the start of the raffle might be viewed as selling property on behalf of others. Such a situation might trigger real estate sale licensing requirements for the non-profit organization.[29]

Restrictions on Sale of Raffle Tickets. A real-estate raffle frequently requires a minimum number of tickets sold so that total ticket proceeds match the market value of the real estate. In some states, raffle laws and regulations may limit how widely a non-profit organization can sell raffle tickets which in turn limits the potential for generating ticket revenue.

Raffles are a form of gambling that some states permit in limited circumstances. An organization can sell tickets for its raffle only in those states in which the raffle is legal. Typically, a non-profit's raffle is legal only in the state in which the non-profit is located. A non-profit that has locations in multiple states may be able to offer a separate raffle in each state but may have more difficulty coordinating compliance with differing state laws to offer one raffle across multiple states.

Quirks of a particular state's law might further impede the wide sale of raffle tickets. For example, Massachusetts regulations require that both the raffle ticket seller and purchaser sign the raffle ticket. (940 Mass. Code Regs. § 12.04(2))

Limitations on Payment to Owner of Real Estate. Proceeds from a non-profit raffle are supposed to go to support the civic and charitable mission of the non-profit. A non-profit organization may lawfully expend raffle proceeds for payment of the raffle prize. Hence, the non-profit organization can apply the raffle proceeds towards the acquisition price of the property to be raffled. However, the non-profit is typically limited to paying only the fair market value of the property. There may be problems if the parties arrange for the non-profit to pay the owner more than the fair market value of the property.

For example, if a raffle awarding a property with a $100,000 fair market value generates $500,000 in raffle ticket sales, many states would not approve the homeowner receiving more than the $100,000 fair market value. In that case, the state would want the remaining $400,000 of the $500,000 to be allocated to the civic and charitable missions of the non-profit organization.

7.3.3. Establish the Promotion Awarding Real Estate as a Skill-Based Contest

As discussed in Section 3.1.3 of this Guide, contests may require consideration for entry. It might be possible to structure a legal real-estate promotion by eliminating the element of chance and making the promotion a skill-based contest. For example, the owner might select the winner of the property through an essay contest.

The contest sponsor must be careful in structuring the rules to make sure that skill rather than chance determines the outcome. In one contest awarding real estate found to be legal under Virginia law a contest sponsor charged each entrant a $100 fee to submit an essay entitled "Why I Should Be Awarded the Property." The sponsor provided specific guidelines for selection of the winner and evaluated each essay for content based on appropriateness, creativity, clarity and sincerity. Students and/or faculty members of an educational institution associated with the contest judged the essays. The Virginia Attorney General found this contest to be based on skill and therefore legal even though proceeds from the promotion benefited an individual who was not affiliated with any civic or charitable organization. (Va. Att'y Gen. Op. (Sept. 19, 1996)).

In contrast, an essay writing contest awarding a house failed to implement specific judging criteria to the satisfaction of South Carolina—resulting in South Carolina labeling the promotion as an illegal lottery. In the South Carolina promotion, contestants paid a $100 entry fee and submitted a written response to the question: "How would winning a home change your life?" According to the contest rules, a panel of judges evaluated the submissions based upon which contestant would benefit most from winning a house and the contestant's writing skills. Instead of identifying the judges or describing their qualifications, the contest materials indicated only that the judges were three independent individuals who were not related in any way to the owner of the home. The South Carolina Attorney General found that the rules lacked clearly established criteria for evaluating the essays and failed to establish the judges' qualifications. The lack of specifics made the attorney general conclude that the winner would be determined by chance, and not by skill. The contest already had the elements of a prize (the house) and consideration (the

$100 entry fee). As a result, the attorney general found the real estate promotion to be an illegal lottery. (S.C. Att'y Gen. Op. (Nov. 19, 2010)).

While states may not regulate a real estate contest as heavily as a real estate raffle, state regulators are alert to any consumer fraud taking place within a real estate contest. To avoid accusations of fraud and misrepresentation from state regulators, best practices for a contest offering real estate as a prize include the sponsor doing all the following:

- provide detailed rules describing the material elements of the promotion,
- establish solid start and end dates,
- be transparent in disclosing the number of entries to be sold before the awarding of the real property can go forward,
- hold entry fees in escrow, and
- return entry money promptly if the sponsor does not sell a sufficient number of tickets within the time-frame indicated in the rules.

7.3.4. Establish the Promotion Awarding Real Estate as an In-Package Sweepstakes

While perhaps not absolutely impossible, the ability to offer legally real estate as part of an in-package sweepstakes opportunity is dubious. For those readers contemplating combining the chance to win the real estate with an in-package sweepstakes opportunity, that idea works only for real products with actual value. Here is how the scenario failed in South Dakota.

A farmer sold a recipe book for $10. The purchase included a chance to win $50,000 cash or eighty acres of land in Union County, South Dakota via a random drawing once the farmer received 20,000 entries. The recipe book consisted of two taped-together photocopied pages and listed thirty-four common recipes ranging from orange jello salad to brownies. Also, even though the rules indicated that no purchase was necessary, the sponsor did not clearly explain how people could enter for free.

Declaring that the recipe book was "not worth one dollar, let alone ten dollars", the South Dakota Attorney General rejected the promotion as a legal sweepstakes and categorized it as an illegal lottery. The attorney general viewed the recipe book as an artifice used by the sponsor-farmer to raffle off his farm in a manner that avoided the provisions of the lottery statute. (S.D. Atty. Gen. Op. No. 86-07 (Mar. 27, 1986)).

7.3.5. Tax Consequences of Promotion Awarding Real Estate

Winning real property in a contest or sweepstakes may have significant tax consequences for the winner. Even if the winner receives the real estate in a raffle sponsored by a non-profit organization or charity, the raffle is considered gambling and the cost of the raffle ticket is not a tax-deductible charitable contribution.

As discussed in Section 5.4 of this Guide, the fair market value of a raffle or promotion prize—in this context, the real estate—is calculated into the winner's gross income and must be reported on the winner's federal income tax return.

7.4. Promotion Using Direct Mail

A promotion incorporating direct mail must comply with the federal Deceptive Mail Prevention and Enforcement Act (DMPEA), 39 U.S.C. §3001 *et seq.* (2014). Individual states may also have parallel requirements in their prize promotion laws. These federal and state prize promotion laws aim to eliminate fraudulent and misleading statements from sweep-stakes, contests, and other prize promotions by ensuring that sponsors give consumers all relevant information and use no deceptive practices.

7.4.1. Compliance with Deceptive Mail Prevention and Enforcement Act

The DMPEA applies only if the sponsor sends information about the promotion through the United States mail. The DMPEA applies to all sweepstakes and to those skill-based contests that charge consideration. The DMPEA does not apply to promotions conducted solely via the internet or telephone since materials about those promotions are not mailed. There is also an exemption for sweepstakes or skill contests advertisements in magazines, newspapers or other periodicals that are mailed as long as those promotions do not seek a purchase or an order on a personalized basis.

When the DMPEA does apply, the sponsor must provide certain disclosures in the promotion mailing. Failure to comply can result in fines of up to two million dollars. In addition, if any mailing violates the DMPEA, the U.S. Postmaster may prohibit its delivery and receipt and a federal court may enjoin the mailing from being sent or received.

DMPEA Rules for Sweepstakes. Under the DMPEA, a sweepstakes sponsor must include the following in any sweepstakes mailing:

- a statement in the mailing, in the rules, and on the order or entry form that no purchase is necessary and that a purchase will not improve the entrant's chances of winning
- all terms and conditions of the sweepstakes promotion, including the rules and entry procedures
- the name and business address of the sponsor
- the estimated odds of winning each prize; the quantity, retail value and nature of each prize; and the schedule for any prize payments to be made over time
- a statement that individuals can halt future mailings by contacting the sponsor via a toll-free number or address provided in the mailing

DMPEA Rules for Contests. Under the DMPEA, a sponsor of a contest that charges consideration must include in any contest mailing the full contest rules as well as the name and business address of the sponsor. The mailing must also include a statement that individuals can halt such mailings by contacting the sponsor via a toll-free number or address. That toll-free number or address must be provided in the mailing. The contest rules must include the following information:

- whether there are multiple rounds in the contest, the number of rounds, the cost to enter each round, whether the difficulty level will increase in subsequent rounds, and the maximum cost to enter all rounds
- an estimate of the number or percentage of entrants who may correctly solve the skill contest or the number or percentage of entrants correctly solving the past three skill contests conducted by the sponsor
- qualifications of the judges if the sponsor is not the judge

- the judging criteria
- the date winners will be announced and the date prizes will be awarded
- the quantity, estimated retail value, and nature of each prize, and the schedule for any payments to be made over time

Other DMPEA Prohibitions. The DMPEA includes several prohibitions to insure that sponsors do not mislead consumers. The sponsor may not suggest or use labels that falsely imply the mailing is from or endorsed by the federal government. The sponsor may not represent that an individual is a winner of a prize unless that individual has won such a prize. The mailing may not contain any statements that contradict or are inconsistent with the rules or the DMPEA disclosures. Technically, the winning representation and inconsistent statement prohibitions are part of only the DMPEA section applying to sweepstakes.[30] However, as a best practice, contest sponsors might also want to heed these prohibitions.

7.4.2. Compliance with State Prize Promotion Laws

Many states have laws that are parallel to the federal Deceptive Mail Prevention and Enforcement Act (DMPEA). While prize promotion protections are most frequently grouped with the state's consumer protection laws, they are sometimes included with a state's criminal laws. A violation of the prize promotions laws is often a violation of the state's deceptive trade practices laws.

Like the DMPEA, state prize promotion laws are often—but not always –applicable only to postal mailings. Which categories of promotions fall under prize promotion laws varies according to the state.

In some states, the prize promotion laws are sufficiently broad to apply to contests. In other states, the prize promotion laws are applicable only to giveaways and/or sweepstakes. While some use the term giveaway to refer to any promotion offering a prize, this Guide uses a narrower definition. A giveaway is an offer of a prize to all individuals who take a specific action. The specific action required to receive the prize is often trying an offered product or taking part in a sales presentation. For example, a sponsor might offer a free dvd player to each consumer who attends a ninety-minute sales presentation for a vacation time share.

Some prize promotion protections are applicable only if chance determines award of the prize. For those giveaways that guarantee the award of a prize to all consumers who take a specific action, a state might still view chance as a determining factor in the giveaway if chance determines which of several potential prizes the consumer receives.

The state summaries in Part Three of this Guide include brief information on the prize promotion laws for each state that has such laws. Here are some of the requirements found in many state prize promotion laws:

Prize Notice Disclosure Requirement. There may be state disclosure requirements for contests, sweepstakes, and other prize promotions. Some states refer to this disclosure requirement as a prize notice requirement. The states' approaches to the prize notice requirements vary. Some states require that certain promotion offers be accompanied by a prize notice with specific disclosures. Other states do not require that sponsors provide a prize notice but do designate what information must be included in a written prize solicitation when sponsors do elect to distribute them.

Not all states that require specific disclosures require that the disclosure be in writing in all circumstances. In some states under certain circumstances, the sponsor can provide the disclosures verbally. Unfortunately, some states prize notice laws do not clearly indicate whether the disclosure must be in writing. Information to be disclosed often includes some or all of the following:

No Purchase Necessary Statement for Sweepstakes. If the promotion is a sweepstakes, the solicitation and informational materials must include a clear and conspicuous statement that no purchase or payment is necessary for participation.

Contest Charging Consideration. When the prize notice laws extend to contests charging consideration, the laws sometimes require disclosure of the maximum amount of money a participant must pay for eligibility to win a prize.

Official Rules. The notice must include the complete rules for the promotion.

Identity of Sponsor. The notice must include the name and address of the sponsor. A sponsor may not deliver a prize notice that falsely identifies who sent the notice. The prohibition includes falsely implying that the notice is from a government agency, public utility, insurance company, brokerage company, consumer reporting agency, debt collector, or law firm.

Accurate Prize Information. Disclosures must include a description of the prize and state the retail value of each prize as well as an explanation of any restrictions or limitations on receiving the prize.

Odds of Winning. Disclosures must include the odds of winning a prize. Some state laws specify the manner in which the sponsor must present these odds. For example in Iowa, the acceptable format requires stating the total number of prizes to be given away and the total number of prize notices distributed using Arabic numerals such as 10 out of 100,000. (Iowa Code §714B.2.3.c (2014)).

Placement and Type Size. Some prize promotion laws specify the placement and type size for the required disclosures and disclaimers. For example, South Dakota requires that disclosures on prize notices not be in less than 12-point boldface type and also requires that the retail value of prizes and the odds of winning a prize be on the first page of the prize notice. (S.D.C.L. §37-32-6 (2014)).

Exemptions. Like the DMPEA, most states exempt from the written disclosure requirements advertisements that appear in a magazine, newspaper, or other periodical if the prize promotion is not directed to a named individual.

Gift as Inducement to Attend Sales Presentation. Many state prize promotion laws target any offer of a prize that includes an invitation or requirement for the consumer to view, listen to, or attend a sales presentation. It applies when the company offers a giveaway or a sweepstakes-winning opportunity to those who attend the company's sales presentation.

Information on Required Sales Presentation. The sponsor must provide a description of any sales presentation at which the person's attendance is required as well as a description of the item being offered for sale.

Opportunity to Return Purchased Item. Some states require that any consumer purchasing an item offered for sale have a certain amount of time in which to cancel the sale. New York is one example. (N.Y. Gen. Bus. § 369-ee(c) (2014)).

Delivery of Prize. If a prize notice requires or invites an individual to a sales presentation, some states prohibit the sales presentation from beginning until the sponsor tells the individual the prize he is to receive and the sponsor actually delivers the prize to the individual. Alternatively, some states require delivery within a certain amount of time with a rain check or cash value replacement if the promised prize is not available.

Representation that a Person Has Won a Prize. In connection with a sales campaign, if a sponsor represents that a person has won a gift or a contest, the sponsor must give the gift to the person without obligation and without shipping or handling charges within a specified period of time.

No Representation of Being Specially Selected. If a sponsor tells a consumer he has won or has been specially selected to receive a prize, the prize cannot be a prize that the sponsor gives to everyone. A common restriction is that the recipient of the prize must have been selected by a method in which no more than ten percent of the persons considered or eligible are selected as winners. Phrases likely to be considered as a representation that a person has been specially selected include "carefully selected", "You have been selected to receive", and "You have been chosen".

No Misrepresentation that a Person Has Won a Prize. If a sponsor tells a person that the person has won a prize, the sponsor must give the person the prize without obligation. Phrases likely to be considered as a representation that a person has won a prize include "Congratulations", "You have won", "You are the winner of" and "You are guaranteed to receive".

Representation that a Person Is Eligible to Win a Prize. In connection with a sales campaign, if a sponsor represents that a person is eligible to win or to receive a prize, the sponsor must provide the disclosures required of a prize notice.

Prohibited Practices. State prize promotion laws often prohibit certain sponsor practices that might defraud or mislead consumers. Common prohibitions in state prize promotion laws include the following:

No False Implication of Winning. The sponsor may not make misleading statements about the recipient's chances of winning a prize. In mailed materials used to sell a product or service, it is unlawful to imply that the recipient has won a prize unless language explaining how the person can actually receive the prize appears on the mailing in clear, easy-to-read, conspicuous print.

No Fake or Simulated Check. Promotional materials may not include documents that simulate a bond, check, or other negotiable instrument, without a disclaimer indicating the document is nonnegotiable and has no cash value.

No False Sense of Urgency. Promotional Materials should not convey a false impression of urgency to prompt consumers to act quickly.

7.5. Promotion Using Telemarketing, Text Messaging, or Faxes

Companies sometimes combine telemarketing calls, text messages, or faxes with promotions. In one real-life example, a company that sells magazine subscriptions sent a text message to thousands of people offering free gift cards or entry into a $1 Million sweepstakes if the receiver called the number included in the text message. When contacted by recipients of its text message, the company attempted to sell them magazine subscriptions.

7.5.1. Compliance with Federal Telemarketing Laws

There are both federal and state laws that regulate telemarketing. This section of the Guide focuses on federal telemarketing laws. Some states have telemarketing laws that are parallel to the federal laws. State telemarketing laws is the subject of Section 7.5.2 of this Guide.

Federal laws designed to protect consumers from annoying and deceptive telemarketing practices include the Telephone Consumer Protection Act of 1991 (TCPA), and the Telemarketing and Consumer Fraud and Abuse

Prevention Act (TCFAPA).[31] The Federal Communications Commission (FCC) issues regulations for the TCPA, and The Federal Trade Commission (FTC) issues the telemarketing sales rule, regulations implementing the TCFAPA.[32]

While the FCC's TCPA regulations focus primarily on whether one can make a telemarketing call, the FTC's telemarketing sales rule focuses primarily on fair business practices while conducting the telemarketing call. The statutory and regulatory provisions of the TCPA and TCFAPA of most relevance to promotion sponsors include the following:

Calls to Mobile Phones. Companies may not use an automatic telephone dialing system or an artificial or prerecorded voice to call a paging number or mobile number without the prior consent of the called party. This prohibition has also been interpreted to mean that companies may not send text messages to mobile phones.[33]

Automated or Prerecorded Calls to Residences. A company may not make a call that is an unsolicited advertisement to a residential number using an artificial or prerecorded voice when the company does not have the prior express written consent of the called party.

Junk Faxes. A company may not send an unsolicited advertisement via facsimile (*i.e.*, fax) unless all of the following three conditions apply:

- the company has an established business relationship with the recipient,
- the recipient voluntarily provides the recipient's fax number within the context of that business relationship,
- and the fax includes a notice with a cost-free mechanism for the recipient to opt out of receiving additional fax communications.

Do Not Call Registry. TCPA and its regulations require companies to honor requests from consumers to stop calling them. These requests come from the federal Do Not Call registry as well as internal company lists that telemarketers are required to maintain.

Promotion as Lead Generator. Promotions can serve as lead generators for a company's products. Consumers who have registered their telephone number in a Do Not Call registry have expressed their preference not to receive telemarketing calls. Pursuant to state and federal law, companies must honor that preference unless the consumer gives his or her express written authorization to receive a call in spite of the registration. If an individual has registered on the federal or a state Do Not Call list and requested no phone calls, the individual's subsequent participation in a sponsor's promotion does not give the sponsor the right to ignore the no-call registrations.

A company may call a consumer's number on the federal registry only if the consumer has signed a written document expressly agreeing to receive the company's calls at that number.[34] The company must obtain the consent in a clear and conspicuous manner. A company cannot attempt to trick the consumer into providing the consent with the use of a prize promotion or sweepstakes entry form.[35]

Obtaining consent through trickery and misrepresentations can generate lawsuits and fines from the FTC and from state attorney general offices. For example, as part of its Kitchen Magic Sweepstakes, A&P sweepstakes entry forms stated that the participant granted Kitchen Magic permission to call the participant with information about Kitchen Magic products and services. According to the entry form, the consent to receive calls from Kitchen Magic was valid even if the participant's telephone number was registered with a state or federal do not call list. New York's Attorney General argued that the A&P Sweepstakes had buried the language in its official rules and, therefore, the rules did not serve as valid consent. To settle the case, A&P and Kitchen Magic paid a $100,000 penalty and agreed to stop the practice.[36]

Consent to Call. There is potential TCPA liability regardless of whether a company makes the calls itself or retains a third party to make the calls on its behalf.[37] Sometimes a company obtains names and telephone or fax numbers from a third party. The third party may represent to the company that the persons on the list have consented to receiving phone calls. That representation by itself is not sufficient for a company to escape potential TCPA liability. Courts expect the company to take additional steps to confirm consent.[38]

When making calls or sending texts based on having consent, the company needs to ensure that it does indeed have the consumer's consent. Validity of consents can be an issue when obtaining names and numbers from a third party. A consumer's consent to receive telephone or fax communications from one company may not qualify as consent to receive communications from a different company. Here is a real-life example illustrating this concept.

Satterfield v. Simon & Schuster, 569 F.3d 946 (9th Cir., 2009). A consumer joined Nextones in order to receive a free ringtone. As part of the online sign-up process, the consumer selected a check-box consenting to receive promotions from Nextones affiliates and brands. Nextones licensed the phone numbers of its subscribers to other companies to use for their own marketing purposes.

Book publisher Simon & Schuster licensed 100,000 Nextone phone numbers and sent text messages to those Nextone numbers as part of its promotional campaign for a Stephen King novel. The text message included "The next call you take may be your . . . Join the Stephen King VIP Mobile Club at www.cellthebook.com. RplySTOP2OptOut. PwdByNexton." The court decided that the consumer had not consented to receiving communications from Simon & Schuster since Simon & Schuster was neither an affiliate nor a brand of Nextones. It did not matter that the text message included the phrase PwdByNextone. According to the court, such logic would mean any company could include "PwdbyNextone" in its text message and be considered a brand of Nextones.

What might have saved Simon & Schuster is broader language in the Nextones consent to include messages about products Nextones believes would be of interest to the consumer. As a best practice, companies licensing numbers for telemarketing should review the form of consent the consumer gave to the third party to ensure the consent covers a communication from the company.

Required Disclosures for Prize Promotions Incorporated into Telemarketing Campaigns. The FTC's telemarketing sales rule contains rules regarding prize promotions incorporated into telemarketing campaigns. The telemarketing sales rule defines a prize promotion to be a sweepstakes; other game of chance; or an oral or written representation that a person has won, has been selected to receive, or may be eligible to win a prize.

A telemarketing call that results in the consumer consenting to buy goods or services triggers certain disclosure requirements. When the telemarketing campaign includes a prize promotion, required disclosures include the odds of winning a prize, an explanation of how to participate without buying anything, a statement that no purchase or payment is required to win, and disclosure of all other material costs or conditions to receive or redeem a prize that is the subject of the prize promotion.[39] There are also record-keeping requirements for prizes awarded.[40]

7.5.2. Compliance with State Telemarketing Laws

Some states have telemarketing laws. Telemarketers sometimes incorporate giveaways and promotion-playing opportunities into their telephone sales campaigns. As a result, the telemarketing laws of several states specifically address giveaways and promotion-playing opportunities combined with telephone solicitations.

The discussion of state telemarketing laws in this Guide focuses on the provisions of those laws specifically related to giveaways and promotion-playing opportunities. The state summaries in Part Three of this Guide include brief information on the telemarketing laws of each state with telemarketing laws that include significant prize promotion provisions. This Guide does not include an in-depth discussion of all registration, bonding, and disclosure requirements commonly incorporated into a state's telemarketing laws.

Applicability of State Telemarketing Laws. State telemarketing laws apply to telephone marketers, sometimes referred to by the state laws as telephonic sellers, telemarketers, telephone solicitors, or other names. A telephone solicitation is a call made to a consumer for the purpose of encouraging the consumer to purchase goods or services. In general, a company is a telemarketer and falls under a state's telemarketing laws if the company makes telephone solicitations from the state or calls potential purchasers located in the state.

When the state's telemarketing laws do apply to a company's telephone activities, the state may have registration, bonding, prohibited practices, and disclosure requirements that apply to the company's telephone sales campaign. Most states include a long list of organizations and telephone activities that are exempt from the state's telemarketing laws. Examples of organizations that may be exempt from a state's telemarketing laws include companies that make telephone solicitations infrequently and companies that make telephone solicitations for religious, political or charitable purposes.

Telemarketing Provisions Specific to Prize Promotions. Some—but not all—states' telemarketing laws include provisions specific to promotions and giveaways incorporated into the telephone solicitation campaign. Here are some of the common characteristics in the prize promotion provisions for those state telemarketing laws that specifically address promotions:

Information Filing Requirements. If, as part of the telemarketing campaign, the telephone seller represents that the purchaser is or might be eligible to receive any gift, premium, bonus, or prize, the telephone seller must submit to the state the material terms of the giveaway or prize-winning opportunity. Required information varies by state but may include a description of the prize and its value, odds of winning, terms and conditions for receiving the prize, and the names and addresses of consumers receiving that prize during the last year. In some states, filing prize-related information is part of the general registration procedure required of telemarketers prior to launching a telemarketing campaign in the state. In other states, it is a separate information filing.

Bonding Requirements. Where prizes or giveaways are offered as part of a telemarketing campaign, some states require the telephone seller to post a bond equal to the value of the prizes.

Disclosure Requirements. The telephone seller must disclose certain information to the consumer as part of the call. Disclosure requirements vary by state and may include a description of the prize, its value, the terms and conditions the consumer must satisfy to receive the prize, and a statement that no purchase is necessary to compete for or receive the prize.

No Misrepresentations or Misleading Statements. Some states' telemarketing laws contain specific prohibitions against misrepresenting that any person has won a contest, sweepstakes or drawing. States also generally prohibit misrepresentations that the person will receive free goods, services or property. These prohibitions against misrepresentation are often similar to the prohibitions included in state prize promotion laws, as discussed in Section 7.4.2 of this Guide.

Record-Keeping Requirements. If the telemarketing campaign includes a prize promotion, there may be record-keeping requirements directly related to the prize promotion. Records to be retained may include copies of promotional materials, information about the prizes awarded, and the name and last-known address of each prize recipient.

7.5.3. Text Messaging and Other Technologies

The extent to which telemarketing restrictions apply to developing technologies is uncertain. For example, the TCPA and FCC regulations define an automatic telephone dialing system as "equipment which has the capacity (A) to store or produce numbers to be called, using a random or sequential number generator; and (B) to dial such numbers."[41] The TCPA prohibits companies from using an automatic telephone dialing system or an artificial or prerecorded voice to call a mobile number without the prior consent of the called party. The FCC as well as courts have interpreted the TCPA prohibition to include a prohibition against sending a text message to a mobile number.

However, some companies have made the argument that internet-to-phone text messaging technology does not qualify as an automatic telephone dialing system and that they can use such technology to send text messages to consumers. Here is how internet-to-phone text messaging works.

Internet-to-phone text messaging initiates text messages via the internet rather than via a telephone system. Suppose the ABC Company wants to contact mobile phone users using internet-to-phone text messaging. ABC Company accomplishes that with the following steps:

- ABC Company collects mobile phone numbers of the consumers it wants to contact.
- ABC Company identifies the carrier for each mobile phone number it has collected (*e.g.*, Verizon, Sprint, *etc.*).
- ABC Company creates an email address for those mobile phone numbers using the domain name assigned by the carrier for mobile service messages. For example, if ABC Company has the cell phone number 202-555-1234 and identifies the carrier for that number as Verizon, the ABC Company can create the email address 2025551234@verizon.messaging.net.
- ABC Company sends an email message to that created email address. As an example, sending an email message to 2025551234@verizon.messaging.net results in the holder of mobile phone number, 202-555-1234, receiving a text message on that mobile telephone line.

While internet to-phone text messaging bypasses the telephone system, it can still result in the recipient of the text message being charged by its carrier for receipt of the text message, a result telemarketing laws are designed to prevent.

In 2012, Revolution Messaging, an agency that relies heavily on digital communications for its works with non-profit organizations and political campaigns, asked the FCC to clarify that the TCPA applied to text messages sent by internet-to-phone text messaging technology. (Revolution Messaging, LLC, Petition for an Expedited Clarification and Declaratory Ruling, CG Dkt No. 02-278 (filed Jan. 19, 2012)). As of the writing of this Guide, the FCC had not issued a ruling in response to Revolution Messaging's petition.

7.6. Broadcast Station Promotions

Broadcast stations—radio stations especially—frequently offer promotions. In addition to complying with all the applicable laws discussed in this Guide, broadcast stations running promotions must comply with certain communications laws and regulations. Specifically, broadcast stations must comply with Section 509 of the Communications Act, 47 U.S.C. §509(b)(1) (2014). Broadcast stations must also comply with

Regulation 73.1216, 47 C.F.R. § 73.1216, issued by the Federal Communications Commission (FCC). For broadcasters offering promotions, FCC Regulation 73.1216 carries much more impact than does Section 509 of the Communications Act.

The texts of the communications laws and regulations do not distinguish between a contest and a sweepstakes. Instead, Section 509 of the Communications Act and FCC Regulation 73.1216 use the general term contest. FCC Regulation 73.1216 defines contest as a scheme in which a prize is offered or awarded, based upon chance, knowledge, diligence, or skill, to members of the public. When describing the applicability of Section 509, the Communications Act says Section 509 is applicable to any contest broadcast by a station in connection with which the program sponsor or other person offers a prize. One can safely interpret these definitions to mean that the communications laws apply to all prize-awarding promotions offered by broadcast stations regardless of whether the promotion is a skill-based contest or a chance-based sweepstakes.

7.6.1. Broadcast Stations Must Announce a Promotion's Material Terms On-Air

FCC Regulation 73.1216 requires that broadcast stations announce on-air all material terms of a promotion and conduct the promotion substantially as announced. Material terms include, but are not limited to, how to enter, any eligibility restrictions, entry deadline dates, time and means of selection of winners, and the extent, nature and value of prizes, tie-breaking procedures, and the basis for the valuation of the prizes.

The FCC expects broadcast stations to disclose the promotion's material terms via periodic on-air announcements throughout the duration of the promotion. While a broadcaster does not need to state the material terms each time it mentions the promotion on the air, the FCC does not specify the number of times a broadcaster must announce the material terms. Instead, the FCC states it is sufficient for the broadcaster to share the material terms in a reasonable number of announcements.

Stations can use disclosure by non-broadcast means to supplement the on-air disclosures. While the FCC will consider the non-broadcast disclosures when evaluating the overall adequacy of the disclosures, the

FCC does not accept non-broadcast disclosure as a substitute for on-air disclosure. If a broadcast station advertises its promotion on the air, it must also periodically announce the material terms on the air. As of the writing of this Guide, there were pending proposals to modify Rule 73.1216 to allow broadcasters to replace on-air announcements with publication via the internet, email, and other methods.[42]

Examples of FCC Penalties. In some respects, broadcast stations face greater risk of penalties for wayward promotions than do other organizations conducting promotions. This is due to the ease with which a consumer can initiate a complaint against a broadcast station. Actions against broadcast stations often begin with a complaint filed with the FCC. Any member of the public or any competitor can easily file a complaint against a station.

It is true that unhappy participants of non-broadcast-station promotions can file complaints with the state attorney general office or with the consumer protection division. However, investigations of promotions by state regulators focus on complaints alleging fraud and egregious violations of anti-gambling and lottery laws. In contrast, the FCC tends to be broader and more aggressive in its selection of promotion-related matters to pursue. The FCC often actively pursues matters that a state regulator, encountering the same matter in a non-broadcast-station promotion, might view as a contract dispute for a court to settle.

In the context of non-broadcast-station promotions, a participant typically pursues legal action only when the stakes are significant. For example, a participant in a non-broadcast-station promotion might be inclined to initiate a legal proceeding if the sponsor's error or misdeed lost the participant a million dollar prize—but less inclined to do so if the sponsor's infraction lost the participant a twenty-five dollar prize. In contrast, the FCC may review and impose monetary fines for relatively minor infractions when dealing with promotions offered by broadcast stations. Here are real-life examples of FCC actions involving promotions offered by broadcast stations:

Ending Promotion Prior to Stated End Date. Station WWEG stopped taking submissions for its Father's Day Contest on June 12. However, in its on-air announcements and its written official rules, the station stated that people could submit entries through June 13. The FCC interpreted this statement to mean that people could enter the contest up to and including June 13. The radio station probably meant to indicate the deadline as "before June 13" as opposed to "through June 13". Nevertheless, the FCC fined the station $4,000 for failing to conduct the promotion as announced. (*In the Matter of Nassau Broadcasting; Licensee of Station WWEG(FM), Myersville, Md.,* 51 Comm. Reg. (P & F) 264 (August 23, 2010)).

Failure to Deliver Prize within Promised Time Frame. In the rules for its promotion, Station WAQY promised delivery of the prize within thirty days. However, the station delivered the prize in seven months without providing any justification for the delay. The FCC fined WAQY $4,000. (*In the Matter of Saga Communications of New England, Licensee of Station WAQY(FM), Springfield, Ma.,* 25 FCC Rcd 3289 (April 1, 2010)).

Failure to Disclose Correctly the Prize to be Awarded. The FCC fined Station KPRR $4,000 for not clarifying that the prize in the So You Want to Win 10,000 Promotion was 10,000 Italian lira and not 10,000 U.S. dollars. At the time of the promotion, 10,000 Italian lira was equivalent to $53 U.S. Dollars. (*Clear Channel Broadcasting Licenses, Licensee of Station KPRR(FM), El Paso, Tx,* 15 FCC Rcd 2734 (Enforcement Bureau 2000)).

Substitution of Online Disclosure for On-Air Announcement. The FCC fined Clear Channel $22,000 for failure to announce contest rules over the air on six of its stations. Clear Channel invited listeners to prepare and submit video commercials for Chevrolet. The prize was an automobile.

In its defense, Clear Channel argued that the promotion had been conducted via the internet and was not an over-the-air promotion. The FCC did not accept this argument in part because Clear Channel had broadcast advertisements for the promotion over-the-air. *In the Matter of Clear Channel Communications, Notice of Apparent Liability for Forfeiture,* File No. EB-08-IH-1738 (Enforcement Bureau, Jan. 19, 2012).

7.6.2. Prohibited Practices in Broadcast Promotions

Section 509 of the Communications Act, entitled "Prohibited Practices in Contests of Knowledge, Skill or Chance", makes it unlawful for any person to manipulate the outcome of a broadcast promotion by doing

such things as supplying contestants with answers or encouraging participants to lose on purpose. Section 509 is a response to the quiz show scandal
of the 1950's during which producers sometimes rigged the outcomes of
televised game shows by giving answers to participants and otherwise
orchestrating who won and who lost.

Section 509 of the Communications Act applies to any bona fide contest
of knowledge, skill, or chance. Since the statute does not define "contest of
intellectual knowledge or skill" and no case law has yet addressed which
contests Section 509 governs, there is uncertainty as to whether the law
applies to contests testing non-intellectual skills and traits such as dancing,
singing, and beauty.

CHAPTER 8

Handling Copyright, Intellectual Property, and Rights Clearance Issues

8.1. How Rights Clearance Issues Arise in Promotions

Rights clearance is what producers and distributors of films, books, music, advertisements, and other creative works do to verify that the material in their productions does not violate the rights of another person and does not violate any relevant laws. Rights clearance also entails acquiring any necessary licenses or permissions required for use of any protected materials. Other terms used to describe the process of clearing rights include vetting a production, getting permission, and licensing.

Rights clearance and licensing issues can arise in a promotion in at least three ways:

- The promotion requests entrants to submit original works that the sponsor shares with the public.
- The sponsor uses its own intellectual property as part of the promotion.
- The sponsor uses the intellectual property of others in connection with the promotion.

This Chapter 8 of this Guide provides a brief overview of the rights clearance and permissions process. For more detailed information on clearing rights and getting permission, refer to my book, *The Permission Seeker's Guide Through the Legal Jungle: Clearing Copyrights, Trademarks, and Other Rights for Entertainment and Media Productions.*

8.1.1. What Is Intellectual Property?

Sponsors must often concern themselves with protecting their own intellectual property as well as with respecting the intellectual property rights of others. The term intellectual property refers to copyrights, trademarks, patents, and trade secrets. Copyright and trademark are the forms of intellectual property most prevalent in most promotions. However, it is possible for patent and trade secret law concerns to arise in a promotion.

With respect to rights of others, there are several areas of concern in addition to intellectual property. If the promotion names or depicts people, the sponsor should be concerned with privacy, publicity, and defamation laws. If the promotion offers descriptions of or comparisons with competing products, the sponsor should be concerned with product disparagement laws.

8.1.2. Rights Clearance Risks in Promotions

As a general rule, when using someone else's material, the sponsor should have permission for that use—whether the material is music, written text, or artwork. As discussed in Section 8.3 of this Guide, there are circumstances in which the law does not require permission to use someone else's material.

However, even when an exception to needing permission applies, using someone else's material without permission always creates risk. This risk falls into two separate categories. There is the risk of being sued. There is the separate risk of losing the lawsuit and having to pay money damages or comply with penalties imposed by a court.

Many rights owners are extremely aggressive about protecting the use of their content. They might challenge the unauthorized use of their content even if there is valid legal justification for the unauthorized use. Many contest and sweepstakes sponsors, deem it not worthwhile to accept any risks associated with the unauthorized use of material and require permissions for the use of any third party material in their promotions.

8.2. Types of Intellectual Property and Rights Clearance Issues

8.2.1. Copyright

Copyright is the form of intellectual property with which most people have the most familiarity. The federal Copyright Act, 17 U.S.C. §101 *et seq.*, protects original works of authorship and extends protection to works such as books, magazines, newspapers, poems, songs, plays, photographs, paintings, sculptures, films, and websites. The originality requirement is met as long as the work is not copied from another source.

Under current copyright law, copyright protects a work as soon as the creator writes down, records, or otherwise fixes the work. While registration maximizes the copyright owner's ability to protect a work, registration of the work with the U.S. Copyright Office is not required for valid copyright protection.

If entrants create an original work such as an essay or video for submission to a sponsor's promotion, each entrant automatically owns the copyright in that submission. If the sponsor wants to display, distribute, reproduce, or otherwise use the submission, the sponsor needs the entrant's permission. Section 8.4.1 of this Guide explains how sponsors can obtain this permission from entrants.

8.2.2. Trademark

Trademarks identify the source of specific goods and services. Trademarks can be words, phrases, logos, graphic symbols, designs, sounds, shapes, colors and even smells. A combination of federal and state laws protect trademarks. Most brand names, logos, and slogans used in product advertisements are protectable trademarks. Examples of protectable trademarks include brand names such as Federal Express and Nabisco; logos such as the McDonald's golden arches; and slogans such as *Snap, Crackle, Pop*; *Don't Leave Home Without It*; and *Finger Lickin' Good*.

As a general rule, a promotion may refer to a trademark as long as the reference does not confuse or deceive consumers as to source, sponsorship or affiliation. In other words, a sponsor may not falsely imply that a product manufacturer or trademark owner is affiliated with or endorses the promotion. As discussed in Section 4.4.9 of this Guide, it is a best practice to include in promotion rules a disclaimer indicating that the manufacturers of any brand-name products offered as prizes are not associated with the promotion.

8.2.3. Patent

Under the U.S. Patent Act, 35 U.S.C. §§1 to 376, patent protection is available for inventions and discoveries that are novel, useful, and nonobvious. The requirements of novelty, usefulness, and nonobviousness have specific meanings within patent law that this Guide mentions only briefly.

To be novel, an invention must be different from all inventions that came before it. To be useful, the invention must be operable and must provide some benefit—even if the benefit is trivial. To be nonobvious, the invention must be sufficiently different from what has been used or described previously that the invention is not evident to a person having ordinary skill in the subject matter area related to the invention.

Patent law issues may arise if the promotion asks entrants to submit entries that might qualify for patent protection, or if the sponsor allows entrants access to the sponsor's patents. For example, the FTC sponsored a Robocall Challenge Promotion inviting entrants to submit solutions to block illegal robocalls. A robocall is an unsolicited telephone call with a prerecorded message. It is possible that some of the submitted robocall solutions might be eligible for patent protection. The promotion left all patent and other intellectual property in each submission to the entrant with the FTC taking only a non-exclusive license in the submission.

8.2.4. Trade Secret

A trade secret is confidential information of a particular company that gives the company a competitive advantage over other businesses. The primary benefit of a trade secret comes from the fact that other companies do not have the same information. Specifically, a trade secret can consist of a practice, a method, a design, computer software, a customer list, a database, a compilation of information, or other know-how. Examples of trade secrets include Google's search algorithm; the methodology behind the New York Times Best Seller list; and recipes for Kentucky Fried Chicken, McDonald's Big Mac's Special Sauce, and Pepsi-Cola.

8.2.5. Rights of Persons—Privacy, Publicity, and Defamation

When handled improperly, mentioning or portraying real people can spark claims of privacy, publicity and defamation violations. Unlike copyright, patent, and much of trademark law, the laws of privacy, publicity, and defamation are governed primarily by state law. As a result, these laws vary significantly from state to state.

- The right of privacy is the right to be left alone and the right to have others stay out of one's personal affairs.
- The right of publicity is the right to prevent others from commercializing or profiting from one's identity.
- Defamation occurs when a false statement is made about a person and the statement damages that person's reputation.

In a promotion, rights of the person arise in at least three distinct ways:

First, if the promoter invites entrants to submit original creative works, entrant submissions might portray, depict, or mention real people in a manner that violates the rights of those real people.

Second, rights of the person might arise with respect to entrants themselves. If sponsors want to publicize the names, images, and other identifying information about the entrants within the context of advertising the promotion and promotion results, sponsors need the entrants' permission.

Third, if the sponsor uses the name of other people to advertise the promotion, such use might violate the persons' publicity rights. As an example, a foundation for famous chef, Julia Child, sued Williams-Sonoma, a manufacturer of culinary products, after Williams-Sonoma used Julia Child's name, photograph and likeness in the operation of a Julia Child's Sweepstakes and for other commercial purposes. (*The Julia Child Foundation v. Williams-Sonoma,* Complaint filed in Sup. Ct. Ca., County of Santa Barbara, Sept. 4, 2013).

8.2.6. Disparagement and False Advertising

Comments about a company or its products that stray too far from fact may result in claims of commercial disparagement or similar claims such as trade libel, product disparagement, slander of goods, unfair competition or interference with prospective business advantage. Commercial disparagement claims are generally state law claims so their elements vary from state to state. To avoid such claims, sponsors should avoid actions that encourage entrants to criticize other products.

A well-known example of a disparagement claim in the context of promotions involved the Quiznos Versus Subway TV Ad Challenge. As part of the promotion, Quiznos invited contestants to submit a video comparing Quiznos to Subway and illustrating why Quiznos is better than Subway. The contest rules did prohibit "any false or misleading statement, or any libelous, slanderous or disparaging statement regarding Quiznos or Subway, or of either companies' products or services." Nevertheless, Subway claimed that the submitted entries made false claims about Subway and otherwise disparaged the Subway brand. Many of the submitted videos depicted Subway products as having no meat. Subway sued Quiznos for false and deceptive advertising. After Quiznos' efforts to obtain a summary judgment ruling in its favor failed, Quiznos and Subway ultimately settled the lawsuit without going to trial. (*Doctor's Assoc. v. QIP Holder*, Memorandum of Decision Denying Defendant's Motion for Summary Judgment, No. 3:06-cv-1710-VLB (D. Conn. Feb. 19, 2010))

8.2.7. Obscenity and Indecency

Obscenity and indecency considerations might arise in promotions inviting the submission of original content. For the benefit of the company and the brand, most sponsors do not want promotion entries to include any material that might be deemed as indecent or obscene.

Obscenity. Supreme Court case law dictates that material is obscene if it appeals to the prurient interest, describes sexual conduct in a patently offensive manner, and lacks value.[43] Congress and each state have discretion to decide what qualifies as prurient, patently offensive, and lacking in value so the response to what material is obscene can differ from one community to the next. While people are allowed to possess obscene materials, they are not allowed to communicate, distribute, sell or transport obscene materials.

Indecency. Indecency laws[44] are of concern if the sponsor wants to broadcast submissions on free radio or television. The Federal Communications Commission (FCC) prohibits the broadcast of indecent programming between 6:00 a.m. and 10:00 p.m. The FCC does not regulate indecency on pay television or the internet.

Material is indecent if it contains patently offensive sexual or excretory references that do not rise to the level of obscenity. For example, many curse words and some forms of nudity are categorized as indecent.

Indecency and Obscenity Considerations for Sponsor. A sponsor can impose stricter, more stringent indecency and obscenity requirements than those imposed by law. In fact, the promotion rules should indicate that the sponsor can disqualify any entries that the sponsor, in its sole discretion, determines to be obscene, indecent or otherwise objectionable or inappropriate. Section 4.4.7 of this Guide has such sample language.

8.3. When Permission Might Not Be Required for Use of Copyrighted and Other Protected Materials

In some instances, the law allows use of copyrighted works and references to people, brand names, and trademarks without the permission of the rights owner. There is a huge caveat. Application of these legal exceptions is subjective, fact-specific, and even fickle at times.

Use of someone else's material in a promotion might qualify as an advertising use to which many of the no-permission-needed exceptions do not apply. While it is not impossible for an advertising use to qualify for fair use, parody, or other First Amendment protection, these exceptions to the need for permission are less available in an advertising context.

Here are the most common circumstances in which permission is not required for use of copyrighted and other works:

First Amendment Use. One cannot use copyright, trademark, and other rights as a means to stop people from expressing themselves, from giving their opinions, and from otherwise using their First Amendment rights. There is always a balancing act between one person's First Amendment rights and another person's right to protect his copyrights, trademarks, publicity, and privacy rights.

Using copyrighted material, depictions of people, and other protected materials for the purpose of reporting the news or other events of public interest; making a commentary about history, society, or culture; critiquing the material; and teaching often qualify as a First Amendment-protected use for which no permission is required. First Amendment rights are the foundation supporting the copyright fair use, trademark fair use, and parody use exceptions discussed below.

Copyright Fair Use. The Copyright Fair Use Doctrine allows one to use a reasonable portion of a copyrighted work without running afoul of copyright law. There is no bright-line rule for what qualifies as a fair use. A use has a better chance of qualifying as a fair use if the use is non-commercial, comprises a small portion of the copyrighted work, is transformative, and does not damage the rights owner's ability to market the work.

The term "transformative" has a specific meaning within copyright law. A use is transformative if the use of the material is creatively different from the copyright owner's intended use. For example, use of copyrighted material in a parody or in a montage might qualify as transformative.

Trademark Fair Use. When one uses a trademark to refer to or describe the trademark owner's goods or services, that is a nominative fair use of the trademark. It is permissible as long as one uses the trademark only as necessary to identify the good or service and does not suggest sponsorship or endorsement by the trademark owner.

Parody. A use that qualifies as a parody does not require the permission of the rights owner. Parody involves the use of materials, depictions of persons or organizations as a target of a joke or commentary.

Public Domain Works. For purposes of copyright law, being in the public domain means that a work, although falling into a subject area eligible for copyright protection, is nevertheless not copyright protected. Typically, works are in the public domain because the copyright in the work expired, the creator of the work deliberately placed the work into the public domain, or no copyright ever existed in the work as is the case for federal government works.

With respect to copyright expiration, due to changes in copyright law, different copyright periods apply to different works depending on the date of creation or publication of the specific work. As a general rule, works published prior to 1923 are in the public domain for United States copyright law purposes.

Federal Government Works. Federal government works are in the public domain. Federal government works include works created by federal government employees within the scope of their employment. They also include works commissioned by the federal government from third party freelancers and independent contractors who transfer rights in those works to the government as a work made for hire. In contrast to federal government works, state and local government works are not always in the public domain and may be protected by copyright.

No Privacy or Defamation Rights for the Deceased. Deceased individuals can not be defamed or have their privacy invaded. In contrast, deceased individuals may have publicity rights which their estates or heirs can enforce.

8.4. Intellectual Property Appearing in Entrant Submissions

A promotion may raise rights clearance issues when participants submit original creative works such as essays, videos, music, photographs, and artwork. Examples of elements that an entrant might put into a submission that create rights clearance concerns include the following:

- background music for a video submission
- a quote from a famous movie in a submitted essay
- the image or name of a real person
- the image of a brand-name product in a submitted photograph
- a submitted writing based on real-life events

When such elements appear in original material created by entrants, the entries might violate copyright, trademark, privacy, publicity, defamation, and other rights clearance laws. If the sponsor plans to post, stream, publish, broadcast, or otherwise share entrant submissions with the public, the sponsor should make certain that the entrant has permission to use these elements in the submission or that the entrant's use of the material qualifies as a use for which no permission is needed. Section 8.3 of this Guide lists circumstances when permission may not be required. The sponsor also needs the entrant's permission to share the submission with the public.

8.4.1. Grant of Rights by Entrant to Sponsor

If the sponsor requests entrants to submit original works that the sponsor will share with the public, the sponsor needs permission from the entrant. The promotion rules or the release to be signed by the winner should cover the scope of rights needed by the sponsor. The sponsor should consider in which media it will use the entry; whether it needs the right to edit the entry; the period for which the sponsor needs rights; and the geographic regions in which the sponsor wants to use the entry.

The sponsor can get permissions for entrant-created material through a license or assignment. The form of permission most typically requested by a sponsor is a non-exclusive license. A license grants permission to use material for a specific purpose. In contrast, an assignment transfers ownership of all or substantially all of the rights in the material.

Characteristics of License Grant. A license can take different forms. It can be verbal or written. It can be expressly granted or implied via conduct. It can take the form of an informal email or a more formal written document. Sponsors typically obtain a written, expressly granted license from entrants conveyed through the promotion rules or a winner's release or affidavit.

Express License or Implied License. The grant of a license or permission to use can be implied through conduct. For example, if the marketing materials for a Best Original Poem Contest indicate that the sponsor will publish all submitted poems on the sponsor's website, anyone submitting a poem arguably grants an implied license allowing posting of the submitted poem on the sponsor's website.

Nevertheless, many sponsors prefer an express license since an implied license does have limitations. An implied license does not suffice if the sponsor wants an exclusive license and might not suffice if the sponsor wants to use the poem in a context outside the promotion. While most sponsors do not need an exclusive license, many do want to use submissions beyond the promotion. Also, the existence of an express license is easier to prove than the existence of an implied license.

For these and other reasons, many sponsors choose to obtain an express license. A sponsor can obtain an express license through the promotion rules and through winner affidavits.

Exclusive or Non-Exclusive License. A license can be exclusive or non-exclusive. If the license is exclusive, the rights owner cannot grant the same rights to anyone else. There are varying degrees of exclusivity. Sometimes exclusivity is absolute meaning that the rights owner may not allow anyone other than the license recipient to use the material. Alternatively, the exclusivity may be limited to a particular industry or product. In practice, an exclusive license can be written so broadly that it captures all or almost all of the rights that a full assignment conveys.

Documentation for Non-Exclusive License. The sponsor can obtain many of the permissions and licenses it needs from an entrant through publication of the promotion's rules. As discussed in Section 4.3 of this Guide, the promotion's rules form a binding contract between the sponsor and the entrants. If the rules contain the appropriate language, the entrants grant the permission by the act of entering the promotion.

Publication of the rules works for grant of a non-exclusive license. For example, the promotion's rules might accomplish a non-exclusive license grant with the following language:

> Entrant retains all intellectual property and other rights in the submission, however, entrant hereby grants sponsor a royalty-free, world-wide, fully paid-up, perpetual, irrevocable, non-exclusive right and license to use the submission for any and all purposes.

Generally, sponsors should not rely on mere publication of the rules as an effective manner of granting an exclusive license or granting an assignment. However, as discussed immediately below, the *Metropolitan Regional Information Systems* case suggests that rules offered as a click-wrap agreement might be sufficient for grant of an exclusive license or an outright assignment.

Documentation for Exclusive License or Transfer of Intellectual Property. An exclusive license, an assignment, or an ownership transfer require a written document signed by the person or entity conveying the rights.[45]

If the sponsor wants to be the only one that can broadcast or distribute the winning entry, the sponsor needs an exclusive license or ownership of the entry. While mere publication of promotion rules is not sufficient for grant of an exclusive license or assignment, there is case law suggesting that rules offered as a click-wrap agreement might be sufficient for this purpose.

Transfer via Online Click-Through Agreement. In the case, *Metropolitan Regional Information Systems v. American Home Realty Network*, 722 F.3d 591 (4th Cir. 2013), the fourth Circuit Court of Appeals ruled that a person can assign a copyright via an online click-through agreement. In this case, Metropolitan Regional (MRIS) offered an online real estate listing service. When a real estate broker or agent uploaded a real estate listing, the broker or agent transferred to MRIS the copyright in each photograph included in the listing. The brokers and agents made the copyright transfer by consenting to the terms of service for the MRIS online service which the brokers and agents did by clicking a button on the screen marked as "yes". The MRIS Terms of Service included the following language:

> All images submitted to the MRIS Service become the exclusive property of [MRIS]. By submitting an image, you hereby irrevocably assign (and agree to assign) to MRIS, free and clear of any restrictions or encumbrances, all of your rights, title and interest in and to the image submitted. This assignment includes, without limitation, all worldwide copyrights in and to the image, and the right to sue for past and future infringements. (*Metropolitan Regional Information Systems v. American Home Realty Network*, 722 F.3d 591, 593 (4th Cir. 2013))

American Home Realty Network, a competitor of MRIS, copied images from the MRIS online service and used the images on its own American Home Realty website. MRIS sued American Home Realty for copyright infringement. In its defense, American Home Realty argued in part that

MRIS could not sue for copyright infringement because MRIS did not own the copyright in the images submitted with the real estate listings.

According to American Home Realty's argument, the brokers' and agents' "yes" click to the MRIS terms of service did not satisfy the Copyright Act's written transfer requirement. The court disagreed and ruled that the "yes" click accepting the MRIS website's terms of service did satisfy the Copyright Act's written transfer requirement.[46]

The *Metropolitan Regional* ruling supports the idea that a sponsor of an online promotion can obtain an exclusive license or assignment from an entrant by publishing rules online which the entrant accepts by checking "yes" or otherwise actively confirming consent. Nevertheless, a recommended best practice for sponsors is to continue using formal documents for transfers until there is additional support for the validity of click-wrap exclusive licenses and assignments. There are two reasons for this recommendation.

First, the *Metropolitan Regional* court opinion is from the U.S. Court of Appeals for the Fourth Circuit. The fourth circuit includes only the states of Maryland, North Carolina, South Carolina, Virginia and West Virginia. Hence, only courts in those states need follow the *Metropolitan Regional* ruling. While courts in other states might choose to adopt and apply the *Metropolitan Regional* analysis, they are not obligated to do so.

Second, the copyright challenge MRIS faced from its competitor in Metropolitan Regional is distinct from the copyright challenge a sponsor would face from an entrant. The requirement that copyright transfers be in writing is designed to protect the copyright owner who transfers the copyright. In the *Metropolitan Regional* case, most of those copyright owners were the real estate brokers and agents who submitted real estate listings. The broker and agent copyright owners did not challenge the validity of the transfer to Metropolitan. Instead, the copyright challenge came from American Home Realty Network, a third party and competitor of MRIS that was not involved in the transfer of the copyright.

The *Metropolitan Regional* court noted that "Section 204(a) was intended to resolve disputes between owners and alleged transferee[s], and was not intended to operate for the benefit of a third-party infringer when there is no dispute between the owner and transferee."[47] In a dispute between the copyright owner (entrant) and transferee (promotion sponsor), a court might scrutinize much more closely the mechanism of a copyright transfer done via an online click-wrap agreement. The *Metropolitan Regional* court acknowledged that the precise manner in which the MBIR terms of use appeared to subscribers was unclear. The lack of clarity was not important to the *Metropolitan Regional* court because the subscribers did not dispute the copyright transfer. The *Metropolitan Regional* court would have been much more interested in the manner of transfer if the dispute about the transfer had been between MRIS, the recipient of the transfer, and the brokers and agents, the grantors of the copyright transfer.

Timing of Assignment or Exclusive License Acquisition. Typically, many sponsors that need an exclusive license or an assignment in submissions acquire exclusive rights only from winners as part of the winner verification process. They obtain non-exclusive licenses from other entrants. A sponsor who wants an exclusive license or ownership transfer from winning entrants should clearly indicate that fact in the promotion rules.

8.4.2. Appearances of Products, People, and Copyrighted Works in Entrant Submissions

When an entrant creates a video or takes a photograph for entry into a promotion, there might be artwork, clothing with logos, brand name products, music and other sounds, and people that get captured as either the primary subject or sometimes as an incidental part of the background. A video with sound also has the potential of picking up music in the background.

In the media industry, when preparing a film or other production, the conservative approach is to obtain authorization for all identifiable people, trademarks, and copyrighted works that appear in the production. However, there are court rulings that support a more relaxed approach.[48]

In some circumstances, it may not be feasible for all entrants to obtain consents for all the people and materials depicted or mentioned in their submissions. There may be good reasons for the sponsors to accept the submissions despite the lack of consents. For example, in a Best Photograph Contest, the Smithsonian invited people to submit photographs of people, travel, Americana, or nature taken in the last two years. A potential entrant might have taken a wonderful photograph before learning of the contest. The Smithsonian recognized that in such situations when a stranger was photographed spontaneously or in another country, it might not be feasible for the entrant to obtain a release. While the Smithsonian had a general requirement for consents submitted with photos, it still allowed photographers to submit photographs with special circumstances impeding consent and invited those entrants to share any concerns regarding the eligibility of any particular photograph. The Smithsonian could then evaluate whether one of the exceptions to requiring consent applied.

Nevertheless, using such material without the authorization of the rights owner introduces the risk of a claim. In some cases, the risk may be minimal but it is never zero. It is for each sponsor to decide how much risk it is willing to accept. Many sponsors choose to follow the conservative approach concluding that it is not worthwhile to risk a claim and negative publicity for a promotional contest or sweepstakes.

Whether or not an unauthorized appearance of a person or other material in an entrant's submission is considered as a fair use or an otherwise permissible use depends on the circumstances. Cases with seemingly similar circumstances have yielded different holdings. Each specific situation requires separate analysis.

Below is a brief introduction to the factors to be considered when evaluating the permissibility of accepting submissions with unauthorized appearances of people, products, and copyrighted works. For a more in-depth description of conducting an analysis of the permissibility of protected materials appearing in the background, readers should consult my book, *The Permission Seeker's Guide Through the Legal Jungle*.

Commercial Use Carries More Risk to Sponsor than Non-Commercial Use. For products, people, and copyrighted works, how the sponsor intends to use the submissions is significant. Commercial uses carry more risk than non-commercial uses.

An example at the low end for risk from unauthorized appearances is a Smithsonian photo contest that accepts and features photographs depicting images associated with American history and culture. Such use might be categorized as editorial or as a commentary on history, culture, and society. Categorized as such, the display and distribution of such photos would be covered by the First Amendment and would not require consent for the depiction of products, people, and copyrighted works.

A contrasting example representing the high end for risk from unauthorized appearances is a Pepsi video contest that accepts commercials featuring Pepsi products. If Pepsi plans to broadcast the commercials on television during the Super Bowl, Pepsi's use is a commercial advertising use. There is significant risk that the unauthorized appearance of a person, product, or copyrighted work would be actionable.

Evaluating the Unauthorized Appearance of a Product in an Entrant Submission. The unauthorized appearance of products does carry some risk. If a trademark owner views the treatment of its trademark as negative, the trademark owner may take some action. For that reason, the rules of many promotions inviting submissions of original photos and videos prohibit any visible brand names, logos, trademarks, or other third party materials in the submitted photos and videos. The prohibition usually extends to logos on clothing. Sponsors usually require entrants to blur out any such markings in their entries. This approach represents the more conservative approach designed to thwart any potential trademark issues.

There is authority supporting the proposition that the fleeting appearance of a brand-name product or other trademark in a submission is not trademark infringement. Most of this legal support comes from court opinions dealing with the film and television industry. There are court rulings holding that the fleeting unauthorized appearance of a brand-name product in a film is permissible as long as the filmmaker is not using the brand or product in a way that promotes his film, the appearance does not make people think that the film is sponsored or supported by the manufacturer of the product, and the appearance does not dilute or tarnish the product's brand name.[49]

Applying this line of case law to promotions, a sponsor's use of submissions with the fleeting unauthorized appearance of a brand-name product is permissible as long as the use does not incorrectly imply that the brand owner endorses or is affiliated with the promotion or entrant in any way and the product is not depicted in a negative manner.

Evaluating the Unauthorized Appearance of a Person in an Entrant Submission. The analysis for the risks associated with the unauthorized appearance of a person in an entrant submission includes several factors.

Is the Person Identifiable? If the person is not identifiable in remarks, images, or by name, there is no privacy, publicity, or defamation violation. Even without using an image or real name, a person can be identifiable through the mention of a nickname, geographic location, physical description, personality trait, or real-life events in which the person was involved.

Who Is the Person? Privacy, publicity, and defamation are the potential claims triggered by the unauthorized appearance of a person in an entrant submission. Public figures and famous people have weaker privacy rights than private citizens. The famous must also meet a higher bar to prove that they have been defamed since public officials and public figures must prove a defamatory remark was made with malice whereas a private person need only prove a defamatory remark was made negligently.

In contrast to their weaker privacy rights, public figures and famous people have stronger publicity rights than private citizens. This is because an image, name, *etc.* of a famous person typically has more commercial value than that of a private person.

Here is an illustration of how those concepts work when applied to promotions. Suppose a sponsor operates a photo contest and plans to display all submitted photos in an online gallery. One of the entries depicts a U.S. president, the Pope, or a well-known movie star in the background. The entrant does not have consent to photograph the president, Pope, or movie star. The U.S. president, the Pope, and well-known movie star are public figures. Using the photo of a public figure in an online gallery carries less risk to the sponsor of a privacy violation than using a similar photo of a private citizen.

It is ideal if the image depicts the public figure in the midst of a truly newsworthy event such as a parade, a festival, or a public debate. However, with famous public figures the "newsworthy" event might be something as mundane as the public figure eating at a restaurant or standing on the street. With a similar photo of a private person, the sponsor would want to scrutinize more diligently whether the photo was truly newsworthy, historical, meant for social commentary, or presented other circumstances that qualify for First Amendment treatment.

The risk of a publicity rights violation requires a different analysis. Publicity rights considerations arise if the sponsor uses the person's image in a commercial manner. For example, using the same photo of the president, Pope, or movie star in the sponsor's televised advertisements and product packaging would likely be considered a commercial use. Both private citizens and public figures can raise a publicity rights claim for the unauthorized commercial use of their image. With similar circumstances, both the famous person and the private citizen may have an equal chance of prevailing on the claim. However, since public figures often have more resources as well as more incentive to control the commercialization of their personas, there is more risk and potentially more expense if the publicity violation claim comes from a public figure.

What Event or Activity Does the Image Depict? There is more latitude for images that depict an activity of public interest or concern. Such images are covered by the First Amendment. For example, a sponsor of a photo contest might feel comfortable accepting photos or a short film of the crowd at a presidential inauguration even if individual members of the crowd were identifiable and provided no releases.

Where Was the Image Taken? For visual works, where the image was taken can be significant. There is wider latitude for photographers and filmmakers to record activity and people in public places. Before using images of persons taken in public places, sponsors should still consider additional factors such as the person depicted, the event depicted, and sponsor intended use of the submission.

Consents from People. Similar to license grants discussed in Section 8.4.1 of this Guide, there are different methods to obtain consent for a person's appearance in an image, film, or audio recording. Consent can be written or verbal or even captured on camera or on audiotape. A person can provide express consent. A person can also give implied consent through his conduct.

Despite the various forms consent can take, written, express consent is preferable especially if the sponsor is relying on a promotion entrant to obtain the consent of third parties. Hence, a sponsor might choose to require express, written consents for all people appearing in an entrant's submission. If the promotion will yield many submissions with identifiable people such as a photo contest or video contest, the sponsor might consider providing a form of consent for entrants to use.

Evaluating the Appearance of a Copyrighted Work in an Entrant Submission. For the unauthorized use of a copyrighted work to be permissible, the use needs to qualify as a fair use. Copyright fair use determinations are very fact specific. A few seconds of music inadvertently picked up while filming an event of public interest might be viewed as a fair use. Similarly, the capture of copyrighted artwork in a photograph or film might in some circumstances also qualify as fair use.

8.4.3. Making the Sponsor's Intellectual Property Available to Entrants

The sponsor must consider the extent to which entrants may use the sponsor's intellectual property. If the promotion challenges entrants to make a video promoting the sponsor's product, the entrants must obviously be allowed to use the name and image of the company's products which may be trademarks. Likewise, if the contest is to create a fan fiction video or essay of the sponsor's work, the entrants must be able to use elements of the sponsor's copyrights and trademarks. One practice worthy of consideration is creating a gallery with a selection of the sponsor's proprietary logos, product images, music, *etc.* and restricting entrants use of sponsor intellectual property to materials within the gallery.

The promotion rules should include limitations on the rights the entrant has in the sponsor's intellectual property. The sponsor should consider whether the sponsor needs to own the rights in the entry and the extent to which the entrant may use an entry incorporating the sponsor's intellectual property for purposes other than the sponsor's promotion.

8.5. Use of Music in Promotions

A sponsor might offer a promotion in which entrants perform music, submit original music, or submit original works that incorporate music such as an original video.

As a first step to understanding the music-related legal issues that might arise in a promotion, one must understand the distinction between a song and a sound recording. A song consists of a melody and any accompanying lyrics. Typically, the copyright in a song is owned by the songwriter or by the songwriter's music publishing company. A sound recording is the recorded rendition of a song. The copyright in a sound recording is typically owned by the record label that released the recording. Within the music industry, a sound recording is often referred to as a master.

8.5.1. Types of Music Licenses

Use of music typically requires a license. The music industry name for a license in music varies according to whether you want to use the song or sound recording, and on how you want to use it. The music licenses most likely to be needed for promotions are public performance, synchronization, and master use licenses. However, sponsors should not be too obsessed by the name of the license. A license for music can be called almost anything. Most relevant is the actual language written into the license document.

Song Public Performance License is the license required to perform or play the recorded version of a song in public. For example, a public performance occurs when a radio station broadcasts a recording of the song, when a television program including the song as background music is broadcast on television, when a singer sings a song at a concert hall or local nightclub, or when a restaurant patron selects a song from a jukebox.

When Might a Promotion Sponsor Need a Song Public Performance License? If entrants provide original work, such as a video, and that original work includes music, the sponsor publicly performs both the video and the music therein when the sponsor offers the video for viewing on the internet, on television, or other public forums. Another situation requiring a public performance license is a singing or music competition in which entrants perform musical selections in public. There are some exceptions to the need for a public performance license.[50]

License to Perform a Sound Recording Publicly by Means of a Digital Audio Transmission. Offering the streaming of a sound recording via the internet or other digital method such as satellite radio requires a license to perform the sound recording publicly via digital audio transmission. This is the license that allows websites such as Pandora and Spotify to offer internet radio. This sound recording public performance license allows only digital audio transmissions. It is not applicable to sound recordings incorporated into a video or audio-visual production. To incorporate a sound recording into a video or audio-visual production, one needs a master use license.

When Might a Promotion Sponsor Need a Sound Recording Public Performance License? A sponsor needs a sound recording public performance license if entrants submit original musical recordings that the sponsor then offers to the public via the internet or via other digital means (such as satellite radio). For an original musical recording created by the entrant, the sponsor can obtain the necessary sound recording public performance license directly from the entrant. As discussed in Section 8.4.1 of this Guide, the sponsor can obtain a non-exclusive version of the sound recording public performance license from the entrant through the promotion rules.

Synchronization License and Master Use License. Synchronization and master use licenses permit the use of music in a film, video, television show, or other audio-visual production. A synchronization license, or synch license for short, grants permission to use the song in the audio-visual production. A master use license grants permission to use the sound recording in the audio-visual production. While related, the two licenses are distinct and not interchangeable. Frequently, the owner of the synchronization rights (the owner of the song) is different than the owner of the master use rights (the owner of the sound recording).

You cannot use a sound recording without also using the underlying song. Hence, when you obtain a master use license in a sound recording and the underlying song is copyright-protected, you must also obtain a synchronization license in the song.

When Might a Promotion Sponsor Need a Synch or Master Use License? For the sponsor, synch and master use licenses are relevant in at least two situations. If an entrant incorporates someone else's music into the entrant's video submission, the entrant would require synch and/or master use licenses from the copyright owners of the music. If an entrant submits the entrant's original music into the promotion and the sponsor desires to use that music in a sponsor-produced audio-visual production, the sponsor would require synch and/or master use licenses from the entrant.

License for Use of Song Lyrics. Song lyrics are protected by copyright law whether used with or without an accompanying melody. For example, displaying lyrics on a card, in a book, or speaking lyrics as part of a film require a license.

When Might a Promotion Sponsor Need a License for Use of Song Lyrics? A sponsor would need a license for the use of song lyrics to display, distribute, or otherwise use song lyrics submitted by an entrant.

Mechanical License. A mechanical license grants permission to make and distribute a recording of an existing song. A record company obtains a mechanical license before releasing a recording of a song. A musical artist who wants to re-record and distribute his own version of an existing song must also obtain a mechanical license.

When Might a Promotion Sponsor Need a Mechanical License? A sponsor needs a mechanical license from the entrant if, for example, the entrant submits an original song of which the sponsor wants to make a recording.

Although probably not applicable to most sponsors' promotion-related music issues, those dealing with mechanical licenses should be aware that a compulsory mechanical license is available for any non-dramatic song that has been commercially released.[51] The Copyright Act dictates license fees and other terms for compulsory mechanical licenses and, thus, eliminates the need to obtain direct permission from or negotiate license terms with the copyright owner.

For recordings of the entrant's original songs, the sponsor can obtain the mechanical license through the promotion rules or winner affidavit and need not rely on the compulsory mechanical license.

8.6. Best Practices to Avoid Rights Clearance Problems in a Promotion

Provide Entrants with Pre-Cleared Materials. Sponsors might minimize the risk of rights clearance problems by providing pre-cleared materials for entrants. For example, in many contests inviting entrants to submit videos, the sponsors reduce the risk of music licensing violations by obtaining necessary licenses in about fifteen music selections in various styles ranging from classical to country to hip-hop to rock and requiring that entrants use only this pre-cleared music in their video submissions.

Benefit from the Digital Millennium Copyright Act Safe Harbors. If the sponsor plans to post entrant submissions on the company's website, the sponsor should provide relevant statements on its website and register a designated agent with the U.S. Copyright Office so the sponsor can take advantage of the safe harbor provisions offered by the Digital Millennium Copyright Act as discussed in Section 6.6.2 of this Guide.

Benefit from the Communications Decency Act. As discussed in Section 6.6.3 of this Guide, the sponsor should benefit from the Communications Decency Act. Here is sample language that a promotion website might use to address this issue:

ENTRIES POSTED TO THE WEBSITE, IF ANY, WERE NOT EDITED BY SPONSOR AND ARE THE VIEWS/OPINIONS OF THE INDIVIDUAL ENTRANT AND DO NOT REFLECT THE VIEWS OF SPONSOR IN ANY MANNER.

Require Entrants/Finalists to Submit Releases. The sponsor should require entrants to obtain releases and permissions for any persons or third party materials appearing in the entrant's submissions. Otherwise, the sponsor should consider prohibiting the appearance of any visible brand names, logos, trademarks, or other third party materials in submissions.

Discourage Comparisons to Competing Products. Sponsors should not encourage entrants to defame other people, disparage products, or provide false advertising. In fact, it is a best practice for promotion rules to dictate that entrants refrain from engaging in such behavior and that their submissions do not depict or mention other products. Entrants should be discouraged from comparing the sponsor's products to any competitive products. Instead, the sponsor should encourage entrants to discuss the benefits of the sponsor's product without making any comparisons to competitors' products.

Use Rules that Clearly Explain Rights Grant and Rights Clearance Requirements. An attorney experienced in licensing issues should review and draft the rules—especially if the promotion requires a transfer of rights in a form other than a non-exclusive license. Such alternative forms of transfer include an assignment, a requirement that entrants place their submissions in the public domain, and a requirement that entrants place their submissions under the terms of a Creative Commons license. An attorney should also review the marketing materials to verify that statements made in the marketing materials are consistent with the rules.

Use Trademark and Copyright Notices on the Sponsor's Own Intellectual Property. The sponsor should clearly communicate that any company materials made available for use to the entrants are the proprietary property of the sponsor. The sponsor can accomplish this by using appropriate trademark and copyright notices and by including such a statement in the promotion rules.

Consider Impact of Guild Issues. Entertainment guilds are labor unions designed to protect creative people. They negotiate and enforce collective bargaining agreements that establish minimum levels of compensation, benefits, and working conditions for their members. A company that employs creative people and has agreed to abide by the contract terms of an entertainment guild is a signatory of that particular guild. One particular guild issue relevant to promotions is the ability of sponsors that are SAG-AFTRA signatories to offer promotions accepting original works. Section 7.1.3 of this Guide has a discussion of SAG-AFTRA Guild issues in this context.

CHAPTER 9

Offering Promotions for Charitable Causes

9.1. For-Profit and Charity Collaborations

Sponsors sometimes connect their promotions to a charitable cause. For example, a sponsor might pledge to make a donation to a charity for every entry received or for each product sold during the promotion period. This is often referred to as a commercial co-venture or as cause marketing.

9.1.1. Legal Requirements

Some states have specific statutes addressing promotional collaborations between charitable organizations and for-profit companies. This includes promotions stating that a purchase from the for-profit company in some manner benefits a charitable organization. These statutes might require that the sponsor take specific steps prior to the collaboration such as a written agreement between the sponsor and charitable organization and specific disclosures that must be made to consumers.

9.1.2. Failure to Disclose

State regulators might take legal actions against cause campaigns deemed to mislead the public. A charitable campaign involving Yoplait Yogurt is an example. While the Yoplait Yogurt campaign did not include a promotion, it does illustrate the danger of not fully disclosing elements of a charitable connection. General Mills, the manufacturer of Yoplait Yogurt, launched a Save Lids to Save Lives Campaign.

On the lid of each Yoplait Yogurt container, General Mills indicated that it would contribute 50 cents to the Breast Cancer Research Foundation for each lid returned by consumers during the campaign. However, General Mills capped its donation to a maximum of $100,000 regardless of the number of lids returned. While General Mills disclosed this $100,000 maximum on the underside of the lids, General Mills did not include the disclosure on the outside packaging where consumers could see it prior to purchase nor did General Mills disclose the maximum in television broadcasts advertising the campaign.

Georgia found the lack of disclosure deceptive and misleading and the Georgia Secretary of State initiated an investigation into the Yoplait Yogurt campaign. The Georgia investigation concluded with a settlement in which General Mills contributed an additional $63,000 to the Breast Cancer Research Foundation, and reimbursed Georgia for its investigative costs. General Mills did not admit any wrongdoing.[52]

9.1.3. Best Practices for Commercial Co-Ventures

Be Transparent. The important guideline for best practices is to be transparent and clear in describing how the promotion benefits the charity. The New York Attorney General's Charities Bureau has offered best practices for cause marketing that are generally useful guidelines for any sponsor even if operating outside of New York:

- Clearly describe the promotion including the name and mission of the charity receiving the donation.
- Clearly describe how and when the charity benefits including any action the consumer must take in order to generate a donation and any restrictions on the giving of a donation.
- Specify a fixed dollar amount to be contributed to the charity— such as one dollar for each entry. This is preferable to a vague statement that the charity will receive a portion of the proceeds.
- Prominently disclose any material information that might not be immediately apparent such as the fact that the sponsor is making a donation of goods or services rather than a monetary donation.[53]

Comply with Co-Venture Laws. Both sponsors and charities should be aware of and heed any co-venture laws of the relevant state.

Vet the Charity. The sponsor should verify that the charitable organization satisfies all applicable legal requirements to be classified as a charity.

Contract with the Charity. Even if state law does not require a contract between the sponsor and charity, it is a good idea to have a contract anyway. The contract should address a description of the charitable promotion; each party's operational and marketing responsibilities; rights of each party to use the other's intellectual property such as charity name, brand names and other trademarks.

Provide Consumers with Advance Disclosure. Place material terms of the promotion on the outside of packaging and in advertising in a clear and prominent manner so consumers know of benefits to charity before purchasing the product.

Contribute to Charity Promptly. The transfer of monies promised to the charity should be prompt and should be a priority of the promotional campaign.

Maintain Accurate Records. The sponsor should maintain accurate inventory and financial records related to the promotion. Some states may request to review such records. The charity might also request a contractual right to examine the records.

Additional Concerns. Characteristics that warrant additional legal review include the following:

- promotional campaigns of long duration
- retention by the sponsor of a percentage of charitable proceeds as a commission, a situation which may subject the sponsor to professional fundraising laws
- an increase in the price of any product during the promotion

9.2. Charitable Gaming—Bingo and Raffles

When people pay to play bingo or participate in a raffle, the bingo or raffle game is a lottery and/or a gambling game. Many states offer an exception in their anti-gambling laws to allow non-profit organizations and other civic and charitable groups to offer bingo games and raffles for fundraising purposes. Many state laws refer to an organization eligible to offer charitable gambling under its laws as a qualified organization.

In some states, the bingo and raffle exceptions are allowances available throughout the state. In other states, raffle and bingo might be permissible in only some localities because such states allow the individual cities and counties to decide whether to allow raffles and bingo. There is information specific to each state's bingo and raffle exceptions in the state summaries in Part Three of this Guide.

9.2.1. State Requirements for Non-Profit Bingo and Raffles

Typically, the exceptions for bingo, raffles, and other charitable gaming come with several requirements. Here are some of the typical requirements found in state bingo and raffle exceptions. This is a general description. Individual states may have differing laws and regulations for bingo and raffles.

Qualified Organization. Most states restrict bingo games, raffles, and other forms of charitable gambling to non-profit, charitable and civic organizations. Some states offer more relaxed eligibility requirements for raffles than for bingo.

Minimum Existence of Organization. Most states require that the organization wishing to offer bingo or raffles have been in existence within the state for a set period of time prior to offering charitable gaming. The period varies by state but is usually no less than one year and no more than five years. With some limited exceptions, the organization typically must be organized under the laws of the state or located in the state in order to offer bingo and raffles in that state.

License Required. Eligible organizations may be required to obtain a license from the state prior to offering bingo games or raffles. Exceptions to the need for a license are more common for raffles than for bingo. A state or county agency administers and issues the licenses, often a department within the Secretary of State or the Department of Revenue. Jurisdictions may issue licenses valid for a specified period of time or for a set number of bingo sessions or raffles.

Financial Records and Reports. Organizations must keep records of gross receipts, expenses, and the use to which the net proceeds are applied. Bingo and raffle licensees must sometimes file periodic financial reports and pay a portion of the proceeds as a tax. Many states have more lenient licensing and reporting requirements for raffles than for bingo.

Definition of Bingo. States construe the bingo game exceptions to the lottery prohibition narrowly. Just because an organization refers to a game as bingo does not necessarily mean the game falls under the bingo exception. Some states restrict the bingo exception to traditional bingo games played on paper or card boards and deny it to bingo games played electronically or as instant bingo.

Use of Proceeds. After paying direct operational expenses of the bingo and raffle, the organization must use the bingo and raffles net proceeds for charitable, civic, community, benevolent, religious, or scholastic works or similar purposes. State laws may have specific rules on how net proceeds are to be calculated and the percentage of proceeds that may be used to cover expenses.

Minimum Age. Bingo participants and individual bingo operators must be of a minimum age. Some jurisdictions allow minors accompanied by a parent or guardian to play.

Location of Game. Bingo games must take place at a location owned or leased by the qualified organization. States may also impose local restrictions on the sale of raffle tickets. For example, Illinois requires that raffle tickets be sold or issued only within the area specified on the license and that winning chances may be determined only at those locations specified on the license. (Ill. Comp. Stat. Ch. 230, § 15/4 (2014)). Nevada requires that tickets or chances for a charitable lottery be sold only in the primary county where the lottery is operated and in the Nevada counties that border the primary county. (Nev. Rev. Stat. § 462.180 (2014)).

Operational Control. The qualified organization must maintain control over bingo and raffle operations. There are limitations on the extent to which the organization can use outside third parties to operate raffles and bingo games. The prohibitions generally do not prohibit employees of the organization from administering the game.

Restrictions on Value and Types of Prizes. States often limit the maximum value of prizes to be awarded in bingo games and raffles. Some states also limit the types of prizes to be awarded. For example, some states prohibit awards of money or real estate.

Bingo Games for Seniors. There are often relaxed licensing and other requirements for bingo games offered in organizations or communities catering to senior citizens. The relaxed requirements are often only available if the payment to play and the value of any prizes are nominal amounts.

Limit on Number of Games. Some states limit the number of bingo sessions within a 24-hour period, week, or month as well as the number of games within a single bingo session. Similarly, some states limit the number of raffles an organization may offer.

Ownership of Raffle Prize. Some states require that the raffle operator have ownership of the raffle prize prior to the commencement of the raffle or prior to the drawing.

Information Printed on Raffle Ticket and Advertisements. Some states specify the information that must be printed on the raffle ticket and advertisement. Required information might include the date and place of the raffle drawing; the three most valuable prizes to be awarded and the total number of prizes to be awarded; and disclosures about the rules, identity of the sponsor, and the source of the funds.

Source of Supplies. Some states require that organizations obtain bingo, raffle, and other charitable gaming supplies only from dealers and manufacturers authorized and/or licensed by the state.

CHAPTER 10

Resolving Problems

10.1. Fraud

10.1.1. Fraud by Sponsor

Fraud or the appearance of fraud in a promotion can generate a lawsuit from the participants or action from a state attorney general. A sponsor commits fraud when the sponsor consciously fails to apply the promotion rules fairly and consistently to all entrants and instead applies the rules in a manner that favors one participant over another.

For example, in one particular contest in which the winner was the fisherman whose total catch had the greatest weight, there was sufficient evidence of fraud. The contest officials allowed one person to weigh his fish prior to entering the contest and then replace three fish with fish of greater weight so that the total weight of his fish would outweigh those of any other entrant. (*In Dobbs v. Plough Broadcasting Company*, 293 S.E.2d 526 (Ga. Ct. of Appeals 1970)).

It is important that sponsors disclose all material terms of the promotion. Failing to share material terms of the promotion can make the sponsor vulnerable to accusations of fraud. The Missouri Attorney General sued a fantasy sports contest operator under Missouri's unfair business practices laws, for making false promises, material omissions, and misrepresentations. According to the Missouri Attorney General, the operator failed to disclose that it used entry fees from a football-themed contest to pay the winners of a previous baseball-themed contest. That shuffling left the contest operator with no funds to pay football contest prizes and, as a result, the contest operator failed to pay at least thirty-two participants over $151,261 of promised prize money. (*Missouri v. Gridiron Fantasy Sports*, No. CC04862 (Mo. 21st Jud. Cir., filed Dec. 8, 2011)).

10.1.2. Fraud by Entrants

Sponsors should carefully think of the potential participant conduct they want to discourage and make certain their rules prohibit such conduct. In *Johnson v. B.P. Oil Company*, 602 So.2d 885 (Ala. 1992), in its License Plate Jackpot, B.P. Oil offered a new BMW valued at over $20,000 to anyone who owned an automobile with a license plate matching exactly to a pre-selected license plate number posted weekly in BP Oil's gasoline stations. The official rules stated that "Promotion materials and prize claims void . . . *if not obtained legitimately*"

After seeing one week's postings, Larry Johnson used public records to determine the current owner of the car with the matching license plate; purchased that car for $650, found to be a fair price for the automobile which was ten years old; and claimed the prize. B.P. Oil attempted to deny Johnson the new BMW arguing that Johnson had not obtained the prize claim legitimately as required by the official rules.

A court disagreed with the B.P. Oil finding that there was no state law requiring Johnson to disclose the promotion at the time of purchasing the automobile. According to the court, the seller of the car had just as much opportunity to learn about the B.P. Oil's publicly advertised promotion as Johnson did and the promotion's rules did not specify how a winner must obtain the car with the matching license plate.

10.1.3. Fraud by Third Parties

A promotion might be at risk of fraud by a third party. One of the most publicized cases of promotion fraud involved the McDonald's restaurant scratch-off, Who Wants to be a Millionaire Promotion. McDonald's outsourced the security for its promotions to Simon Marketing. A criminal ring comprised of Simon Marketing employees stole winning McDonald's game pieces and embezzled more than thirteen million dollars from the McDonald's promotions over a multi-year period. The conspiracy resulted in an FBI investigation leading to the arrests of dozens of people.

Such fraud can be devastating to the sponsor in terms of public relations. Hence, the sponsor's legal and marketing departments should work together in finding ways to restore good will. In the McDonald's situation, after discovering the fraud, McDonald's gave away $10 million in store visit promotions to restore customer goodwill. Here is sample rule language that can aid in insulating the sponsor from negative legal liability stemming from fraud and provide flexibility in salvaging the integrity of a promotion:

> *Example One.* Sponsor reserves the right, without prior notice and at any time, to terminate or suspend the promotion, in whole or in part, or to modify the promotion in any way, should any factor (including but not limited to fraud or security breach) interfere with the promotion's proper conduct as contemplated by these official rules, or if the sponsor believes that the promotion has been or will be compromised in any way.

> *Example Two.* Sponsor reserves the right to void any game card submitted for a prize, if sponsor believes such game card was obtained other than through regular channels of business as contemplated by the official rules or that the game card has been tampered with in any manner.

10.2. Disputes among Winners

It is possible for two or more people to claim the same prize. When a sponsor anticipates awarding a large monetary sum or an expensive prize to one winner, it does not want to find itself in the position of owing the prize to two different individuals. The sponsor wants to handle a dispute in a manner that avoids double liability.

A risk-minimizing solution is for the sponsor to let the entrants resolve the dispute among themselves—even if that resolution must come from a lawsuit among the potential winners. The sponsor then defers to the court's decision, either refraining from awarding the prize until the court renders a decision or delivering the prize to the custodianship of the court.

If the parties do not initiate a lawsuit themselves, the sponsor can initiate an interpleader action. An interpleader is a legal proceeding in which the sponsor has in its possession property to which two or more people claim a right and in which the sponsor itself claims no interest.

Real-Life Example of a Promoter Confronted with Two Winners Demanding the Grand Prize.

Pepsi-Cola Globe Bucks Million Dollar Prize (Anderson v. Yeats, Complaint filed March 20, 1998, Case No. 98A386066). During the Pepsi-Cola Globe Bucks Bottle Cap Promotion, Judy Richardson purchased a bottle of Pepsi-Cola during her work day and left the unopened bottle on a counter where she normally kept her possessions. Later in the day, a co-worker, Sindy Allen, opened the bottle and discovered the bottle-cap for the grand prize worth $1,000,000. When Allen tried to claim the prize money from Pepsi-Cola, Richardson sued both Allen and Pepsi-Cola to retrieve the prize money. Richardson also warned Pepsi-Cola that if Pepsi-Cola paid the money to Allen prior to a court resolution of the matter and if the court subsequently decided that Richardson was due the money, Richardson would pursue Pepsi-Cola for payment if she could not collect from Allen.

As a result of Richardson's actions, Pepsi-Cola refused to pay the $1,000,000 to Allen. In response, Allen filed her own lawsuit against Pepsi-Cola alleging a breach of contract and breach of the covenant of good faith and fair dealing. Allen argued that Pepsi-Cola owed her the award money since Allen had supplied Pepsi-Cola with the winning bottle cap as stipulated in the Globe Bucks Official Rules.

Pepsi-Cola took no position on the rightful owner of the prize money and left it to the court to decide the matter. Pepsi-Cola won against Allen's breach of contract claim basing its legal argument on language in the official rules that stipulated as follows:

- All game pieces were subject to verification at the sole discretion of the Pepsi-Cola Company.
- A person claiming a prize was not a winner until that person's game piece was timely received and verified by the Pepsi-Cola Company and the person had complied with the official rules.

- All participants agreed to be bound by the official rules and the decisions of the Pepsi-Cola Company which are final and binding in all respects of the promotion.

Pepsi-Cola was involved in the litigation from 1998 until June 2000 when it won a dismissal of all claims against it by both potential winners. Richardson ultimately won the right to claim the grand prize after a jury trial.

Endnotes for Part Two, Overview

1. No state is on record as explicitly adopting the pure chance test. Research for this Guide indicated that Arkansas, Idaho, and Kentucky are the only states that might apply the pure chance test. Even within these three states, it is likely that the dominant factor doctrine or material element test would be preferred.

2. Order Denying Defendants' Motions and Joint Motions to Dismiss, case nos. cv 07-3916 fmc, cv 07-3537 fmc, cv 07-3643 fmc, and cv 07-3647 fmc (C.D. Ca. Nov. 30, 2007). At the time of the dismissal motion, the case included four consolidated cases: Couch v. Telescope; Herbert v. Endemol USA; Cunningham v. Endemol USA; and Bentley v. NBC Universal. Subsequently, three additional cases were added: Glass v. NBC Universal, Snelson v. Endemol USA, and Miller v. Upper Ground Enterprises. The seven cases were consolidated for pre-trial purposes.

3. *Hardin v. NBC Universal*, 660 S.E.2d 374 (Ga. 2008).

4. *Couch v. Telescope, supra* note 2.

5. *E.g.*, *Sun Light Prepaid Phonecard Co. v. South Carolina*, 600 S.E. 2d 61 (2004); *Midwestern Enters. v. Stenehjem*, 625 N.W.2d 234 (N.D. 2001); KY Att'y Gen. Op. No. 10-007 (Nov. 3, 2010).

6. Research for this Guide indicated that Arizona and Michigan are among the few states expressing a willingness to find the existence of a lottery in a scheme missing one of the elements of a prize, consideration, and chance.

7. Office of the Att'y Gen. and the Colo. Dep't of Law, *Common Legal Questions/Gambling*, http://www.coloradoattorneygeneral.gov/initiatives/consumer_resource_guide/common_legal_questions#gambling (last visited Sept. 8, 2014).

8. For example, the Unlawful Internet Gambling Enforcement Act indicates that "[n]o provision of [the Unlawful Internet Gambling Enforcement Act] shall be construed as altering, limiting, or extending . . ." any federal or state gambling law. 31 U.S.C. § 5361(b) (2014).

9. The U.S. Department of Justice has expressed the opinion that the Interstate Wire Act of 1961 applies only to bets or wagers on sporting events or contests. Virginia A. Seitz, U.S. Dep't of Justice, *Whether Proposals by Illinois and New York to Use the Internet and Out-of-State Transaction Processors to Sell Lottery Tickets to In-State Adults Violate*

the Wire Act (Sept. 9, 2011) http://www.justice.gov/sites/default/files/olc/opinions/2011/09/31/state-lotteries-opinion.pdf (last visited Sept. 9, 2014).

10. A characteristic of a skill contest governed by the DMPEA is a contest that requires a purchase, payment, or donation or implies that a purchase, payment, or donation is required to enter. 39 U.S.C. § 3001(k)(1)(C) (2014).

11. *See e.g., Cudd. v. Aschenbrenner*, 377 P. 2d 150, 157 (Or. 1962); *N.J. Att'y Gen. Op. No. 6-1983 (June 1, 1983)*.

12. *See e.g., Johnson v. B.P. Oil Company*, 602 So.2d 885, 888 (Ala. 1992).

13. Email from Iris Alonzo, Creative Director, American Apparel to Nancy Upton (Sept. 13, 2011), http://extrawiggleroom.tumblr.com/post/10193626169/american-apparel-responds, (last visited May 20, 2014).

14. *See e.g., Trannel v. Prairie Ridge Media*, 987 N.E.2d 923 (Ill. App. Ct. 2013).

15. *See e.g.*, Fla. Att'y Gen. Op. No. 1991-03 (Jan 8, 1991); Mass. Att'y Gen., *Advisory on Poker Tournaments* (June 30, 2005), http://www.mass.gov/ago/doing-business-in-massachusetts/public-charities-or-not-for-profits/soliciting-funds/raffles-and-other-gaming-activity/poker-advisory.html (last visited Sept. 9, 2014).

16. See current versions of Internal Revenue Service, Instructions for Forms W-2G and 5754.

17. In its regulations and instructional publications, the IRS does not clearly classify a sweepstakes as a promotion that charges no consideration. Similarly, the IRS does not describe a contest as a promotion that might or might not charge consideration. The IRS does explain that a Form 1099 Misc ordinary income is appropriate for a sweepstakes not involving a wager and that a Form W-2G gambling income is appropriate for a promotion involving a wager. Internal Revenue Service, Instructions for Form 1099-MISC, p. 5 (2014).

18. Definitions and Implementation Under the CAN-SPAM Act, 73 Fed. Reg. 29654, § II.A.5 (May 21, 2008). *See also* FTC, *The Can-Spam Act: A Compliance Guide for Business* (Sept. 2009), http://business.ftc.gov/documents/bus61-can-spam-act-compliance- guide-business (last visited Sept. 9, 2014). The CAN-SPAM rules issued by the FTC are codified at 16 C.F.R. §316.1-316.6.

19. Closing letter from Mary K. Engle, Assoc. Dir., Div. of Advertising Practices, Federal Trade Commission to Christie Grymes Thompson, Counsel for Cole Haan, Inc., FTC File No. 142-3041 (Mar. 20, 2014), http://www.ftc.gov/enforcement/cases-proceedings/closing-letters/cole-haan-inc (last visited Sept. 9, 2014)

20. 16 C.F.R. § 312.4(c)(1) (2013). The required content for the direct notice varies depending upon the personal information collected and the purposes for its collection. Circumstances recognized as distinct and triggering variation in required notice content include a circumstance where an operator voluntarily seeks to provide notice to a parent of a child's online activities that do not involve the collection, use or disclosure of personal information, 16 C.F.R. § 312.4(c)(2) (2013); a circumstance where an operator intends to communicate with the child multiple times via the child's online contact information and collects no other information, 16 C.F.R. § 312.4(c)(3) (2013); and a circumstance where the operator collects a child's and a parent's name and online contact information to protect a child's safety and does not use or disclose the information for any other purpose, 16 C.F.R. § 312.4(c)(4) (2013).

21. Federal Trade Commission, *Complying with COPPA: Frequently Asked Questions, A Guide for Business and Parents and Small Entity Compliance Guide*, §I.1 (July 2013), http://www.business.ftc.gov/documents/0493-Complying-with-COPPA-Frequently-Asked-Questions (last visited Sept. 10, 2014).

22. *See e.g.*, S.B. 568, 2013-2014 Leg. (Cal. 2014), codified in Cal. Bus. & Prof. Code §§ 22580 to 22582, which became effective on January 1, 2015.

23. Both the FTC and the California Attorney General have expressed the belief that COPPA does not preempt state laws that protect the privacy rights of teenagers. Brief for Fed. Trade Comm. as Amicus Curiae Supporting Neither Party, Batman v. Facebook, Civ. No. 13-16819 (9th Cir., appeal filed Sept. 11, 2013); Brief for the State of California as Amicus Curiae Supporting Neither Party, Schachter v. Facebook, 13-16918 (9th Cir., appeal filed Sept. 24, 2013).

24. While not illegal under federal and state laws, specific social media networks might prohibit or limit like-gating. For example, effective as of November 5, 2014, Facebook placed limits on the use of the like feature. In communicating the platform change to developers, Facebook indicated, "You must not incentivize people to use social plugins or to

like a Page. This includes offering rewards, or gating apps or app content based on whether or not a person has liked a Page. It remains acceptable to incentivize people to login to your app, checkin at a place or enter a promotion on your app's Page." *Graph API v2.1 and updated iOS and Android SDKs/Changes to Platform Policy*, (Aug. 7, 2014) https://developers.facebook.com/blog/post/2014/08/07/Graph-API-v2.1/

25. Although to this writer's knowledge never challenged, this claim is arguable—based on the structure of the promotion. While being selected as a grand prize winner carries no immediate monetary prize, the grand prize winners do have additional opportunities to win contest prizes. If the finalist's video ranks as one of the top three best Super Bowl commercials, Frito-Lay gives that finalist an additional monetary bonus of between $400,000 and $1,000,000. Video ranking for best Super Bowl commercials is determined by the USA Today Ad Meter rankings. Frito-Lays is not affiliated with and does not control the outcome of the USA Today Ad Meter rankings.

26. A broad reading of the state statutory language suggests that Connecticut, Georgia, or Tennessee might use the any chance test. However, no authority clearly supports adoption of the any chance test in any of these three states. See state summaries for Connecticut, Georgia, and Tennessee in Part Three of this Guide.

27. For example, in Colorado, prior to offering real estate as a raffle prize, the raffle licensee must take several steps: file proof of ownership (such as a bill of sale) with the state; secure an enforceable contract with the real estate owner in which the real estate owner commits to transferring the real estate to the winner; disclose any encumbrances on the real estate prize such as a mortgage; and secure a bond for an amount that would allow the raffle licensee to provide an equivalent real estate property to the winner in the event the real estate owner defaults on the transfer. 8 Colo. Code Reg. § 1505-2-9.0.C (2008).

28. *See e.g.*, N.D. Cent. Code § 53-06.1-10.1. North Dakota explicitly states that real estate may not be a raffle prize.

29. *See, e.g.*, N.C. Att'y Gen. Op. (Dec. 18, 1981).

30. The Deceptive Mail Prevention and Enforcement Act (DMPEA) contains the winning representation and inconsistent statement prohibitions in the provision related to sweepstakes. 39 U.S.C. §3001(k)(3)(A)(ii) (2014).

However, there are no parallel prohibitions in the DMPEA provision dealing with contests. 39 U.S.C. §3001(k)(3)(B) (2014).

31. The Telephone Consumer Protection Act of 1991 (TCPA), Pub. L. No. 102-243, 1052 Stat. 2394 is codified in 47 U.S.C. 237 and other sections of 47 U.S.C. (2014). The Telemarketing and Consumer Fraud and Abuse Prevention Act (TCFAPA) is codified in 15 U.S.C. §§6101 to 6108 (2014).

32. Regulations for the Telephone Consumer Protection Act of 1991 TCPA, issued by the Federal Communications Commission are codified at 16 C.F.R. §§310.1 to 310.9. The telemarketing sales rule are the regulations issued by the Federal Trade Commission to implement the Telemarketing and Consumer Fraud and Abuse Prevention Act (TCFAPA). The TCFAPA regulations are codified at 16 C.F.R. §§310.1 to 310.9.

33. Federal Communications Commission, *In Re Rules and Regulations Implementing the Telephone Consumer Protection Act of 1991*, 58 Fed. Reg. 44144, 44165, ¶ 116 (2003). *See also, Satterfield v. Simon & Schuster*, 569 F.3d 946, 952 (9th Cir. 2009).

34. 16 C.F.R. § 310.4(b)(1)(iii)(B)(i); 68 Fed. Reg. 4580, 4634 (2003).

35. Federal Trade Commission, *Complying with the Telemarketing Sales Rule*, p. 44, available at http://www.business.ftc.gov/documents/bus27-complying-telemarketing-sales-rule (last visited Sept. 10, 2014).

36. Press Release, N.Y. Att'y Gen., Promotion to Stop Requiring Waiver of Do Not Call Protection (May 3, 2005), http://www.ag.ny.gov/press-release/promotion-stop-requiring-waiver-do-not-call-protection (last visited Sept. 10, 2014).

37. Joint Petition Filed by DISH Network, LLC, the United States, and the States of California, Illinois, North Carolina, and Ohio for Declaratory Ruling Concerning the Telephone Consumer Protection Act (TCPA) Rules, Declaratory Ruling, 28 FCC Rcd 6574 (2013)(FCC clarifying that a seller may be held vicariously liable under federal common law principles of agency for TCPA violations committed by third-party telemarketers). *See also, Thomas v. Taco Bell*, 879 F. Supp. 2d 1079, 1084 (C.D. Cal. 2012).

38. *See, e.g., Silbaugh v. Viking Magazine*, No. 1:11 CV 1299 (N.D. OH. Jan. 10, 2012).

39. 16 C.F.R. §§ 310.3(a)(1)(iv)—(v); 310.3(a)(2)(v); and 310.4(d)(4) (2013).

40. 16 C.F.R. § 310.5(a)(2) (2013).

41. 47 U.S.C. § 227(A)(1) (2014). The definition in the FCC regulations for automatic telephone dialing system, 47 C.F.R. 64.1200(f)(2) (2013), is substantially similar to the definition in the United States Code.

42. *See e.g.,* In the Matter of Entercom Communications Corp. Petition to Amend Section Sec. 73.1216 Licensee-conducted Contests, RM-11684 (filed Jan. 20, 2012).

43. *Miller v. California,* 413 U.S. 15 (1973).

44. The FCC has the statutory authority under 18 U.S.C. § 1464 to regulate the broadcast of obscene, indecent or profane material. 47 CFR 73.3999 (2013) is the FCC regulation enforcing obscene and indecent broadcast prohibition.

45. 17 U.S.C. § 204(a) (2014) requires that the assignment of a copyright be in writing; 15 U.S.C. § 1060(a)(3) (2014) requires that the assignment of a trademark registration be in writing; 35 U.S.C. § 261 (2014) requires that the assignment of a patent be in writing.

46. In making its decision, the court also relied on the Electronic Signatures in Global and National Commerce Act (the E-Sign Act), 15 U.S.C. § 7001 *et seq.* (2014). Effective since October 1, 2000, the E-Sign Act mandates that no signature be denied legal effect simply because it is in electronic form.

47. *Metropolitan Regional Information Systems v. American Home Realty Network,* 722 F.3d 591, 601 (4th Cir. 2013), citing *Kindergartners Count v. Demoulin,* 249 F. Supp. 2d 1213, 1221 n.22 (D.Kan. 2003).

48. *See e.g., Caterpillar v. Walt Disney Company,* 287 F. Supp. 2d 913 (C.D. Ill. 2003) (finding that appearance of Caterpillar-branded bulldozers in eight minutes of scenes in Disney's *George of the Jungle 2* was not trademark infringement and was not confusing to consumers); *Delan by Delan v. CBS,* 458 N.Y.S.2d 608 (1983) (concluding that four-second appearance of a man in a documentary was not a right of publicity violation); *Sandoval v. New Line Cinema, Corp.,* 147 F.3d 215 (2nd Cir. 1998) (ruling that on-screen appearance of photographic transparencies lasting for only 35.6 seconds in the movie *Seven* was a *de minimis* use and was not a copyright infringement violation).

49. See e.g., *Caterpillar v. Walt Disney Company, supra* note 48.

50. These exceptions are in Section 110 of the Copyright Act. 17 U.S.C. §110 (2014). Section 110(3) of the Copyright Act allows the no-license performance of a nondramatic literary or musical work or of a

dramatico-musical work of a religious nature during religious worship services. Section 110(4) of the Copyright Act allows the no-license performance of a nondramatic literary or musical work as long as there is no fee paid to the performers, promoters, or organizers. Additionally, for the Section 110(4) exception, if there is any direct or indirect admission fee paid for the performance, all proceeds remaining after payment of reasonable expenses must be used solely for educational, religious or charitable purposes. Section 110(10) of the Copyright Act allows the no-license performance of a nondramatic literary or musical work at a social function organized by a nonprofit veterans' or fraternal organization open to invitees of the organization (but not open to the general public) as long as the net proceeds from the performance are used for charitable purposes and not for financial gain.

51. The mechanical license provision is in Section 115 of the Copyright Act. 17 U.S.C. §115 (2014). For many songs, non-statutory equivalents to the Section 115 compulsory mechanical license can be obtained through Harry Fox and Rights Flow.

52. Press Release, Cathy Cox, Ga. Sec'y of State, Agreement with General Mills to Conclude Investigation into Yoplait Charitable Promotion Results in Additional $63,000 for Breast Cancer Research (Dec. 21, 1999).

53. N.Y. Att'y Gen. Eric T. Schneiderman Charities Bureau, *Five Best Practices for Transparent Cause Marketing*, http://www.charitiesnys.com/Five%20 Best%20Practices%20for%20Transparent%20Cause%20Marketing.pdf (last visited Nov. 15, 2014).

PART THREE

Summaries of State Laws

Part Three provides a separate summary for each state and for the District of Columbia discussing the laws most relevant to contests and sweepstakes in that state.

Structure of Part Three:

1. How Each State Summary Is Organized
2. State Summaries (in alphabetical order)

How Each State Summary Is Organized

This Part Three offers a separate summary for each state and the District of Columbia outlining the specific laws most relevant to promotions in that state. Familiarity with the concepts presented in Part Two, Overview of this Guide is helpful in understanding the material within the state summaries. The discussion within each state summary is organized with the following headings:

State Attorney General Office. This portion of the state summary lists the address, phone number and website of the state's Office of the Attorney General. The attorney general is usually the administrator within the state who initiates legal actions against sponsors whose contests and sweepstakes violate the state's laws. Attorney generals often issue opinion letters on how the state's laws apply to specific promotions.

Selected State Laws, Regulations, and Constitutional Provisions. This portion of the state summary provides the reference number and a descriptive name for some of the state's legal provisions most relevant to contests and sweepstakes. A state's promotion-related laws are often (but not always) codified with the state's criminal laws and/or consumer protection laws.

Not all legal provisions have helpful descriptive names. Hence, I often add wording to the descriptive name of the legal provision to give readers a better idea of what the provision covers. Portions of the descriptive name provided by me—rather than by the state—appear in parenthesis.

Summary of State Law. The Summary of State Law discussion is further divided into four primary headings:

Prohibition of Lotteries and Gambling: This portion of the state summary indicates the state's position on lotteries and gambling. It highlights the state's legal provisions that prohibit lotteries and gambling and how the state defines lottery. Most states define lottery as a promotion that combines a prize, chance, and consideration.

Contests: This portion of the state summary provides the state's position on contest promotions. Typically, states permit contests as long as the contest does not conflict with anti-gambling laws. If the contest includes an element of consideration, most states require that the sponsor award the contest prize based on skill and not on chance. This portion of the state summary indicates, when known, the test used by the state when evaluating whether chance or skill prevails in a promotion that combines elements of both.

The potential tests used for a chance-skill determination include the dominant factor doctrine, the material element test, the any chance test, and the pure chance test. Section 3.4.3 of this Guide describes each of these four chance-skill determination tests. Appendix A.2 of this Guide lists in table form the chance-skill determination test used by each of the states.

The *Contests* portion of the state summary also indicates whether the state places any restrictions or limitations on contest sponsors charging consideration. Appendix A.3 of this Guide compiles a list of the states that prohibit or restrict consideration in skill-based contests.

Sweepstakes: This portion of the state summary indicates the state's position on sweepstakes promotions. Typically, states permit sweepstakes as long as participants do not pay consideration and the sweepstakes does not otherwise violate anti-gambling laws. The *Sweepstakes* portion of the state summary provides a discussion of any insight the state offers on what it deems to be consideration in a contest or sweepstakes promotion. Sections of the Part Two, Overview that are helpful for understanding the *Sweepstakes* portion of the state summary include the discussions of consideration and alternative methods of entry in Sections 3.5 and 3.6, respectively, of this Guide.

Prize Promotion Laws: If applicable, the state summary includes a discussion of the state's prize promotion laws. All states do not have prize promotion laws. This *Prize Promotions Laws* portion of the state summary also includes a discussion of any state telemarketing laws that have significant prize promotion protection provisions.

Sections of the Part Two, Overview that are helpful for understanding this portion of the state summary include the general discussion of compliance with state prize promotion laws and the general discussion of compliance with state telemarketing laws in Sections 7.4.2 and 7.5.2, respectively, of this Guide.

Gambling Exceptions for Non-Profits and Other Qualified Organizations/*Raffles, Lotteries, and Bingo.* This portion of the state summary explains the state's exceptions to anti-gambling laws that allow non-profit organizations and other civic and charitable groups to offer raffles and bingo games. Many state laws refer to an organization eligible to offer non-profit raffles and bingo games as a qualified organization.

Section 9.2 of this Guide includes a general discussion of the typical requirements found in state raffle and bingo exceptions. Appendix A.4 of this Guide summarizes in table form the raffle laws of each of the states. Appendix A.5 of this Guide summarizes in table form the bingo laws of each of the states.

Resources. The state summary indicates where the reader can obtain copies of opinion letters issued by the state's attorney general. Many states provide a free searchable online database of attorney general opinions, typically on the website of the Office of the Attorney General. The website of the state's Office of the Attorney General is indicated at the beginning of the state summary.

Endnotes. The majority of—but now all—case law, statutory, and regulatory citations is included as endnotes at the end of each individual state summary. See Section 1.4 of this Guide for an explanation of the citation system used in this book.

Alabama

State Attorney General Office
Office of the Attorney General
501 Washington Avenue
Montgomery, Alabama 36130
Consumer Protection Section
(334) 242-7335 or (800) 392-5658
Website: http://www.ago.state.al.us/

Selected State Laws, Regulations, and Constitutional Provisions

Alabama's anti-gambling laws (Title 13A, Chapter 12, Article 2, Sections 13A-12-20 *et seq.* of the Alabama Code), which contain provisions related to promotions, are in its criminal code. As part of its commercial and consumer protection laws, Alabama includes laws prohibiting deceptive sweepstakes solicitations (Title 8, Chapter 19D, Sections 8-19D-1 and 2 of the Alabama Code). Specific Alabama legal provisions frequently cited in court cases and interpretive opinions related to promotions include the following:

Reference No.	Descriptive Name
Ala. Const. art. IV, §65	Lotteries and gift enterprises prohibited
Ala. Code § 13A-12-20	Definitions (for anti-gambling laws including definitions for contest of chance, gambling, lottery and something of value)
Ala. Code § 13A-12-21	Simple Gambling (prohibited as misdemeanor)
Ala. Code § 13A-12-22	Promoting Gambling (prohibited as misdemeanor)
Ala. Code § 8-19D-1	Definitions (for laws against deceptive sweepstakes solicitations)
Ala. Code § 8-19D-2	Deceptive solicitations; action for damages

Summary of State Law

Prohibition of Lotteries and Gambling: Alabama's Constitution as well as its statutory laws prohibit lotteries.[1] A promotion combining a prize, chance, and consideration is a lottery in Alabama.[2] Alabama also has a general prohibition against gambling.[3] Exceptions to the lottery and gambling prohibitions include some forms of charitable bingo.

Contests: Alabama permits contests as long as the contest does not conflict with anti-gambling laws. If the contest includes an element of consideration, the sponsor must award the contest prize based on skill and not on chance.

The statutory definition for contest of chance implies that Alabama applies the material element test[4] when evaluating whether or not chance determines the outcome of a promotion. In its anti-gambling statute, Alabama defines contest of chance as "Any contest, game, gaming scheme or gaming device in which *the outcome depends in a material degree upon an element of chance*, notwithstanding that skill of the contestants may also be a factor therein".[5]

Sweepstakes: Alabama permits sweepstakes as long as participants do not pay consideration and the sweepstakes does not violate anti-gambling laws. Alabama does not consider any of the following activities as consideration:

- A participant paying postage to request or return an entry form
- A participant advertising the promotion to friends and relatives
- A participant going to a retail store
- A sponsor benefiting from increased sales as a result of the promotion[6]

To meet the no consideration requirement, each sweepstakes must include a free method of entry.[7] In a 1994 opinion, the Alabama Attorney General indicated that the sponsor of a package sweepstakes must make the free alternative method of entry available at the point of purchase.[8] In a subsequent 1998 opinion, the Alabama Attorney General explicitly overruled that interpretation concluding that it is acceptable for consumers to get free entry by making a request by mail even if the consumer must include a self-addressed, stamped envelope with the request.[9] The postage for the envelope is not consideration.

Prize Promotion Laws: Alabama's prize promotion law is called the Deceptive Sweepstakes Solicitation law (Title 8, Chapter 19D, Sections 8-19D-1 and 2 of the Alabama Code). The law applies to sweepstakes that are advertised in mailed materials in conjunction with the offer of a product or service. The mailed materials can not include any misleading statements that the recipient has won a sweepstakes prize. Any statement about winning a prize must include qualifying language that explains any circumstances or actions required for the person to receive the prize. Alabama does not provide many specifics for the wording, content, and format of this qualifying language. Instead, the Alabama law requires simply that the qualifying language appear on the mailing in clear, easy-to-read, conspicuous print.[10]

Alabama also includes prize promotion provisions in its telemarketing laws. Under the Alabama Telemarketing Act (Title 8, Chapter 19A, Sections 18-19A-1 to 18-19A-24 of the Alabama Code), if a commercial telephone seller represents that a purchaser is or may be eligible to receive any gift, premium, bonus, or prize, the commercial telephone seller must submit to the state information related to the prize promotion component of the campaign.[11] The information filing is not required in circumstances in which the telemarketing gift offer is unconditional.[12]

Gambling Exceptions for Non-Profits and Other Qualified Organizations

Raffles and Lotteries: Alabama offers no exceptions to its anti-gambling laws that allow non-profits and other charitable institutions to hold raffles or lotteries. The only exception to the anti-gambling laws for non-profits is the operation of bingo games, discussed below.

Bingo. Alabama views the game of bingo as a lottery.[13] While lotteries are generally prohibited in the state, Alabama has adopted constitutional amendments allowing bingo in certain towns and counties. Instead of a state-wide exception for bingo, there is a separate constitutional amendment for each individual town or county allowing non-profit bingo games. The individual town or county issues rules and regulations for the licensing and regulation of bingo within its jurisdiction. Hence, the rules and licensing requirements for Alabama non-profit bingo vary depending on the location of the game. In general, each Alabama town or county with a bingo amendment allows non-profit organizations to sponsor bingo games as long as the non-profit uses the bingo proceeds for charitable or educational purposes.[14]

Resources

Alabama offers copies of its attorney general opinions from 1979 through the present online in the official opinions section of the website of the Office of the Attorney General.

Endnotes

1. Ala. Const. art. IV, § 65; Ala. Code §§ 13A-12-20 – 13A-12-22 (2013).
2. *Pepsi Cola Bottling v. Coca Cola Bottling*, 534 So. 2d 295, 296 (Ala. 1988).
3. Ala. Code § 13A-12-20 *et seq.* (2013).
4. *See generally*, Section 3.4.3 of this Guide for a discussion of tests used when evaluating whether chance or skill prevails in a promotion combining elements of both.
5. Ala. Code § 13A-12-20(3) (emphasis added) (2013).
6. Ala. Att'y Gen. Op. No. 99-00028, *3 (Oct. 29, 1998) *citing Opinion of the Justices*, 397 So. 2d 546, 547 (Ala. 1981).
7. *See generally*, Section 3.6 of this Guide for a discussion of effective free alternative methods of entry.
8. Ala. Att'y Gen. Op. No. 94-00249 (July 20, 1994).
9. Ala. Att'y Gen. Op. No. 99-00028, *3 (Oct. 29, 1998).
10. Ala. Code § 8-19D-2 (2013).
11. Ala. Code § 8-9A-13 (2013). *See generally*, discussion of state telemarketing laws in Section 7.5.2 of this Guide.
12. Ala. Code § 8-9A-13(c) (2013).
13. *Barber v. Cornerstone Cmty. Outreach, Inc.*, 42 So. 3d 65, 78 (Ala. 2009).
14. *See generally*, discussion of bingo and raffles in Section 9.2 of this Guide.

Alaska

State Attorney General Office
Office of the Attorney General
P.O. Box 110300
Juneau, Alaska 99811-0300
(907) 465-2133 / fax: (907) 465-2075
Website: http://www.law.state.ak.us

Selected State Laws, Regulations, and Constitutional Provisions

Alaska's anti-gambling laws (Title 11, Chapter 11.66, Article 02, Sections 11.66.200 *et seq.* of the Alaska Statute), which are in its criminal code, contain provisions related to promotions. There are also statutory provisions relevant to promotions located in the amusements and sports code (Title 5, Chapter 05.15, Sections 050.15.010 *et seq.* of the Alaska Statute). Specific Alaska legal provisions frequently cited in court cases and interpretive opinions related to promotions include the following:

Reference No.	Descriptive Name
Alaska Stat. § 11.66.200	Gambling (prohibited as a violation or misdemeanor)
Alaska Stat. § 11.66.210	Promoting gambling in the first degree (prohibited as a felony)
Alaska Stat. § 11.66.220	Promoting gambling in the second degree (prohibited as a misdemeanor)
Alaska Stat. § 11.66.280	Definitions (for anti-gambling laws including definitions for contest of chance, gambling, promoting gambling, and something of value)
Alaska Stat. § 05.15.690	Definitions (for charitable gaming laws)

Summary of State Law

Prohibition of Lotteries and Gambling: Alaska prohibits lotteries as illegal gambling.[1] A promotion combining a prize, chance, and consideration is a lottery in Alaska.[2] Alaska also has a general prohibition against gambling and promoting gambling.[3] Exceptions to the lottery and gambling prohibitions include certain charitable lotteries.

Contests: Alaska permits contests as long as the contest does not conflict with anti-gambling laws. If the contest includes an element of consideration, the sponsor must award the contest prize based on skill and not on chance.

According to an Alaska Attorney General opinion, Alaska uses the material element test[4] when evaluating whether or not chance determines the outcome of a promotion.[5] Alaska's preference for the material element test is also incorporated into the statutory definition of *contest of chance*. According to Alaska's anti-gambling statute, a "'contest of chance' means a contest, game, gaming scheme, or gaming device *in which the outcome depends in a material degree upon an element of chance*, notwithstanding that the skill of the contestants may also be a factor".[6]

Sweepstakes: Alaska permits sweepstakes as long as participants do not pay consideration and the sweepstakes does not violate anti-gambling laws. To meet the no consideration requirement, the sweepstakes must include a free method of entry. Alaska has a strict interpretation of the alternative free method of entry. According to the Alaska Attorney General, if a sweepstakes ticket is combined with a product that has never been offered for sale outside of the sweepstakes, the sweepstakes is illegal gambling.[7]

Gambling Exceptions for Non-Profits and Other Qualified Organizations

Raffles, Bingo, and Charitable Gaming. There are exceptions to the gambling prohibitions for raffles, bingo, and other charitable gaming activities in which the proceeds support municipalities or qualified charitable organizations.[8] Organizations eligible to offer charitable gaming include civic, service, religious, charitable, fraternal, labor, political, and educational organizations, police or fire departments, and non-profit trade associations.[9] Individual municipalities and villages can vote to prohibit charitable gaming within their jurisdiction.[10]

Operation of bingo games and raffles must meet several statutory and regulatory requirements.[11] Eligible organizations wishing to offer charitable gaming need a license issued by the Alaska Department of Revenue. Organizations must also file with the Alaska Department of Revenue periodic reports of their charitable gaming activities including gross receipts, expenses, and the value of prizes awarded.[12]

The charitable gaming laws are in the Alaska Gaming Reform Act, which is codified in Title 5, Chapter 05.15, Sections 05.15.010 *et seq.* of the Alaska Code. Regulations for charitable gaming are in Sections 15 AAC 160.010 *et seq.* of the Alaska Administrative Code.

Additional information, registration and report forms are available online in the gaming section of the website of the Alaska Department of Revenue, Tax Division, http://www.tax.alaska.gov/gaming. The state gaming group has multiple physical locations throughout the state.

Resources

Alaska offers a searchable database for its attorney general opinions from the mid 1980's through the present in the law resources section of the Alaska Attorney General website. The office acknowledges that there are gaps in the online database from the mid-1980's until 1990.

Endnotes

1. *Morrow v. Alaska*, 511 P.2d 127 (Alaska 1973).
2. *Id.*
3. Alaska Stat. §§ 11.66.200, 11.66.210, 11.66.220 (2014).
4. *See generally,* Section 3.4.3 of this Guide for a discussion of tests used when evaluating whether chance or skill prevails in a promotion combining elements of both.
5. Alaska Att'y Gen. Op. No. 663-01-0183 (May 22, 2001). This result contradicts the earlier analysis in *Morrow v. State of Alaska.* In *Morrow,* the Alaska Supreme Court indicated "We agree that the sounder approach is to determine the character of the scheme under the dominant factor

rule." 511 P.2d 127, 129 (1973). As explained in the 2001 attorney general opinion, the Alaska legislature rejected the *Morrow* determination in favor of the material element test finding that ". . . gambling occurs even if skill is the dominant factor, as long as chance is a material element." Alaska Att'y Gen. Op. No. 663-01-0183, *4 (May 22, 2001)

6. Alaska Stat. § 11.66.280(1) (2014) (emphasis provided).

7. Alaska Att'y Gen. Op. No. 663-00-0212, *6 (Oct. 17, 2000). *See generally,* Section 3.6 of this Guide for a discussion of effective free alternative methods of entry.

8. Alaska Stat. § 11.66.280(2)(C) (2014).

9. Alaska Stat. § 05.15.690(39) (2014).

10. Alaska Stat. § 05.15.620 (2014).

11. See generally, discussion of bingo and raffles in Section 9.2 of this Guide.

12. Alaska Stat. § 05.15.083 (2014).

Arizona

State Attorney General Office
Office of the Attorney General
1275 W. Washington St.
Phoenix, Arizona 85007-2926
(602) 542-5025
Website: http://www.azag.gov

Selected State Laws, Regulations, and Constitutional Provisions

Arizona has anti-gambling laws (Title 13, Chapter 33, Sections 13-3301 *et seq.* of the Arizona Revised Statutes) in its criminal code. Specific Arizona legal provisions frequently quoted in court cases and interpretive opinions related to promotions include the following:

Reference No.	Descriptive Name
Ariz. Rev. Stat. § 13-3301	Definitions (for anti-gambling laws including definitions for amusement gambling, gambling, and gamble)
Ariz. Rev. Stat. § 13-3302	Exclusions (from gambling prohibitions)
Ariz. Rev. Stat. § 13-3303	Promotion of gambling; classification (prohibited as felony)
Ariz. Rev. Stat. § 13-3304	Benefiting from gambling; classification (prohibited as misdemeanor)
Ariz. Rev. Stat. § 13-3305	Betting and wagering; classification (prohibited as misdemeanor)
Ariz. Rev. Stat. § 13-3311	Amusement gambling intellectual contests or events; registration; filing of rules; sworn statement; exceptions

Summary of State Law

Prohibition of Lotteries and Gambling: Arizona prohibits gambling which the statute defines as the "act of risking or giving something of value for the opportunity to obtain a benefit from a game or contest of chance or skill or a future contingent event . . . "[1] The statutory definition encompasses the three commonly recognized elements of a lottery: consideration (*i.e.*, expressed as something of value), prize (*i.e.*, expressed as a benefit), and chance.

In contrast to the approach used by many other states, Arizona's definition of gambling does not distinguish between games of chance and games of skill. Both skill-based games and chance-based games can potentially be categorized as gambling under Arizona law if the game offers a prize and requires consideration for participation.[2] Exceptions to the lottery and gambling prohibitions include state-operated lotteries and certain charitable lotteries.

Contests: Skill-based contests that charge no consideration are permissible in Arizona. The permissibility of contests that charge consideration is less clear. As a consequence, many practitioners view it as risky to charge consideration for a contest in Arizona—unless the contest qualifies as an intellectual skill-based contest and has been registered with the state (See discussion of Intellectual Skill-Based Contests below).

The statutory definition of gambling indicates that a game in which participants risk something of value (*i.e.*, consideration) for the opportunity to obtain a benefit (*i.e.*, a prize) can qualify as gambling, regardless of whether or not the game is skill-based or chance-based.[3] This lack of distinction between skill-based and chance-based games has led some to conclude that sponsors of skill-based contests may not charge consideration in Arizona. Research for this Guide suggests that this conclusion is incorrect.

Arizona's gambling definition means that a skill-based game with a prize and consideration can potentially be characterized as a gambling game under Arizona law. However, Arizona case law indicates that this definition of gambling does not mean that *every* skill-based game with a prize and consideration qualifies as gambling. Hence, if one structures a skill-based contest so it is not gambling, it is permissible to charge contest participants payment or other consideration. This analysis is based primarily on the Arizona Supreme Court decision, *Arizona v. American Holiday Association*, 727 P.2d 807 (Ariz. 1986), discussed immediately below.

ARIZONA SUPREME COURT DECISION, *ARIZONA V. AMERICAN HOLIDAY ASSO-CIATION*, RULES THAT SKILL-BASED CONTESTS MAY CHARGE CONSIDERATION IN ARIZONA. In the 1986 decision, *Arizona v. American Holiday Association*, the Arizona Supreme Court explicitly said that entrance fees for contests can be legal and that reasonable entrance fees charged by the sponsor of a contest to participants competing for prizes are not bets or wagers. The Arizona Supreme Court held that the payment of entry fees does not constitute illegal wagering (a requirement for a finding of gambling in Arizona) under Arizona law when the entry fees are paid unconditionally and the prizes do not depend on the number of participants.[4]

In *American Holiday*, the Arizona Supreme Court considered whether a skill-based puzzle contest that charged a monetary payment was illegal gambling in Arizona. The court concluded that the puzzle contest was not illegal gambling. The court's analysis focused on whether the puzzle contest violated a statutory provision prohibiting any person from benefiting from taking bets or wagers for any race, sporting event, or other contingent future event.[5] To complete its analysis, the court needed to decide how to characterize the monetary payment made by the puzzle contest participants. One potential option was characterizing the fee as an illegal bet placed on the winner of the puzzle contest. Alternatively, the fee could be viewed as a legal entry fee for the privilege of competing in the puzzle contest. The Arizona Supreme Court chose the latter option concluding that the fee charged was a legal entry fee.

In its opinion, the court said "Obviously it is not illegal for the directors of a contest, for example the national spelling bee or the local rodeo, to charge an entrance fee. We think it equally obvious that not every contest charging an entry fee *and* awarding a prize becomes an illegal gambling operation."[6] The court added that golf tournaments, bridge tournaments, local and state rodeos or fair contests, and literary and essay competitions are not illegal gambling just because they combine an entry fee with a prize.

More specifically, the Arizona Supreme Court found that the payments charged by the puzzle contest sponsor were legal entry fees and not illegal bets because the payments lacked the attributes of gambling as follows:

- Only contest participants were eligible to receive prizes.
- The outcome of the contest was determined by the participants themselves and not by the outcome of an event involving third parties.
- The sponsor awarded the prize and the sponsor had no opportunity to win the prize.
- The prize was known from the start of the contest.
- The prize was not dependent on the number of participants or amount of entry fees actually received by the sponsor.
- The contest did not involve bets among participants. Instead, the sponsor, who did not compete for the prize, awarded the prize.
- The competition was one between participants for prizes. The sponsor was obligated to pay a guaranteed prize out of its own funds, regardless of whether the entrance fees or additional entrance fees equal the prize money.

Hence, the *American Holiday* case supports the argument that contests charging consideration are legal in Arizona where the contest is a competition among contest participants for a prize known at the start of the contest, the sponsor provides the prize and has no opportunity to win the prize, and the winner of the prize is determined by actions of participants and not by any outside force.

There is a wrinkle in the above analysis that places some uncertainty in one's ability to rely on *American Holiday* to support the argument that contest sponsors may charge consideration in Arizona. The Arizona Supreme Court issued its holding in September 1986. Accordingly, the *American Holiday* decision pre-dates the current definition of gambling in Section 13-3301.4 of the Arizona Revised Statutes. As explained above, Arizona's gambling definition indicates that a game with a prize and consideration can be characterized as gambling—regardless of whether chance or skill determines the outcome of the game.

It is uncertain whether the *American Holiday* ruling suffers any adverse impact due to Arizona's subsequent adoption of the statutory definition for gambling. The *American Holiday* court did state that the characterization of the puzzle contest as skill-based or chance-based had little relevance on whether the fees charged by the sponsor were illegal bets or legal entrance fees.[7] That statement supports the argument that *American Holiday* remains good law despite the subsequent adoption of a statutory gambling definition that views both skill-based and chance-based games as potential illegal gambling games.

INTELLECTUAL SKILL-BASED CONTEST REQUIRING PRODUCT PURCHASE. Amusement gambling is not unlawful under Arizona law.[8] Arizona defines four categories of amusement gambling.[9] The amusement gambling category most relevant to the type of promotions discussed in this Guide is an intellectual contest played for entertainment in which the entry fee is part of an established purchase price for a product and the winner is not determined by a drawing or lottery.[10]

Sponsors of contests that qualify as intellectual contests must register those contests with the Arizona Attorney General's Office prior to the start of the contest.[11] The registration information the sponsor must provide includes sponsor name and address, the value of the prizes, and a copy of the rules. After completion of the contest, the sponsor must file the names and addresses of the winners. Certain tax-exempt organizations and school districts offering skill-based intellectual contests are not required to make the filing.[12]

Sweepstakes: Arizona permits sweepstakes as long as participants do not pay consideration and the sweepstakes does not violate anti-gambling laws. Arizona does not require registration for sweepstakes.

Gambling Exceptions for Non-Profits and Other Qualified Organizations

Raffles and Lotteries. Arizona allows raffles to be conducted by certain tax-exempt, non-profit organizations[13], by historical societies[14], and by non-profit organizations that are booster clubs, civic clubs, political clubs or political organizations[15]. The requirements to offer a raffle differ significantly depending upon which of these categories applies to the raffle sponsor.[16]

The most significant distinction is the requirement for the raffle sponsor to have been in existence continuously in Arizona for five years immediately before conducting the raffle.[17] This five-year existence requirement applies to raffle sponsors relying on the exemption for tax-exempt, non-profit organizations or the exemption for historical societies. There is no such five-year existence requirement for raffle sponsors relying on the exemption for booster/civic/political organizations.

However, organizations conducting a raffle in reliance on the booster/civic/political organization exemption are limited to a ten thousand dollar annual maximum benefit from raffle activities.[18] There is no annual maximum limitation for organizations relying on the raffle exceptions for non-profit organizations and for historical societies.

Research for this Guide uncovered no legal provisions indicating that offering a raffle under any of the exceptions requires a license or permit.[19] The Arizona Attorney General has accepted an interpretation that raffles are synonymous with lotteries.[20] Hence, each raffle exception could arguably be applied to allow these same organizations to offer forms of lotteries other than traditional raffles.

The following chart illustrates the distinctions among the available raffle exceptions:

Applicable Raffle Exception	tax-exempt, non-profit organizations[21]	historical societies[22]	booster clubs, civic clubs, political clubs or political organizations[23]
Annual Maximum	None	None	$10,000
Registration or License Required	No	No	No
Five-year existence requirement	Yes	Yes	No

Bingo: Bingo is legal in Arizona for recreational purposes and for certain civic and non-profit organizations. Organizations eligible to offer bingo games include certain homeowners associations; charitable, fraternal, religious, social, veterans' or volunteer fire fighters organizations; non-profit ambulance services; and a branch or chapter of non-profit national or state organizations.[24]

The operation of the bingo game must meet several statutory and regulatory requirements.[25] The organization must have a bingo license, issued by the Arizona Department of Revenue. The organization must devote all net bingo proceeds to charitable purposes or to uses consistent with its organizational purposes.[26] All bingo licensees must file periodic financial reports and pay a portion of bingo proceeds as a bingo tax.

Laws addressing non-profit bingo are codified in Title 5, Chapter 4, Sections 5-401 *et seq.* of the Arizona Revised Statutes. Bingo regulations, issued by the Arizona Department of Revenue, are codified in Sections 15-7-201 *et seq.* of the Arizona Administrative Code. More information on bingo licensing in Arizona is available from the Bingo Section of the Arizona Department of Revenue, 1600 W Monroe, Phoenix, Arizona 85007-2650, (602) 716-7801, www.azdor.gov, bingo@azdor.gov.

Resources

Arizona attorney general opinions issued from 1999 to the present are available online in the Opinions section of the website of the Office of the Attorney General. Attorney general opinions issued prior to 1999 are available and searchable at the Arizona State Library, Archives and Public Records archival website, http://azmemory.azlibrary.gov/cdm/

Endnotes

1. Ariz. Rev. Stat. § 13-3301.4 (2014).
2. *See generally,* discussion of requirements for gambling in Sections 3.7.1 and 3.7.2 of this Guide.
3. Ariz. Rev. Stat. § 13-3301.4 (2014).
4. *Arizona v. Am. Holiday Ass'n,* 727 P.2d 807, 812 (Ariz. 1986).
5. In its analysis, the Arizona Supreme Court evaluated whether the puzzle contest violated Section 13-3307 of the Arizona Revised Statute. That statutory provision was subsequently re-numbered and is now Section 13-3305.A. The statutory provision prohibits any person from benefiting

from taking bets or wagers on any race, sporting event, contest or other game of skill or chance or any other unknown or contingent future event.

6. *Arizona v. Am, Holiday Ass'n, supra* note 4, at 809.
7. *Id.* at 809.
8. Ariz. Rev. Stat. § 13-3302.A.1 (2014).
9. Ariz. Rev. Stat. § 13-3301.1 (2014).
10. Ariz. Rev. Stat. § 13-3301.1(d)(iii) (2014).
11. Ariz. Rev. Stat. § 13-3311 (2014).
12. Ariz. Rev. Stat. § 13-3311.D (2014).
13. Ariz. Rev. Stat. § 13-3302.B (2014).
14. Ariz. Rev. Stat. § 13-3302.C (2014).
15. Ariz. Rev. Stat. § 13-3302.D (2014).
16. Ariz. Rev. Stat. § 13-3302 (2014).
17. Ariz. Rev. Stat. § 13-3302.B & C (2014).
18. Ariz. Rev. Stat. § 13-3302.D.3 (2014).
19. The Arizona Attorney General's form for registration of intellectual contests is titled, Amusement Gambling and Raffle Registration Form. However, this form does not appear to be intended for use with the non-profit, historical society, and booster/civic/political organization raffles permitted by Ariz. Rev. Stat. §13-3302. Instead, the Amusement Gambling and Raffle Registration Form references itself as a requirement for the intellectual contests permitted pursuant to Ariz. Rev. Stat. §§ 13-3301.1(d)(iii) and 13-3311.
20. Ariz. Att'y Gen. Op. I84-018, note 1. (Jan. 25, 1984).
21. Ariz. Rev. Stat. § 13-3302.B (2014).
22. Ariz. Rev. Stat. § 13-3302.C (2014).
23. Ariz. Rev. Stat. § 13-3302.D (2014).
24. Ariz. Rev. Stat. § 5-401.25 (2014).
25. *See generally*, discussion of bingo and raffles in Section 9.2 of this Guide.
26. Ariz. Rev. Stat. §§ 5-401.11 and 5.401.12 (2014).

Arkansas

State Attorney General Office
Office of the Attorney General
323 Center Street, Suite 200
Little Rock, Arkansas 72201
(501) 682-2007
Website: http://www.arkansasag.gov

Selected State Laws, Regulations, and Constitutional Provisions

Arkansas' anti-gambling laws (Title 5, Subtitle 6, Chapter 66, Sections 5-66-101 *et seq.* of the Arkansas Code), which are in its criminal offenses code, contain provisions related to promotions. In its business and commercial law code, Arkansas includes its prize promotion laws (Title 4, Subtitle 7, Chapter 102, Sections 4-102-101 *et seq.*). Specific Arkansas legal provisions frequently quoted in court cases and interpretive opinions related to promotions include the following:

Reference No.	Descriptive Name
Ark. Const. art. 19, § 14	Lotteries prohibited
Ark. Code § 4-102-105	Prohibited practices (for promotions)
Ark. Code § 4-102-106	Disclosures required (for promotions)
Ark. Code § 4-70-102	Advertisement by giving away prizes lawful
Ark. Code § 5-66-113	Games of hazard or skill—Betting
Ark. Code § 5-66-118	Lottery, etc.—Tickets

Summary of State Law

Prohibition of Lotteries and Gambling: Arkansas' Constitution as well as its statutory laws prohibit lotteries.[1] A promotion that combines a prize, chance, and consideration is a lottery in Arkansas.[2] Arkansas also has a general prohibition against gambling.[3] Exceptions to the lottery and gambling prohibitions include state-operated lotteries and certain charitable lotteries.

Contests: Arkansas permits contests as long as the contest does not conflict with anti-gambling laws. If the contest includes an element of consideration, the sponsor must award the contest prize based on skill and not on chance. Contests offered in conjunction with sales campaigns must comply with Arkansas prize promotions laws, discussed below.

Court opinions suggest that Arkansas applies the dominant factor doctrine[4] when evaluating whether or not chance determines the outcome of a promotion. In *Longstreth v. Cook*, 220 S.W.2d 433, 437 (Ark. 1949), the Arkansas Supreme Court determined that pari-mutuel betting of horseracing did not constitute a lottery.[5] In its conclusion, the *Longstreth* court reasoned that "while the element of chance no doubt enters into these races, *it does not control them,* and that there is therefore no lottery."[6]

Although subsequent court opinions and attorney general opinions wholly follow the *Longstreth* holding,[7] some of the language used in those subsequent opinions seems to overstate *Longstreth's* characterization of the required role of chance in a lottery and could be interpreted as supporting Arkansas' use of the pure chance test.[8] Nevertheless, it seems likely that Arkansas law would favor the dominant factor doctrine over the pure chance test.

ARKANSAS LAW GOVERNING BEAUTY PAGEANTS. Arkansas has laws that deal with beauty pageants (Title 17, Chapter 21, Sections 17-21-101 to 17-21-205 of the Arkansas Code). If a beauty pageant operator charges an entry fee or an audience admission fee, or sells tickets or chances in connection with the pageant, the operator must register with the Director of the Department of Finance and Administration and obtain a bond in the amount of $10,000.

The beauty pageant laws do not apply to an operator that has existed for at least twenty-five years and whose continuing primary function involves the annual operation of a statewide pageant in which contestants compete for scholarships and for the opportunity to represent Arkansas in an annual nationwide pageant with which the operator is affiliated.[9] Civic, non-profit, and religious organizations as well as local government entities and schools are exempt from the bond requirement.

Sweepstakes: Arkansas permits sweepstakes as long as participants pay no consideration and the sweepstakes does not violate the anti-gambling laws. Sweepstakes offered in conjunction with sales campaigns must comply with the Arkansas prize promotion laws, discussed below.

The Arkansas Attorney General has commented on indirect consideration in a sweepstakes. Indirect consideration occurs when a participant receives a sweepstakes ticket with the purchase of a non-gaming product and the participant pays an inflated price for the non-gaming product. Arkansas views the premium paid for the non-gaming product as consideration paid for the sweepstakes ticket. Other indirect consideration methods identified by Arkansas include payment of an annual fee.[10] For example, there is indirect consideration for a bingo game held at a club when the only people allowed to play are members of the club and their guests (where club membership requires payment of a membership fee).[11]

Arkansas law explicitly legalizes in-package sweepstakes as long as there is a free alternative method of entry.[12] The Arkansas Attorney General has emphasized that this in-package sweepstakes allowance is for sweepstakes combined with pre-existing products. According to the Arkansas Attorney General, the in-package sweepstakes provision was enacted with the intent of allowing promotional advertising for products that are typically sold independent of a promotional scheme and that cost the same before, during, and after the promotion.[13]

Prize Promotion Laws: The Arkansas Prize Promotion Act (Title 4, Subtitle 7, Sections 4-102-101 *et seq.* of the Arkansas Code) applies when a company combines a prize offer with the sale of products or services. It does not apply to a promotion in which there is no opportunity for money to pass from the participant to the sponsor.[14] The Arkansas Prize Promotion Act includes disclosure requirements, prohibited practices designed to thwart misrepresentation[15], and a requirement to award any prize promised[16].

OFFER OF A PRIZE REQUIRES A WRITTEN DISCLOSURE. If the Arkansas Prize Promotion Act applies, a company must provide people to whom it offers a prize with certain disclosures in a written prize notice.[17] The written prize notice requirement applies regardless of whether the company makes the prize offer in writing, verbally, or by telephone.[18] There are specific requirements for the wording, appearance and placement of the disclosures in the prize notice.[19]

APPLICABILITY OF THE ARKANSAS PRIZE PROMOTION ACT TO CONTESTS CHARGING CONSIDERATION. A literal reading of the Arkansas Prize Promotion Act indicates the act applies whenever a company charges Arkansas residents money as a condition of receiving or competing for, or learning information about a prize.[20] Nevertheless, in *Burford Distributing v. Starr*, 20 S.W.3d 363 (Ark. 2000), the Arkansas Supreme Court concluded that the Arkansas Prize Promotion Act was not applicable in a skill-based contest where the participant paid an entry fee but was not required to purchase any of the sponsor's products in order to compete in the contest. In *Burford Distributing*, the Burford Distributing Company sponsored a golf tournament that charged a $40 entry fee and promised the prize of a car to the first person to score a hole-in-one. Danny Starr sued Burford Distributing for breach of contract and violation of the Arkansas Prize Promotion Act after he shot a hole in one and was refused the car.[21]

Among the facts convincing the court that the Arkansas Prize Promotion Act was inapplicable to the golf tournament contest were Starr's admissions that he never received any communication from Burford Distributing encouraging him to participate in the tournament, that he learned about the tournament through an acquaintance, and that he had no knowledge of the car giveaway at the time he entered the tournament. It is noteworthy that the dissenting opinion in *Burford Distributing* argues that the Arkansas Prize Promotion Act should apply to the Burford Distributing golf tournament precisely because payment of an entry fee was a requirement to competing in the tournament.

PRIZE PROMOTION PROVISIONS OF TELEMARKETING LAWS. Arkansas has telemarketing laws (Title 4, Subtitle 7, Chapter 99, Sections 4-99-101 to 4-99-408 of the Arkansas Code) which include disclosure requirements for sweepstakes and giveaways offered as part of a telephone solicitation.[22] The Arkansas Mail and Telephone Consumer Product Promotion Fair Practices Act (Title 4, Subtitle 7, Chapter 95, Sections 4-95-101 to 4-95-108 of the Arkansas Code) also contains disclosure requirements for prizes and gifts offered by telephone or mail in conjunction with a consumer product sales campaign.[23]

Gambling Exceptions for Non-Profits and Other Qualified Organizations

Bingo and Raffles: A constitutional amendment allows certain non-profit, tax-exempt organizations to conduct bingo games and raffles as long as the organization uses all net receipts over and above the actual cost of conducting the bingo game or raffle for charitable, religious, or philanthropic purposes.[24]

Qualified organizations able to offer bingo games and raffles include religious, educational, veterans, fraternal, service, civic, medical, volunteer rescue services, volunteer firefighters, and volunteer police organizations.[25] The operation of raffles and bingo games must meet several statutory and regulatory requirements.[26] Organizations operating bingo and raffle games must have a license issued by the Arkansas Department of Finance and Administration.[27]

The Charitable Bingo and Raffles Game Enabling Act is codified in Title 23, Chapter 114 of the Arkansas Code. The raffle and bingo regulations are in Rule 2007-4 of the Arkansas Administrative Code. Additional information, registration and report forms are available from the Arkansas Department of Finance and Administration, Revenue Division, Miscellaneous Tax, P. O. Box 896 - Room 2340, Joel Y. Ledbetter Building, Little Rock, Arkansas 72203, Phone: 501-682-7187, Fax: 501-683-3699, http://www.state.ar.us/dfa

Resources

Arkansas offers a searchable database for its attorney general opinions online at http://www.arkansasag.gov/opinions/

Endnotes

1. Ark. Const. art. 19, § 14; Ark. Code § 5-66-118 (2013).
2. Ark. Att'y Gen. Op. 2006-052 (June 28, 2006) *citing Scott v. Dunaway*, 311 S.W.2d 305 (1958).
3. *See generally,* Ark. Code §§ 5-66-101, 5-66-113 *et seq.* (2013).
4. *See generally,* Section 3.4.3 of this Guide for a discussion of tests used when evaluating whether chance or skill prevails in a promotion combining elements of both.
5. However, the court did conclude that such pari-mutuel betting constitutes a form of gambling other than a lottery. At the time of the *Longstreth* case (1949), the legislature's authorization of a form of gambling (other than a lottery) would have been constitutional. In contrast, the legislature's authorization of a lottery in 1949 would have been unconstitutional. *Longstreth v. Cook*, 220 S.W.2d 433, 435 (Ark. 1949).
6. *Longstreth, supra* note 5, at 438 (Ark. 1949) (emphasis added).
7. *See e.g., Scott v. Dunaway*, 311 S.W.2d 305 (Ark. 1958); Ark. Att'y Gen. Op. 93-437 (Jan. 5, 1994).
8. For example, in *Scott v. Dunaway, supra* note 7, at 306, the Arkansas Supreme Court references the *Longstreth* decision as holding "it is essential to a lottery that the winners be determined by chance alone". In a 1994 opinion, the Arkansas Attorney General citing the *Scott* and *Longstreth* decisions, says "in order to constitute a lottery, it is essential that the winners be determined by 'chance alone,' and that the outcome be 'wholly dependent upon the element of chance,' and the type of betting be 'completely controlled by chance.' Such wording seems to be an overstatement of the *Longstreth* decision, which characterized the role of chance in a lottery as the controlling element or the determining element, *Longstreth, supra* note 5, at 437 and 438, and not as the sole element.
9. Ark. Code § 17-21-101 (2013).
10. Ark. Att'y Gen. Op. No. 2004-357 (March 9, 2005).
11. Ark. Att'y Gen. Op. No. 99-318 (Dec. 9, 1999).
12. Ark. Code § 4-70-102 (2013).
13. Ark. Att'y Gen. Op. No. 2006-052 (June 28, 2006).
14. Ark. Code § 4-102-104(b)(1) (2013). There are additional exemptions in Ark. Code §4-102-104.
15. See Ark. Code § 4-102-105 (2013).
16. Ark. Code § 4-102-107 (2013).
17. Ark. Code § 4-102-106 (2013).

18. Ark. Code §§ 4-102-106(a) and 4-102-108 (2013).
19. See Ark. Code § 4-102-106(b) and (c) (2013). *See generally,* discussion of prize promotion laws in Section 7.4.2 of this Guide.
20. *See e.g.,* Ark. Code §§ 4-102-102(3) and 4-102-106 (2013).
21. Starr shot his hole-in-one on Hole No. 8 of the golf course. Evidently, Burford Distributing was offering the car for a hole-in-one from Hole No. 17. Hole No. 17 and Hole No. 8 shared the same green; however, Hole No. 17 had a tee box located farther away from the hole than the tee box for Hole No. 8. Hence, a hole-in-one from Hole No. 17 was more difficult than a hole-in-one from Hole No. 8.
22. Ark. Code § 4-99-108 (2013). *See generally,* discussion of state telemarketing laws in Section 7.5.2 of this Guide.
23. Ark. Code § 4-95-105 (2013).
24. Ark. Const., amend. no. 84.
25. Ark. Code § 23-114-102(1) (2013).
26. *See generally,* discussion of bingo and raffles in Section 9.2 of this Guide.
27. Ark. Code § 23-114-103(b)(2) (2013).

California

State Attorney General Office
Office of the Attorney General
1300 "I" Street
Sacramento, California
95814-2919
(916) 445-9555
Website: http://oag.ca.gov/

Selected State Laws, Regulations, and Constitutional Provisions

California's anti-gambling laws (Part 1, Title 9, Chapters 9 and 10, Sections 319 to 337z of the California Penal Code) include provisions related to promotions. California law also includes prize promotion protections (Division 7, Part 3, Chapter 1, Article 2, Section 17533.8 *et seq.* of the California Business and Professions Code). Specific California legal provisions frequently quoted in court cases and interpretive opinions related to promotions include the following:

Reference No.	Descriptive Name[1]
Cal. Const. art. IV, § 19,	(prohibition against lotteries)
Cal. Penal Code § 319	(definition of lottery)
Cal. Penal Code § 320	(preparing or drawing a lottery is a misdemeanor)
Cal. Penal Code § 326.5	(exemption for charitable bingo)
Cal. Bus. & Prof. Code §§ 17533.8, 17537, 17537.1, 17537.2, 17537.11	(required disclosures for gifts given as inducement to attend sales presentations or take other commercial action)
Cal. Bus. & Prof. Code §§17539-17539.3, 17539.35	(disclosure and procedural requirements for contests charging consideration)

Summary of State Law

Prohibition of Lotteries and Gambling: California's Constitution and its statutory laws prohibit lotteries.[2] A promotion that combines a prize, chance, and consideration is a lottery in California.[3] California also has a general prohibition against gambling in its penal code.[4] Exceptions to the lottery and gambling prohibitions include lotteries operated by the state and certain charitable lotteries.

Contests: California permits contests as long as the contest does not conflict with anti-gambling laws. If the contest includes an element of consideration, the sponsor must award the contest prize based on skill and not on chance. Contests charging consideration must also comply with California's prize promotion laws, discussed below.

Court opinions indicate that when evaluating whether or not chance determines the outcome of a promotion, California applies the dominant factor doctrine[5] and has explicitly rejected the pure chance test. In *Bell Gardens Bicycle Club v. Dept. of Justice*, 42 Cal. Rptr. 2d 730, 747-748 (Cal. Ct. App. 1995), the court explained that when determining whether a particular game or scheme is a lottery, the test in California is whether the game is dominated by chance and not whether the winner of the game is determined solely by chance.

Sweepstakes: California permits sweepstakes as long as participants do not pay consideration and the sweepstakes does not conflict with anti-gambling laws. Sweepstakes must comply with prize promotion laws discussed below. The California statutory definition of lottery indicates that the consideration paid for a lottery must be valuable.[6] California authorities have interpreted this definition to mean that consideration for a contest or sweepstakes does not include requiring a ticket holder to go to the sponsor's place of business to deposit an entry.[7]

Prize Promotion Laws: California has prize promotion laws in its business and promotions code. The following discussion separates prize promotion laws into four separate categories: contests that charge consideration; sweepstakes; gifts given to motivate sales or attendance at sales presentations; and gifts given as part of telemarketing campaigns.

When the prize promotion laws require a disclosure statement, there are typically specific statutory requirements for the disclosures' placement, font, and wording.[8]

Most of California's prize promotion laws are codified in Division 7, Part 3, Chapter 1, Article 2, Section 17533.8 *et seq.* of the California Business and Professions Code. The prize promotion provisions related to telemarketing are codified in Division 7, Part 3, Chapter 1, Article 1.4, Sections 17511 to 17514 of the California Business and Professions Code.

PRIZE PROMOTION LAWS FOR CONTESTS THAT CHARGE CONSIDERATION. If contest participants pay consideration, the contest sponsor must provide certain disclosures and comply with other requirements.[9] One requirement found in California law that is not common in the prize promotion laws of other states is the requirement to provide a refund to any participant who is unable to participate in the contest through no fault of his own and who requests a refund in writing within one year.[10] The award of the prize cannot be conditioned upon a minimum number of entries or contest participants.[11]

Certain contests do not have to comply with these requirements—even if they do require consideration. Exempted contests include sporting events, performances, or tournaments of skill, power or endurance between participants who are actually present at the contest.[12]

PRIZE PROMOTION LAWS FOR SWEEPSTAKES. The prize promotion laws specific to sweepstakes implement numerous prohibited practices and mandatory disclosures for sweepstakes.[13] California prohibits soliciting or selling an information-access service in conjunction with a sweepstakes.[14] However, a sponsor can use a 900 or 976 number to administer a sweepstakes as long as the sponsor registers with the Department of Justice within ten days after advertising the sweepstakes in California.[15]

PRIZE PROMOTION LAWS FOR GIFTS GIVEN AS A SALES INCENTIVE. There is a set of California prize promotion laws for prize giveaways designed as an inducement to encourage consumer purchases or attendance at sales presentations.[16] A company offering a gift or prize as an incentive for a consumer to attend or listen to a sales presentation must disclose the sales presentation attendance requirement and make other specific written disclosures.[17]

The law also prohibits certain practices that might mislead consumers.[18] As an example, it is misleading for a company to tell a consumer that the consumer has won a gift if in order to receive the gift, the consumer must make a purchase or pay unreasonable shipping or handling charges.[19]

PRIZE PROMOTION PROTECTIONS IN TELEMARKETING LAWS. California has telephonic sellers laws that include a prize notice component.[20] If a prize or gift is offered to consumers as part of a telephone solicitation campaign, the telephone solicitor must disclose certain information both to the state as part of the required telemarketing registration and to the consumer as part of the call.[21]

Gambling Exceptions for Non-Profits and Other Qualified Organizations

Raffles and Lotteries: An exception to the constitutional lottery prohibition allows certain private, tax-exempt, non-profit organizations to conduct raffles as long as the organization uses at least ninety percent of the raffle proceeds for charitable purposes within California.[22]

The operation of the raffle must meet several statutory and regulatory requirements.[23] Eligible organizations wishing to conduct raffles must register annually with the California Office of the Attorney General and must file an annual report of receipts, costs, and charitable uses of the receipts.[24] Certain organizations, including religious corporations, educational institutions, and hospitals, are exempt from the registration and report filing requirements.[25]

The raffle law is codified in Section 320.5 of the California Penal Code. Raffle regulations are codified in Title 11, Division 1, Chapter 4.6, Sections 410 to 426 of the California Code of Regulations. Raffle registration and report forms are available from the Office of the Attorney General, Registry of Charitable Trusts, 1300 I Street, Sacramento, CA 94203, (916) 445-2021, http://ag.ca.gov/charities/. Online information offered by the Registry of Charitable Trusts includes a searchable database of information about non-profit raffles (such as the amount of money collected and dates on which a non-profit intends to hold a raffle).

Bingo: An exception to the constitutional lottery prohibition allows cities and counties to authorize certain organizations to operate bingo games for charitable purposes.[26] Eligible organizations able to offer bingo games include certain tax-exempt organizations, mobile home park associations, senior citizens organizations, and charitable organizations affiliated with a school district.

The operation of the bingo game must meet several statutory requirements.[27] The constitutional allowance for bingo is codified in Section 326.5 of the California Penal Code.[28] Traditional bingo is not regulated at the state level.[29] Instead, bingo regulation is the responsibility of the local jurisdictions. Cities and counties permitting bingo games within their jurisdiction can require that the sponsoring organization obtain a license from the city or county.[30]

Resources

California offers a searchable database for its attorney general opinions from 1986 through the present online at the website of the Office of the Attorney General.

The California Department of Consumer Affairs offers several free short legal guides explaining California law related to prizes, promotions, giveaways and lotteries. The legal guides are available online in the Publication section of the website of the California Department of Consumer Affairs at http://www.dca.ca.gov/

Endnotes

1. California's code does not provide narrative titles for its statutory provisions. The author has provided all the section descriptions in the parentheticals.
2. Cal. Const. art. IV, § 19; Cal. Penal Code § 320 (2014).
3. Cal. Att'y Gen. Op. No. 02-809 (Dec. 10, 2002) *citing Cal. Gas. Retailers v. Regal Petroleum Corp.*, 50 Cal. 2d 844, 851 (Cal. 1958) and previous attorney general opinions; Cal. Penal Code § 319 (2014).
4. Cal. Penal Code §§ 330 to 337z (2014).
5. *See generally*, Section 3.4.3 of this Guide for a discussion of tests used when evaluating whether chance or skill prevails in a promotion combining elements of both.

6. Cal. Penal Code § 319 (2014).
7. Cal. Att'y Gen. Op. No. 98-1101 (Feb. 4, 1999) *citing Cal. Gas. Retailers, supra* note 3, at 861-862.
8. *See generally,* discussion of state prize promotion laws in Section 7.4.2 of this Guide.
9. Cal. Bus. & Prof. Code §§ 17539.1, 17539.2, and 17539.35 (2014).
10. Cal. Bus. & Prof. Code § 17539.2(b) (2014).
11. Cal. Bus. & Prof. Code § 17539.35 (2014).
12. Cal. Bus. & Prof. Code § 17539.3(e) and (f) (2014).
13. Cal. Bus. & Prof. Code §§ 17539.15, 17539.5, and 17539.55 (2014).
14. Cal. Bus. & Prof. Code § 17539.5(d) (2014).
15. Cal. Bus. & Prof. Code § 17539.55 (2014).
16. Cal. Bus. & Prof. Code §§ 17533.8, 17537, 17537.1, and 17537.11 (2014).
17. Cal. Bus. & Prof. Code §§ 17533.8 and 17537.1 (2014).
18. Cal. Bus. & Prof. Code § 17537.1(g) (2014).
19. Cal. Bus. & Prof. Code § 17537 (2014).
20. *See generally,* discussion of state telemarketing laws in Section 7.5.2 of this Guide.
21. Cal. Bus. & Prof. Code §§ 17511.5(a) and 17511.4(l) (2014).
22. Cal. Const., Art. IV § 19, subd. (f).
23. *See generally,* discussion of bingo and raffles in Section 9.2 of this Guide.
24. Cal. Penal Code § 320.5(h) (2014).
25. Cal. Penal Code § 320.5(h)(7) (2014).
26. Cal. Const., art IV, § 19, subd. (c).
27. *See generally,* discussion of bingo and raffles in Section 9.2 of this Guide.
28. California also allows remote caller bingo (wherein a live bingo game from a single location is transmitted to multiple locations) pursuant to a separate statutory section, Cal. Penal Code, §326.3 (2014).
29. The California Gambling Control Commission does issue regulations for remote caller bingo. Regulations for remote caller bingo are codified in Title 4, Division 18, Chapter 8, Sections 12480 to 12514 of the California Code of Regulations.
30. Cal. Penal Code § 326.5(l) (2014).

Colorado

State Attorney General Office
Office of the Attorney General
Ralph L. Carr Colorado Judicial Center
1300 Broadway, 10th Floor
Denver, Colorado 80203
(720) 508-6000
Website: www.coloradoattorneygeneral.gov

Selected State Laws, Regulations, and Constitutional Provisions

Colorado's anti-gambling laws (Title 18, Article 10, Sections 18-10-101 *et seq.* of the Colorado Revised Statute), which are in its criminal code, contain provisions related to promotions. Colorado also has laws relevant to direct mail contests and sweepstakes in its Consumer Protection Act (Title 6, Article 1, Part 8, Sections 6-1-801 to 6-1-804 of the Colorado Revised Statute). Specific Colorado legal authorities frequently quoted in court cases and interpretive opinions related to promotions include the following:

Reference No.	Descriptive Name
Colo. Const. art. XVIII, § 2	Lotteries prohibited—exceptions
Colo. Rev. Stat. § 18-10-102	Definitions (for anti-gambling laws)
Colo. Rev. Stat. § 18-10-103	Gambling—professional gambling—offenses
Colo. Rev. Stat. § 6-1-803	Prohibited practices and required disclosures

Summary of State Law

Prohibition of Lotteries and Gambling: The Colorado Constitution prohibits lotteries.[1] A promotion that combines a prize, chance, and consideration is a lottery in Colorado.[2] Colorado also has a general prohibition against gambling.[3] Exceptions to the lottery and gambling prohibitions include state-supervised lotteries and certain charitable lotteries.

Contests: Colorado allows contests as long as the contest does not conflict with anti-gambling laws. The Colorado anti-gambling laws specifically recognize that a contest does not qualify as gambling if the contest sponsor awards the prize based on skill, speed, strength, or endurance.[4] According to the Colorado Attorney General and Colorado court opinions, Colorado applies the dominant factor doctrine[5] when evaluating whether or not chance determines the outcome of a promotion.[6]

If the contest includes an element of consideration, the sponsor must award the contest prize based on skill and not on chance. Colorado does place additional restrictions on a contest sponsor's ability to charge consideration. Under the Colorado Consumer Protection Act, a contest implemented by direct mail solicitation may not require the purchase of a product or payment of any fee.[7]

Sweepstakes: Colorado permits sweepstakes as long as the participants pay no consideration and the sweepstakes does not conflict with anti-gambling laws. Any sweepstakes implemented by direct mail must comply with the prize promotion laws in the Colorado Consumer Protection Act.

Free Giveaways at Events Charging Admission: If a product giveaway is for the purpose of commercial advertisement, the creation of goodwill, the promotion of new products or services, or the collection of names, the giveaway is not considered an illegal lottery.[8] While this statutory provision for giveaways is grouped with the charitable/non-profit bingo and raffle laws, staff of the Bingo-Raffles Licensing Division of the Colorado Department of State explain that the provision is not limited to organizations that qualify as charitable organizations nor to organizations that have a bingo-raffle license from the state.[9]

Under this giveaway exception, an organization can offer prize give-aways by random drawing even if the organization conducts the giveaway at an event charging admission. This giveaway provision is designed for events like the Colorado stock show (an agricultural exhibition) to allow vendors participating in the stock show to conduct random drawings. According to an informal inquiry to the Colorado Department of State staff, there is no license or other regulatory filing requirement for the offering of a drawing or giveaway in reliance on this giveaway provision.[10]

Prize Promotion Laws: Colorado includes prize promotion protections in the sweepstakes and contests portion of its Consumer Protection Act (Title 6, Article 1, Part 8, Sections 6-1-801 to 6-1-804 of the Colorado Revised Statute). These prize promotion protections apply to contests and sweepstakes that are offered by direct mail, that require consideration and that are combined with the sponsors' sale of goods and services.[11]

As a general rule, any direct mail solicitation that *requires* the purchase of a product or payment of a fee as a condition to entering or winning a contest or sweepstakes is illegal in Colorado.[12] A company may incor-porate a contest or sweepstakes into a direct mail campaign offering the company's goods or services if the company includes specific disclosures in the direct mail piece. The required disclosures include a statement that no purchase is necessary. There are specific requirements for the place-ment, font, and wording of the required disclosures.[13] Colorado prize promotion protections also prohibit numerous practices and representa-tions that might mislead direct mail recipients or that negatively impact the chances of winning for those consumers who enter the promotion without making a purchase.[14]

In the portion of its consumer protection laws addressing telemarketing (Title 6, Article 1, Part 3, Sections 6-1-301 to 6-1-305 of the Colorado Revised Statute), Colorado prohibits telemarketers from misrepresenting that a person has won a contest, sweepstakes, or drawing, or that the person will receive free goods, services, or property.[15]

Other Colorado consumer protection laws make it a deceptive trade practice for a company to tell a person that the person has won or is eligible to win a prize as the result of a promotion or eligible to receive a free giveaway if the company does not have the present ability to supply the promised prize or giveaway.[16] It is also a deceptive trade practice to fail to disclose clearly the retail value of a prize offered in connection with any oral or written solicitation.[17]

Gambling Exceptions for Non-Profits and Other Qualified Organizations

Bingo and Raffles: The Colorado constitutional provision prohibiting lotteries contains an exception allowing certain charitable organizations to engage in bingo, lotto, and raffles under certain conditions.[18] Non-profit organizations eligible to operate bingo games and raffles include a branch, lodge, or chapter of a national or state organization or any religious, charitable, labor, fraternal, educational, voluntary firefighters', or veterans' organization.[19]

The operation of raffles and bingo games must meet several statutory and regulatory requirements.[20] The organization must have a license issued by the Colorado Secretary of State[21] and must file quarterly reports of proceeds, expenses, and use of proceeds[22]. Certain federally tax-exempt community chest organizations are exempt from the reporting requirements.[23]

The bingo and raffle laws in Title 12, Article 9, Sections 12-9-101 *et seq.* of the Colorado Revised Statutes implement the constitutional exemption. Bingo and raffle regulations, issued by the Colorado Department of State, are located in Sections 8 Colo. Code Regs. 1505-2-1.1 *et seq.* of the Colorado Code of Regulations. Forms, rules, requirements and fee information for the necessary licenses are available in the bingo and raffles section of the Secretary of State's website, http://www.sos.state.co.us/pubs/bingo_raffles/apply.html

Resources

Colorado attorney general opinions issued from 1984 to the present are available online in the AG Opinions portion of the website of the Office of the Attorney General. Copies of opinions issued prior to 1984 can be obtained by contacting the Office of the Attorney General.

Endnotes

1. Colo. Const. art. XVIII, § 2.
2. *Interrogatories of Governor Regarding Sweepstakes Races Act*, 585 P.2d 595, 598 (Colo. 1978).
3. Colo. Rev. Stat. § 18-10-103 (2014).
4. Colo. Rev. Stat. § 18-10-102(2)(a) (2014).
5. *See generally*, Section 3.4.3 of this Guide for a discussion of tests used when evaluating whether chance or skill prevails in a promotion combining elements of both.
6. *Interrogatories of Governor, supra* note 2, at 598; Colo. Att'y Gen. Op. No. 93-05, *4 (April 21, 1993).
7. Colo. Rev. Stat. §§ 6-1-802(4) and 6-1-803(1) (2014).
8. Colo. Rev. Stat. § 12-9-102.5(1) and (2) (2014).
9. Telephone Interview with Program Manager, Bingo-Raffle Licensing Program, Colorado Dept. of State (August 7, 2014).
10. *Id.* The actual wording of the giveaway statutory provision is murky on this point. Colo. Rev. Stat. § 12-9-102.5(1) reads in part that "The giveaways described in this subsection (1) are exempt from regulation under [the Bingo and Raffle laws] when all of the conditions set forth in *this section* [arguably, a reference to the entirety of Section 12-9-102.5] are satisfied" (emphasis added). Unfortunately, the Colorado Legislature chose wording arguably indicating required compliance with Section 12-9-102.5 in its entirety rather than wording clearly indicating compliance with only a few subsections of Section 12-9-102.5. When Section 12-9-102.5 is referenced in its entirety, it includes subsection 12-9-102.5(4) which requires a filing with the state describing the prize within ten days of the prize award. Colorado Dept. of State staff explained that this Section 12-9-102.5(4), which does refer to bingo-raffle licensees is not applicable to giveaways permitted under Sections 12-9-102.5(1) and (2).
11. *See e.g.,* Colo. Rev. Stat. § 6-1-802(5) and (9) (2014).
12. Colo. Rev. Stat. § 6-1-803(1) (2014).
13. Colo. Rev. Stat. § 6-1-803(5) and (6) (2014). *See generally*, discussion of prize promotion laws in Section 7.4.2 of this Guide.
14. Colo. Rev. Stat. § 6-1-803 (2014).
15. Colo. Rev. Stat. § 6-1-304(1)(e) (2014). *See generally*, discussion of state telemarketing laws in Section 7.5.2 of this Guide.
16. Colo. Rev. Stat. § 6-1-105(1)(jj) (2014).
17. Colo. Rev. Stat. § 6-1-105(1)(y) (2014).

18. Colo. Const. art. XVIII, § 2.
19. Colo. Rev. Stat. §12-9-104(1) (2014).
20. *See generally*, discussion of bingo and raffles in Section 9.2 of this Guide.
21. Colo. Rev. Stat. §12-9-106(1) (2014).
22. Colo. Rev. Stat. §12-9-108 (2014).
23. Colo. Rev. Stat. §§12-9-102(5.5) and 12-9-108 (2014).

Connecticut

State Attorney General Office
Office of the Attorney General
55 Elm Street
Hartford, Connecticut 06106
Phone: (860) 808-5318
Website: http://www.ct.gov/ag/

Selected State Laws, Regulations, and Constitutional Provisions

Connecticut's anti-gambling laws (Title 53, Chapter 946, Sections 53-278a to 53-278g of the Connecticut General Statutes) which are in its criminal code contain provisions related to promotions. Specific authorities frequently quoted in Connecticut court cases and interpretive opinions related to promotions include the following:

Reference No.	Descriptive Name
Conn. Gen. Stat. § 53-278a	Gambling: Definitions (including definition for gambling)
Conn. Gen. Stat. § 53-278b	Gambling; professional gambling; penalties (prohibited as misdemeanor)
Conn. Gen. Stat. § 53-278g	Gambling: Excepted activities
Conn. Gen. Stat. § 53-290a	Disclosures re promotional drawings

Summary of State Law

Prohibition of Lotteries and Gambling: Connecticut has a general prohibition against gambling[1] and includes conducting a lottery among the forms of prohibited professional gambling.[2] In its attorney general opinions and case law, Connecticut defines a lottery as a game combining the elements of prize, chance, and consideration.[3] Exceptions to the lottery and gambling prohibitions include state-operated lotteries and certain charitable lotteries.

Contests: Connecticut permits contests as long as the contest does not conflict with anti-gambling laws. If the contest includes an element of consideration, the sponsor must award the contest prize based on skill and not on chance. Connecticut law explicitly exempts from its gambling prohibitions a contest of skill, speed, strength or endurance in which the sponsor gives awards only to the entrants or to the owners of entries (*e.g.*, the owner of an animal entered in a contest).[4]

Opinions issued by the Connecticut Attorney General suggest that Connecticut applies the dominant factor doctrine[5] when evaluating whether chance determines the winner of a promotion.[6] In a 2004 opinion, after acknowledging that the Connecticut statute does not define the term lottery, the Connecticut Attorney General indicated that Connecticut accepts the traditional definition of lottery. The attorney general then explained that in a traditional lottery, skill is almost totally absent in determining the winner. Instead, a lottery awards its prize based solely upon random chance.[7] The Connecticut Attorney General's description of the role of chance is consistent with the dominant factor doctrine.

A comparison of Connecticut opinion letters and the Connecticut statute suggests that Connecticut might use a different standard when evaluating the existence of chance in a lottery from the standard used when evaluating the existence of chance in the broader category of gambling. According to the Connecticut anti-gambling laws, gambling can exist if the winner is determined *in whole or in part by chance*.[8] This suggests that when evaluating the existence of chance in a gambling game, Connecticut might apply the material element test or even the any chance test, both of which require lower levels of chance than the dominant factor doctrine which Connecticut seems to apply to lottery questions.

Through its prize promotion laws, Connecticut places restrictions on the ability of contest sponsors to charge consideration. The restriction applies if the contest offers a prize with a retail value over $200.[9]

Connecticut implements the restriction in an unusual manner. Rather than explicitly prohibiting the operation of a contest charging consideration, Connecticut prohibits the advertising of any contest that charges consideration.[10] Advertising is defined broadly to include the use of the media, mail, computer, telephone or personal contact.[11] The prohibition on advertising does not apply when the participant pays consideration for the purchase of a consumer product or service and the primary purpose of the contest is to promote those products or services.[12]

Sweepstakes: Connecticut permits sweepstakes as long as participants do not pay consideration and the sweepstakes does not otherwise violate anti-gambling laws. Connecticut law indicates that consideration does not include a visit to a retail establishment within the participant's local marketing area as long as the visit does not include a requirement to attend a sales presentation.[13]

Connecticut law explicitly exempts from the gambling prohibition any promotional drawing open to the general public in which no purchase is necessary.[14] The exemption does not apply if the sponsor of the drawing is a retail grocer or retail grocery chain. Each ticket for a promotional drawing under this exemption must include a disclosure of the actual number and dollar amount of prizes to be awarded and the number of winners per each thousand tickets to be distributed.[15]

Sweepstakes must provide certain disclosures mandated by Connecticut's prize promotion laws. There are more details on Connecticut's prize promotion laws below in the *Prize Promotions Laws* portion of this Connecticut State Summary.

Prize Promotion Laws: Connecticut has prize promotion laws codified with its laws regarding business selling trading and collection practices. The prize promotion laws are in Title 42, Chapter 743n, Sections 42-295 to 42-300 of the Connecticut General Statutes.

PRIZE PROMOTION LAWS FOR CONTESTS CHARGING CONSIDERATION. While the Connecticut prize promotion laws are most relevant to sweepstakes, they do include restrictions on contests charging consideration.[16] The prize promotion laws relevant to contests are discussed above in the section on contests.

PRIZE PROMOTION LAWS FOR SWEEPSTAKES. Any advertisement for a sweepstakes must include certain disclosures.[17] The prize promotion laws define advertising for a sweepstakes as the use of the media, mail, computer, telephone or personal contact to offer a specifically named person the opportunity to participate in a sweepstakes.[18]

The Connecticut prize promotion requirements for sweepstakes are unclear in at least two respects. First, it is unclear whether the notice must be in writing. The font and typeface requirements for the disclosures to accompany sweepstakes advertisements certainly imply that Connecticut expects the disclosures to be in writing.[19] However, as defined by the statute, advertising can include contact by telephone, media (which one assumes includes radio or television), and in-person contact. Connecticut never says that an offer initiated by telephone or verbally must be followed by a written disclosure. Second, the words "offer a specifically named person" imply that these requirements are not applicable to mass advertising not directed to a specific individual in Connecticut; however, there is no explicit statement to that effect in the law.

Gambling Exceptions for Non-Profits and Other Qualified Organizations

Raffles and Lotteries: The Connecticut Bazaar and Raffle Act allows each Connecticut municipality to choose by vote whether non-profit raffles can be held within that municipality. Once the municipality approves the offering of raffles within its jurisdiction, non-profit organizations eligible to offer raffles include veterans' organizations; churches; religious organizations; civic, service or social clubs; fraternal societies; educational or charitable organizations; volunteer fire companies; and political party and municipality anniversary-planning committees.

There are statutory and regulatory requirements for raffles.[20] The organization offering the raffle must have a permit issued by the municipality's chief of police or chief executive officer. There are limits on the raffle prizes that may be awarded, requirements for information to be printed on the raffle ticket, and certain restrictions on advertising. Raffle sponsors must also file with the chief of police or chief executive officer a report of the gross receipts, raffle tickets sold, expenses, prizes awarded, and use of net receipts.

The Connecticut Bazaar and Raffle Act is codified in the municipalities code at Title 7, Chapter 98, Sections 7-170 to 7-186 of the Connecticut General Statutes. Raffle regulations, issued by the Division of Special Revenue, are codified in Sections 7-185-1a to 7-185-16b of the Regulations of Connecticut State Agencies.

Bingo: Each municipality may choose by vote to permit bingo within its jurisdiction.[21] Once the municipality approves bingo games within its jurisdiction, non-profit organizations eligible to offer bingo games are charitable, civic, educational, fraternal, veterans' or religious organizations; volunteer fire departments; or granges.[22]

The operation of the bingo game must meet several statutory and regulatory requirements.[23] Bingo operators must have a permit issued by the Connecticut Commissioner of Consumer Protection. Bingo operators must maintain records of bingo receipts and disbursements and make those records available for inspection by the Commissioner of Consumer Protection or their municipality's chief law enforcement officer.[24] There are relaxed registration requirements for organizations offering recreational bingo games to senior citizens and parent-teacher organizations.

The bingo laws are in the municipalities code at Title 7, Chapter 98, Sections 7-169 to 7-169e of the Connecticut General Statutes. Bingo regulations, issued by the Division of Special Revenue, are codified in Sections 7-169-1a to 7-169-35a and Sections 169c-1 to 169c-6 of the Regulations of Connecticut State Agencies.

Resources

Connecticut offers a searchable database for its attorney general opinions from 1990 through the present online in the formal opinions section of the website of the Office of the Attorney General.

Endnotes

1.   Conn. Gen. Stat. § 53-278b (2013).
2.   Conn. Gen. Stat. § 53-278a(3) (2013).

3. Conn. Att'y Gen. Op. (May 21, 2004) *citing Connecticut v. Bull Inv. Group.*, 351 A.2d 879 (Conn. Super. Ct. 1974).

4. Conn. Gen. Stat. § 53-278a(2) (2013).

5. *See generally*, Section 3.4.3 of this Guide for a discussion of tests used when determining whether chance or skill prevails in a promotion combining elements of both.

6. Conn. Att'y Gen. Op. (May 21, 2004).

7. *Id.*

8. Conn. Gen. Stat. § 53-278a(2) (emphasis provided) (2013).

9. Conn. Gen. Stat. § 42-298 (2013).

10. *Id.*

11. Conn. Gen. Stat. § 42-295(1) (2013). Due to the qualifications in the statutory definition for advertise, one could interpret the statute to allow the use of advertising for a contest with a $200 prize if the advertisement clearly states that there is not a strong likelihood that the participant will be awarded the prize. The Connecticut statute is unclear on how the qualifications in Conn. Gen. Stat. §§ 42-295(1) and 42-298 are to be applied. As practical guidance, sponsors should be aware that charging consideration for a contest in Connecticut with a prize valued at over $200 introduces risk.

12. Conn. Gen. Stat. § 42-298 (2013).

13. Conn. Gen. Stat. § 42-296 (2013).

14. Conn. Gen. Stat. § 53-278g (2013).

15. Conn. Gen. Stat. § 53-290a (2013).

16. *See* the discussion of Conn. Gen. Stat. § 42-298 under portion on contests in this Connecticut State Summary.

17. Conn. Gen. Stat. § 42-297 (2013). See general discussion of state prize promotion laws in Section 7.4.2 of this Guide.

18. Conn. Gen. Stat. § 42-295(1) (2013).

19. Conn. Gen. Stat. § 42-297 (2013).

20. *See* generally, discussion of bingo and raffles in Section 9.2 of this Guide.

21. Conn. Gen. Stat. § 7-169(b) (2013).

22. *Id.*

23. *See generally*, discussion of bingo and raffles in Section 9.2 of this Guide.

24. Conn. Gen. Stat. § 7-169(h) (2013).

Delaware

State Attorney General Office
Office of the Attorney General
Wilmington Office
Carvel State Office Bldg
820 N. French Street
Wilmington, Delaware 19801
Fraud & Consumer Protection: (302) 577-8600
Website: http://attorneygeneral.delaware.gov/

Selected State Laws, Regulations, and Constitutional Provisions

Delaware's anti-gambling laws, which are in its crimes and criminal procedures code (Title 11, Chapter 5, Subchapter VII, Sections 1401 to 1432 of the Delaware Code), contain provisions related to promotions. In its commerce and trade code, Delaware incorporates prize promotion protections into its Telemarketing Fraud Act (Title 6, Chapter 25A, Sections 2501A to 2509A of the Delaware Code). Specific Delaware legal provisions frequently quoted in court cases and interpretive opinions related to promotions include the following:

Reference No.	Descriptive Name
Del. Const. art. II, § 17	Lotteries and other gambling
Del. Const. art. II, § 17A	Bingo games; organizations authorized to conduct; submission to referendum; districts; regulation; penalties
Del. Const. art. II, § 17B	Lotteries not under State control; organizations authorized to conduct; submission to referendum; districts; regulation; penalties

Del. Code tit. 11, § 1401	Advancing gambling in the second degree; Class A misdemeanor
Del. Code tit. 11, § 1403	Advancing gambling in the first degree; Class A misdemeanor
Del. Code tit. 11, § 1408	Merchandising plans are not gambling
Del. Code tit. 11, § 1432	Gambling; Definitions (including definition for gambling offense)
Del. Code tit. 6, § 2503A	Registration of sellers, telemarketers, and telemarketing businesses

Summary of State Law

Prohibition of Lotteries and Gambling: The Delaware Constitution prohibits lotteries.[1] A promotion that combines a prize, chance, and consideration is a lottery in Delaware.[2] Delaware also has a general prohibition against gambling.[3] Exceptions to the lottery and gambling prohibitions include state-operated lotteries and certain charitable lotteries.

Contests: Delaware permits contests as long as the contest does not conflict with anti-gambling laws. If the contest includes an element of consideration, the sponsor must award the contest prize based on skill and not on chance in order to avoid characterization of the contest as a lottery. As discussed below under the Sweepstakes heading, Delaware may take a broader view of what constitutes consideration when determining whether a promotion should be characterized as a lottery or a gambling game.

Court opinions suggest that Delaware applies the dominant factor doctrine[4] when evaluating whether or not chance determines the outcome of a promotion. In *National Football League v. Governor of the State of Delaware*, 435 F. Supp. 1372, 1384 (D. Del. 1977), a Delaware federal court expressed the viewpoint that the Delaware Supreme Court would be inclined to adopt the dominant factor doctrine when determining the existence of a lottery.

Sweepstakes: Delaware permits sweepstakes as long as participants do not pay consideration. The Delaware legislature has passed a statutory provision indicating that a merchandising or advertising plan awarding a prize by chance is not gambling or a lottery unless the chance to win the prize requires payment in money, a purchase, or something of pecuniary value.[5] The merchandising plan promotion described in the Delaware statute meets the definition of a sweepstakes.

DELAWARE'S BROADER VIEW OF CONSIDERATION. Court opinions suggest that Delaware might take a broader view of what constitutes consideration for the existence of a lottery or a gambling game. As a result, Delaware might characterize certain activities required for participation in a promotion as qualifying as consideration when other states would not view those same activities as consideration.

This characterization of Delaware law is based on a 1939 case, *Affiliated Enterprises v. Waller*, 5 A.2d 257 (Del. Super. 1939). In the *Affiliated Enterprises* case, the Delaware court concluded that filling out a registration and appearing at a particular lobby, at a particular time, was sufficient to constitute consideration for entering a contest. In a subsequent 1960 decision in *Delaware v. Eckerd's Suburban*, 164 A.2d 873 (Del. 1960), the Delaware Supreme Court declined to overrule the *Affiliated Enterprises* decision and held that a drugstore's award of a prize to a winner selected by a random drawing could constitute a lottery—even though no payment or purchase was required for the chance to win.

Neither the *Affiliated Enterprises* nor the *Eckerd's Suburban* holdings has been overruled by a court. Nevertheless, as discussed above, the merchandising plans statute explicitly authorizes a chance-based advertising promotion as long as participants need not pay money, make a purchase, or pay anything else of pecuniary value.

Prize Promotion Laws: Delaware incorporates prize promotion protections into its Telemarketing Fraud Act.[6] During a telemarketing call, the company must disclose to the consumer all material elements of any offered prize promotion.[7] As part of the record keeping requirements, the telemarketer must maintain records of the advertising materials used, the prizes awarded, and the name and last known address of each recipient of a prize valued at twenty-five dollars or more.[8]

Gambling Exceptions for Non-Profits and Other Qualified Organizations

Raffles, Bingo, and Charitable Gaming: Constitutional provisions allow individual geographic districts to authorize certain non-profit organizations to operate raffles[9], bingo[10], and other charitable gambling games within the district. The organizations must use net receipts from such activities for charitable and beneficial purposes. Organizations eligible to offer raffles, bingo and charitable gaming include veterans', religious or charitable organizations; volunteer fire companies; and fraternal societies.[11]

There are statutory and regulatory requirements for the operation of bingo games and raffles.[12] Eligible organizations offering bingo and raffles must have a license issued by the Delaware Gaming Control Board[13] and must file periodic reports[14]. However, there is no license or report-filing requirements for eligible organizations offering raffles if the raffle ticket is five dollars or less *and* the total retail value of raffle prizes is less than five thousand dollars.[15]

The charitable gambling laws are in Title 28, Chapter 15, Sections 1501 to 1570 of the Delaware Code. Bingo and raffle regulations, issued by the Delaware Gaming Control Board, are in Title 10, Sections 101 and 102 of the Delaware Administrative Code. Licensing forms and regulations for charitable bingo and raffles are available online at the website of the Division of Professional Regulation: Board of Charitable Gambling at http://dpr.delaware.gov/boards/gaming/.

Resources

Delaware offers a database for its attorney general opinions from 1995 through the present online in the Public Resource portion of the website of the Office of the Attorney General.

Endnotes

1. Del. Const. art. II, § 17.
2. *Nat'l Football League v. Gov. of State of Del.*, 435 F. Supp. 1372 (D. Del. 1977).
3. Del. Code tit. 11, § 1432(d) (2014).

4. *See generally*, Section 3.4.3 of this Guide for a discussion of tests used when evaluating whether chance or skill prevails in a promotion combining elements of both.

5. Del. Code tit. 11, § 1408 (2014).

6. Del. Code tit. 6, §§ 2501A to 2509A (2014). *See generally*, Section 7.5.2 of this Guide for discussion of state telemarketing laws.

7. Del. Code tit. 6, § 2506A(a)(2)f (2014).

8. Del. Code tit. 6, § 2504A (2014).

9. Del. Const. art. II, § 17B.

10. Del. Const. art. II, § 17A.

11. Del. Const. art. II, §§ 17A and 17B; Del. Code, tit. 28 § 1502(4) (2014).

12. *See generally*, discussion of bingo and raffles in Section 9.2 of this Guide.

13. Del. Code tit. 28, §§ 1501 and 1502 (2014).

14. Del. Code tit. 28, § 1521 (2014).

15. 10 Del. Admin. Code § 102; Raffle Event Information, Website of Delaware Division of Professional Regulation, http://dpr.delaware.gov/boards/gaming/raffle.shtml (last visited Oct. 19, 2014).

District of Columbia

Attorney General Office
Office of the Attorney General
441 4th Street, NW
Washington, District of Columbia 20001
Phone: (202) 727-3400
Website: http://oag.dc.gov

Selected State Laws, Regulations, and Constitutional Provisions

The District of Columbia's anti-gambling laws (Title 22, Subtitle I, Chapter 17, Sections 22-1701 *et seq.* of District of Columbia Code), which are in its criminal offenses and penalties code, contain provisions related to promotions. Specific District of Columbia authorities frequently quoted in court cases and interpretive opinions related to promotions include the following:

Reference No.	Descriptive Name
D.C. Code § 22-1701	Lotteries; promotion; sale or possession of tickets (prohibited)
D.C. Code § 22-1704	Gaming; setting up gaming table; inducing play
D.C. Code § 22-1705	Gambling premises; definition; prohibition against maintaining; forfeiture; liens; deposit of moneys in Treasury; penalty; subsequent offenses

Summary of State Law

Prohibition of Lotteries and Gambling: The District of Columbia prohibits lotteries.[1] A promotion that combines a prize, chance, and consideration is a lottery in the District of Columbia.[2] The District of Columbia also has a general prohibition against gaming and gambling devices.[3] Exceptions to the lottery and gambling prohibitions include state-operated lotteries and certain charitable lotteries.

Contests: No provisions in its laws indicate that the District of Columbia prohibits contests as long as the contest does not conflict with anti-gambling laws. If the contest includes an element of consideration, the sponsor must award the contest prize based on skill and not on chance. Court opinions suggest that the District of Columbia applies the dominant factor doctrine[4] when determining whether or not a promotion incorporates chance.[5]

Sweepstakes: No provisions in its laws indicate that the District of Columbia prohibits sweepstakes as long as participants do not pay consideration and the sweepstakes does not conflict with anti-gambling laws.

Gambling Exceptions for Non-Profits and Other Qualified Organizations

Bingo, Raffles and Charitable Gaming: The District of Columbia allows certain qualified organizations to operate lotteries, raffles, bingo, and charitable gambling games for educational and charitable purposes.[6] Organizations eligible to offer bingo games and raffles are non-profit organizations that can accept tax-deductible contributions and that are organized for charitable, benevolent, eleemosynary, humane, religious, philanthropic, recreational, social, educational, civic, fraternal, or other non-profit purposes.[7] Certain Virginia and Maryland non-profit groups with similar purposes can also obtain licenses to sell raffle tickets in the District of Columbia provided that the non-profit group uses at least thirty percent of the raffle net proceeds for beneficial purposes in the District of Columbia.[8]

The operation of the bingo games and raffles must meet several statutory and regulatory requirements.[9] To offer bingo games or raffles, the organization must have a license issued by the D.C. Lottery & Charitable Games Control Board, Charitable Games Division.[10] Laws authorizing raffles and bingo games are codified in Title 3, Chapter 13 of the District of Columbia Code. Regulations related to bingo games and raffles are codified at Title 30 of the District of Columbia Municipal Regulations.

Licensing information and forms for bingo, raffles, and charitable gambling are available from the Charitable Games Division, 2101 Martin Luther King Jr., Ave. SE, Washington, DC 20020, and from the Charitable Games portion of the website, www.dclottery.com/

Resources

District of Columbia offers copies of its attorney general opinions issued from 1982 through the present in the Laws and Regulations portion of the website of the Office of the Attorney General.

Endnotes

1. D.C. Code § 22-1701 (2013).
2. *Forte v. United States*, 83 F.2d 612 (D.C. Cir. 1936).
3. D.C. Code §§ 22-1704 to 22-1705 (2013).
4. *See generally*, Section 3.4.3 of this Guide for a discussion of tests used when determining whether chance or skill prevails in a promotion combining elements of both.
5. *Boosalis v. Crawford*, 99 F.2d 374 (D.C. 1938) (concluding that a pay-to-play gaming machine was a gambling device for which winning depended on chance since chance predominated over skill and chance was present in such manner as to thwart the exercise of skill.)
6. D.C. Code § 22-1717 (2013).
7. D.C. Code § 3-1323(b) (2013).
8. D.C. Code § 3-1323(b-1)(1) (2013).
9. *See generally*, discussion of bingo and raffles in Section 9.2 of this Guide.
10. D.C. Code § 3-1323(a) (2013).

Florida

State Attorney General Office
Office of Attorney General
State of Florida
The Capitol PL-01
Tallahassee, Florida 32399
(850) 414-3300
Website: http://www.myfloridalegal.com/

Selected State Laws, Regulations, and Constitutional Provisions

Florida's anti-gambling laws, which are in its crimes code (Title 46, Chapter 849, Sections 849.01 *et seq.* of the Florida Statutes), contain provisions related to promotions. Specific Florida legal authorities frequently quoted in court cases and interpretive opinions related to promotions include the following:

Reference No.	Descriptive Name
Fla. Const. art. X, § 7	Lotteries prohibited—exceptions
Fla. Stat. § 849.08	Gambling
Fla. Stat. § 849.09	Lottery prohibited; exceptions
Fla. Stat. § 849.0931	Bingo authorized; conditions for conduct; permitted uses of proceeds; limitations
Fla. Stat. § 849.0935	Charitable, non-profit organizations; drawings by chance; required disclosures; unlawful acts and practices; penalties
Fla. Stat. § 849.094	Game promotion in connection with sale of consumer products or services
Fla. Stat. § 849.14	Unlawful to bet on result of trial or contest of skill, etc.

Summary of State Law

Prohibition of Lotteries and Gambling: Florida's Constitution as well as its statutory laws prohibit lotteries.[1] A promotion that combines a prize, chance, and consideration is a lottery in Florida.[2] Florida also has a general prohibition against gambling.[3] Exceptions to the lottery and gambling prohibitions include state-operated lotteries and certain charitable lotteries.

Contests: Florida permits contests as long as the contest does not conflict with anti-gambling laws. If the contest includes an element of consideration, the sponsor must award the contest prize based on skill and not on chance. According to the Florida Attorney General, Florida applies the dominant factor doctrine[4] when evaluating whether or not chance determines the outcome of a promotion.[5]

While a contest sponsor may charge consideration, Florida authorities indicate that the prize may not consist solely of the contestants' entry fees.[6] In such a case, Florida would deem the contest as illegal gambling.

Sweepstakes: Instead of using the term sweepstakes, Florida statutes use the term game promotion. Florida defines game promotion to include a promotion (whether it be called a contest, sweepstakes, gift enterprise, or some other term) that combines chance and a prize and that is conducted in connection with the sale of consumer goods and services.[7] A promotion combining chance and a prize is the traditional definition for a sweepstakes.

The legislative staff analysis provided when Florida amended its game promotion law (discussed in the next paragraph of this Florida State Summary) provides insight on Florida's view of consideration within the context of promotions. According to that analysis, Florida views consideration broadly, as the conferring of any benefit. For example, if a sponsor offers a prize-winning opportunity and, as a result, the sponsor receives an increase in patrons for the sponsor's business, Florida might deem that benefit to the sponsor as consideration and label the promotion an illegal lottery—even if the promotion participants pay no money or other tangible asset for a chance to win the prize.[8]

2013 AMENDMENTS TO GAME PROMOTION LAWS. Florida amended its game promotion law and other gambling-related laws with amendments that became effective on April 10, 2013.[9] The goal for the 2013 legislation was to prohibit internet cafes. To achieve that goal, Florida narrowed the categories of permissible game promotions. The legislation explains that the intent of Section 849.094 (*i.e.*, the game promotion law) is ". . . to regulate certain game promotions or sweepstakes conducted by *for-profit commercial entities on a limited and occasional basis* . . ."[10] The 2013 legislation also modified the definitions of game promotion operators (*i.e.*, types of sponsors that may offer game promotions) in a manner placing emphasis on the for-profit status of game promotion operators.[11]

The language in the legislation and amended statutes has introduced confusion. It is unclear how Florida will apply the requirement that game promotions be implemented on a limited and occasional basis. It is also unclear whether the 2013 amendments allow non-profits to continue operating sweepstakes in Florida.[12] While media reports suggest that the prohibition on non-profit sweepstakes was an unintended consequence of the legislation, some non-profits have taken the position that they may not offer sweepstakes in Florida.[13] As of the writing of this Guide, Florida has not clarified the impact of these 2013 legislative modifications.

REGISTRATION, BONDING, AND OPERATIONAL REQUIREMENTS FOR SWEEPSTAKES WITH PRIZES OVER $5,000. Florida has registration, bonding, and operational requirements for sweepstakes offering prizes with an aggregate retail value over $5,000.[14]

- Registration Requirements. Sponsors of sweepstakes with aggregate prizes valued at more than $5,000 must register with the Florida Department of Agriculture and Consumer Services.[15] To fulfill the registration requirement, the sponsor must provide a completed application, a copy of the official sweepstakes rules, and payment of a filing fee.

- Bonding Requirements. The sweepstakes registration process also has a financial component. At least seven days prior to the start of the promotion, the sweepstakes sponsor must establish a trust account or provide a bond equal to the retail value of the prizes and notify the Department of Agriculture and Consumer Services that it has such trust account or bond.[16] A sponsor which has conducted promotions in Florida for five consecutive years without incident is eligible for a waiver to the bonding requirement.[17]

- Operational Requirements. The most significant operational requirement for sweepstakes include publication of the rules and filing of a winners' list. The sweepstakes rules must be posted in retail outlets where the game is available and be included in advertising.[18] Printed advertisements may include an abbreviated version of the rules. An acceptable abbreviated version includes the sweepstakes' material terms along with information indicating where entrants can obtain a complete copy of the rules such as a website address, toll-free telephone number, or mailing address.[19] Radio and television announcements may indicate that the rules and regulations are available at retail outlets or from the operator of the promotion.[20] Within sixty days of determining winners, the sponsor must file a certified list of winners for all prizes valued at more than twenty-five dollars.[21]

  Sponsors may not modify a sweepstakes' official rules after the Florida registration.[22] As discussed in Section 4.4.7 of this Guide, states usually allow a sponsor to change the promotion rules (such as the prize to be awarded) if the sponsor reserves its right to make such changes in the promotion's rules. It is unclear from the statute whether Florida allows a sponsor to reserve this right in its rules.

Prize Promotion Laws: The Florida Telemarketing Act (Title XXXIII, Chapter 501, Part IV, Sections 501.601 to 501.626 of the Florida Statutes) includes disclosure requirements for sellers combining promotions with telemarketing campaigns. If a commercial telephone seller represents that a prospective purchaser is or may be eligible to receive a gift, the commercial telephone seller must file with the state an information statement about the gift including a description, its value, odds of winning, and the terms and conditions for receiving the prize.[23]

The Florida Free Gift Advertising Law[24] prohibits deceptive use of the word *free* and similar words such as *award* and *prize*. Any advertisement offering items for free must include a clear and conspicuous disclosure of all conditions or obligations necessary to obtain the free item.

Gambling Exceptions for Non-Profits and Qualified Organizations

Raffles and Lotteries: Florida allows organizations that are federally tax-exempt[25] to conduct raffles and other drawings of chance.[26] While the sponsoring organization cannot require consideration for participation, the organization can suggest and accept a minimum donation for participation.[27]

There are specific disclosures that the tickets and advertisements must have.[28] There is a laundry list of prohibited practices for conducting the drawing. The prohibited practices include that the sponsor may not condition the drawing on distributing a minimum number of tickets, the sponsor may not fail to award all the advertised prizes, and the sponsor may not condition any prize giveaway upon the receipt of a donation or other fee.[29] The raffle statute does not indicate that the sponsor must have a license.

Bingo: The Florida bingo exception extends to more organizations than does the raffle and lotteries exemption. Florida allows certain charitable, non-profit, and veterans' organizations to conduct bingo games.[30] Organizations that do not qualify as a charitable, non-profit, or veterans' organization may also conduct bingo games as long as all the proceeds are returned to players in the form of prizes, donated to charity, or used to cover the actual expenses of conducting the game.[31] While the Florida state statute includes several operational requirements for bingo games, it does not contain a licensing requirement.[32] However, local governments may impose licensing and other requirements for bingo games taking place within their jurisdictions.[33]

Resources

Florida offers a searchable database for its attorney general opinions from 1971 through the present online in the Legal Resources portion of

the website of the Office of the Attorney General at http://myfloridalegal.
com/ago.nsf/Opinions

Endnotes

1. Fla. Const. art. X, § 7; Fla. Stat. § 849.09 (2014).
2. Fla. Att'y Gen. Op. No. 2008-35 (July 8, 2008) *citing Little River Theatre Corp. v. State ex rel. Hodge,* 185 So. 855 (Fla. 1939).
3. Fla. Stat. § 849.08 (2014).
4. *See generally,* Section 3.4.3 of this Guide for a discussion of tests used when evaluating whether chance or skill prevails in a promotion combining elements of both.
5. Fla. Att'y Gen. Op. No. 1990-58 (July 27, 1990).
6. *See e.g.,* Fla. Att'y Gen. Op. No. 1991-03 (Jan. 8, 1991).
7. Fla. Stat. § 849.094(a) (2014).
8. Fla. House of Representatives Final Bill Analysis for Prohibition on Electronic Gambling Devices, Bill CS/HB 155, p. 2, (Apr. 19, 2013).
9. Fla. H.R. CS/HB 155, 2013 Leg. (Fla. 2013) (amending Fla. Stat. §§ 849.0935, 849.094 and other sections of the Florida Statute).
10. *Id.* at Section 1(3) (emphasis added).
11. *Id.* at Section 3 (codified at Fla. Stat. § 849.094(1)(a) and (b)).
12. During an interview conducted shortly after the amendment's April 10, 2013 effective date, Liz Compton, the Chief of the Bureau of Compliance at the Department of Agriculture and Consumer Services, explained that ". . . the amendments to [Section 849.094, the game promotion statute] prohibit a non-profit or charitable organization from operating a game promotion. This includes nationally advertised game promotions. Only for-profit entities may operate game promotions in Florida." *EXCLUSIVE: Florida's top sweepstakes regulator discusses recent changes to Florida's game promotion statute,* Thompson Coburn LLP Sweepstakes Law Blog, http://www.thompsoncoburn.com/ (follow Blogs) (last visited Oct. 14, 2014).
    There is at least some doubt as to whether the department still holds this view. Within the same time-frame as Ms. Compton's interview, the Department of Agriculture and Consumer Services explained some of the effects of the 2013 changes in the Frequently Asked Questions portion of its website. The department explained that non-profit entities and charitable organizations may continue to offer skill-based contests, raffles, and bingo games in Florida; however, such non-profit entities and charitable organizations may not operate a game promotion

(*i.e.*, sweepstakes or promotions based on chance). That explanatory language was subsequently removed (on or before July 11, 2013) and the department's FAQ on game promotions became silent on whether non-profit and charitable organizations may offer game promotions and sweepstakes. As of the writing of this Guide, the department's FAQ remains silent on this topic.

13. *See e.g.*, Marc Caputo, *AARP cancels Florida sweepstakes, blames new state gambling law*, Miami Herald, May 17, 2013, http://www.miamiherald.com/news/politics-government/article1951646.html, (last visited Oct. 14, 2014).
14. Fla. Stat. § 849.094 (2014).
15. Fla. Stat. § 849.094(4) (2014).
16. Fla. Stat. § 849.094(4)(a) (2014).
17. Fla. Stat. § 849.094(4)(b) (2014).
18. Fla. Stat. § 849.094(3) (2014).
19. *Id.*
20. *Id.*
21. Fla. Stat. § 849.094(5) (2014).
22. Fla. Stat. § 849.094(3) (2014).
23. Fla. Stat. § 501.614 (2014). *See generally*, discussion of state telemarketing laws in Section 7.5.2 of this Guide.
24. Fla. Stat. § 817.415 (2014).
25. Specifically, the organization must be qualified under 26 U.S.C. § 501(c)(3), (4), (7), (8), (10), or (19). Fla. Stat. 849.0935(1)(b) (2014).
26. Fla. Stat. § 849.0935(2) (2014).
27. Fla. Stat. § 849.0935(4)(b) (2014).
28. Fla. Stat. § 849.0935(3) (2014).
29. Fla. Stat. § 849.0935(4) (2014).
30. Fla. Stat. § 849.0931(2) (2014).
31. Fla. Stat. § 849.0931(3) and (4) (2014).
32. Fla. Stat. § 849.0931. *See generally*, discussion of bingo and raffles in Section 9.2 of this Guide.
33. *See e.g.*, *F.Y.I. Adventures, Inc. v. City of Ocala*, 698 So.2d 583 (Fla. Dist. Ct. App. 1997); Pinellas County Bingo Ordinance (Pinellas County Code Section 10-61); Polk County Bingo Ordinance, Ordinance No. 94-36.

Georgia

State Attorney General Office
Office of the Attorney General
40 Capitol Square, SW
Atlanta, Georgia 30334
(404) 656-3300
Website: http://www.law.ga.gov/

Selected State Laws, Regulations, and Constitutional Provisions

Georgia's anti-gambling laws, which are in its criminal code (Title 16, Chapter 12, Article 2, Part 1, Sections 16-12-20 *et seq.* of the Georgia Code), contain provisions related to promotions. In its commerce and trade code, Georgia includes its prize promotion laws (Title 10, Chapter 1, Article 15, Part 2, Sections 10-1-390 *et seq.* of the Georgia Code) as part of the Fair Business Practices Act. Specific Georgia authorities frequently quoted in court cases and interpretive opinions related to promotions include the following:

Reference No.	Descriptive Name
Ga. Const. art. I, § II, para. VIII	Lotteries and non-profit bingo games
Ga. Code § 10-1-393	Unfair or deceptive practices in consumer transactions unlawful; examples
Ga. Code § 16-12-20	Definitions (for anti-gambling laws including definitions for lottery)
Ga. Code § 16-12-21	Gambling (defined and prohibited as misdemeanor)
Ga. Code § 16-12-22	Commercial gambling (defined; prohibited as felony)

Ga. Code § 16-12-35 Applicability of part; penalty for violation
(providing meaning of "some skill" and
provisions related to free plays)

Ga. Code § 16-12-36 Lawful promotional and giveaway contests

Summary of State Law

Prohibition of Lotteries and Gambling: Georgia's Constitution as well as its statutory laws prohibits lotteries.[1] A promotion that combines a prize, chance, and consideration is a lottery in Georgia.[2] In 2012, Georgia adopted legislation designed to prohibit retail internet cafes. As part of that legislation, the definition of lottery was expanded to include payment of consideration to play a no-skill game on a computer, mechanical device, or electronic device for a chance to win a prize.[3]

Georgia also has a general prohibition against gambling in its constitution as well as in its statutory laws.[4] Exceptions to the lottery and gambling prohibitions include state-operated lotteries and certain charitable lotteries.

Contests: Georgia permits contests as long as the contest does not conflict with anti-gambling laws. If the contest includes an element of consideration, the sponsor must award the contest prize based on skill and not on chance.

It is uncertain which approach Georgia uses when evaluating whether or not chance determines the outcome of a promotion.[5] Language in the Georgia anti-gambling laws suggests that Georgia might apply the any chance test. The anti-gambling laws include as an illegal lottery any promotional contest involving *an element of chance* if the promotional contest has the other elements of a lottery[6] (the other elements being a prize and consideration[7]).

Some practitioners assert that Georgia applies the dominant factor doctrine. This is a reasonable assertion given that the majority of states apply the dominant factor doctrine. However, research for this Guide yielded no Georgia statutory or case law authority confirming Georgia's adoption of the dominant factor doctrine.

GEORGIA LAW GOVERNING BEAUTY PAGEANTS. Georgia has laws that deal with beauty pageants. These beauty pageant laws are in Title 10, Chapter 1, Article 30, Sections 10-1-830 *et seq.* of the Georgia Code. The law applies to beauty pageants that charge an entry fee. An entry fee includes any requirement for the beauty pageant participants to pay money, sell advertisements or tickets, or obtain sponsors.[8] Before accepting any entry fee, the beauty pageant operator must obtain a bond in the amount of $10,000[9]; and provide each entrant a disclosure statement with information about the operator, its previous pageants, and its compliance with the bonding requirement.[10]

The following groups are exempt from the bonding requirement:

- non-profit organizations
- bona fide civic clubs in existence for at least one year
- churches and religious organizations
- groups, fairs, or festivals affiliated with schools or political subdivisions
- any other pageant which confers no benefit upon any participant other than any or all of the following: a beauty title, a crown, a trophy, a ribbon, or a sash.[11]

In lieu of obtaining the bond, a beauty pageant operator may place all entrants' fees in an escrow account from which the operator does not withdraw any funds until the pageant has been held and all awards have been made.[12]

Sweepstakes: Georgia permits sweepstakes as long as participants do not pay consideration and the sweepstakes does not otherwise violate anti-gambling laws. Georgia implicitly excludes certain sweepstakes from the definition of illegal lottery.[13] Without explicitly using the term sweepstakes, the Georgia law permits a sponsor to give away prizes by chance to promote its business as long as the prize offering meets the following criteria:

- No participants pay consideration. Consideration includes a requirement that the participant give something of value to the sponsor, purchase anything from the business, or participate in a seminar or sales presentation.

- The prizes are non-cash prizes.
- The prizes are not awarded based upon the playing of a game on a computer, mechanical device, or electronic device at a place of business in Georgia.[14]

The non-cash and electronic device restrictions were added in 2012 with other modifications designed to prohibit internet cafes.[15] The 2012 internet cafe legislation also explicitly legalized a national or regional promotion, contest, or sweepstakes conducted by a corporation, its wholly owned subsidiary or valid franchisee if at the time of the promotion the corporation is registered under the federal Securities Exchange Act of 1934 and has assets of at least $100 million.[16]

Prize Promotion Laws: Georgia includes prize promotion protections in its Fair Business Practices Act (Title 10, Chapter 1, Article 15, Part 2, Sections 10-1-390 to 10-1-407 of the Georgia Code). The Georgia prize promotion laws apply to promotions in which companies offer consumers prizes as an incentive to attend a seminar or sales presentation.[17] These laws do not apply to promotional schemes if receipt of the prize does not involve an element of chance even if receipt of the prize requires purchase of an item sold by the sponsor.[18] As part of its amendments for implementing internet café prohibitions, Georgia added an additional statutory provision prohibiting cash prizes for any promotions subject to the Georgia prize promotion laws.[19]

Persons who receive an opportunity to participate in a promotion (governed by the prize promotion laws) must also receive a written notice prior to the person's traveling to the sponsor's place of business. Alternatively, if travel by the participant is unnecessary, the sponsor must provide the notice prior to any seminar or presentation.[20] The promotion must be an advertising and promotional undertaking solely for the purpose of advertising the goods, services, or property, real or personal, of the sponsor.[21] Other than the expense of traveling to the sponsor's place of business or allowing the presentation in his or her home, the participant may not be required to pay any money in exchange for the offered prize.[22] This prohibition on consideration includes payments for service fees, mailing fees, and handling fees.

Gambling Exceptions for Non-Profits and Other Qualified Organizations

Raffles and Lotteries: A constitutional exception to the lottery prohibition allows certain non-profit organizations to conduct raffles.[23] Organizations eligible to offer raffles include non-profit, tax-exempt churches, schools, and civic organizations; nonprofit, 501(c) federally tax-exempt organizations; and other bona fide non-profit organizations approved by a county sheriff.[24] Prior to conducting the raffle, the eligible organization must obtain a license from the sheriff of the county in which the organization is located.[25] Organizations licensed to hold raffles must submit an annual report to the county sheriff disclosing all raffle receipts and expenditures.[26]

Bingo: A constitutional exception to the lottery prohibition allows the operation of non-profit bingo games.[27] With the exception of recreational bingo, only non-profit, tax-exempt organizations with a bingo license, issued by the Georgia Bureau of Investigation, may operate bingo games in Georgia.[28]

The operation of the bingo game must meet several statutory and regulatory requirements.[29] A bingo licensee must file an annual report with the Georgia Bureau of Investigation reporting all bingo receipts and expenditures.[30] The bingo law is codified in Title 16, Chapter 12, Article 2, Part 2, Sections 16-12-50 to 16-12-62 of the Georgia Code. The Georgia bingo regulations are codified in Sections 92-2-.01 to 92-2-.29 of the Official Compilation Rules and Regulations of the State of Georgia.

Additional information, forms, and regulations are available from the Georgia Bureau of Investigation, 3121 Panthersville Road, Decatur, Georgia 30034, (404) 244-2600, website: www.gbi.georgia.gov

Resources

Georgia offers a searchable database for its attorney general opinions in the Opinions section of the website of the Office of the Attorney General.

Endnotes

1. Ga. Const. art. I, § II, para. VIII.; Ga. Code §§ 16-12-22(6); 16-12-26; 16-12-27 (2013).

2. Ga. Code § 16-12-20(4) (2013).

3. 2012 Ga. Act, SB 431, § 2 (2012) (codified at Ga. Code § 16-12-20(4) (2013)).

4. Ga. Const. art. I, § II, para. VIII.; Ga. Code §§ 16-12-21, 16-12-22 (2013).

5. *See generally*, Section 3.4.3 of this Guide for a discussion of tests used when evaluating whether chance or skill prevails in a promotion combining elements of both.

6. Ga. Code § 16-12-36 (2013) (emphasis added).

7. Ga. Code § 16-12-20(4) (2013).

8. Ga. Code §§ 10-1-830(2) and 10-1-831(1) (2013).

9. Ga. Code § 10-1-832 (2013).

10. Ga. Code § 10-1-831 (2013).

11. Ga. Code § 10-1-833 (2013).

12. Ga. Code § 10-1-837 (2013).

13. Ga. Code § 16-12-20(4)(B) (2013).

14. Ga. Code § 16-12-20(4)(B) (2013).

15. 2012 Ga. Act, SB 431 (2012) (codified in sections of titles 10, 12, and 48 of Ga. Code).

16. 2012 Ga. Act, SB 431, § 2 (2012) (codified at Ga. Code § 16-12-20(4)(D) (2013)).

17. Ga. Code § 10-1-392(a)(27) (2013).

18. *Id.* The purchase requirement must be clearly and conspicuously disclosed in the advertising and promotional literature. Note that a purchase requirement for a prize where the prize involves an element of chance is an illegal lottery under Ga. Code § 16-12-20(4).

19. 2012 Ga. Act, SB 431, § 1 (2012) (codified at Ga. Code § 10-1-393(b)(16) (N.1) (2013)).

20. Ga. Code § 10-1-393(b)(16)(A.1) (2013).

21. Ga. Code § 10-1-393(b)(16)(B) (2013).

22. Ga. Code § 10-1-393(b)(16)(C) (2013).

23. Ga. Const. art. I, § II, para. VIII(d); Ga. Code § 16-12-22.1.

24. Ga. Code § 16-12-22.1(b) (2013).

25. Ga. Code § 16-12-22.1(c) (2013).

26. Ga. Code § 16-12-22.1(j) (2013).

27. Ga. Const. art. I, § II, para. VIII(b).

28. Ga. Code § 16-12-52 (2013).

29. *See generally*, discussion of bingo and raffles in Section 9.2 of this Guide.

30. Ga. Code § 16-12-59 (2013).

Hawaii

State Agency Regulating Promotions
Office of the Attorney General
425 Queen Street
Honolulu, Hawaii 96813
(808) 586-1500
Website: http://hawaii.gov/ag

Selected State Laws, Regulations, and Constitutional Provisions

Hawaii's anti-gambling laws (Title 37, Chapter 712, Sections 712-1220 *et seq.* of the Hawaii Revised Statute), which are in its penal code, contain provisions related to promotions. Specific authorities frequently quoted in court cases and interpretive opinions related to promotions include the following:

Reference No.	Descriptive Name
Haw. Rev. Stat. § 712-1220	Definitions of terms in this part (for anti-gambling laws including definitions for contest of chance, gambling, lottery, and something of value)
Haw. Rev. Stat. § 712-1221	Promoting gambling in the first degree (prohibited as a felony)
Haw. Rev. Stat. § 712-1222	Promoting gambling in the second degree (prohibited as a misdemeanor)
Haw. Rev. Stat. § 712-1223	Gambling (prohibited as misdemeanor)

Summary of State Law

Prohibition of Lotteries and Gambling: Gambling and promoting gambling are illegal in Hawaii.[1] A lottery is characterized by the Hawaii statute as a type of gambling scheme.[2] A promotion that combines a prize, chance, and consideration is a lottery in Hawaii.[3]

Contests: There are no provisions in its laws to indicate that Hawaii prohibits contests as long as the contest does not conflict with anti-gambling laws. If the contest includes an element of consideration, the sponsor must award the contest prize based on skill and not on chance.

Hawaii's statutory definition of contest of chance implies that Hawaii applies the material element test[4] when determining whether or not a promotion incorporates chance. Under Hawaii state law, a contest of chance means "any contest, game, gaming scheme, or gaming device in which the outcome *depends in a material degree* upon an element of chance, notwithstanding that skill of the contestants may also be a factor therein".[5]

Sweepstakes: There are no provisions in its laws to indicate that Hawaii prohibits sweepstakes as long as participants do not pay consideration and the sweepstakes does not conflict with anti-gambling laws. Hawaii state law defines consideration as something of value including money, property, anything exchangeable for money or property, or involving extension of a service or entertainment.[6]

Prize Promotion Laws: Hawaii's trade regulation and practice laws include prize promotion provisions (Title 26, Chapter 481B, Part I, Section 481B-1.6 and Chapter 481C, Sections 481C-1 to 481C-6 of the Hawaii Revised Statute). When offering a gift as part of a direct mail or telephone campaign to sell or lease a consumer product, the seller must disclose all material terms for purchase or lease of the consumer product including the price and handling and shipping fees.[7] There are similar requirements if the consumer must call a 900 number or pay any money to redeem a prize offered by direct mail or telephone.[8] There are specific disclosures that must be included in any offer of a prize made by means of written notice sent through the mail or by telephone.[9] If the sponsor of a chance-based promotion will not award all prizes offered, it must disclose that fact to participants in writing.[10]

If an advertisement includes a giveaway offer as an inducement for consumers to visit the sponsor's place of business, Hawaii may classify sales resulting from that advertisement as a door-to-door sale.[11] A door-to-door sale carries certain consumer protection requirements including notifying the purchaser of the right to cancel the transaction.[12]

Gambling Exceptions for Non-Profits and Other Qualified Organizations

Raffles and Lotteries: Hawaii views raffles as a type of lottery and lotteries are illegal in the state. There is no general exception for non-profits to hold raffles. However, in a written statement, the Hawaii Attorney General indicated that charities[13] may request—but not require—donations in connection with a raffle as long as every participant realizes that the raffle is free of charge and donations are voluntary.[14] The attorney general statement also indicates that a charity may conduct a raffle ancillary to another fundraising event for which there is a charge to participate. For example, if the charity holds an event for which there is a charge such as a banquet, the charity may hold a raffle as part of the banquet event as long as no additional charge is required for participation in the raffle.[15]

Bingo: Bingo is not legal in Hawaii. There is no exception for non-profits or other organizations to operate bingo games.

Resources

Hawaii offers a searchable database for its attorney general opinions from 1987 through the present online at http://hawaii.gov/ag/main/publications/opinions/. Research for this Guide uncovered no opinion letters relevant to contests and sweepstakes.

Endnotes

1. Haw. Rev. Stat. §§ 712-1221 to 712-1222, 712-1223 (2014).
2. Haw. Rev. Stat. § 712-1220 (2014).

3. Haw. Rev. Stat. § 712-1220(6) (2014).

4. *See generally*, Section 3.4.3 of this Guide for a discussion of tests used when determining whether chance or skill prevails in a promotion combining elements of both.

5. Haw. Rev. Stat. § 712-1220(3) (2014) (emphasis added).

6. Haw. Rev. Stat. § 712-1220(11) (2014).

7. Haw. Rev. Stat. § 481B-1.6(b) (2014).

8. Haw. Rev. Stat. § 481B-1.6(c) (2014).

9. Haw. Rev. Stat. § 481B-1.6(d) (2014). ". . . written notice sent . . . by telephone" is language directly from the statute. It is unclear what this language means.

10. Haw. Rev. Stat. § 481B-1.6(e) (2014).

11. Haw. Rev. Stat. § 481C-1 (2014).

12. Haw. Rev. Stat. § 481C-2 (2014).

13. The Hawaii statutory definition for charitable organization is codified at Haw. Rev. Stat. § 467B-1 (2014).

14. Haw. Att'y Gen., *Guidance Regarding Charitable Raffles*, available at http://ag.hawaii.gov/tax/files/2013/01/DOC018.pdf (last visited on May 26, 2014.)

15. *Id.*

Idaho

State Attorney General Office

Office of the Attorney General
700 W. Jefferson Street
P.O. Box 83720
Boise, Idaho 83720-0010
(208) 334-2400
Website: http://www.ag.idaho.gov/

Selected State Laws, Regulations, and Constitutional Provisions

Idaho's anti-gambling laws (Title 18, Chapter 38, Sections 18-3801 to 18-3810 and Chapter 49, Sections 18-4901 *et seq.* of the Idaho Code), which are in the crimes and punishment portion of the Idaho Code, contain provisions related to promotions. Specific authorities frequently quoted in court cases and interpretive opinions related to promotions include the following:

Reference No.	Descriptive Name
Idaho Const. art. III, § 20	Gambling Prohibited
Idaho Code § 18-3801	Gambling Defined
Idaho Code § 18-3802	Gambling Prohibited (misdemeanor)
Idaho Code § 18-4901	Lottery Defined
Idaho Code § 18-4902	Engaging in Lottery (prohibited as misdemeanor)
Idaho Admin. Code r. 04.02.080	No Purchase Required for Chance Promotions

Summary of State Law

Prohibition of Lotteries and Gambling: Idaho prohibits gambling in its constitution and in its statutory laws.[1] Idaho law also prohibits engaging or assisting in lotteries and distributing lottery tickets.[2] While recognizing that a lottery is a form of gambling, Idaho is one of the states that analyzes gambling differently than it analyzes lotteries.[3] A promotion that combines a prize, chance, and consideration is a lottery in Idaho.[4] Exceptions to the gambling and lottery prohibitions include state-operated lotteries and certain charitable lotteries.

Contests: Idaho permits contests as long as the contest does not conflict with anti-gambling laws. Idaho law explicitly exempts from the definition of gambling "bona fide contests of skill, speed, strength or endurance in which awards are made only to entrants or the owners of entrants".[5] Owners of entrants refers to owners of things such as racehorses, greyhounds, or race cars.[6] According to the Idaho Attorney General, "this [exemption for contests testing skill, speed, strength or endurance] permits contestants to pay a fee to enter a contest, such as a golf tournament, and gain a prize or award depending on the contestant's performance . . . "[7]

If the contest includes an element of consideration, the sponsor must award the contest prize based on skill and not on chance. Court opinions suggest that Idaho might apply the pure chance test[8] when determining whether or not a promotion incorporates sufficient chance to make it an illegal lottery. In *Oneida County Fair Board v. Smylie*, 386 P.2d 374, 391 (Idaho 1963), the Idaho Supreme Court adopted the viewpoint that an essential requisite of a lottery is having an outcome based solely on chance and an outcome in which neither merit nor skill play a part in the award determination.

As part of a subsequent 2003 decision in *MDS Investments, LLC v. Idaho*, 65 P.3d 197 (2003), the Idaho Supreme Court revisited the *Oneida County Fair Board* decision. While the 2003 Idaho Supreme Court did not directly re-evaluate the *Oneida County* holding related to chance, the Idaho Supreme Court did leave the reasonable impression that the rulings by the *Oneida County Fair Board* court are still applicable in Idaho.

Sweepstakes: Idaho permits sweepstakes as long as participants do not pay consideration and the sweepstakes does not violate anti-gambling laws. The Idaho statute explicitly exempts from the definition of gambling any "merchant promotional contests and drawings conducted incidentally to bona fide nongaming business operations, if prizes are awarded without consideration being charged to participants."[9] Similarly, the statutes prohibiting lotteries exempt from anti-lottery laws any "... advertising and promotional activities, whether or not conducted by mass media techniques, in which prizes may be awarded."[10]

Prize Promotion Laws: Idaho has prize promotion protections in the consumer protection regulations issued by the Idaho Office of the Attorney General (Rules 04.02.081 to 04.02.082 of the Idaho Administrative Code). If a seller offers a gift to a consumer as an inducement for the consumer to attend a sales presentation or for the consumer to telephone the seller, the seller must provide certain disclosures and refrain from acts that might mislead consumers.[11]

Gambling Exceptions for Non-Profits and Other Qualified Organizations

The Idaho constitutional provision prohibiting gambling contains an exception allowing charitable raffles and bingo games under certain conditions.[12] Organizations that satisfy the Idaho statutory definitions for charitable organizations or non-profit organizations may operate raffles and bingo games.[13]

Raffles: An eligible organization holding a raffle must use at least eighty percent of the net raffle proceeds for charitable or non-profit purposes.[14] If the organization wants to raffle merchandise with an aggregate value over five thousand dollars, it must obtain a raffle license from the Idaho State Lottery Commission.[15] Raffle licensees must periodically file financial statements and reports with the Idaho State Lottery Commission.[16]

Bingo. Any bingo proceeds remaining after payment of expenses must be used for charitable, civic, or beneficial purposes which may include the maintenance and construction of buildings to be used by the charitable organization, the fostering of amateur sports competition, or the prevention of cruelty to children or animals.[17] Eligible organizations that generate gross annual bingo sales of $10,000 or more must obtain a bingo license from the Idaho State Lottery Commission.[18] All eligible organizations offering bingo in reliance on the statutory exemption must file financial statements and reports with the Idaho State Lottery Commission.[19]

Additional Information about Raffles and Bingo: The operation of raffles and bingo games must meet several statutory and regulatory requirements.[20] The laws enacting the constitutional exception for raffles and bingo games are in Title 67, Chapter 77, Sections 67-7701 *et seq.* of the Idaho Code. Raffle and bingo regulations, issued by the Idaho State Lottery Commission, are in Rules 52.01.02.000 *et seq.* of the Idaho Administrative Code. Additional information and forms are available online at the website of the Idaho State Lottery Commission, 1199 Shoreline Lane, Suite 100, Boise, ID 83702, www.idaholottery.com

Resources

Idaho offers a database for its attorney general opinions from 1985 through the present online in the opinions portion of the website of the Office of the Attorney General. Tables of citation are available at the website for opinions issued between 1975 and 1984.

Endnotes

1. Idaho Const. art. III, § 20; Idaho Code § 18-3802 (2014).
2. Idaho Stat. §§ 18-4902 to 18-4904 (2014).
3. *See, MDS Invs. v. State of Idaho*, 65 P.3d 197 (Idaho 2003). Idaho addresses gambling in a different chapter of the criminal code (Idaho Stat. § 18-3801 to 18-3810 (2014)) than it addresses lotteries (Idaho Stat. § 18-4901 to 18-4909 (2014)).
4. Idaho Stat. § 18-4901 (2014).
5. Idaho Stat. § 18-3801(1) (2014).
6. *See e.g.,* Idaho Att'y Gen. Op. (Sept. 17, 1993).
7. *Id.* at 4.

8. *See generally*, Section 3.4.3 of this Guide for a discussion of tests used when determining whether chance or skill prevails in a promotion combining elements of both.
9. Idaho Stat. § 18-3801(4) (2014).
10. Idaho Stat. § 18-4909 (2014).
11. *See generally*, discussion of prize promotion laws in Section 7.4.2 of this Guide.
12. Idaho Const. art. III, § 20(1)c.
13. Idaho Stat. §§ 67-7702(3) and (10), 67-7707, 67-7710(1) (2014).
14. Idaho Stat. § 67-7710(3) (2014).
15. Idaho Stat. §§ 66-7711, 67-7713 (2014).
16. Idaho Stat. § 67-7710(4) (2014).
17. Idaho Stat. § 66-7709(c) (2014).
18. Idaho Stat. §§ 66-7711 and 67-7713 (2014).
19. Idaho Stat. § 67-7709(2) (2014).
20. *See generally*, discussion of bingo and raffles in Section 9.2 of this Guide.

Illinois

Attorney General Office
Office of the Attorney General
Chicago Main Office
100 West Randolph Street
Chicago, IL 60601
(312) 814-3000
Website: www.illinoisattorneygeneral.gov

Selected State Laws, Regulations, and Constitutional Provisions

Illinois anti-gambling laws (Chapter 720, Title III, Part D, Article 28, Sections 5/28-1 *et seq.* of the Illinois Compiled Statute) which are part of Illinois' criminal code, contain provisions related to promotions. Illinois includes its prize promotion laws, referred to as the Prizes and Gifts Act (Chapter 815, Sections 525/1 *et seq.* of the Illinois Compiled Statute), with its business transactions laws. Specific Illinois authorities frequently quoted in court cases and interpretive opinions related to promotions include the following:

Reference No.	Descriptive Name
Ill. Comp. Stat. Ch. 720, § 5/28-1	Gambling (activities that do and do not constitute gambling; act of gambling is misdemeanor or felony)
Ill. Comp. Stat. Ch. 720, § 5/28-2	Definitions (for anti-gambling laws including definition for lottery)

Summary of State Law

Prohibition of Lotteries and Gambling: Illinois' statutory laws prohibit promoting and advertising lotteries.[1] A promotion that combines a prize, chance, and consideration is a lottery in Illinois.[2] Illinois also has a general prohibition against gambling.[3] Exceptions to the anti-lottery and anti-gambling prohibitions include lotteries operated by the state and certain charitable lotteries.[4]

Contests: Illinois permits contests as long as the contest does not conflict with anti-gambling laws. Illinois laws explicitly exempt from the definition of gambling any contest for which a prize is awarded based on skill, speed, strength or endurance or awarded to the owner of an animal or vehicle entered in the contest.[5] Research for this Guide uncovered no authority indicating which test Illinois uses when determining whether or not chance determines the outcome of a promotion.[6]

Some interpret Illinois law as prohibiting contests from charging consideration. A provision of the Illinois Prizes and Gifts Act does indeed prohibit any promotion sponsor from requiring any person to pay money to the sponsor as a condition to receive, use, compete for, or obtain information about a prize.[7] However, the payment prohibition has some ambiguity.

First, the statute refers to money. One could infer that a sponsor could require forms of non-monetary consideration.[8] Also, the Prizes and Gifts Act defines a prize as an item or service of value awarded to a participant in a contest, competition, sweepstakes, or other selection process that *involves an element of chance*.[9] The definition of prize seems to nullify the payment prohibition for contests awarding a prize based on skill. Hence, there is a reasonable argument that the sponsor of a skill-based contest can charge money-consideration in Illinois.

Research for this Guide uncovered no Illinois authorities clarifying the permissibility of contest sponsors charging consideration. Hence, any contest sponsor charging any type of consideration in Illinois should exercise caution.

Sweepstakes: Illinois permits sweepstakes as long as participants do not pay consideration and the sweepstakes does not conflict with anti-gambling laws. Sweepstakes advertised with written advertisements must also comply with the disclosure requirements of the Illinois prize promotion laws discussed below.

Like other states, Illinois expects the sponsor to offer a free alternative method of entry when opportunities to play are dispensed with the purchase of a product or service.[10] Illinois examines closely what motivates the consumer to purchase the product. If the consumer buys the product or service essentially only to play the game, Illinois may re-characterize the sweepstakes as an illegal lottery. "The controlling fact in the determination of whether a given scheme or business is a lottery is determined by the nature of the appeal which the business makes to secure the patronage of its customers. If, as [with the purchase of phone cards sold with a sweepstakes opportunity], the controlling inducement is the lure of an uncertain prize, then the business is a lottery."[11]

Prize Promotion Laws: Illinois incorporates prize promotion protections into its Prizes and Gifts Act.[12] The prize notice component of the law does not require sponsors to provide a written disclosure in all circumstances. However, if the sponsor uses print advertisements or marketing materials to offer promotional prizes, those printed documents must include certain disclosures.[13]

The law applies to a written promotional offer used to induce or invite a person to claim a prize, attend a sales presentation, conduct any business in Illinois, or meet or contact the sponsor or its agent.[14] As discussed above in the contest section of this Illinois State Summary, the Prizes and Gifts Act arguably does not apply to contests that are skill-based. Nevertheless, conservative sponsors of skill-based contests might choose to comply with the disclosure requirements in the Prize and Gifts Act when using print advertisements.

The list of prohibited practices in the Illinois Prizes and Gifts Act is not as long as the list of prohibited practices in the prize promotion laws of other states. One Illinois consumer protection provision worthy of mention is the requirement that the sponsor deliver either the prize, a voucher or certificate awarding the prize, or the retail value of the prize within thirty days of telling a person that the person has won a prize.[15]

Gambling Exceptions for Non-Profits and Other Qualified Organizations

Raffles: The Illinois Raffles Act authorizes counties and municipalities to license certain non-profit organizations to operate raffles. Organizations eligible to offer raffles are religious, charitable, labor, business, fraternal, educational or veterans' organizations; and certain non-profit fund-raising organizations. The organization must use all raffle net proceeds exclusively for the lawful purposes of the organization[16] and must obtain a raffle license.[17]

The Raffles Act is in Chapter 230, Sections 15/0.01 *et seq.* of the Illinois Compiled Statute. Each county and municipality establishes its own licensing mechanism within the parameters of the Raffles Act.

There is a separate section of the Raffles Act specifically for political committees that want to hold raffles. The State Board of Elections issues raffle licenses to political committees.[18] The remaining provisions for political committee raffles are parallel to the general raffle exemption.

Bingo: The Illinois Bingo License and Tax Act allows certain organizations to operate bingo games. Organizations eligible to offer bingo games include religious, charitable, labor, fraternal, youth athletic, senior citizen, educational and veterans' organizations.

The operation of the bingo game must meet several statutory and regulatory requirements.[19] Bingo operators must have a license issued by the Illinois Department of Revenue. There is an exemption to the bingo license requirement for senior citizens' organizations provided that certain conditions are met. The conditions include requirements that the game be held at a local-government-owned facility used to service senior citizens or federally assisted rental housing for the elderly, that bingo cards be distributed at nominal charge, and that the retail value of prizes be nominal.[20]

The Bingo License and Tax Act is in Chapter 230, Sections 25/1 *et seq.* of the Illinois Revised Statute. Bingo regulations, issued by the Illinois Department of Revenue, are codified in Title 86, Sections 435-100 to 435-220 of the Illinois Administrative Code. Additional information, forms, and regulations are available through the Illinois Department of

Revenue, Office of Bingo & Charitable Games, P.O. Box 19480 Springfield, Illinois 62794-9480, website: http://tax.illinois.gov/CharityGaming/

Resources

Illinois offers a searchable database for its attorney general opinions from 1971 through the present online in the opinions section of the website of the Office of the Attorney General.

Endnotes

1. Ill. Comp. Stat. Ch. 720, §§ 5/28-1(a)(7), 9, and (10) (2014).
2. Ill. Comp. Stat. Ch. 720, § 5/28-2(b) (2014).
3. Ill. Comp. Stat. Ch. 720, § 5/28-1(c) (2014).
4. Ill. Comp. Stat. Ch. 720, § 5/28-1(b) (2014).
5. Ill. Comp. Stat. Ch. 720, § 5/28-1(b)(2) (2014).
6. *See generally*, Section 3.4.3 of this Guide for a discussion of tests used when determining whether chance or skill prevails in a promotion combining elements of both.
7. Ill. Comp. Stat. Ch. 815, § 525/20(a) (2014).
8. *See generally*, discussion of what qualifies as consideration in Section 3.5.2 of this Guide.
9. Ill. Comp. Stat. Ch. 815, § 525/10 (2014) *(emphasis added)*.
10. *See generally*, discussion of alternative methods of entry in Section 3.6 of this Guide.
11. *G.A. Carney, Ltd. v. Brzeczek*, 453 N.E.2d 756, 757-758 (Ill. App. Ct. 1983).
12. Ill. Comp. Stat. Ch. 815, § 525/1 *et. seq.* (2014).
13. *See generally*, discussion of state prize promotion laws in Section 7.4.2 of this Guide.
14. Ill. Comp. Stat. Ch. 815, § 525/15 (2014).
15. Ill. Comp. Stat. Ch. 815, § 525/30 (2014).
16. Ill. Comp. Stat. Ch. 230, § 15/4(a)(1) (2014).
17. Ill. Comp. Stat. Ch. 230, § 15/3 (2014) (2014).
18. The general raffle exemption is in Ill. Comp. Stat. Ch. 230, §15/3 (2014). The political committee raffle exemption is in Ill. Comp. Stat. Ch. 230, § 15/8.1 (2014).
19. *See generally*, discussion of bingo and raffles in Section 9.2 of this Guide.
20. Ill. Comp. Stat. Ch. 230, § 25/1.3(9) (2014).

Indiana

State Attorney General Office
Indiana Attorney General's Office
302 W. Washington St., 5th Floor
Indianapolis, Indiana 46204
(317) 232-6201
Website: http://www.in.gov/attorneygeneral

Selected State Laws, Regulations, and Constitutional Provisions

Indiana's anti-gambling laws, which are codified with its criminal law and procedure laws (Title 35, Article 45, Chapter 5, Sections 35-45-5-1 *et seq.* of the Indiana Code), contain provisions related to promotions. Specific Indiana legal authorities frequently quoted in court cases and interpretive opinions related to promotions include the following:

Reference No.	Descriptive Name
Ind. Code § 35-45-5-1	Definitions (for anti-gambling laws including definition for gambling)
Ind. Code § 35-45-5-2	Unlawful gambling (prohibited as misdemeanor; felony if conducted over the internet)
Ind. Code § 35-45-5-3	Professional gambling; professional gambling over the Internet (defined and prohibited as felony)

Summary of State Law

Prohibition of Lotteries and Gambling: Indiana has a general prohibition against gambling.[1] Prohibited gambling practices include conducting lotteries.[2] A promotion that combines a prize, chance, and consideration is a lottery in Indiana.[3] Exceptions to the gambling and lottery prohibitions include lotteries operated by the state and certain charitable lotteries.

Contests: Indiana permits contests as long as the contest does not conflict with anti-gambling laws. If the contest includes an element of consideration, the sponsor must award the contest prize based on skill and not on chance.

The anti-gambling statutes explicitly exclude from the definition of gambling "bona fide contests of skill, speed, strength, or endurance in which awards are made only to entrants or the owners of entries".[4] Court opinions indicate that Indiana applies the dominant factor doctrine[5] when evaluating whether chance determines the outcome of a promotion.[6]

Sweepstakes: Indiana permits sweepstakes as long as participants do not pay consideration and the sweepstakes does not violate anti-gambling laws. Like many other states, for there to be no consideration attributed to the promotion, Indiana insists that any free alternative method of entry be effective.[7] It also insists that participants purchasing any products that come with the sweepstakes entry make the purchase due primarily to an interest in the product and not an interest in the opportunity to win a prize.[8]

Prize Promotion Laws: The promotional gifts and contests laws (Title 24, Article 8, Sections 24-8-1-1 to 24-8-6-3 of the Indiana Code), which are part of the trade regulation laws, are Indiana's version of prize promotion laws. If an individual or organization delivers a written notice that offers something of value and that represents that the notice recipient has been awarded or may have been awarded a prize, the written notice must include certain disclosures and information. The disclosure requirement is applicable whether the written notice is delivered by hand, mail, newspaper or other periodical or via email or other electronic communication.[9] There are specific statutory requirements for placement, font, and wording of the notice.[10]

Gambling Exceptions for Non-Profits and Other Qualified Organizations

Raffles, Bingo, and Charitable Gaming: Indiana allows certain non-profit and civic organizations to operate raffles, bingo, charity game nights, and other gambling games as a fundraising activity.[11] The organization must use the net proceeds in a manner consistent with the lawful purposes of the organization.[12] Organizations eligible to offer charitable games include religious, educational, senior citizens, veterans, or civic organizations; certain tax-exempt political organizations; and educational institutions.[13] A broader category of non-profit business organizations may obtain licenses to hold door prize events.[14]

The operation of raffles and bingo games must meet several statutory and regulatory requirements.[15] Organizations offering raffles and bingo games must obtain a license issued by the Indiana Gaming Commission.[16] There is an exception to the license requirement if the aggregate value of the prizes to be awarded falls below $1,000 for a single event and $3,000 for the calendar year.[17] However, even if the licensing exception applies, the organization must still maintain accurate records of all financial transactions of the event and may be required to file an informational notice with the Indiana Gaming Commission.[18]

The charity gaming laws are with Indiana's state offices and administration laws and are codified in Title 4, Article 32.2, Sections 4-32.2-1-1 *et seq.* of the Indiana Code. Charitable gaming regulations, issued by the Indiana Gaming Commission, are codified in Title 68, Article 21, Sections 21-1-1 *et seq.* of the Indiana Administrative Code. Additional information, application forms, and regulations for charitable gaming are available online at the website of the Indiana Gaming Commission, East Tower, Suite 1600, 101 W. Washington Street, Indianapolis, Indiana 46204, website: http://www.in.gov/igc/.

Resources

Indiana offers a database for its attorney general opinions from 2001 through the present online in the advisory and opinion portion of the website of the Office of the Attorney General.

Endnotes

1. Ind. Code §§ 35-45-5-2 and 35-45-5-3 (2014).
2. Ind. Code § 35-45-5-3 (2014); *Lashbrook v. Indiana*, 550 N.E.2d 772, 776 and n. 6 (Ind. Ct. App. 1990).
3. *See Lashbrook*, 550 N.E.2d at 774-777.
4. Ind. Code § 35-45-5-1-1(d)(1) (2014).
5. *See generally*, Section 3.4.3 of this Guide for a discussion of tests used when determining whether chance or skill prevails in a promotion combining elements of both.
6. *See Lashbrook*, 550 N.E.2d at 775-776.
7. *See e.g., F.A.C.E. Trading v. Carter*, 821 N.E.2d 38, 42 (Ind. Ct. App. 2005). *See also*, Sections 3.5.2 and 3.6 of this Guide for a discussion of what qualifies as consideration and what qualifies in a sweepstakes as an effective free alternative method of entry.
8. *See e.g., F.A.C.E. Trading v. Carter*, 821 N.E.2d at 42-43.
9. Ind. Code § 24-8-3-1 (2014).
10. Ind. Code §§ 24-8-3-2 to 24-8-3-7 (2014). *See generally*, discussion of state prize promotion laws in Section 7.4.2 of this Guide.
11. Ind. Code §§ 4-32.2-1-1 and 4-32.2-1-2 (2014).
12. Ind. Code § 4-32.2-5-3 (2014).
13. Ind. Code § 4-32.2-2-24 (2014).
14. Ind. Code §§ 4-32.2-2-24(c) and 4-32.2-4-10 (2014).
15. *See generally*, discussion of bingo and raffles in Section 9.2 of this Guide.
16. Ind. Code § 4-32.2-4-2 (2014).
17. Ind. Code § 4-32.2-4-3 (2014).
18. *Id.*

Iowa

State Attorney General Office
Office of the Attorney General
1305 E. Walnut Street
Des Moines, Iowa 50319
(515) 281-5164
Website: http://www.iowa.gov/government/ag/

Selected State Laws, Regulations, and Constitutional Provisions

Iowa's anti-gambling laws (Title XVI, Subtitle 1, Chapter 725, Sections 725.5 to 725.19 of the Iowa Code) contain provisions relevant to promotions and are codified with the state's criminal law and procedure laws. Iowa has additional anti-gambling laws in its public services and regulation code (Title III, Subtitle 4, Chapter 99B, Sections 99B.1 *et seq.* of the Iowa Code). Specific Iowa legal provisions frequently quoted in court cases and interpretive opinions related to promotions include the following:

Reference No.	Descriptive Name
Iowa Code § 725.7	Gaming and betting—penalty
Iowa Code § 725.12	Lotteries and lottery tickets—definition— prosecution (lotteries prohibited as misdemeanor)
Iowa Code § 725.15	Exceptions for legal gambling
Iowa Code § 99B.11	Bona fide contests
Iowa Code § 99B.21	Tax on prizes

Summary of State Law

Prohibition of Lotteries and Gambling: Iowa's statutory laws prohibit lotteries.[1] A promotion combining a prize, chance, and consideration is a lottery in Iowa.[2] Iowa also has a general prohibition against gambling.[3] Exceptions to the lottery and gambling prohibitions include lotteries operated by the state and certain charitable lotteries.

Contests: Iowa permits skill-based contests. Contests charging consideration must provide a written disclosure notice in compliance with the Iowa prize promotion laws, discussed below. Iowa statutory language suggests that Iowa applies the material element test[4] when evaluating whether or not chance determines the outcome of a promotion. For the purpose of its anti-gambling statute addressing lotteries and lottery tickets, Iowa defines lottery to mean an arrangement where a prize is awarded by chance or any process involving *a substantial element of chance* to a participant, and where some or all participants have paid or furnished a consideration for such chance.[5]

The Iowa statute includes several exceptions to a gambling offense.[6] One exception is a bona fide contest.[7] The statutory provision for bona fide contest indicates that it is lawful for a person to conduct contests specified in the provision, and to offer and pay awards to persons winning in those contests regardless of whether the sponsor charges consideration. The contest may not be held at a school or amusement concession and the contest may not utilize a gambling device.[8] The contests specified in the provision as qualifying for this exception include several categories of athletic and sporting events; contests and exhibitions of cooking, horticulture, animals, artwork, hobbywork, and craftwork; and contests and tournaments for bridge, chess, checkers, and similar games.[9]

Sweepstakes: Iowa permits sweepstakes as long as participants do not pay consideration and the sweepstakes does not violate anti-gambling laws.

WHAT IS CONSIDERATION UNDER IOWA LAW? The Iowa statute is generous in the amount of information provided concerning what constitutes consideration in a promotion.

There is consideration if some or all participants spend money or something of monetary value through a purchase, payment of an entry or admission fee, or other payment. Consideration also exists if participants must expend substantial effort in order to participate in the promotion.

However, none of the following activities or activities similar to them qualify as a substantial expenditure of effort:

- registering one's name, address, and related information
- obtaining an entry blank or participation sheet
- permitting or taking part in a demonstration of any article or commodity
- making a personal examination of posted lists of prize winners
- submitting free entries via the internet or through the regular mail[10]

The acts may be performed in person at any store, place of business, or other designated location; through the mail; or by telephone. A sponsor may not require that the winner be present at a designated location for the selection of the winner. Instead, the sponsor must notify the winner either by the same method used to communicate the prize offer or by regular mail.[11]

ALLOWANCE FOR PROMOTIONAL SWEEPSTAKES. The Iowa statute has an exception for the advertising of (but not explicitly the operation of) a lottery, game of chance, contest, or promotional activity operated by a commercial organization that offers occasional lotteries as ancillary to its primary business.[12] To fall under this exception, the sponsor must include the effective dates of the promotion in all advertising materials.[13] To be considered occasional, the promotional activity can be in effect for no more than ninety days during any one-year period.[14]

The exception does not allow commercial organizations *to sell* pull-tabs, instant tickets, or other tokens that represent a chance to obtain a cash prize to be paid on the premises where the chance to win such prize was obtained.[15] However, the commercial organization can *give away* such pull-tabs and instant tickets.[16] Although the Iowa statute provision does not explicitly use the term sweepstakes, given that there can be no consideration for the chance-based prize opportunity, one can reasonably interpret this exception as an allowance for promotional sweepstakes.

Prize Promotion Laws: Iowa prize promotion laws are in Title XVI, Subtitle 1, Chapter 714B, Section 714B.1 *et seq.* of the criminal law and procedure law of the Iowa Code. A sponsor of a prize may not require a person to purchase merchandise or pay or donate money as a condition of awarding a prize or as a condition of allowing the person to receive, use, compete for, or obtain information about a prize, unless the sponsor first gives the person a written disclosure statement.[17] The statute refers to this written disclosure statement as a prize notice. Iowa prize promotion laws and their accompanying regulations list specific information that must be included in the prize notice and prohibit certain practices that might mislead consumers.[18]

Gambling Exceptions for Non-Profits and Other Qualified Organizations

Raffle, Bingo, and Charitable Gaming: Iowa allows certain tax-exempt, non-profit organizations to engage in games of skill, games of chance, and raffles as long as the organization uses at least seventy-five percent of the net receipts for educational, civic, public, charitable, patriotic, or religious uses in Iowa.[19] Organizations eligible to offer raffles, bingo, and charitable gaming include federal-tax exempt organizations, government agencies, certain parent-teacher organizations, political parties, and political party organizations.[20]

The operation of raffles, bingo games, and other charitable gaming must meet several statutory and regulatory requirements.[21] Charitable gaming requires a license issued by the Iowa Department of Inspections and Appeals.[22] Licensees must also file periodic reports of gross receipts, expenses, and the cost of prizes awarded.

The primary statutory provision for charitable gaming is in Title III, Subtitle 4, Chapter 99B, Section 99B.7 of the Iowa Code. Regulations for charitable gambling, issued by the Department of Inspections and Appeals, are codified in Sections 481-100.1 *et seq.* of the Iowa Administrative Code.[23] Licensing information and forms are available from the Iowa Department of Inspections and Appeals, Lucas State Office Building, 321 East 12th Street, Des Moines, Iowa, 50319-0083, website: http://dia.iowa.gov/.

Resources

Iowa offers an online searchable database of its attorney general opinions from 1898 through the present. The database is accessible via the website of the Office of the Attorney General.

Endnotes

1. Iowa Code § 725.12 (2014).
2. Iowa Code § 725.12.3 (2014).
3. Iowa Code § 725.7 (2014).
4. *See generally*, Section 3.4.3 of this Guide for a discussion of tests used when evaluating whether chance or skill prevails in a promotion combining elements of both.
5. Iowa Code § 725.12.3 (2014) (emphasis added).
6. Iowa Code § 725.15, 99B.3 to 99B.12 (2014).
7. Iowa Code § 99B.11 (2014).
8. Iowa Code § 99B.11.1 (2014).
9. Iowa Code § 99B.11.2 (2014).
10. Iowa Code § 725.12.4 (2014).
11. *Id.*
12. Iowa Code § 725.12.1 (2014).
13. *Id.*
14. *Id.*
15. Iowa Code § 725.12.2 (2014).
16. *Id.*
17. Iowa Code § 714B-2.1 (2014).
18. Iowa Code §§ 714B.2 to 714B.4 (2014); Iowa Admin. Code r. 61-32.1 (2014). *See generally*, discussion of state prize promotion laws in Section 7.4.2 of this Guide.
19. Iowa Code § 99B.7.3.b (2014).
20. Iowa Code §§ 99B.7.1.m, 99B.7.6 (2014).
21. *See generally*, discussion of bingo and raffles in Section 9.2 of this Guide.
22. Iowa Code §§ 99B.7.1.a and 99B.7.3 (2014).
23. Iowa Admin. Code r. 481-100.1 *et seq.* (2014).

Kansas

State Attorney General Office
Office of the Attorney General
120 SW 10th Street
Memorial Hall, 2nd Floor
Topeka, Kansas 66612
(785) 296-2215
Website: http://www.ksag.org

Selected State Laws, Regulations, and Constitutional Provisions

Kansas has anti-gambling laws (Chapter 21, Article 64, Sections 21-6403 to 21-6409 of the Kansas Statute) in the crimes against the public morals portion of its state code. In its unfair trade and consumer protection laws, Kansas includes its prize promotion laws (Chapter 50, Article 6, Section 50-692 of the Kansas Statute). Specific Kansas legal authorities frequently quoted in court cases and interpretive opinions related to promotions include the following:

Reference No.	Descriptive Name
Kan. Const. art. XV, § 3	Lotteries (prohibited)
Kan. Stat. § 21-6403	Definitions (for anti-gambling laws including definitions for consideration and lottery)
Kan. Stat. § 21-6404	Gambling (includes making a bet and participating in a lottery and is prohibited as a misdemeanor)
Kan. Stat. § 21-6406	Commercial gambling (includes conducting a lottery and is prohibited as a felony)
Kan. Stat. § 50-692	Prize notification; definitions; requirements of notice and solicitation; violations

Summary of State Law

Prohibition of Lotteries and Gambling: Both Kansas' Constitution and statutory laws prohibit lotteries.[1] A promotion that combines a prize, chance, and consideration is a lottery in Kansas.[2] Kansas also has a general prohibition against gambling.[3] Exceptions to the lottery and gambling prohibitions include lotteries operated by the state and non-profit bingo games.

Contests: Kansas permits contests as long as the contest does not conflict with anti-gambling laws. If the contest includes an element of consideration, the sponsor must award the contest prize based on skill and not on chance. Court opinions suggest that Kansas prefers to apply the dominant factor doctrine[4] when evaluating whether or not chance determines the outcome of a promotion.[5]

Sweepstakes: Kansas permits sweepstakes as long as participants do not pay consideration and the sweepstakes does not conflict with anti-gambling laws. Kansas takes a broad view of consideration. In its anti-gambling laws, Kansas indicates that consideration within a lottery can be anything which is a commercial or financial advantage to the promoter or a disadvantage to the participant.[6] The Kansas statute does offer some specific exclusions from consideration. None of the following activities alone qualifies as consideration in Kansas for purposes of a lottery or promotion:

- completing a registration as long as there is no purchase of goods or services;
- attending a place or event as long as there is no admission fee;
- listening to or watching radio and television programs;
- answering the telephone or making a telephone call; and
- participating in similar activities.[7]

Prize Promotion Laws: Kansas unfair trade and consumer protection laws include prize promotion provisions (Chapter 50, Article 6, Section 50-692 of the Kansas Statute). The law does not apply to traditional contests and sweepstakes. Instead, the Kansas prize promotion law targets giveaways that include consideration or any type of required contact with the sponsor for receipt of the prize. If a sponsor tells a person, either verbally or in writing, that the person has been selected or may be eligible to receive a prize, the sponsor must provide the person with a written prize notice prior to requesting or accepting payment of any kind. There are specific statutory requirements for the placement, font, and wording of the disclosures. Kansas' prize promotion law also prohibits practices that might mislead consumers.[8]

Gambling Exceptions for Non-Profits and Other Qualified Organizations

Raffles and Lotteries: Kansas views raffles as lotteries and offers no exceptions allowing charitable or non-profit organizations to operate a raffle or any other promotion that combines prize, chance, and consideration. However, in a raffle policy statement, the Sedgwick County District Attorney suggested that charitable and non-profit organizations wishing to hold raffle fundraisers may do so by inviting raffle participants to make a donation for the raffle ticket as long as it is clear that making a donation or any other sort of payment is not a requirement for participating in the raffle.[9]

The policy statement is an interpretation of the law from a district attorney in one county of Kansas. The statement is not official Kansas state law. Hence, some Kansas counties might choose not to follow the policy statement. As a best practice, any non-profit organization relying on the statement to offer a raffle should verify that all raffle promotional materials, tickets, signs and advertisements include a statement that all contributions are strictly voluntary.

Bingo: A Kansas constitutional amendment allows certain non-profit organizations to operate bingo games for charitable purposes.[10] Organizations eligible to offer bingo games include non-profit religious, charitable, fraternal, educational and veterans organizations.[11]

The operation of the bingo game must meet several statutory and regulatory requirements.[12] Bingo operators must obtain a license[13], file periodic operational reports[14], and use net proceeds in a manner consistent with the licensee's lawful purposes.[15]

Kansas enacted this constitutional amendment for bingo as the Bingo Act. The Bingo Act is codified in the taxation chapter of the Kansas statute (Chapter 79, Article 47, Sections 79-4701 *et seq.* of the Kansas Statute). The bingo regulations, issued by the Kansas Department of Revenue, are codified in Sections 92-23-9 *et seq.* of the Kansas Administrative Regulations.

The Administrator of Charitable Gaming, a position within the Kansas Office of the Secretary of Revenue, coordinates all licensing, compliance and tax collection activities relating to charitable bingo in Kansas. Additional licensing information, regulations and forms are available from the Kansas Administrator of Charitable Gambling, Docking State Office Building, 915 SW Harrison Street, Topeka, KS 66625-3512, (785) 296-6127, website: http://www.ksrevenue.org/bustaxtypesbingo.html

Resources

Kansas offers a searchable database for its attorney general opinions from 1974 through the present available online at http://ksag.washburnlaw.edu

Endnotes

1. Kan. Const. art. XV, § 3; Kan. Stat. §§ 21-6403(b), 21-6404(2), 21-6406 (2013).
2. Kan. Stat. § 21-6403(b) (2013).
3. Kan. Stat. §§ 21-6404 and 21-6406 (2013).
4. *See generally*, Section 3.4.3 of this Guide for a discussion of tests used when evaluating whether chance or skill prevails in a promotion combining elements of both.
5. *Three Kings Holdings v. Six*, 255 P.3d 1218, 1223 (Kan. Ct. of App. 2011).
6. Kan. Stat. § 21-6403(c) (2013).
7. *Id.*
8. *See generally*, discussion of state prize promotion laws in Section 7.4.2 of this Guide.
9. Nola Tedesco Foulston, District Attorney of Sedgwick County, *Raffle Policy Statement*, http://sedgwickcounty.org/da/lottery_casino_night.asp (last visited Sept. 17, 2014).
10. Kan. Const. art. XV, § 3a.
11. *Id.*
12. *See generally*, discussion of bingo and raffles in Section 9.2 of this Guide.
13. Kan. Stat. § 79-4703 (2013).
14. Kan. Stat. § 79-4705 (2013).
15. Kan. Stat. §§ 79-4701(n) and 79-4706(a) (2013); Kan. Admin. Regs. § 92-23-15(e).

Kentucky

State Attorney General Office
Office of the Attorney General
700 Capitol Avenue, Suite 118
Frankfort, Kentucky 40601
(502) 696-5300
Website: http://ag.ky.gov/

Selected State Laws, Regulations, and Constitutional Provisions

Kentucky's anti-gambling laws, which are in its penal code (Title L, Chapter 528, Sections 528.010 *et seq.* of the Kentucky Revised Statute), contain provisions related to promotions. Specific legal provisions frequently quoted in court cases and interpretive opinions related to promotions include the following:

Reference No.	Descriptive Name
Ky. Const. § 226	State lottery—Charitable lotteries and charitable gift enterprises—Other lotteries and gift enterprises forbidden
Ky. Rev. Stat. § 528.010	Definitions for chapter (on anti-gambling laws including definitions for gambling, lottery, gift enterprise)
Ky. Rev. Stat. § 528.020	Promoting gambling in the first degree (defined and prohibited as felony)
Ky. Rev. Stat. § 528.030	Promoting gambling in the second degree (defined and prohibited as misdemeanor)

Summary of State Law

Prohibition of Lotteries and Gambling: Kentucky's Constitution as well as its statutory laws prohibit lotteries.[1] A promotion that combines a prize, chance, and consideration is a lottery in Kentucky.[2] Kentucky also has a general prohibition against promoting gambling.[3] Exceptions to the lottery and gambling prohibitions include lotteries operated by the state and certain charitable lotteries.

Contests: Kentucky permits contests as long as the contest does not conflict with anti-gambling laws. If the contest includes an element of consideration, the sponsor must award the contest prize based on skill and not on chance. The Kentucky gambling laws explicitly exempt from the definition of gambling a contest or game in which eligibility to participate is determined by chance and the ultimate winner is determined by skill.[4]

Kentucky authorities do not clearly state which test Kentucky applies when evaluating whether or not chance determines the outcome of a promotion.[5] In a 2010 opinion, the Kentucky Attorney General acknowledged that previous attorney general opinions had evaluated the existence of a lottery by analyzing the nature of chance and the significance of skill versus luck in the selection of a lottery winner.[6] The Kentucky Attorney General then concluded that Kentucky case law is clear that in order to be a "'lottery' the winner must be chosen 'purely by chance'".[7] Although these words suggest that Kentucky applies the pure chance test, there is no conclusive, explicit statement by a Kentucky legal authority that Kentucky uses the pure chance test. Given the wide rejection of the pure chance test in the United States, it is reasonable to interpret the attorney general's use of "purely by chance" as signaling that Kentucky would be inclined to apply the dominant factor doctrine or material element test.

Sweepstakes: Kentucky permits sweepstakes as long as participants do not pay consideration and the sweepstakes does not otherwise conflict with anti-gambling laws. The sweepstakes-playing opportunity can accompany a purchase as long as there is a clearly available and disclosed free alternative method of entry.[8] However, an advertisement of no purchase necessary, without more, is unfair and misleading if the advertisement fails to disclose the free alternatives for obtaining sweepstakes tickets and participating in the promotion.[9] The mere fact that some participants make a purchase "does not, in and of itself, constitute consideration supporting a lottery, where chances to participate in the scheme are also freely given away on a reasonably equal basis without respect to the purchase of merchandise."[10]

Prize Promotion Laws: In its unfair trade practice laws (Title XXIX, Chapter 365, Sections 365.020 *et seq.* of the Kentucky Revised Statute), Kentucky has a provision related to prize promotions. If a company mails to members of the public a product advertisement with the representation that the recipient has won a prize, the advertisement must include prominent, conspicuous, and clearly stated disclosure of exclusions or conditions to receiving the prize.[11]

As part of its telephone solicitation laws (Title XXIX, Chapter 367, Sections 367.461 to 367.46999 of the Kentucky Revised Statute), if a telemarketer represents or implies that a consumer will receive one prize from a selection of multiple prizes, the telemarketer must provide certain disclosures related to the prize award.[12]

Gambling Exceptions for Non-Profits and Other Qualified Organizations

Raffles, Bingo, and Charitable Gaming: Kentucky allows certain charitable organizations to operate raffles, bingos, and other charity games.[13] The organization must use the net proceeds exclusively for purposes consistent with its charitable and civic objectives.[14] Organizations eligible to offer raffles and bingos in Kentucky include non-profit entities organized for charitable, religious, educational, literary, civic, fraternal, or patriotic purposes.[15]

There are statutory and regulatory requirements for the operation of raffles and bingo games.[16] Typically, a charitable gaming operator needs a license issued by the Kentucky Department of Charitable Gaming, a division within the Kentucky Public Protection Cabinet.[17] Exceptions to the licensing requirement include the following:

GAMING RECEIPTS OF NO MORE THAN $25,000. A charitable organization with annual gross receipts for charity gaming activities of no more than $25,000 does not need a license for a bingo, raffle, or other permissible game.[18] However, even with the licensing exemption, the charitable organization must still file with the Department of Charitable Gaming a notice of licensing exemption and financial reports of its gaming activities.[19]

RAFFLES WITH RECEIPTS OF NO MORE THAN $150. Any organization or group of individuals may hold three raffles per year as long as the gross receipts of any single raffle do not exceed $150 and all proceeds from the raffles are distributed to a charitable organization.[20] Organizations qualifying for this license exemption are also exempt from notification and financial reporting requirements.[21]

The charitable gambling laws are in Title XIX, Chapter 238, Sections 238.500 *et seq.* of the Kentucky Revised Statutes. The regulations issued by the Department of Charitable Gambling are in Sections 1:001 *et seq.* of Title 820 of the Kentucky Administrative Regulations. Additional information, application forms, and regulations for charitable gaming are available at the website of the Kentucky Department of Charitable Gaming, 132 Brighton Park Boulevard, Frankfort, KY 40601-3714, website: http://dcg.ky.gov/

Resources

Kentucky offers its attorney general opinions from 1993 through the present available in the opinions portion of the website of the Office of the Attorney General. The Office of the Attorney General office will also mail free of charge copies of opinions requested by reference number.

Endnotes

1. Ky. Const. § 226(3); Ky. Rev. Stat. §§ 528.010(5), 528.020 to 528.030 (2014).
2. Ky. Att'y. Gen. Op. No. 81-146, *1 (Apr. 14, 1981) *citing A.B. Long Music Co. v. Kentucky*, 429 S.W. 2d 391, 394 (Ky. 1968).
3. Ky. Rev. Stat. §§ 528.020 to 528.030 (2014).
4. Ky. Rev. Stat. § 528.010(3) (2014).
5. *See generally*, Section 3.4.3 of this Guide for a discussion of tests used when evaluating whether chance or skill prevails in a promotion combining elements of both.
6. Ky. Att'y Gen. Op. No. 05-003 (March 21, 2005).
7. *Id.* at *7.

8. Ky. Att'y Gen. Op. No. 81-259, *2-3 (July 14, 1981); 2 Ky. Op. Att'y Gen. No. 81-146, *2 (Apr. 14, 1981).
9. Ky. Att'y Gen. Op. No. 81-259, *3 (July 14, 1981).
10. *Id.* at *2.
11. Ky. Rev. Stat. § 365.055 (2014). *See generally,* discussion of state prize promotion laws in Section 7.4.2 of this Guide.
12. Ky. Rev. Stat. § 367.46977 (2014). *See generally,* discussion of state telemarketing laws in Section 7.5.2 of this Guide.
13. Ky. Rev. Stat. § 238.500 (2014).
14. Ky. Rev. Stat. § 238.536 (2014).
15. Ky. Rev. Stat. § 238.505(3) (2014).
16. *See generally,* discussion of bingo and raffles in Section 9.2 of this Guide.
17. Ky. Rev. Stat. § 238.535 (2014).
18. *Id.*
19. Ky. Rev. Stat. § 238.535(2) (2014).
20. Ky. Rev. Stat. § 238.535(10) (2014).
21. *Id.*

Louisiana

State Attorney General Office
Office of the Attorney General
1885 N. Third Street
Baton Rouge, Louisiana 70802
(225) 326-6079
Website: http://www.ag.state.la.us/

Selected State Laws, Regulations, and Constitutional Provisions

Louisiana's anti-gambling laws (Title 14, Chapter 1, Part V, Sections 14-90 *et seq.* of the Louisiana Revised Statute) are in its criminal code. With its trade and commerce laws, Louisiana includes prize promotion laws (Title 51, Chapter 19-A, Section 1721 *et seq.* of the Louisiana Revised Statute). Specific legal provisions frequently quoted in court cases and interpretive opinions related to promotions include the following:

Reference No.	Descriptive Name
LA. Const. art. XII, § 6	Lotteries; Gaming, Gambling or Wagering
LA. Rev. Stat. § 14:90	Gambling (prohibited)
LA. Rev. Stat. § 51:1721	Promotional contests; prerequisites for lawful promotion
LA. Rev. Stat. § 51:1725	Mail solicitations for contest participation

Summary of State Law

Prohibition of Lotteries and Gambling: Louisiana has a general prohibition against conducting lotteries or other forms of gambling.[1] A promotion that combines a prize, chance, and consideration is a lottery in

Louisiana.[2] Exceptions to the lottery and gambling prohibitions include state-operated lotteries and certain charitable lotteries.

Contest: Louisiana permits contests as long as the contest does not conflict with anti-gambling laws. Contests must comply with Louisiana's prize promotion laws, discussed below. If the contest includes an element of consideration, the sponsor must award the contest prize based on skill and not on chance. Research for this Guide did not uncover any authorities indicating which doctrine Louisiana applies when evaluating whether or not chance determines the outcome of a promotion.[3]

Sweepstakes: Louisiana permits sweepstakes as long as participants do not pay consideration and the sweepstakes does not conflict with anti-gambling laws. Sweepstakes must comply with Louisiana's prize promotion laws, discussed below.

Prize Promotion Laws: Louisiana has prize promotion protections with its trade and commerce laws (Title 51, Chapter 19-A, Sections 1721 to 1727 of the Louisiana Revised Statute).

NOTIFICATION OF SWEEPSTAKES AND CONTEST WINNERS. Louisiana requires that winners of certain promotions be announced by one of the following methods: through posting on a printed list, through the use of scratch-off tickets or cards, through the use of pull-tab tickets or cards, or through written or telephone contact with the winner.[4] According to the statute, the winner notification requirement applies to sweepstakes promotions. However, the definition for sweepstakes used by the provision is sufficiently broad to encompass both sweepstakes and contests, regardless of whether participants pay consideration and regardless of whether chance or skill determines the winner. The provision defines sweepstakes promotion as "any game, contest, or other offering where entry . . . whether [free] or through a bargained for exchange, is offered in connection with the promoting or advertising of . . ." a business, product, investment opportunity, charitable contribution or service.[5] The requirement does not apply to promotions open only to the sponsor's employees.[6]

GIFT AS INDUCEMENT TO ATTEND SALES PRESENTATION. If a company makes a prize offer to a consumer that includes an invitation or requirement for the consumer to participate in a sales presentation or promotional program in order to claim the prize, the offer must include a disclosure.[7] A written prize offer requires a written disclosure. A verbal prize offer requires a verbal disclosure. There is specific information that must be included in the disclosure.[8] The provision also lists mandatory and prohibited acts designed to prevent consumer deception such as a requirement for the company to deliver the promised gift and a prohibition on the company charging shipping and handling charges for gifts advertised as free.

OBLIGATION TO AWARD PROMISED PRIZE. If in conjunction with a sales campaign, a company represents that a person has won a prize or gift, the company must deliver the gift within ten days of making the representation without further obligation to the person and without charging the person for shipping or handling costs.[9]

DIRECT MAIL USED WITH CONTEST. When using direct mail to solicit entries in a contest, the contest sponsor must include the odds of winning each prize offered.[10] The statutory provision does not define contest so it is not clear if this provision applies to both chance-based sweepstakes and skill-based contests.[11] Hence, conservative sweepstakes sponsors might choose to comply with this disclosure requirement when using direct mail for a sweepstakes offer in Louisiana.

PRIZE PROMOTION PROVISIONS OF TELEMARKETING LAWS. A company that offers gifts or prizes in conjunction with a telephone sales or advertising campaign may be subject to Louisiana's telephone solicitation laws (Title 45, Chapter 8-C, Sections 821 - 833 of the Louisiana Revised Statute) which contain registration, bonding, and disclosure requirements.[12]

Exceptions for Non-Profits and Other Qualified Organizations

Raffles, Bingo, and Charitable Gaming: Louisiana allows certain non-profit charitable and civic organizations to offer raffles, bingo games, and other charitable gambling games as long as the organization uses the net proceeds for charitable causes.[13] The governing authority of each municipality or parish decides whether charitable raffles, bingo, and keno can take place within the municipality or parish.[14]

There are statutory and regulatory requirements for the operation of raffles and bingo games.[15] Typically, offering a raffle or bingo game in Louisiana requires a license issued by the Division of Charitable Gaming Control.[16] The local government authority in which the bingo or raffle takes place may also choose to impose local licensing requirements and regulations.[17] Each licensee must provide quarterly reports to the local government authority indicating receipts, expenses, winners, prizes awarded, and use of net proceeds.[18]

There are some exemptions to the state licensing and reporting requirements. There are no licensing or reporting requirements for fundraising raffles conducted by associations of elementary and secondary school students and 501(c)(3) conservation organizations.[19] Louisiana also allows any person over twenty-one to conduct a raffle for any purpose provided that the value of the prize does not exceed two hundred fifty dollars.[20]

The Charitable Raffles, Bingo and Keno Licensing Law is codified in Title 4, Chapter 11, Sections 4:701 *et seq.* of the Louisiana Revised Statute. Regulations for charitable gaming are in Title 42 of the Louisiana Administrative Code. Forms, regulations, and additional information are available from the Louisiana Office of Charitable Gaming, 8585 Archives Ave., Ste. 301, Baton Rouge, LA 70809, website: http://www.ocg.louisiana.gov/.

Resources

Louisiana offers a searchable database for its attorney general opinions from 1977 through the present online at http://www.ag.state.la.us/Opinions.aspx

---

Endnotes

1. LA. Rev. Stat. § 14:90 (2013).
2. *Gandolfo v. Louisiana State Racing Com'n*, 78 So.2d 504 (La. 1954).

3. *See generally*, Section 3.4.3 of this Guide for a discussion of tests used when evaluating whether chance or skill prevails in a promotion combining elements of both.

4. LA. Rev. Stat. §51:1726.A. This seems to be an attempt to discourage and prohibit internet cafes and electronic gambling. *See also* LA. Rev. Stat. §51:1727 which limits the type of information that may be displayed on a computer used as part of a sweepstakes promotion.

5. LA. Rev. Stat. §51:1726.B(5) (2013).

6. LA. Rev. Stat. §51:1726.D (2013).

7. LA. Rev. Stat. §51:1721 (2013).

8. LA. Rev. Stat. §51:1721.B (2013). *See generally*, discussion of state prize promotion laws in Section 7.4.2 of this Guide.

9. LA. Rev. Stat. §51:1723 (2013).

10. LA. Rev. Stat. §51:1725 (2013).

11. In another section of these prize promotion laws, LA. Rev. Stat. §51:1726 (Sweepstakes promotions), contest is defined as " . . . any activity that involves competition between one or more persons". However, it is not clear that this same definition for contest is applicable to LA. Rev. Stat. §51:1725 (Mail solicitations for contest participation).

12. LA. Rev. Stat. §§ 45:823, 45:829, and 45:831 (2013). *See* discussion of state telemarketing laws in Section 7.5.2 of this Guide.

13. LA. Rev. Stat. § 4:707.C (2013).

14. LA. Rev. Stat. § 4:706 (2013).

15. See general discussion of bingo and raffles in Section 9.2 of this Guide.

16. LA. Rev. Stat. § 4:707.H (2013).

17. LA. Rev. Stat. §§ 4:706.C and 4:707.B (2013).

18. LA. Rev. Stat. § 4:716 (2013).

19. LA. Rev. Stat. § 4:707.F(2)-(4) (2013).

20. LA. Rev. Stat. § 27:502. While the wording of the statute allows "conduct of a raffle for any purpose" staff at the Louisiana Office of Charitable Gaming indicate that the statutory intent is to allow raffles for civic and humanitarian causes such as payment of funeral expenses and aid for a sick person. While there is no reporting requirement, the person must complete an application for a license exemption to conduct charitable gaming and must complete a raffle accountability form that is subject to audit. Telephone interview with Licensing Coordinator, Louisiana Office of Charitable Gaming (Aug. 5, 2014).

Maine

State Attorney General Office
Office of the Attorney General
6 State House Station
Augusta, Maine 04333
(207) 626-8800
Website: http://www.maine.gov/ag/

Selected State Laws, Regulations, and Constitutional Provisions

Maine's anti-gambling laws (Title 17-A, Chapter 39, Sections 951 *et seq.* of Maine Revised Statute), which are in its criminal code, contain provisions related to promotions. In its laws regulating professions, Maine includes some prize promotion protections (Title 32, Chapter 128, Sections 14701 *et seq.* of Maine Revised Statute). Specific authorities frequently quoted in court cases and interpretive opinions related to promotions include the following:

Reference No.	Descriptive Name
Me. Rev. Stat. tit 17-A, § 952	Definitions (for anti-gambling laws including definitions for contest of chance, gambling, lottery and something of value)
Me. Rev. Stat. tit 17-A, § 953	Aggravated unlawful gambling (prohibited)
Me. Rev. Stat. tit 17-A, § 954	Unlawful gambling (prohibited)

Summary of State Law

Prohibition of Lotteries and Gambling: Maine has a general prohibition against gambling.[1] The gambling prohibition prohibits lotteries which the Maine statute defines as a category of unlawful gambling scheme.[2] A promotion that combines a prize, chance, and consideration is a lottery in Maine.[3]

Contests: Maine permits contests as long as the contest does not conflict with anti-gambling laws. If the contest includes an element of consideration, the sponsor must award the contest prize based on skill and not on chance.

Research for this Guide uncovered no authoritative sources indicating which test Maine applies when evaluating whether or not chance determines the outcome of a promotion.[4] However, Maine law indicates that one element of both a contest of chance and a game of chance is a situation where "chance enters as an element that influences the outcome in a manner that can not be eliminated through the application of skill".[5] The contest of chance and game of chance definitions suggest Maine might apply either the material element test or the dominant factor doctrine.

Sweepstakes: Maine permits sweepstakes as long as participants do not pay consideration and the sweepstakes does not otherwise conflict with anti-gambling laws. In its statutes, Maine uses the term game of chance. Essentially, Maine characterizes a game of chance as a scheme having a prize, chance, and consideration.[6]

IN-PACKAGE SWEEPSTAKES IS PERMISSIBLE. Maine's game of chance regulations provide guidance on the criteria for a permissible in-package sweepstakes promotion. According to Maine regulations, a game promotion is not a game of chance if it meets the following criteria:

- No entry fee, payment, donation, or proof of purchase is required as a condition of entering to win or becoming eligible to receive a prize.
- The game promotion is occasional and of limited duration.
- During the game promotion, there is no increase in the price of the products or services being promoted.
- There is a demand for the products or services independent of the demand for the game promotion and the chance to win its prize.[7]

DOOR PRIZE IS PERMISSIBLE. A door prize giveaway as part of an event is not considered to be a game of chance if the prize giveaway is not promoted in the advertising for the event and is not mentioned on the event ticket.[8]

Prize Promotion Laws: To protect consumers, Maine has laws governing anyone deemed to be a *transient seller of consumer merchandise*.[9] The term includes sellers who sell merchandise via personal or telephone contact and who have no permanent place of business in Maine. The term is relevant to contests and sweepstakes because a transient seller of consumer merchandise includes a seller who incorporates prize give-aways into its direct mail campaigns if recipients of the giveaway offer must pay something in order to receive the prize, even if the recipient's payment is an entrance fee, processing fee or handling charge.[10]

Companies that qualify as transient sellers of consumer merchandise must obtain a license from the Maine Department of Professional and Financial Regulation and pay a security deposit.[11]

Gambling Exceptions for Non-Profits and Other Qualified Organizations

Raffles and Lotteries: Maine allows certain non-profit and civic organizations to conduct raffles. Organizations eligible to offer raffles include agricultural societies; non-profit organizations that are charitable, educational, political, civic, recreational, fraternal, patriotic or religious; volunteer police forces, fire departments or ambulance corps; classes or organizations of a Maine-affiliated educational institution; and state agencies conducting a raffle to benefit fish and wildlife conservation projects.[12]

The operation of the raffle must meet several statutory requirements.[13] To operate a raffle with a prize valued at more than $10,000, the organization must obtain a license from the Maine State Police.[14] No license is required by the eligible organization if the raffle prizes have a value of no more than $10,000.[15]

Maine's Game of Chance laws, in Title 17, Chapter 62, Sections 1831 to 1846 of the Maine Revised Statute, include provisions related to raffles.[16] Game of Chance regulations, issued by the Maine State Police, are codified in 16-222/Chapter 2, Sections 2.01 to 2.05 of the Code of Maine Rules. Additional information and license application forms are available online from the Non-Profit Gaming Licenses section of the Maine State Police website (www.maine.gov/dps/msp/).

Bingo: Maine allows certain non-profit organizations to operate bingo games for charitable purposes. Maine refers to bingo as beano. Qualified organizations able to offer bingo games include volunteer fire departments; agricultural fair associations; and non-profit charitable, educational, political, civic, recreational, fraternal, patriotic, religious or veterans' organizations.[17]

There are statutory and regulatory requirements that bingo game operators must follow.[18] Eligible organizations wishing to offer bingo games must obtain a license from the Maine State Police.[19] Clubs, groups or organizations, offering recreational bingo games to senior citizens on a non-profit basis are exempt from the bingo application and licensing provisions.[20]

Bingo licensees must also file periodic reports with the Maine State Police. The bingo exemption is codified in Title 17, Chapter 13A, Sections 311 to 329 of the Maine Revised Statute. Bingo regulations, issued by the Maine State Police, are codified in 16-222/Chapter 3, Sections 3.01 to 3.09 of the Code of Maine Rules. Additional information, license applications, and copies of the regulations for bingo are available from the Non-Profit Gaming Licenses section of the Maine State Police website (www.maine.gov/dps/msp/).

Resources

Maine offers at least some of its most recent attorney general opinions online at http://www.maine.gov/ag/about/ag_opinions.html.

Endnotes

1. Me. Rev. Stat. tit 17-A, §§ 953 and 954 (2014).
2. Me. Rev. Stat. tit 17-A, § 952(6) (2014).
3. *State v. Bussiere*, 154 A.2d 702, 707 (1959); Me. Rev. Stat. tit. 17-A, § 952(6) (2014).

4. *See generally,* Section 3.4.3 of this Guide for a discussion of tests used when evaluating whether chance or skill prevails in a promotion combining elements of both.

5. Me. Rev. Stat. tit 17-A, § 952.3.C; Me. Rev. Stat. tit 17, § 1831.5.C (2014).

6. Me. Rev. Stat. tit 17, § 1831(5) (2014).

7. 16-222 Me. Code R. § 2.05.

8. Me. Rev. Stat. tit 17, § 1835(6) (2014).

9. Me. Rev. Stat. tit 32, § 14701 *et seq.* (2014).

10. Me. Rev. Stat. tit 32, § 14701(8) (2014).

11. Me. Rev. Stat. tit 32, §§ 14702 and 14708.3 (2014).

12. Me. Rev. Stat. tit 17, § 1837(1) (2014) .

13. See generally, discussion of bingo and raffles in Section 9.2 of this Guide.

14. Me. Rev. Stat. tit 17, § 1837(2) (2014) .

15. Me. Rev. Stat. tit 17, § 1837(1) (2014).

16. Me. Rev. Stat. tit 17, § 1831(13) (2014) defines raffles as a category of *game of chance* so all the game of chance operational requirements apply to raffles. *See* Me. Rev. Stat. tit 17, §§ 1835, 1837 to 1839 (2014), for some specific requirements related to raffles.

17. Me. Rev. Stat. tit 17, § 314 (2014).

18. *See generally,* discussion of bingo and raffles in Section 9.2 of this Guide.

19. Me. Rev. Stat. tit 17, § 312(1) (2014).

20. Me. Rev. Stat. tit 17, § 313-A (2014).

Maryland

State Attorney General Office
Office of the Attorney General
200 St. Paul Place
Baltimore, Maryland 21202
(410) 576-6300
Website: http://www.oag.state.md.us

Selected State Laws, Regulations, and Constitutional Provisions

Maryland's anti-gambling laws (Criminal Law, Title 12, Sections 12-101 *et seq.* of the Maryland Code), which are part of its criminal laws, contain provisions related to promotions. With its commercial laws, Maryland includes its prize promotion protections (Commercial Law, Title 13, Section 13-305 of the Maryland Code) as part of the Consumer Protection Act. Specific Maryland authorities frequently quoted in court cases and interpretive opinions related to promotions include the following:

Reference No.	Descriptive Name
Md. Const. art. III, § 36	(prohibiting lotteries unless operated by the state)
Md. Code, Crim. Law § 12-101	Definitions (for anti-gambling laws including definition for gaming event)
Md. Code, Crim. Law § 12-102	Betting, wagering, gambling, etc. (prohibited as misdemeanor)
Md. Code, Crim. Law § 12-114	Online Fantasy Competition (permissible; state anti-gambling prohibitions do not apply to fantasy sports or other online fantasy competitions)
Md. Code, Crim. Law § 12-203	Sales and draw of lottery devices (prohibited as misdemeanor)

| Md. Code, Crim. Law § 12-212 | Barter, trade, or sale of gift enterprise (prohibited) |

Summary of State Law

Prohibition of Lotteries and Gambling: Maryland's Constitution as well as its statutory laws prohibit lotteries.[1] A promotion that combines a prize, chance, and consideration is a lottery in Maryland.[2] Maryland also has a general prohibition against gambling.[3] Exceptions to the lottery and gambling prohibitions include state-operated lotteries and certain charitable lotteries.

Contests: Maryland permits contests as long as the contest does not conflict with anti-gambling laws. Opinions from the Maryland Attorney General suggest that Maryland applies either the dominant factor doctrine or the material element test[4] when evaluating whether or not chance determines the outcome of a promotion. In an opinion letter assessing whether poker qualifies as a gambling game, the Maryland Attorney General remarked that " . . . poker, despite elements of skill or judgment, is a game of chance that depends in substantial part on the hand a player is dealt and the placement of cards."[5] In other words, poker is a game of chance because chance or luck (*i.e.*, the deal of the cards) plays a substantial role in determining the winners. One can reasonably interpret a substantial part as a material part in support of the material element test or as a dominant part in support of the dominant factor doctrine.

Maryland places prohibitions on charging consideration in a contest; however, the applicability of the prohibitions is unclear. Contest sponsors should exercise caution when charging consideration in Maryland. See further discussion about contests charging consideration below in the discussion of prize promotion laws.

Sweepstakes: Maryland permits sweepstakes as long as participants do not pay consideration and the sweepstakes does not violate anti-gambling laws. Maryland courts have said that the consideration must be money or other thing of value in order for a sweepstakes to be re-characterized as an illegal lottery.[6] This means that a sweepstakes sponsor may require a participant to visit a store, make a phone call, or perform a similar activity.

Such a required act would not qualify as consideration and would not result in the state characterizing the sweepstakes as an illegal lottery.

Sweepstakes must comply with the written disclaimer and other requirements set forth in the Maryland Consumer Protection Act, discussed with prize promotion laws below.

Prize Promotion Laws: Within the Maryland Consumer Protection Act, the state includes prize promotion protections.

GENERAL PROHIBITION ON CONSIDERATION AND MANDATORY PURCHASE. The Maryland Consumer Protection Act prohibits a company from notifying a person that the person has won a prize or is eligible to receive a prize if in order to claim the prize, the person must purchase goods or services, pay any money, or submit to a sales promotion effort.[7] According to the statutory language, this prohibition on consideration applies to "a notification that takes place *by any means*, as part of an advertising scheme or plan".[8] Hence, the prohibition is not limited to offers made by direct mail or even to offers made in writing.

EXCEPTIONS TO THE CONSIDERATION PROHIBITION

Activities to which Consideration Prohibition Does Not Apply. Section 13-305 of the Maryland Consumer Protection Act contains the general prohibition on consideration. The opening part of Section 13-305 contains a list of activities to which Section 13-305 does not apply.[9] The list includes "games of skill competition not involving sales promotion efforts".[10] The statute does not define game of skill or sales promotion efforts. Hence, when a sponsor of a contest charging consideration evaluates this exception, it must rely on other Maryland authorities to provide definitions for game of skill[11] and sales promotion efforts.

Contests with Retail Price Limitation on Prize Offered. Another exception to the consideration prohibition is available to a company sponsoring a non-sweepstakes promotion. To qualify for the exception, the promotion must satisfy certain conditions.[12]

- The sponsor may not require the consumer to pay consideration for participation in the promotion or to submit to a sales promotion effort (*e.g.*, a sales presentation).[13]

- The retail price of the prize offered can not exceed a statutorily-mandated maximum. The applicable retail price maximum varies and is determined on a sliding scale.[14] The permissible maximum retail price of the prize offered increases proportionately with the purchase price of the goods and services to be purchased in order to win the prize. The permissible maximum on the sliding scale is $400.
- The sponsor may not award the prize based on chance.[15]

GIFT AS INDUCEMENT TO ATTEND SALES PRESENTATION. While some states regulate promotions in which an incentive is offered in exchange for attending a seminar or sales presentation, Maryland prohibits such promotions altogether. As noted in the above discussion, the Retail Price Limitation exemption from the general consideration prohibition is not available for promotions that require participants to attend a sales presentation in order to receive the gift.[16]

DISCLOSURE REQUIREMENT. Section 13-305 of the Maryland Consumer Protection Act includes written disclosure requirements for contests, sweepstakes, and other prize promotions.[17] One of the disclosures for both contests and sweepstakes is a statement that in order to receive the prize offered in the promotion, the sponsor may not require the consumer to pay money, purchase goods or services (unless covered by the Retail Price Limitation exception discussed above), or submit to a sales promotion.[18]

APPLICABILITY OF PRIZE PROMOTION LAWS TO CONTESTS CHARGING CONSIDERATION. There is ambiguity concerning whether the Maryland prize promotion laws prohibit contest sponsors from charging consideration. As discussed above, the prize promotion provision begins with a statement that the prize promotion statutory exception does not apply to "games of skill competition not involving sales promotion efforts". Since the statute offers no definitions for games of skill and sales promotion efforts, it is unclear whether this exception applies to all skill-based contests.

One of the disclosure requirements for a contest "not involving the award of prizes by chance" is a statement that in order to receive the offered prize, the participant may not be required to purchase goods or services (unless the Retail Price Limitation exemption applies); pay any money; or submit to a sales promotion effort.[19]

Many interpret this provision to prohibit a contest promoter not falling into the Retail Price Limitation exemption from charging consideration in Maryland. However, there is at least some doubt surrounding this interpretation. This interpretation seems to contradict the opening provision of the prize promotion statutory provision exempting from the provision "games of skill competition not involving sales promotion efforts".

It is unclear the extent to which the general exemption in the opening provision provides an exemption to the written disclaimer requirements for a contest, sweepstakes, or other sales promotion effort not prohibited by Section 13-305. Research for this Guide yielded no resolution for this issue. As a result, contest sponsors charging consideration in Maryland should exercise caution.

Gambling Exceptions for Non-Profits and Other Qualified Organizations

Raffles, Bingo, and Charitable Gaming:

COUNTY PROVISIONS. There are twenty-six counties in Maryland. Each county has its own statutory code section legislating the conduct by non-profits of raffles, bingos, bazaars, and other charitable gaming events. The rules vary significantly from county to county. Some require that the non-profit obtain a permit for some or all gaming events; some do not. The county laws are codified in Title 13 of the Maryland Criminal Law Code.[20]

STATE-WIDE RAFFLE EXEMPTIONS. In addition to the county provisions, Maryland has some state-wide anti-gambling exceptions for non-profits. When applicable, the state-wide provisions override the county provisions. That means a non-profit may offer a game covered by the following state-wide exemptions even if the county laws have conflicting provisions.

- A charitable organization may conduct up to two raffles per calendar year for which the prize is real property provided that the charitable organization holds title to the property and the raffle proceeds are for the exclusive benefit of the charitable organization.[21]
- A political committee or candidate may hold a raffle where the prize is cash or merchandise as long as the cost for a raffle ticket is no

more than five dollars and participants can not purchase more than fifty dollars in tickets.[22]

OTHER REQUIREMENTS FOR CHARITABLE PROMOTIONS. There are certain disclosures required if, in connection with a written charitable solicitation, a person offers a contest, sweepstakes, or other promotion.[23] Also, as part of an advertising plan in connection with a charitable solicitation, one may not notify a person that the person has won a prize, has received an award, or has been chosen or is eligible to receive a thing of value if the person is required to buy goods or services, pay money, or submit to a promotion.[24] This disclosure and prohibition do not apply to a raffle or other game of chance that a charitable organization holds in a county under the laws applicable to the county.

Resources

Maryland offers a searchable database for its attorney general opinions from 1993 through the present in the Opinions portion of the website of the Office of the Attorney General.

Endnotes

1. Md. Const. art. III, § 36; Md. Code, Crim. Law § 12-203 (2013).
2. *Mid-Atlantic Coca-Cola Bottling Co. v. Chen, Walsh & Tecler*, 460 A.2d 44, 47 (1983).
3. Md. Code, Crim. Law § 12-102 (2013).
4. *See generally*, Section 3.4.3 of this Guide for a discussion of tests used when evaluating whether chance or skill prevails in a promotion combining elements of both.
5. Md. Att'y. Gen. Op. No. 91-64, 65 (Mar. 2, 2006).
6. *Mid-Atlantic Coca-Cola Bottling Co., supra* note 2.
7. Md. Code, Com. Law § 13-305(b) (2013).
8. Md. Code, Com. Law § 13-305(b) (2013) (emphasis added).
9. Md. Code, Com. Law § 13-305(a) (2013).
10. Md. Code, Com. Law § 13-305(a)(4) (2013).
11. *See generally*, Md. Att'y. Gen. Op. No. 91-64 (Mar. 2, 2006).
12. Md. Code, Com. Law § 13-305(c) (2013).
13. Md. Code, Com. Law § 13-305(d) (2013).

14. Md. Code, Com. Law § 13-305(c) (2013).
15. Md. Code, Com. Law § 13-305(d) (2013).
16. *See* Md. Code, Com. Law § 13-305(b) to (d) (2013).
17. Md. Code, Com. Law § 13-305(g) and (h) (2013). *See also,* the discussion of prize notice disclosures in Section 7.4.2 of this Guide.
18. Md. Code, Com. Law §§ 13-305(g)(7) and 13-305(h)(3) (2013).
19. Md. Code, Com. Law § 13-305(h) (2013).
20. Allegany County, Md. Code, Crim. Law § 13-301 *et seq.* (2013); Anne Arundel County, Md. Code, Crim. Law § 13-401 *et seq.* (2013); Baltimore City, Md. Code, Crim. Law § 13-501 *et seq.* (2013); Baltimore County, Md. Code, Crim. Law §§ 13-601 *et seq.* (2013); Carroll County, Md. Code, Crim. Law § 13-901 *et seq.* (2013); Cecil County, Md. Code, Crim. Law § 13-1001 *et seq.* (2013); Charles County, Md. Code, Crim. Law § 13-1101 *et seq.* (2013); Dorchester County, Md. Code, Crim. Law § 13-1201 *et seq.* (2013); Frederick County, Md. Code, Crim. Law § 13-1301 *et seq.* (2013).; Garrett County, Md. Code, Crim. Law § 13-1401 *et seq.* (2013); Harford County, Md. Code, Crim. Law § 13-1501 *et seq.* (2013); Kent County, Md. Code, Crim. Law § 13-1701 *et seq.* (2013); Montgomery County, Md. Code, Crim. Law § 13-1801 *et seq.* (2013); Prince George's County, Md. Code, Crim. Law § 13-1901 *et seq.* (2013); Queen Anne's County, Md. Code, Crim. Law § 13-2001 *et seq.* (2013); St. Mary's County, Md. Code, Crim. Law § 2101 *et seq.* (2013); Wicomico County, Md. Code, Crim. Law § 2503 *et seq.* (2013); Worcester County Md. Code, Crim. Law § 13-2619 *et seq.* (2013). Except as otherwise provided in Title 13, Md. Code, Crim. Law § 201 *et seq.* applies to Allegany County, Anne Arundel County, Baltimore County, Calvert County, Caroline County, Carroll County, Dorchester County, Frederick County, Garrett County, Howard County, Prince George's County, St. Mary's County, Somerset County, Talbot County; and Washington County.
21. Md. Code, Crim. Law § 12-106(a) (2013).
22. Md. Code, Crim. Law § 12-106(b) (2013).
23. Md. Code, Bus. Reg. § 6-503 (2013).
24. Md. Code, Bus. Reg. § 6-618 (2013).

Massachusetts

State Attorney General Office
Office of the Attorney General
One Ashburton Place
Boston, Massachusetts 02108 -1518
(617) 727-2200
Website: www.mass.gov/ag

Selected State Laws, Regulations, and Constitutional Provisions

Massachusetts has anti-lottery laws (Part IV, Title I, Chapter 271, Sections 1 *et seq.* of the General Laws of Massachusetts) in the criminal law chapter titled Crimes Against Public Policy. Specific authorities frequently quoted in court cases and interpretive opinions related to promotions include the following:

Reference No.	Descriptive Name
Mass. Gen. Laws ch. 271, § 7	Lotteries; disposal of property by chance (prohibited)
Mass. Gen. Laws ch. 271, § 9	Lottery tickets; sale, or possession (prohibited)
Mass. Gen. Laws ch. 271, § 11	Lottery tickets; advertising
Mass. Gen. Laws ch. 271, § 16A	Organizing or promoting gambling facilities or services
Mass. Gen. Laws ch. 271, § 17	Place for registering bets or dealing in pools; owner or occupant; custodian or depository
Mass. Gen. Laws ch. 271, § 29	Sale, exchange or disposition of property; misrepresentation (offering award to induce purchase of separate, unrelated item prohibited)

Mass. Regs. Code
tit. 940, § 30.00

Illegal Lotteries, Sweepstakes and *De Facto*
Gambling Establishments

Summary of State Law

Prohibition of Lotteries and Gambling: Massachusetts statutory laws prohibit lotteries.[1] A promotion that combines a prize, chance, and consideration is a lottery in Massachusetts.[2] Massachusetts also has a general prohibition against gambling.[3] Exceptions to the lottery and gambling prohibitions include state-operated lotteries and certain charitable lotteries.

Contests: Massachusetts permits contests as long as the contest does not conflict with anti-lottery and anti-gambling laws. If the contest includes an element of consideration, the sponsor must award the contest prize based on skill and not on chance. Massachusetts applies the dominant factor doctrine[4] when evaluating whether or not chance determines the outcome of a promotion.[5]

One provision of the Massachusetts' anti-lottery laws prohibits anyone from registering bets, or buying or selling pools, on the result of poker hands, games or tournaments.[6] The Massachusetts Attorney General has interpreted this statutory provision as preventing anyone—even a qualifying non-profit organization—from operating a tournament or contest in which players or spectators bet money or anything else of value on hands, or in which prizes come from a pool of money or something else of value based on the number of people who play, or the amount of proceeds collected.[7]

Sweepstakes: Massachusetts permits sweepstakes as long as participants do not pay consideration and the sweepstakes does not violate anti-lottery and anti-gambling laws. The Massachusetts' Attorney General has indicated that consideration can be an entry fee, a required charitable contribution, or a payment of money or anything else of value.[8]

Massachusetts does allow sponsors to distribute sweepstakes-playing opportunities with the sponsors' sale of products and services. Like most states, Massachusetts requires that the sweepstakes promotion be a vehicle to sell the sponsor's legitimate good or service. In its regulations, Massachusetts indicates that when a promotion combines both a chance to win a prize and the sale or purported sale of a good or service, it is an unfair and deceptive act if the promotion's gambling purpose is stronger than the promotion's purpose to sell bona fide goods or services.[9] The regulation lists specific criteria which Massachusetts examines to determine whether the gambling purpose is stronger than the promotional purpose.[10]

The criteria used by Massachusetts are similar to the criteria used by other states when evaluating whether or not a sweepstakes is a valid sweepstakes or an illegal lottery. Section 3.6.2 of this Guide contains a discussion of how incidental product purchases can invalidate an in-package sweepstakes.

Gambling Exceptions for Non-Profits and Other Qualified Organizations

Raffles: Massachusetts anti-gambling and anti-lottery laws include a provision that allows certain non-profit organizations to conduct raffles. The organization must use raffle proceeds for educational, charitable, religious, fraternal or civic purposes or for veterans' benefits.[11] Organizations eligible to offer raffles consist of a veterans' organization; a church or religious organization; a fraternal or fraternal benefit society; an educational or charitable organization; a civic or service club or organization; and other organizations operated exclusively for pleasure, recreation and other non-profit purposes.[12]

The operation of the raffle must meet several statutory and regulatory requirements.[13] Eligible organizations wishing to conduct raffles must obtain a permit from the clerk of the city or town in which the raffle drawing takes place.[14] The non-profit raffle sponsor must also file with the city clerk an annual report of its raffle receipts, costs, winners, and charitable uses of the receipts.[15] Within ten days after each raffle, the non-profit raffle sponsor must also file a return with the state lottery commission and pay a tax of five per cent of the gross proceeds.[16]

The statutory provision permitting raffles is named Raffles and bazaars; conduct by certain organizations and is codified at Part IV, Title I, Chapter 271, Section 7A of the General Laws of Massachusetts. Regulations governing raffles are in Title 940, Sections 12.01 et seq. and 13.01 *et seq.* of the Massachusetts Code of Regulations.

Bingo: Massachusetts allows a variety of non-profit organizations to offer bingo games, which the statute refers to as beano, in a city or town which has voted to allow it. Organizations eligible to offer bingo include fraternal organizations, religious organization, veterans' organization, volunteer, non-profit fire company, and non-profit athletic associations.

The operation of the bingo game must meet several statutory and regulatory requirements.[17] An organization offering bingo must obtain a license from the Massachusetts State Lottery Commission[18], use all bingo profits for charitable, religious or educational purposes[19], and pay a tax equal to five percent of the gross bingo proceeds[20]. Senior citizens' organizations may operate recreational bingo games without a license and do not need to pay the bingo tax; however, they must still obtain an identification number from the state lottery commission.[21]

The bingo exemption is codified in Part I, Title II, Chapter 10, Sections 38 to 39A of the Massachusetts General Laws. Bingo regulations, issued by the Massachusetts' State Lottery Commission, are codified at Title 961, Sections 3.0 *et seq.* of the Massachusetts Code of Regulations. Additional information, regulations, registration and report forms for non-profit bingo are available through the Charitable Gaming Division of the State Lottery Commission, 60 Columbian Street, Braintree, MA 02184, (781) 849-5555, website: http://www.masslottery.com/games/charitable-games/.

Resources

Massachusetts makes a few attorney general opinions available in the Government Resources portion of the website of the Office of the Attorney General.

Endnotes

1. Mass. Gen. Laws ch. 271, § 7 (2014).
2. *Mobil Oil Corp. v. Att'y Gen.*, 280 N.E.2d 406, 411 (1972).
3. Mass. Gen. Laws ch. 271, § 16A (2014).
4. *See generally*, Section 3.4.3 of this Guide for a discussion of tests used when evaluating whether chance or skill prevails in a promotion combining elements of both.

5. Office of Att'y Gen. of Mass., *Advisory on Poker Tournaments* (June 30, 2005), http://www.mass.gov/ago/doing-business-in-massachusetts/public-charities-or-not-for-profits/soliciting-funds/raffles-and-other-gaming-activity/poker-advisory.html (last visited Sept. 17, 2014), *citing Commonwealth v. Plissner, 295 Mass. 457, 463-64 (1936).*

6. Mass. Gen. Laws ch. 271, § 17 (2014).

7. *Advisory on Poker Tournaments, supra* note 5.

8. *Id.*

9. Mass. Regs. Code tit. 940, § 30.04.

10. Mass. Regs. Code tit. 940, § 30.05.

11. Mass. Gen. Laws ch. 271, §7A (2014).

12. *Id.*

13. *See generally,* discussion of bingo and raffles in Section 9.2 of this Guide.

14. Mass. Gen. Laws ch. 271, §7A (2014).

15. *Id.*

16. *Id.*

17. *See generally,* discussion of bingo and raffles in Section 9.2 of this Guide.

18. Mass. Gen. Laws ch. 10, § 38 (2014).

19. *Id.*

20. Mass. Gen. Laws ch. 10, § 39 (2014).

21. Mass. Gen. Laws ch. 10, § 38 (2014).

Michigan

Attorney General Office
Office of the Attorney General
G. Mennen Williams Building, 7th Floor
525 W. Ottawa St.
P.O. Box 30212
Lansing, Michigan 48909
Website: http://www.michigan.gov/ag/

Selected State Laws, Regulations, and Constitutional Provisions

In its penal code, Michigan has specific anti-lottery laws (Chapter 750, Sections 750.372 *et seq.* of the Michigan Compiled Laws) as well as more general anti-gambling laws (Chapter 750, Sections 750.301 *et seq.* of the Michigan Compiled Laws). Both sets of laws contain provisions related to promotions. Specific Michigan legal authorities frequently cited in court cases and interpretive opinions related to promotions include the following:

Reference No.	Descriptive Name
Mich. Const., art IV, § 41	Lotteries
Mich. Comp. Laws § 750.301	Accepting money or valuable thing contingent on uncertain event (prohibited as misdemeanor)
Mich. Comp. Laws § 750.372	Lotteries and gift enterprises; prohibited acts; applicability of subsection (1); "promotional activity" defined; violation as misdemeanor; penalty

| Mich. Comp. Laws § 750.372a | "Game promotion" defined; force or coercion to purchase, presumption; predetermining identity of one entitled to prize; disclosing description, amount, number of prizes; penalty, misdemeanor. |
| Mich. Comp. Laws § 750.373 | Game promotion; tickets; selling, possession, exchange (selling lottery tickets prohibited as misdemeanor) |

Summary of State Law

Prohibition of Lotteries and Gambling: Michigan's Constitution and its statutory laws prohibit lotteries.[1] Michigan also has general prohibitions against gambling.[2] Lotteries authorized by the legislature are permissible exceptions to the lottery and gambling prohibitions.

Michigan's statute does not include a definition for lottery. Court opinions indicate that Michigan is willing to go beyond the commonly accepted definition of lottery as a scheme that combines a prize, chance, and consideration. The absence of one of those elements does not prevent Michigan from characterizing a promotion as an illegal lottery if the promotion otherwise meets the commonly understood definition of lottery.[3] Michigan has applied this principle in expanding the range of activities that qualify as consideration.[4]

Contests: Michigan permits contests as long as the contest does not conflict with anti-gambling laws. If the contest includes an element of consideration, the sponsor must award the contest prize based on skill and not on chance.

Court opinions suggest that Michigan applies the dominant factor doctrine[5] when evaluating whether or not chance determines the outcome of a promotion. In *Att'y Gen. v. PowerPick Club of Michigan*, 783 N.W.2d 515 (Mich. Ct. App. 2010), a Michigan court decided that a promotion was determined by chance even though the promotion mixed elements of chance and skill since "the element of skill as compared with the element of chance is slight."[6]

Sweepstakes: Michigan permits sweepstakes as long as participants do not pay consideration and the sweepstakes does not otherwise violate anti-gambling laws. Sweepstakes must also comply with the game promotion disclosure laws[7] codified with the anti-lottery laws, discussed below in the Prize Promotion Laws portion of this Michigan State Summary.

MICHIGAN'S BROADER VIEW OF CONSIDERATION. Michigan takes a broader view of what constitutes consideration than other states do. If participants are required to be present at a place of business for a chance to win a prize, Michigan labels that requirement as consideration that can turn a sweepstakes into an illegal lottery.[8]

In Michigan, consideration in a promotion can exist if the promotion yields an indirect benefit to the sponsor. For example, in some cases involving drawings at movie theaters, Michigan found consideration. In those cases, often referred to as bank night cases, a theater distributed coupon tickets to its customers. At a specified time during the evening, the theater randomly drew from the tickets to select a winner of a cash prize. Even though patrons received the tickets for free, the Michigan Supreme Court found consideration in the drawing because the fact that the theater distributed prizes attracted more people and the theater reaped a direct financial benefit from their attendance.[9]

Although these bank night cases are from the 1930s, more recent opinions indicate Michigan courts' continued willingness to follow this broader view of consideration.[10] The 2010 decision, *PowerPick Club of Michigan*, involved PowerPick, a company that organized lottery pools. PowerPick offered games of chance in its newsletter, giving a prize to the first three randomly drawn tickets that correctly answer a question. For example, one question asked readers to name the number of hidden Shamrocks located within the newsletter. Although the periodic drawings were available at no additional cost to the newsletter's readers, a Michigan court found that the drawings were used to induce people to become or to remain PowerPick customers and that, therefore, the drawings attracted customers that PowerPick otherwise might not have had. Thus, PowerPick profited from the drawing and the drawing was deemed to have consideration.

STATUTORY EXCEPTION FOR PROMOTIONAL SWEEPSTAKES. Michigan law offers an explicit statutory exception to the lottery prohibition for promotional activities that a company uses to promote its products or services and that are occasional and ancillary to the company's primary business.[11] The activity is not occasional and ancillary if the activity is conducted consistently and is a part of the company's primary business.[12] Specifically, the exception requires that the product or service that comes with the chance to win not be sold for a price substantially more than its fair market value.[13] In essence, this means that a company can distribute chances to win along with products or services it sells. A Michigan court has held that the exception applies only if the promotional activity promotes only one business or the products of that business; the exception does not apply if the activity promotes several businesses.[14]

REGULATION OF GAME PROMOTIONS. Michigan has laws in its penal code addressing game promotions, defined as " . . . any game or contest in which the elements of chance and prize are present but in which the element of consideration is not present."[15] No lessee, agent or franchise dealer may be forced or coerced into purchasing game promotions. Game promotion sponsors must provide participants with the following disclosures:

- the geographic area or number of outlets in which the game promotion is proposed to be conducted,
- an accurate description of each type of prize to be made available,
- the minimum number and minimum amount of cash prizes to be made available, and
- the minimum number of each other type of prize to be made available.[16]

The disclosures must appear on a poster for games taking place within a retail outlet. If the game promotion does not take place in a retail outlet, the disclosures must appear on any card, promotional pieces, entry blanks or other paraphernalia used for the game.

Prize Promotion Laws: As part of its consumer protection laws, Michigan prohibits offering a consumer a prize as an inducement to attend a sales presentation unless the prize offer comes with a written disclosure statement.[17]

Gambling Exceptions for Non-Profits and Other Qualified Organizations

Raffle, Bingo and Charitable Games: The Michigan Bingo Act allows certain non-profit organizations to conduct raffles, bingo games, and other charitable gaming events. Eligible organizations include non-profit, federally tax-exempt religious, educational, service, senior citizens, fraternal, or veterans' organizations.[18] Michigan explicitly excludes candidate and political committees from participating in charitable gaming.[19] The organization must devote the net proceeds exclusively to uses consistent with its lawful purposes.[20]

Eligible organizations wishing to offer raffles or bingo games must obtain a license from the bureau of state lottery.[21] There are some exemptions to the need for a license. There is no license requirement for recreational bingo conducted by a senior citizens club, group, or home consisting of members who are 60 years of age or older.[22] There is no license requirement for a qualified organization sponsoring a single gathering and conducting a raffle during the event as long as there is no sale of tickets prior to the event and the total aggregate retail value of the raffle prize is no more than one hundred dollars.[23]

The operation of the games must meet several statutory and regulatory requirements.[24] Bingo and raffle licensees must file periodic financial statements, maintain records, and make those records available for state inspection upon request.[25] The Bingo Act is codified in Chapter 432, Sections 432.101 to 432.120 of the Michigan Compiled Laws. Bingo and raffle regulations, issued by the Charitable Gaming Division of the Bureau of State Lottery are codified as Rules 432.21101 *et seq.* of the Michigan Administrative Code.

Additional information, registration and report forms are available online from the Charitable Gaming Division, c/o Fund Accounting, 101 E. Hillsdale, Box 30023, Lansing, MI 48909, (517) 335-5780, www.michigan.gov/cg.

Resources

Michigan offers a searchable database for its attorney general opinions from 1963 through the present in the Opinions portion of the website of the Michigan Office of the Attorney General.

Endnotes

1. Mich. Const., art IV, § 41; Mich. Comp. Laws § 750.372 (2014).
2. *See e.g.*, Mich. Comp. Laws §§ 750.301, 750.314, and 750.315 (2014).
3. *See e.g., Att'y Gen. v. PowerPick Club of Michigan*, 783 N.W.2d 515, 528 (Mich. Ct. App. 2010).
4. *Id.*
5. *See generally*, Section 3.4.3 of this Guide for a discussion of tests used when evaluating whether chance or skill prevails in a promotion combining elements of both.
6. *PowerPick Club of Michigan*, 783 N.W.2d at 530-531, *citing United-Detroit Theaters v. Colonial Theatrical Enterprise, Inc.*, 273 N.W. 756 (Mich. 1937).
7. Mich. Comp. Laws § 750.372a (2014).
8. *See e.g.*, Mich. Gaming Control Board, Guide: Internet Sweepstakes Cafes, Internet Cafes, and Cyber Cafes, http://www.michigan.gov/documents/mgcb/ INTERNET_CAFE_GUIDE-final_372838_7.pdf, sidebar (last visited Oct. 19, 2014).
9. *Sproat-Temple Theatre Corp. v. Colonial Theatrical Enterprise*, 267 N.W. 602 (1936). *See* similar conclusion in *United-Detroit Theaters Corp. v. Colonial Theatrical Enterprise, Inc.*, 273 N.W. 756 (1937).
10. *See generally*, Mich. Att'y Gen. Op. No. 6755 (March 29, 1993); Mich. Att'y Gen. Op. No. 5692 (Apr. 23, 1980).
11. Mich. Comp. Laws § 750.372(2) (2014).
12. *Face Trading Inc. v. Dept. of Consumer and Industry Services & Liquor Control Comm.*, 717 N.W.2d 377, 389 (Mich. Ct. App. 2006).
13. Mich. Comp. Laws § 750.372(2) (2014).
14. *Face Trading Inc. v. Dept. of Consumer and Industry Services & Liquor Control Comm.*, supra, note 12.
15. Mich. Comp. Laws § 750.372a(a) (2014).
16. Mich. Comp. Laws § 750.372a(d) (2014).
17. Mich. Comp. Laws § 445.903(1)(ff) (2014). *See generally*, discussion of state prize promotion laws in Section 7.4.2 of this Guide.

18. Mich. Comp. Laws § 432.103(g) (2014). A component of the military or the Michigan national guard may also conduct raffles.
19. Mich. Comp. Laws § 432.103(h) (2014).
20. Mich. Comp. Laws § 432.109 (2014).
21. Mich. Comp. Laws § 432.104 (2014).
22. Mich. Comp. Laws § 432.105(a) (2014).
23. Mich. Comp. Laws § 432.105d (2014).
24. *See generally*, discussion of bingo and raffles in Section 9.2 of this Guide.
25. Mich. Comp. Laws § 432.114 (2014).

Minnesota

State Attorney General Office
Minnesota Attorney General Office
1400 Bremer Tower
445 Minnesota Street
St. Paul, Minnesota 55101
(651) 296-3353
Website: http://www.ag.state.mn.us/

Selected State Laws, Regulations, and Constitutional Provisions

As part of its criminal code, Minnesota has anti-gambling laws (Chapter 609, Sections 609.75 to 609.763 of the Minnesota Statute) which contain provisions related to promotions. Specific Minnesota authorities frequently quoted in court cases and interpretive opinions related to promotions include the following:

Reference No.	Descriptive Name
Minn. Stat. § 609.75	Definitions (for anti-gambling laws including definition for lottery and bet)
Minn. Stat. § 609.755	Acts of or relating to gambling (prohibited as misdemeanor)
Minn. Stat. § 609.76	Other acts related to gambling

Summary of State Law

Prohibition of Lotteries and Gambling: Minnesota prohibits selling or distributing chances to play in a lottery and also prohibits distributing information about lotteries.[1] A promotion that combines a prize, chance, and consideration is a lottery in Minnesota.[2] Minnesota implements its anti-gambling laws by prohibiting specific activities related to gambling including a prohibition on making bets.[3] Exceptions to the lottery and gambling prohibitions include state-operated lotteries and certain charitable lotteries.

Contests: Minnesota permits contests as long as the contest does not conflict with anti-gambling laws. If the contest includes an element of consideration, the sponsor must award the contest prize based on skill and not on chance. Contests requiring payment of money must comply with Minnesota's prize notice and solicitation laws.[4] Opinions issued by the Minnesota Attorney General indicate that Minnesota applies the dominant factor doctrine[5] when evaluating whether or not chance determines the outcome of a promotion.[6]

Sweepstakes: Minnesota permits sweepstakes as long as participants do not pay consideration and the sweepstakes does not otherwise conflict with anti-gambling laws. Minnesota anti-gambling laws expressly state that in-package chance promotions are not lotteries, provided that the promotion satisfies certain requirements.[7] An in-package chance promotion is a sweepstakes opportunity included with purchased products.[8] For the lottery exclusion to apply to the in-package sweepstakes promotion, the promotion must be coupled with a legitimate, valuable product. The sponsor must meet other conditions including the following:

- there is a free method of entry available through the retailer, by toll-free phone call, or by mail;
- the label of the promotional packaging and any advertising clearly states the methods of play and the sweepstakes end date;
- the sponsor provides the retailer with an adequate number of free play forms;
- the sponsor does not misrepresent chances of winning;
- the sponsor randomly distributes all game pieces and retains records of the random distribution for at least one year;
- the sponsor randomly awards all prizes, if game pieces are not used; and
- the sponsor maintains name and address information for winners of prizes over $100 and makes those records available to a Minnesota state agency upon request.[9]

The criteria—particularly the requirements for a free method of entry, clear communication of play rules, and no misrepresentation of odds—provide helpful guidance for all sweepstakes sponsors operating in Minnesota, regardless of whether the sponsor is attempting to qualify for the in-package promotion exception.

Prize Promotion Laws: Minnesota's prize promotion law is the Prize Notices and Solicitations statute codified with the state's consumer protection laws.[10] The law applies to any promotions that require payment of money.

PRIZE OFFERINGS REQUIRING PAYMENT OF MONEY REQUIRE WRITTEN DISCLOSURE. If a company requires a person in Minnesota to pay money as a condition of receiving, competing for, or obtaining information about a prize, the sponsor must provide the person with a written disclosure statement, referred to as a prize notice.[11] There is specific information that must be included in the prize notice and specific requirements for the placement, font, and wording of the required disclosures.[12]

OBLIGATION TO AWARD PROMISED PRIZE. If in conjunction with a prize promotion requiring money from a person, a company represents to the person that the person has won a prize, the company must deliver to the person one of the following within thirty days of the representation:

- the promised prize,
- a voucher for the promised prize,
- an alternate prize of equal or greater value, or
- a monetary payment equal to the retail value of the promised prize.[13]

Gambling Exceptions for Non-Profits and Other Qualified Organizations

Raffles, Bingo and Charitable Gambling: Minnesota allows certain non-profit organizations to conduct bingos, raffles, and other forms of charitable gambling.[14] The organizations must spend gross gaming profits on statutorily designated permissible expenses and on charitable and civic purposes.[15] Organizations eligible to conduct charitable gambling include fraternal, religious, veterans, and other non-profit organizations.[16]

The operation of the games must meet several statutory and regulatory requirements.[17] In most instances, an eligible organization must obtain a license issued by the Minnesota Gambling Control Board prior to engaging in charitable gambling.[18] Organizations must also maintain records and file periodic reports of receipts, expenses, profits, and expenditure of profits from lawful gambling.[19]

The exemption for charitable gambling is codified in Chapter 349, Section 349.11 *et seq.* of the Minnesota Statute. Regulations for charitable gambling, issued by the Minnesota Gambling Control Board, are in Sections 7861.0210 of the Minnesota Rules. Additional licensing information, forms, and regulations are available from the Minnesota Gambling Control Board, 1711 West County Road B, Suite 300 South, Roseville, Minnesota 55113, (651) 639-4000, website: http://www.gcb.state.mn.us/

EXCEPTIONS TO LICENSING REQUIREMENT. Minnesota allows some forms of charitable and lawful gambling to occur without a license and/or with greatly relaxed regulatory requirements. Raffles may be conducted by a qualified organization without a license if the value of all raffle prizes awarded by the organization in a calendar year does not exceed $1,500.[20] Qualified non-profit organizations may conduct bingo without a license if the bingo game is at a fair or civic organization or if the organization conducts fewer than four bingo games in a calendar year.[21] There are no licensing, reporting, or operational requirements for organizations housing or serving senior citizens to offer bingo games as long as the prize value does not exceed certain amounts.[22] There are also relaxed licensing and reporting requirements for school districts and related non-profit organizations conducting raffles at a school-district-sponsored high school event if the proceeds are used to send event participants to high school activities held at other locations.[23]

Resources

Minnesota offers a searchable database for its attorney general opinions from 1993 to the present online in the resources section of the Minnesota Attorney General's website at http://www.ag.state.mn.us/resources/resourcesattgenopinion.asp

Endnotes

1. Minn. Stat. § 609.755(2) and (3) (2014).
2. Minn. Stat. § 609.75, subd. 1 (a) (2014). *See also Minnesota Souvenir Milkcaps v. Minnesota*, 687 N.W.2d 400, 402-403 (Minn. Ct. App. 2004).
3. Minn. Stat. § 609.755(1) (2014).
4. Minn. Stat. § 325F.755 (2014).
5. *See generally*, Section 3.4.3 of this Guide for a discussion of tests used when evaluating whether chance or skill prevails in a promotion combining elements of both.
6. Minn. Att'y Gen. Op. No. 510-C-3 (Sept. 24, 1947).
7. Minn. Stat. § 609.75, subd. 1(b) (2014).
8. *See generally*, discussion of in-package sweepstake promotions included in Section 3.6 of this Guide
9. Minn. Stat. § 609.75, subd. 1(b) (2014).
10. Minn. Stat. § 325F.755 (2014).
11. *Id.*
12. Minn. Stat. § 325F.755, subd. 2(b) and (c) (2014). *See generally*, discussion of state prize promotion laws in Section 7.4.2 of this Guide.
13. Minn. Stat. § 325F.755, subd. 3 (2014).
14. Minn. Stat. § 349.16 (2014).
15. Minn. Stat. § § 349.12, subd. 3a & 25, 349.15 (2014).
16. Minn. Stat. § 349.12(28) (2014).
17. *See generally*, discussion of bingo and raffles in Section 9.2 of this Guide.
18. Minn. Stat. § 349.16 (2014).
19. Minn. Stat. § 349.19 (2014).
20. Minn. Stat. § 349.166 (2014).
21. *Id.*
22. *Id.*
23. Minn. Stat. § 609.761, subd. 5 (2014).

Mississippi

State Attorney General Office
Mississippi Attorney General's Office
Walter Sillers Building
550 High Street, Suite 1200
Jackson, Mississippi 39201
(601) 359-3680
Website: http://www.ago.state.ms.us

Selected State Laws, Regulations, and Constitutional Provisions

Mississippi's crime code includes a chapter on gambling and lotteries (Title 97, Chapter 33, Sections 97-33-1 *et seq.* of the Mississippi Code). Specific Mississippi authorities frequently quoted in court cases and interpretive opinions related to promotions include the following:

Reference No.	Descriptive Name
Miss. Code § 97-33-1	Betting, gaming or wagering; exception from prohibition; penalty
Miss. Code § 97-33-31	Lotteries; penalty for putting on
Miss. Code § 97-33-33	Lotteries; advertising prohibited
Miss. Code § 97-33-39	Lotteries; sale of tickets (prohibited)
Miss. Code § 97-33-41	Lotteries; buying tickets in state prohibited
Miss. Code § 97-33-47	Lotteries; acting as agent for (prohibited)
Miss. Code § 97-33-49	Raffles (prohibited except for non-profit raffles)

Summary of State Law

Prohibition of Lotteries and Gambling: Mississippi's statutory laws include several prohibitions against operating, advertising, and buying lottery tickets.[1] A promotion that combines a prize, chance, and consideration is a lottery in Mississippi.[2] Mississippi also has a general prohibition against gambling.[3] Exceptions to the lottery and gambling prohibitions include state-operated lotteries and certain charitable lotteries.

Contests: Mississippi permits contests as long as the contest does not conflict with anti-gambling laws. If the contest includes an element of consideration, the sponsor must award the contest prize based on skill and not on chance.

The Mississippi statute suggests that Mississippi applies the dominant factor doctrine[4] when evaluating whether or not chance determines the outcome of a promotion. When defining lottery, the Mississippi legislature indicated that a lottery consists of players paying something of value for a chance to win where the winner is "determined by a drawing or similar selection method *based predominately upon the element of chance* or random selection rather than upon the skill or judgment of the player or players".[5]

Sweepstakes: Mississippi permits sweepstakes as long as participants do not pay consideration and the sweepstakes does not conflict with anti-gambling laws. Mississippi indicates it closely scrutinizes alternative methods of entry (AMOE) to ensure that the AMOE effectively removes consideration.[6] In that regard, the Mississippi Attorney General has indicated that when chances to win are distributed with a product for sale, the ability to obtain via mail a free chance to play is relevant to, but is not conclusive to the question of whether there is consideration.[7] Sponsors do not have to make free entry available at the location at which the promotion is held and can instead require people to mail in a request for a free method of entry.[8]

Gambling Exceptions for Non-Profits and Other Qualified Organizations

Raffles and Lotteries: Mississippi allows non-profit civic, educational, wildlife conservation or religious organizations to offer raffles.[9] The statute provides that all raffle proceeds must go to the non-profit organization.[10] Otherwise, Mississippi does not provide great detail on how the non-profit organization must use the proceeds. According to an informal inquiry to the state's charitable gaming division, there are no license or reporting requirements for an eligible organization operating a raffle.[11]

Bingo: Non-profit, federally tax-exempt charitable organizations may conduct bingo games provided that the organization expends the net proceeds only for the purposes for which the organization is created.[12] The operation of the bingo game must meet several statutory and regulatory requirements.[13] The non-profit bingo operator needs a license, issued by the Mississippi Gaming Commission.[14] Bingo licensees must file quarterly reports with information including receipts, expenses, use of receipts, and prizes awarded.[15]

The Charitable Bingo Law is codified in Title 97, Chapter 33, Sections 97-33-50 to 97-33-203 of the Mississippi Code. The Mississippi Gaming Commission issues regulations for charitable gaming.[16]

Additional information, application forms, and regulations for charitable bingo are available at the website of the Mississippi Gaming Commission Charitable Gaming Division, 620 North Street, Suite 200, Jackson, MS 39202, (601) 576-3800, website: http://www.mgc.state.ms.us/

Resources

Mississippi offers a searchable database for its attorney general opinions online at http://government.westlaw.com/msag/help.asp.

Endnotes

1. Miss. Code §§ 97-33-31 to 97-33-47 (2013).
2. Miss. Code § 75-76-3(6) (2013). This section contains the declaration to the Mississippi Gaming Control Act, which provided a regulatory framework for legalized gambling in Mississippi. Section 92 of the Mississippi Constitution prohibited lotteries until its repeal in 1992. In the declaration to the Mississippi Gaming Control Act, the legislature describes the characteristics of a lottery prohibited by the state constitution as an activity in which: (a) players pay something of value for chances to win, (b) the winner is determined by random selection method based predominately upon the element of chance rather than upon the

skill of the player; (c) the winner receives a prize; and (d) the activity is conducted and participated in without regard to geographical location, with the player or players not being required to be present upon any particular premises or at any particular location in order to participate or to win.

3. Miss. Code § 97-33-1 (2013).

4. *See generally*, Section 3.4.3 of this Guide for a discussion of tests used when evaluating whether chance or skill prevails in a promotion combining elements of both.

5. Miss. Code § 75-76-3(6)(b) (2013) (emphasis added). *See also, supra*, note 2, for additional discussion of Section 75-76-3.

6. *See generally*, discussion of free alternative methods of entry for sweepstakes in Section 3.6 of this Guide.

7. Miss. Att'y Gen. Op. No. 94-0725 (Dec. 16, 1994).

8. *Miss. Gaming Comm. v. Treasured Arts*, 699 So.2d 936, 940 (Miss. 1997).

9. Miss. Code § 97-33-51 (2013).

10. *Id.*

11. Telephone interview with staff person, Mississippi Gaming Commission Charitable Gaming Division, (Nov. 4, 2011). The lack of a license requirement is not clearly stated in the statute. Staff also indicated that the raffle operator should be a 501(c)(3) federally exempt organization; however, this requirement is not indicated in the statute.

12. Miss. Code § 97-33-52 (2013).

13. *See generally*, discussion of bingo and raffles in Section 9.2 of this Guide.

14. Miss. Code § 97-33-55 (2013).

15. Miss. Code § 97-33-71 (2013).

16. Mississippi Gaming Commission, Charitable Gaming Regulations, 2012 edition, available at http://www.msgamingcommission.com/index.php/regulations/charitable_gaming/ (last visited Sept. 20, 2014).

Missouri

State Attorney General Office

Missouri Attorney General
Supreme Court Building
207 W. High St.
P.O. Box 899
Jefferson City, MO 65102
Phone: 573-751-3321
Website: http://ago.mo.gov/

Selected State Laws, Regulations, and Constitutional Provisions

Missouri's anti-gambling laws (Title XXXVIII, Chapter 572, Sections 572-010 *et seq.* of the Missouri Revised Statute), codified with its laws of crimes and punishment, contain provisions related to promotions. Specific Missouri authorities frequently quoted in court cases and interpretive opinions related to promotions include the following:

Reference No.	Descriptive Name
Mo. Const. art. III, § 39(9)	(limitation on lotteries)
Mo. Rev. Stat. § 572.010	Definitions (for anti-gambling laws including definitions for contest of chance, gambling, lottery, and professional player)
Mo. Rev. Stat. § 572.020	Gambling (prohibited as misdemeanor; felony for professional players)
Mo. Rev. Stat. § 572.030	Promoting gambling in the first degree (prohibited as a felony)
Mo. Rev. Stat. § 572.040	Promoting gambling in the second degree (prohibited as a misdemeanor)
Mo. Rev. Stat. § 572.080	Lottery offenses--no defense

Summary of State Law

Prohibition of Lotteries and Gambling: Missouri's State Constitution as well as its anti-gambling laws prohibit lotteries.[1] A promotion that combines a prize, chance, and consideration is a lottery in Missouri.[2] Missouri also has a general prohibition against gambling.[3] Exceptions to the lottery and gambling prohibitions include lotteries operated by the state and certain charitable lotteries.

Contests: Missouri permits contests as long as the contest does not conflict with anti-gambling laws. If the contest includes an element of consideration, the sponsor must award the contest prize based on skill and not on chance.

Conflicting authorities make it uncertain as to whether Missouri applies the material element test or the dominant factor doctrine when evaluating whether or not chance determines the outcome of a promotion.[4] Court opinions suggest that Missouri applies the dominant factor doctrine. For example, in *Harris v. Missouri Gaming Commission*, 869 S.W.2d 58, 62 (Mo. 1994), the Missouri Supreme Court indicated that a game is not a lottery if skill is predominant.[5] In contrast, current Missouri anti-gambling laws suggest that Missouri uses the material element test. In the anti-gambling laws, game of chance is defined as a contest or game "in which *the outcome depends in a material degree upon an element of chance*, notwithstanding that the skill of the contestants may also be a factor therein".[6]

Sweepstakes: Missouri permits sweepstakes as long as participants do not pay consideration and the sweepstakes does not conflict with anti-gambling laws. The attorney general has indicated that in the context of a lottery, services or efforts expended as a condition for entrance into a drawing qualify as consideration only if the services or efforts are more than trivial.[7] Specific situations in which Missouri has found consideration include the following:

- A university alumni association provided a chance to win an expense-paid trip in a drawing. To be eligible for the drawing, each alumnus had to enroll three new members into the association. Association membership required the payment of dues.[8]

- Participants were required either to go to a store selling the sponsor's product or buy a magazine in order to obtain an entry blank for a chance drawing.[9]
- Manufacturer of merchandise conducted a drawing of product registration cards for a prize when such cards could only be obtained by purchasing merchandise.[10]

Gambling Exceptions for Non-Profits and Other Qualified Organizations

Raffles and Lotteries: The Missouri Constitution provides that raffles and sweepstakes may be conducted by organizations recognized as charitable or religious pursuant to federal law.[11] Missouri has no raffle licensing requirements and has not issued any laws or regulations to govern the operation of charitable raffles. The Consumer Protection Division of the Attorney General's Office does informally recommend that eligible organizations planning to offer raffles notify Missouri of its status as a charitable or religious organization.[12] The notification is informal and can be a simple letter stating the organization's status and providing supporting evidence of its status as a charitable or religious organization such as an IRS Letter of Determination.[13]

Bingo: A constitutional amendment allows the Missouri legislature to authorize bingo games for religious, charitable, fraternal, veteran or service organizations.[14] The organization must use the net bingo receipts for purposes consistent with the charitable, religious or philanthropic purposes of the organization.[15]

There are statutory and regulatory requirements for the operation of charitable bingo games.[16] Eligible organizations wishing to offer bingo games must obtain a license from the Missouri Gaming Commission.[17] Most licensees must file quarterly reports with information about the number and location of bingo games, gross receipts, and use of proceeds.[18]

The laws enabling the constitutional bingo exemption are codified in Title XXI, Chapter 313, Sections 313.005 to 313.085 of the Missouri Revised Statute. Bingo regulations issued by the Missouri Gaming Commission are codified in Title 11, Sections 45-30.020 *et seq.* of the Missouri Code of State Regulations. Additional information, registration and report forms are available online from the Missouri Gaming Commission, 3417 Knipp Drive, P.O. Box 1847, Jefferson City, MO 65102, Telephone: (573) 526-5370, website: http://www.mgc.dps.mo.gov/

Resources

Missouri offers a searchable database for its attorney general opinions from 1968 through the present online in the Opinions portion of the website of the Missouri Attorney General's Office. The Missouri Attorney General's Office will provide paper copies of opinions issued from 1933 through 1967 upon request.

Endnotes

1. Mo. Const. art. III, § 39(9); Mo. Rev. Stat. §§ 572.020 to 572.040 (2013).
2. Mo. Rev. Stat. § 572.010(7) (2013).
3. Mo. Rev. Stat. §§ 572.020 to 572.040 (2013).
4. *See generally*, Section 3.4.3 of this Guide for a discussion of tests used when evaluating whether chance or skill prevails in a promotion combining elements of both
5. *Harris v. Missouri Gaming Commissioner*, 869 S.W.2d 58, 62 (Mo. 1994) *citing* McKittrick v. Globe-Democrat Pub., 110 S.W.2d 705, 713 (Mo. 1937).
6. Mo. Rev. Stat. § 572.010(3) (2013) (emphasis added).
7. Mo. Att'y Gen. Op. No. 70-83 (May 23, 1983) (citations omitted).
8. *Id.*
9. Mo. Att'y Gen. Op. No. 424-69 (Oct. 30, 1969).
10. Mo. Att'y Gen. Op. No. 217-91 (Dec. 30, 1991).
11. Mo. Const. art. III, § 39(f).
12. Telephone inquiry to staff of Missouri Attorney General Office, Consumer Protection Division (Sept. 23, 2014).
13. *Id.*
14. Mo. Const. art. III, § 39(a).
15. Mo. Const. art. III, § 39(a); Mo. Rev. Stat. § 313.010(1)(a) (2013).
16. *See generally*, discussion of bingo and raffles in Section 9.2 of this Guide.
17. Mo. Rev. Stat. § 313.010 (2013).
18. Mo. Rev. Stat. § 313.045 (2013).

Montana

State Attorney General Office
Montana Department of Justice
Office of the Attorney General
215 N. Sanders, Third Floor
P.O. Box 201401
Helena, Montana 59620-1401
(406) 444-2026
Website: http://www.dojmt.gov/

Selected State Laws, Regulations, and Constitutional Provisions

Montana's anti-gambling laws (Title 23, Chapter 5, Sections 18-3801 *et seq.* of the Montana Code) are in its criminal code and contain provisions related to promotions. As part of its consumer protection laws, Montana includes prize promotion protections applicable to telemarketing campaigns. Specific Montana legal provisions frequently cited in court cases and interpretive opinions related to promotions include the following:

Reference No.	Descriptive Name
Mont. Const. art. III, § 9	Gambling (prohibited)
Mont. Code § 23-5-112	Definitions (for anti-gambling laws including definitions for promotional game of chance, gambling, lottery and raffle)
Mont. Code § 23-5-151	Gambling prohibited (unless authorized by statute)
Mont. Code § 23-5-801	Fantasy sports league defined
Mont. Code § 23-5-802	Fantasy sports league authorized
Mont. Code § 23-5-413	Raffle prizes—investigations—rulemaking

Mont. Admin. R. 23.16.2602	Raffle General Requirements, Authorized Random Selection Processes, and Record Keeping Requirements

Summary of State Law

Lotteries and Gambling: Montana prohibits all forms of gambling and lotteries that have not been explicitly authorized by law.[1] A promotion that combines a prize, chance, and consideration is a lottery in Montana.[2]

LIBERAL ALLOWANCE FOR RAFFLES. Unlike most states, Montana has liberal laws that do not limit raffles (a form of lottery) to charitable and non-profit organizations. Any person or organization may offer a raffle if the raffle conforms with the applicable Montana law and regulation. Montana law defines a raffle as a "form of lottery in which each participant pays valuable consideration for a ticket to become eligible to win a prize."[3]

While no license or permit is required to offer a raffle, there are several record-keeping and operational requirements.[4] Except for non-profit and certain educational institutional raffles where raffle proceeds are used for charitable purposes, the raffle sponsor must own all prizes before selling any raffle tickets[5] and the value of a raffle prize may not exceed $5,000.[6] Raffle sponsors may sell tickets only at events and only to participants within Montana. While sponsors may use the internet to advertise raffles, Montana explicitly prohibits the sale of raffle tickets over the internet.[7] All raffle rules must be available to the public prior to the sale of any tickets.[8] Raffle operators must retain records for twelve months related to proceeds, prizes awarded, and distribution of charitable proceeds (if applicable); and the raffle sponsor must provide those records to the Montana Department of Justice upon request.[9] The raffle sponsor must select the winner by a random selection process consistent with guidelines issued by the Montana Department of Justice.[10] The random selection process cannot be tied to an event with its own intrinsic significance (*e.g.*, a sports event, game of chance, *etc.*).[11]

Contests: Montana permits skill-based contests as long as the contest does not otherwise violate the anti-gambling laws. Court opinions suggest that Montana applies the dominant factor doctrine[12] when determining whether or not a promotion is based on chance or skill.[13]

Sweepstakes: Montana permits chance-based promotions as long as the promotion does not violate any anti-gambling laws. If the chance-based promotion does not meet the criteria of a raffle or other authorized gambling, as discussed above in the *Lotteries and Gambling* portion of this Montana State Summary, the sponsor may not charge consideration for participation.

Prize Promotion Laws: Montana incorporates prize promotion protections into the Montana Telemarketing Registration and Fraud Prevention Act (Title 30, Chapter 14, Part 14, Sections 30-14-1401 to 30-14-1414 of the Montana Code). The Telemarketing Registration and Fraud Prevention Act applies broadly to any companies using telemarketing, which Montana defines as a campaign conducted by telephone to induce the purchase of goods or services and involving more than one telephone call to a consumer.[14]

If the telemarketing campaign includes a prize promotion, there are record keeping and disclosure requirements related directly to the prize promotion.[15] Prize promotion is defined by the statute as a sweepstakes or other game of chance. Under the statute, prize promotion also includes any oral or written representation, express or implied, that a person has won, has been selected to receive, or is eligible to receive a prize.[16]

Gambling Exceptions for Non-Profits and Other Qualified Organizations

Raffles and Lotteries: As discussed above under the *Lotteries and Gambling* portion of this Montana State Summary, it is not necessary to be a charitable or non-profit organization in order to offer a raffle in Montana. However, the statutory and regulatory requirements are more relaxed when a non-profit organization or certain educational institutions offer the raffle and use the raffle proceeds exclusively for charitable purposes and for the payment of raffle prizes.[17] Unlike raffles sponsored by for-profit organizations, qualifying non-profit organizations sponsoring raffles do not need to own all raffle prizes prior to selling raffle tickets and are not subject to the $5,000 limitation on the value of raffle prizes.

Bingo: Montana allows bingo to be offered by those other than charitable and non-profit organizations. Bingo operators need a bingo permit. Having a gambling operator license is a condition to securing the bingo permit. Any person or organization with a gambling operator's license may apply for a permit to conduct live bingo on specified premises.[18]

The operation of the bingo game must meet several statutory requirements.[19] Licensed bingo operators must pay a tax on proceeds, maintain records of proceeds, and report proceeds and taxes due in periodic filings to the Montana Department of Justice.[20] There are exemptions from the taxes, from all or a portion of the permit fee, and from the record retention and reporting requirements for charitable organizations and for organizations that serve senior citizens.[21]

The bingo and raffle laws are codified in Title 23, Chapter 5, Part 4, Sections 23-5-401 to 23-5-431 of the Montana Code. Bingo Regulations, issued by the Montana Gambling Control Division, are codified primarily in Title 23, Chapter 16, Subchapters 23 and 24 of the Administrative Rules of Montana. Additional information, regulations, and forms are available from the Gambling Control Division of the Montana Department of Justice, 2550 Prospect Avenue, Helena, Montana, (406) 444-1971, www.dojmt.gov/gaming.

Resources:

Montana offers copies of attorney general opinions and letters of advice[22] issued from 1993 through the present online at http://doj.mt.gov/agooffice/attorney-generals-opinions/. Opinions from 1977 to 1992 are available at the website of the Montana Association of Counties (www.mtcounties.org).

Endnotes

1. Mont. Const. art. III, § 9; Mont. Code Ann.§ 23-5-151 (2014).
2. Mont. Code § 23-5-112(27) (2014); *Montana v. Cox*, 349 P.2d 104, 105 (Mont. 1960).

3. Mont. Code § 23-5-112(36) (2014).
4. Mont. Code §§ 23-5-112 and 23-5-413 (2014); Mont. Admin. R. 23.16.2602 (2014); Angela Nunn, Operations Bureau Chief, Montana Gambling Control Division, *Bingo and Raffle Information*, (Nov. 1, 2011, updated Dec. 17, 2012).
5. Mont. Code § 23-5-413 (2014).
6. *Id.*
7. *Id.*
8. Mont. Admin. R. 23-16-2602 (2014).
9. *Id.*
10. *Id.*
11. *Id.*
12. *See generally*, Section 3.4.3 of this Guide for a discussion of tests used when evaluating whether chance or skill prevails in a promotion combining elements of both.
13. *See Montana v. Hahn*, 72 P.2d 459, 461 (Mont. 1937).
14. Mont. Code § 30-14-1403(12) (2014).
15. Mont. Code §§ 30-14-1408(1)(b)(ii), 30-14-1410 (2014). *See generally*, discussion of state telemarketing laws in Section 7.5.2 of this Guide.
16. Mont. Code § 30-14-1403(7) (2014).
17. Mont. Code § 23-5-413(2)(c) (2014).
18. Mont. Code § 23-5-407 (2014).
19. *See generally*, discussion of bingo and raffles in Section 9.2 of this Guide.
20. Mont. Code § 23-5-409 (2014).
21. Mont. Code §§ 23-5-406 and 23-5-410 (2014).
22. While Montana Attorney General opinions have the force of law (unless and until overturned by a court or new statute), letters of advice do not have binding force of law.

Nebraska

State Attorney General Office
Nebraska Attorney General Office
2115 State Capitol
Lincoln, Nebraska 68509
(402) 471-2682
Website: http://www.ago.ne.gov/

Selected State Laws, Regulations, and Constitutional Provisions

Nebraska's anti-gambling laws (Chapter 28, Article 11, Sections 28-1101 *et seq.* of Nebraska Revised Statute), which are in its criminal code, contain provisions related to promotions. With its telecommunication and technology laws, Nebraska includes prize promotion laws (Chapter 86, Sections 86-212 to 86-235 of Nebraska Revised Statute). Specific authorities frequently quoted in court cases and interpretive opinions related to promotions include the following:

Reference No.	Descriptive Name
Neb. Const. art. III, § 24	Games of chance, lotteries, and gift enterprises; restrictions; pari-mutuel wagering on horse races; bingo games; use of state lottery proceeds
Neb. Rev. Stat. § 28-1101	Terms, defined (for anti-gambling laws including definitions for gambling and prize contest)
Neb. Rev. Stat. § 28-1102	Promoting gambling, first degree; penalty
Neb. Rev. Stat. § 28-1103	Promoting gambling, second degree; penalty
Neb. Rev. Stat. § 28-1104	Promoting gambling, third degree; penalty

Summary of State Law

Prohibition of Lotteries and Gambling: Nebraska's Constitution as well as its statutory laws prohibit lotteries.[1] A promotion that combines a prize, chance, and consideration is a lottery in Nebraska.[2] Nebraska also has a general prohibition against promoting gambling.[3] Exceptions to the anti-lottery and anti-gambling prohibitions include lotteries operated by the state and certain charitable lotteries.

Contests: Nebraska permits contests as long the contest does not conflict with anti-gambling laws. If the contest includes an element of consideration, the sponsor must award the contest prize based on skill and not on chance. Court opinions indicate that Nebraska applies the dominant factor doctrine[4] when evaluating whether or not chance determines the outcome of a promotion.[5]

Nebraska exempts prize contests from the definition of gambling.[6] According to the Nebraska statutory definition, a prize contest may have the elements of prize and consideration.[7] The statutory definition does not explicitly say that the award of the prize in the prize contest must be based on skill. Instead, the statute indicates the prize is awarded to a participant as a consequence of winning or achieving a certain result in the competition. Based on Nebraska court opinions[8], a reasonable interpretation is that awards in prize contests with consideration must be based predominantly on skill. Although all contests may not fall into Nebraska's statutory definition of prize contest, the statute provides some best practice guidelines for all sponsors offering contests in Nebraska:

- The contest promoter should publish the value and identity of prizes before the competition begins.
- The prize can not depend upon chance, upon the number of contest participants, or upon the amount of consideration paid by contest participants.[9]

Sweepstakes: Nebraska permits sweepstakes as long as participants do not pay consideration and the sweepstakes does not otherwise violate anti-gambling laws. Sponsors that conduct sweepstakes as part of a tele-marketing sales campaign must comply with the disclosure and other requirements of the Nebraska Telemarketing and Prize Promotions Act, the state's prize promotion law, discussed below.

Nebraska law includes a provision that explicitly allows a category of promotions referred to in the Nebraska statutes as gift enterprises.[10] As used in the Nebraska statute, gift enterprises are essentially sweepstakes. Nebraska law defines a gift enterprise as a business promotion which is conducted in connection with the sale of consumer products or services and which includes the elements of prize and chance.[11]

Sponsors can view the gift enterprises law provisions as requirements for sweepstakes combined with product and service sales and as suggested guidelines (as applicable) for other sweepstakes. The statute includes provisions to ensure a fair process for the gift enterprise. For example, gift enterprise sponsors must award all prizes and disclose all terms of the promotion. Prohibited practices include arbitrarily disqualifying an entry or using deceptive advertising materials.

While gift enterprise sponsors cannot require consideration, they can require evidence of the purchase of a product or service as long as the purchase price charged for such product or service is not greater than it would have been without the promotion.[12] Consideration does not include filling out an entry blank or entering by mail or telephone as long as the associated fees are no greater than the postage for a first-class letter weighing one ounce or less.[13]

Prize Promotion Laws: Nebraska includes prize promotion protections as a component of its Telemarketing and Prize Promotions Act (Chapter 86, Sections 86-212 to 86-235 of Nebraska Revised Statute). The prize promotion component of the act applies to companies that offer a prize or gift as part of a telemarketing campaign to sell consumer goods and services.[14] A company must provide certain disclosures and refrain from certain prohibited practices when, in conjunction with its telemarketing sales campaign, the company offers a sweepstakes or tells a consumer that the consumer has won or may be eligible to receive a prize.[15]

For purposes of the Telemarketing and Prize Promotions Act, a prize is anything offered and given to a person by chance.[16] Hence, by its plain language, these prize promotion provisions are not applicable to skill-based contests.

The statute suggests that the initial disclosure (*i.e.*, the disclosure made during the telemarketing call) can be verbal. However, the sponsor must deliver a written disclosure statement (referred to in the statute as a prize notice) prior to requesting or accepting any money from a consumer if the sponsor has told the consumer that the consumer has won or may receive a prize.[17]

Gambling Exceptions for Non-Profits and Other Qualified Organizations

Raffles and Lotteries: Nebraska allows certain non-profit and federally tax-exempt organizations to conduct raffles and lotteries as long as the organization uses the proceeds solely for charitable or community betterment purposes, for prizes, or for expenses. Nebraska distinguishes a raffle from a lottery. In a lottery, the prize consists of cash (referred to by the statute as something of value). In a raffle, at least eighty percent of the prizes (as determined by market value) must be merchandise.[18] Nebraska further bifurcates non-profit promotions by regulating larger raffles and lotteries as one group and smaller raffles and lotteries as a separate group.

LARGE RAFFLES AND LOTTERIES. The Nebraska Lottery and Raffle Act governs larger raffles and lotteries. This category includes lotteries with gross proceeds greater than one thousand dollars and certain raffles with gross proceeds greater than five thousand dollars.

The operation of the large raffles must meet several statutory and regulatory requirements.[19] Organizations conducting such lotteries and raffles must obtain a license from the Nebraska Department of Revenue.[20] These raffle sponsors must file an annual report of activities and comply with specific operational procedures.

The Nebraska Lottery and Raffle Act is codified at Chapter 9, Sections 9-401 to 9-437 of the Nebraska Revised Statute. Regulations for the Nebraska Lottery and Raffle Act, issued by the Nebraska Department of Revenue, are codified in Title 316, Chapter 35, Sections 35-400 to 34-409 of the Nebraska Administrative Code.

Additional information, registration and report forms are available online from the Department of Revenue, Charitable Gaming Division,

1800 "O" Street, Suite 101, PO Box 94855, Lincoln, NE 68509, 402-471-5937, website: http://www.revenue.ne.gov/gaming/

SMALL RAFFLES AND LOTTERIES. The Nebraska Small Lottery and Raffle Act governs smaller raffles and lotteries. This category includes lotteries with gross proceeds no greater than one thousand dollars and raffles with gross proceeds no greater than five thousand dollars. Nebraska extends eligibility to operate small raffles and licenses to non-profit organizations that do not have federally tax-exempt status as long as the organization conducts its activities primarily for charitable or community betterment purposes. An eligible organization does not need a license to offer a small raffle or lottery.

The Nebraska Small Lottery and Raffle Act is codified at Chapter 9, Sections 9-501 to 9-513 of the Nebraska Revised Statute. Regulations for the Nebraska Small Lottery and Raffle Act, issued by the Nebraska Department of Revenue, are codified at Title 316, Chapter 35, Sections 35-500 to 35-504 of the Nebraska Administrative Code.

Bingo: Nebraska allows certain non-profit and civic organizations to offer bingo games. Organizations eligible to offer bingo games are federally-tax exempt non-profit organizations or any volunteer fire company or volunteer first-aid, rescue, ambulance, or emergency squad. Eligible organizations must use proceeds for a list of lawful purposes consistent with the organizations' mission and other charitable and civic purposes. The bingo operator must have a license issued by the Nebraska Department of Revenue.

The operation of the bingo game must meet several statutory and regulatory requirements.[21] The Nebraska Bingo Act is codified in Chapter 9, Sections 9-201 to 9-266 of the Nebraska Revised Statute. Bingo regulations issued by the Nebraska Department of Revenue are codified in Title 316, Chapter 35, Sections 35-200 *et seq.* of the Nebraska Administrative Code.

Additional information, application forms, and regulations for bingo are available online at the website of the Department of Revenue, Charitable Gaming Division, 1800 "O" Street, Suite 101, PO Box 94855, Lincoln, NE 68509, 402-471-5937, website: http://www.revenue.ne.gov/gaming/

Resources

Nebraska offers a searchable database for its attorney general opinions from 1981 through the present in the opinions portion of the website of the Office of the Attorney General.

Endnotes

1. Neb. Const. art. III, § 24; Neb. Rev. Stat. § 28-1101 *et seq.* (2013).
2. *Contact v. Nebraska*, 324 N.W.2d 804 (Neb. 1982); *Hunter v. Fox Beatrice Theatre Corp.*, 275 N.W. 605, 606 (Neb. 1937).
3. Neb. Const. art. III, § 24; Neb. Rev. Stat. § 28-1102 – 28-1104 (2013).
4. *See generally,* Section 3.4.3 of this Guide for a discussion of tests used when evaluating whether chance or skill prevails in a promotion combining elements of both.
5. *American Amusements Co. v. Neb. Dep't of Revenue*, 807 N.W.2d 492, 501-502 (Neb. 2011); *Indoor Recreation Enter. v. Douglas*, 235 N.W.2d 398, 400 (Neb. 1975).
6. Neb. Rev. Stat. § 28-1101(4)(c) (2013).
7. Neb. Rev. Stat. § 28-1101(7) (2013).
8. *Baedaro v. Caldwell*, 56 N.W.2d 706 (Neb. 1953). *See also, American Amusements Co. v. Neb. Dep't of Rev*, 807 N.W.2d 492 (2011).
9. Neb. Rev. Stat. § 28-1101(4)(c) and 28-1101(7) (2013).
10. Neb. Rev. Stat. § 9-701 (2013).
11. *Id.*
12. Neb. Rev. Stat. § 9-701(3)(e) (2013).
13. *Id.*
14. The provisions pertain to sellers that initiate unsolicited telephone sales calls to consumers. Neb. Rev. Stat. § 86-219 (2013).
15. Neb. Rev. Stat. §§ 86-228 to 86-229 (2013). *See generally,* discussion of state prize promotion laws in Section 7.4.2 of this Guide.
16. Neb. Rev. Stat. § 86-217 (2013).
17. Neb. Rev. Stat. § 86-229(4) (2013).
18. Neb. Rev. Stat. §§ 9-411, 9-415, 9-507 and 9-509 (2013). See also Neb. Dep't of Revenue, Nebraska Lottery and Raffle Information Guide (Sept, 22, 2010) available at www.revenue.nebraska.gov/gaming/infoguide/raffle.pdf *(last visited Sept. 25, 2014).*
19. *See generally,* discussion of bingo and raffles in Section 9.2 of this Guide.
20. Neb. Rev. Stat. § 9-422 (2013).
21. *See generally,* discussion of bingo and raffles in Section 9.2 of this Guide.

Nevada

State Attorney General Office
Office of the Attorney General
100 North Carson Street
Carson City, Nevada 89701
(775) 684-1100
Website: http://ag.state.nv.us

Selected State Laws, Regulations, and Constitutional Provisions

Nevada's laws on gaming, horse racing, and sporting events contain provisions related to promotions in the chapter on lotteries (Title 41, Chapter 462 of the Nevada Revised Statute) and the chapter on licensing and control of gaming (Title 41, Chapter 463 of the Nevada Revised Statute). With its deceptive trade practice laws, Nevada includes prize promotion laws (Title 52, Chapter 598, Sections 598.131 to 598.139 of the Nevada Revised Statute). Specific authorities frequently quoted in court cases and interpretive opinions related to promotions include the following:

Reference No.	Descriptive Name
Nev. Const. art. IV, § 24	Lotteries
Nev. Rev. Stat. § 462.035	Definitions (for lotteries laws including definitions for lottery)
Nev. Rev. Stat. § 462.105	Lottery defined
Nev. Rev. Stat. § 462.250	Penalty for unauthorized lottery (prohibited as misdemeanor)
Nev. Rev. Stat. § 463.0152	Game and gambling game defined
Nev. Rev. Stat. § 463.160	Licenses required; unlawful to permit certain gaming activities to be conducted without license; exceptions

Summary of State Law

Prohibition of Lotteries and Gambling: Nevada's Constitution prohibits lotteries—even those lotteries operated by the state.[1] A promotion that combines a prize, chance, and consideration is a lottery in Nevada.[2] Paradoxically, Nevada is the only state that prohibits lotteries while it permits licensed casino gambling. Nevada does have a general prohibition against gaming and gambling activity that is not licensed.[3] Nevada does allow charitable raffles and bingo games.

Contest: Nevada permits contests as long as the contest does not conflict with anti-gambling laws. If the contest includes an element of consideration, the sponsor must award the contest prize based on skill and not on chance.

Court opinions indicate that Nevada applies the dominant factor doctrine[4] when evaluating whether or not chance determines the outcome of a promotion. In *Las Vegas Hacienda v. Gibson*, 359 P.2d 85, 87 (Nev. 1961), the Nevada Supreme Court considered whether a promotion offering a prize for shooting a hole in one in golf qualified as a gambling game. The *Las Vegas Hacienda* court found that the promotion was not a gambling game, basing its decision in part on the fact that the game required skill. In its analysis, the *Las Vegas Hacienda* court remarked that "The test of the character of a game is not whether it contains an element of chance or an element of skill, but which is the *dominating element*."[5]

Sweepstakes: Nevada permits sweepstakes as long as participants do not pay consideration and the sweepstakes does not violate anti-gambling laws. The definition of lottery includes some indications on what Nevada considers to be consideration.[6] The statutory definition of lottery provides as follows:

- There is no consideration simply because a person engages in a transaction in which the person receives fair value for the payment. This provision seems to contemplate and to permit in-package sweepstakes.[7]
- There is no consideration simply because a person accepts a product or service on a trial basis.

- There is no consideration simply because a person is present at a particular time and place. This seems to permit a sponsor requiring that a sweepstakes participant be present at a drawing, drop off an entry at a store, and potentially visit a store for other purposes.

Prize Promotion Laws: With its deceptive trade practice laws, Nevada has prize promotion protections. The prize promotion laws are codified in Title 52, Chapter 598, Sections 598.131 to 598.139 of the Nevada Revised Statute. The prize promotion protections apply to giveaways and promotions offered as part of a campaign for the sale or lease of goods, services, or property. The prize promotion protections do not apply to contests that are based on skill and that do not involve the sale or lease of goods, services, or property.[8] The protections include disclosure requirements and prohibited practices for giveaways and for promotional opportunities to win a prize. There is some variation in requirements depending on the type of promotion offered.

REPRESENTATION THAT A PERSON HAS WON A PRIZE. If, in conjunction with a company sales campaign, a company tells a consumer that the consumer has won a prize, the company must provide a disclaimer and refrain from certain prohibited practices.[9] A sales campaign includes the sale or lease of goods, services, or property. The company must give the prize to the person without obligation within thirty days of making the representation. The disclosures can be given verbally. If given in writing, there are specific statutory requirements for placement and type size.[10]

REPRESENTATION THAT A PERSON HAS A CHANCE TO WIN A PRIZE. If, in conjunction with a company sales campaign, a company tells a consumer that the consumer has a chance to win a prize, the company must make certain disclosures and refrain from certain prohibited practices.[11] The disclosure requirements and prohibitions do not apply if consumers can participate in the prize-winning opportunity solely by submitting an entry by mail, phone, or at a local retail store, and if consumers are not required to listen to a sales presentation.[12] While this statutory provision does not explicitly say the disclosure must be in writing, it does indicate that the disclosure must be displayed, clearly and conspicuously, adjacent to the description of the prize. Hence, it is reasonable to assume that Nevada expects the disclosure to be in writing.

PRIZE PROMOTION PROVISIONS OF TELEMARKETING LAWS. Nevada's laws regarding telephone solicitations (Title 52, Chapter 599B, Sections 599B.005 to 599B.300 of the Nevada Revised Statute) also include prize promotion protections.[13] If a company offers prizes or gifts to consumers as part of the company's telephone solicitation campaign, the company must disclose certain information about the gift to the consumer as part of the call and in an information statement filed with the state.[14] There are additional disclosure requirements and prohibitions for use of a chance-based promotion with telephone solicitations.[15]

Gambling Exceptions for Non-Profits and Other Qualified Organizations

Raffles and Lotteries: The Nevada constitutional prohibition on lotteries includes an exception for charitable and non-profit lotteries in the form of raffles or drawings.[16] This exception is codified in Title 41, Chapter 462, Section 462.015 *et seq.* of the Nevada Revised Statute. The raffle sponsor must use net proceeds from the raffle to benefit charitable or non-profit activities in Nevada.

Organizations eligible to offer raffles consist of non-profit charitable, civic, educational, fraternal, patriotic, political, religious and veterans' organizations.[17] An eligible organization does not need a license to offer a raffle if one of two conditions applies:

- the raffle prizes do not exceed $2,500 in value and the organization offers no more than two raffles per year or
- the annual aggregate value of raffle prizes does not exceed $15,000 and either the organization sells raffle tickets only to members of the organization or only to attendees at its member events.[18]

Eligible organizations whose raffles fall outside those parameters must either register with or obtain approval from the Nevada State Gaming Control Board, depending on the annual aggregate value of the raffle prizes.[19] Organizations that need approval for their raffles must also file annual financial reports with the Nevada State Gaming Control Board.[20] Raffle registration and report forms are available online from the Nevada State Gaming Control Board, http://gaming.nv.gov/, (775) 684-7700.

Bingo: Nevada allows charitable bingo as long as the bingo sponsor uses net bingo proceeds on charitable and non-profit activities within Nevada.[21] Organizations eligible to offer bingo games consist of non-profit charitable, civic, educational, fraternal, patriotic, political, religious or veterans' organizations.[22] There is no license required for the eligible organization to operate bingo games if the value of the prizes offered in a calendar quarter does not exceed $2,500.[23] Eligible organizations operating bingo games outside of these parameters must register with or be approved by the Nevada State Gaming Control Board. Eligible organizations that need approval for bingo must also file annual financial reports with the Nevada State Gaming Control Board.[24] Bingo registration and report forms are available online from the Nevada State Gaming Control Board, http://gaming.nv.gov/, (775) 684-7700.[25]

Resources

Nevada offers archives of its attorney general opinions from 1914 through the present in the Opinions portion of the website of the Office of the Attorney General.

Endnotes

1. Nev. Const. art. IV, § 24.
2. Nev. Rev. Stat. § 462.105 (2014).
3. Nev. Rev. Stat. § 463.160 (2014).
4. *See generally*, Section 3.4.3 of this Guide for a discussion of tests used when evaluating whether chance or skill prevails in a promotion combining elements of both.
5. *Las Vegas Hacienda v. Gibson*, 359 P.2d 85, 87 (Nev. 1961) (emphasis added).
6. Nev. Rev. Stat. § 462.105(3) (2014).
7. *See generally*, the discussion of in-package sweepstakes included in Section 3.6 of this Guide.
8. Nev. Rev. Stat. § 598.135 (2014).

9. Nev. Rev. Stat. § 598.136 (2014).
10. Nev. Rev. Stat. § 598.136 (2014). See general discussion of state prize promotion laws in Section 7.4.2 of this Guide.
11. Nev. Rev. Stat. § 598.137 (2014).
12. *Id.*
13. *See generally,* discussion of state telemarketing laws in Section 7.5.2 of this Guide.
14. Nev. Rev. Stat. §§ 599B.170 and 599B.180 (2014).
15. Nev. Rev. Stat. § 599B.187 (2014).
16. Nev. Const. art. IV, § 24.
17. Nev. Rev. Stat. § 462.125 (2014).
18. Nev. Rev. Stat. § 462.140 (2014).
19. *Id.*
20. Nev. Rev. Stat. § 462.200 (2014).
21. Nev. Rev. Stat. §§ 463.4091 to 463.40965 (2014).
22. Nev. Rev. Stat. § 463.4093 (2014).
23. Nev. Rev. Stat. § 463.4094 (2014).
24. Nev. Rev. Stat. § 463.40965 (2014).
25. *See generally,* discussion of bingo and raffles in Section 9.2 of this Guide.

New Hampshire

State Attorney General Office
New Hampshire Department of Justice
Office of the Attorney General
33 Capitol Street
Concord, New Hampshire 03301
(603) 271-3658
Website: http://doj.nh.gov

Selected State Laws, Regulations, and Constitutional Provisions

New Hampshire's anti-gambling laws (Title LXII, Chapter 647, Sections 647:2 *et seq.* of the New Hampshire Revised Statutes) which are in the state's criminal code contain provisions related to promotions. With its trade and commerce laws, New Hampshire includes its prize promotion laws (Title XXXI, Chapter 358-O, Sections 358-O:1 *et seq.* of the New Hampshire Revised Statutes). Specific New Hampshire authorities frequently quoted in court opinions and interpretive opinions related to promotions include the following:

Reference No.	Descriptive Name
N.H. Rev. Stat. § 647:1	Lotteries (prohibited)
N.H. Rev. Stat. § 647:2	Gambling (prohibited; includes definition for gambling)

Summary of State Law

Prohibition of Lotteries and Gambling: New Hampshire prohibits lotteries.[1] A promotion that combines a prize, chance, and consideration is a lottery in New Hampshire.[2] New Hampshire also has a general prohibition against gambling.[3] Exceptions to the lottery and gambling prohibitions include state-operated lotteries and certain charitable lotteries.

Contests: There are no provisions in its laws to indicate that New Hampshire does not permit contests as long as the contest does not conflict with anti-gambling laws. If the contest includes an element of consideration, the sponsor should award the contest prize based on skill and not on chance. Research for this Guide uncovered no indication of which test New Hampshire uses[4] when determining whether or not a promotion incorporates chance.[5]

Sweepstakes: There are no provisions in its laws to indicate that New Hampshire does not permit sweepstakes as long as participants pay no consideration and the sweepstakes does not conflict with anti-gambling laws.

Prize Promotion Laws: New Hampshire's trade and commerce laws include the state's version of a prize promotion law, the Prizes and Gifts Act (Title XXXI, Chapter 358-O, Sections 358-O:1 *et seq.* of the New Hampshire Revised Statutes). The law applies to companies that use promotions and giveaways in conjunction with the sale of goods and services.

REPRESENTATION OF HAVING CHANCE TO WIN A PRIZE. If as part of its sales campaign a company represents that a consumer has a chance to win or to receive a prize, the company must make certain disclosures.[6] The provision does not explicitly state that the disclosure must be in writing and implies that a verbal disclosure of all material conditions is adequate for a verbal solicitation.[7] There are specific placement, font, and other requirements for disclosures in written materials.[8] No disclosure is necessary if to be eligible for the chance to win, the following conditions apply:

- Participants are asked only to complete and mail, or deposit at a local retail commercial establishment, an entry blank obtainable locally or by mail, or to call in their entry by telephone.
- Participants are never required to listen to a sales presentation and never requested or required to pay any sum of money for any merchandise, service or item of value.[9]

REPRESENTATION THAT A PERSON HAS WON A PRIZE. If a company represents that a person has won a prize, the company must award the prize within ten days without obligation or expense to the winner.[10]

The New Hampshire Prize and Promotion Act also prohibits sponsors from engaging in certain unfair practices that might mislead consumers.

Gambling Exceptions for Non-Profits and Other Qualified Organizations

Raffles and Lotteries: New Hampshire allows charitable organizations to offer raffles to promote the organization's charitable purposes.[11] Charitable organizations eligible to offer raffles include 501(c)(3) non-profit organizations as well as any person or entity established for charitable purposes; a political committee or political party; or any person who in any manner employs a charitable appeal as the basis of any solicitation.[12] Eligible organizations wishing to conduct raffles must obtain a permit from the designated local government representative of the town or city where the raffle is to be held.[13]

Bingo: New Hampshire allows charitable organizations to offer bingo games and use those proceeds to promote the organization's charitable purposes.[14] Organizations eligible to offer bingo games are charitable organizations to which contributions are exempt from federal income tax.[15]

The operation of the bingo games must meet several statutory and regulatory requirements.[16] Organizations offering bingo games must have a license issued by the New Hampshire Racing and Charitable Gaming Commission[17] and must file periodic financial reports.[18] Senior citizens' organizations conducting bingo games are not subject to the licensing and reporting requirements under certain circumstances.[19]

The bingo exemption is codified in Title XXIV, Chapter 287-E, Sections 287-E:1 *et seq.* of the New Hampshire Revised Statutes. Bingo regulations, issued by the New Hampshire Racing and Charitable Gaming Commission, are codified in Sections 1001.01 *et seq.* of the New Hampshire Code of Administrative Rules.

Licensing information, application forms, and the bingo regulations are available from the New Hampshire Racing and Charitable Gaming

Commission, 21 South Fruit Street, Concord, New Hampshire, 03301, (603) 271-2158, website: http://www.racing.nh.gov.

Endnotes

1. N.H. Rev. Stat. § 647:1 (2014).
2. *New Hampshire v. Powell*, 567 A.2d 562, 566-567 (N.H. 1989) *citing New Hampshire v. Eames, 183 A. 590, 591 (N.H. 1936)*.
3. N.H. Rev. Stat. § 647:2 (2014).
4. *See generally*, Section 3.4.3 of this Guide for a discussion of tests used when evaluating whether chance or skill prevails in a promotion combining elements of both.
5. Some commentators indicate that New Hampshire follows the dominant factor doctrine; however, no such comments located during the research for this Guide provide any New Hampshire legal authority confirming this statement.
6. N.H. Rev. Stat. § 358-O:4(I) (2014). *See generally*, discussion of state prize promotion laws in Section 7.4.2 of this Guide.
7. N.H. Rev. Stat. § 358-O:4(I) (2014).
8. N.H. Rev. Stat. §§ 358-O:4 to 358-O:7 (2014).
9. N.H. Rev. Stat. § 358-O:4(IV) (2014). The provision does not indicate whether both conditions must be met or only one. A conservative approach is to rely on this exception only if both conditions are met.
10. N.H. Rev. Stat. § 358-O:3 (2014).
11. N.H. Rev. Stat. § 287-A:2 (2014).
12. N.H. Rev. Stat. § 287-A:1 (2014).
13. N.H. Rev. Stat. § 287-A:7 (2014).
14. N.H. Rev. Stat. §§ 287-E:1(V) and 287-E:6 (2014).
15. *Id.*
16. *See generally*, discussion of bingo and raffles in Section 9.2 of this Guide.
17. N.H. Rev. Stat. §§ 287-E:2 and 287-E:6 (2014).
18. N.H. Rev. Stat. § 287-E:9 (2014).
19. N.H. Rev. Stat. § 287-E-11 (2014).

New Jersey

State Attorney General Office
Office of the Attorney General
RJ Hughes Justice Complex
25 Market Street, P.O. Box 080
Trenton, NJ 08625-0080
(609) 292-4925
Website: http://www.nj.gov/oag/

Selected State Laws, Regulations, and Constitutional Provisions

New Jersey's anti-gambling laws (Title 2C, Chapter 37, Sections 2C:37-1 *et seq.* of the New Jersey Statute), which are in its criminal justice code contain provisions related to promotions. There are additional anti-gaming laws in Title 2A, Chapter 40. Specific New Jersey authorities frequently quoted in judicial and interpretive opinions related to promotions include the following:

Reference No.	Descriptive Name
N.J. Const. art. IV, § VII, para. 2	(state legislature's power to authorize gambling)
N.J. Stat. § 2A:40-1	Gaming transactions unlawful
N.J. Stat. § 2A:40-8	Penalty for erecting, *etc.*, lottery; action by common informer, disposition of penalty; jurors and witnesses
N.J. Stat. § 2C:37-1	Definitions (for anti-gambling laws including definitions for contest of chance, gambling, lottery, and something of value)
N.J. Stat. § 2C:37-2	Promoting gambling (prohibited with grading dependent on number of bets and/or their dollar amount)

N.J. Stat. § 5:19-1 Participation in contests of skill not deemed unlawful gambling

Summary of State Law

Prohibition of Lotteries and Gambling: The New Jersey statute defines lottery as an illegal gambling scheme.[1] A promotion that combines a prize, chance, and consideration is a lottery in New Jersey.[2] New Jersey makes it illegal to engage in gambling transactions and to promote gambling.[3] Exceptions to the lottery and gambling prohibitions include state-operated lotteries and certain charitable lotteries.

Contests: New Jersey permits contests as long as the contest does not conflict with anti-gambling laws. If the contest includes an element of consideration, the sponsor must award the contest prize based on skill and not on chance.

The statutory definition of contest of chance implies that New Jersey applies the material element test[4] when evaluating whether or not chance determines the outcome of a promotion.[5] The New Jersey statute defines a contest of chance as a contest or game "in which *the outcome depends in a material degree* upon an element of chance, notwithstanding that skill of the contestants or some other persons may also be a factor therein."[6]

Some sponsors have interpreted New Jersey law as prohibiting contests with consideration and have refused New Jersey residents entry into such contests.[7] New Jersey legislators have referred to this interpretation as incorrect[8] and passed legislation to correct the misinterpretation. Legislation adopted by the New Jersey legislature in January 2014 clarifies that participation by New Jersey residents in contests of skill does not constitute unlawful gambling, regardless of whether the contest charges consideration.[9] The 2014 legislation defines contest of skill as any baking or photography contest or similar contest approved by the New Jersey Attorney General as a contest of skill where the winner or winners are selected solely on the quality of an entry in the contest as determined by a panel of judges using uniform criteria to assess the quality of entries.[10]

The legislature adopted into law a definition of contest of skill narrower than previously proposed definitions.[11] With respect to the narrower definition adopted into law, it is unclear whether the statutory permission extends to a skill-based contest with consideration other than those contests within the subject matters of baking and photography and those contests explicitly approved by the New Jersey Attorney General. It is also unclear whether the statutory permission extends to a skill-based contest with consideration where the winner is determined by a format other than a panel of judges such as via public voting.

Sweepstakes: New Jersey permits sweepstakes as long as participants do not pay consideration. The New Jersey Attorney General has expressed the view that the consideration for an illegal promotion or gambling must be greater than the type of personal inconvenience that suffices for consideration under a contract.[12] Whether or not personal effort qualifies as something of value or consideration is determined by considering all relevant circumstances.

Prize Promotion Laws: New Jersey includes a prize promotion protection with its unfair business practices laws. As part of an advertising campaign, a company may not notify a person by any means that the person has won a prize and require the person to do any act, purchase any other item, or submit to a sales promotion effort to obtain the prize.[13]

Gambling Exceptions for Non-Profits and Other Qualified Organizations

Raffles and Bingo: A constitutional provision allows municipalities to authorize the offering of raffles and bingo games by certain organizations.[14] Organizations eligible to offer raffles are veterans, charitable, educational, religious or fraternal organizations, civic and service clubs, senior citizen associations or clubs, volunteer fire companies and first-aid or rescue squads.[15] Raffle and bingo game operators must devote all net proceeds to educational, charitable, patriotic, religious or public-spirited uses, and in the case of veterans' and senior citizen organizations to the support of such organizations. Typically, the organization offering the raffle or bingo game needs a license from the governing body of the municipality in which it is located.[16]

LICENSING EXCEPTION FOR DOOR PRIZE RAFFLES. There is a door prize exception to the licensing requirement. An eligible organization may offer a door prize raffle or drawing at an event or gathering without a license as long as the raffle prize is donated merchandise valued at less than fifty dollars; there is no additional charge for participation in the raffle; and there are no other games of chance offered at the event.[17]

LICENSING AND OPERATIONAL INFORMATION. There are statutory and regulatory operational requirements for both raffles and bingo games.[18] Every organization interested in conducting bingo games or a raffle must first apply to the Legalized Games of Chance Control Commission for eligibility. If the Commission determines that the applicant is eligible, the Commission issues the organization an identification number. The organization must then obtain a license for each separate type of game of chance it intends to conduct from the municipality where the games are to be held.

Eligible organizations wishing to conduct raffles and bingo games must file periodic reports of receipts, costs, and charitable uses of the receipts.[19] There are fewer restrictions for senior citizen associations or clubs holding, operating and conducting raffles or bingo games solely for the amusement and recreation of its members.[20]

The Raffles Licensing Act, codified in Title 5, Chapter 8, Sections 5:8-50 *et seq.* of the New Jersey Statute, enacts the constitutional raffle exemption. The Bingo Licensing Law, codified in Title 5, Chapter 8, Sections 5:8-24 *et seq.* of the New Jersey Statute, enacts the constitutional amendment permitting bingo. Regulations for raffles, bingo, and other forms of licensed games of chance, issued by the Legalized Games of Chance Control Commission, are in Sections 13:47-1.1 *et seq.* of the New Jersey Administrative Code and are available on the commission's website.

Additional information, license applications, and report forms are available from the Legalized Games of Chance Control Commission, P.O. Box 46000, Newark, New Jersey 07101, (973) 273-8000, website: http://www.state.nj.us/lps/ca/lgccc/index.htm

Resources

New Jersey offers its attorney general opinions from 1949 through the present online in the opinions portion of the website of the Office of the Attorney General.

Endnotes

1. N.J. Stat. § 2C:37-1.h (2014).
2. N.J. Stat. § 2C:37-1.h (2014); *New Jersey v. Horn,* 1 A.2d 51, 53 *(N.J. 1938).*
3. N.J. Stat. § 2A:40-1 (2014); N.J. Rev. Stat. § 2C:37-2.
4. *See generally,* Section 3.4.3 of this Guide for a discussion of tests used when evaluating whether chance or skill prevails in a promotion combining elements of both.
5. N.J. Stat. § 2C:37-1.a (2014).
6. *Id.* (emphasis added).
7. Statement included with Assemb. A3624, 215th Leg. 2012-2013, Reg. Sess. (N.J. 2014). *See also, New Jersey bakers in pie contests do not violate state gaming regulations,* Shore News Today, Jan. 6, 2014, http://www. shorenewstoday.com/snt/news/index.php/regional/atlantic-county/48118-new-jersey-bakers-in-pie-contests-do-not-violate-state-gaming-regulations.html; Chad Halloway, *New Jersey Assembly Passes Bill to Define Contests of Skill,* PokerNews.com, Jan. 9, 2014, http://www.pokernews.com/news/2014/01/new-jersey-assembly-passes-bill-to-define-contests-of-skill-17210.htm.
8. According to an email to author from Chris A. Brown, N.J. Assemb. and sponsor of A3624, (Feb. 13, 2014) (email on file with author), this misunderstanding originates from misinterpretations of the N.J. Superior Ct. decision in *Boardwalk Regency Corp. v. Att'y Gen of N.J.,* 457 A.2d 847 (1982) and of N.J. Att'y Gen. Op. 1-1980 (Jan. 10, 1980).
9. N.J. Stat. § 5:19-1 (2014).
10. *Id.*
11. A previous version of the legislation proposed a broader definition for contest of skill as "any contest where the winner or winners are selected solely on the quality of an entry in the contest as determined by a panel of judges using uniform criteria to assess the quality of entries. A 'contest of skill' shall not include any contest, game, pool, gaming scheme or gaming device in which the outcome depends in a material degree upon an element of chance." S2643, 215th Leg. 2012-2013, Reg. Sess. (N.J. 2014)

(Replaced by Assemb. A3624, 215th Leg. 2012-2013, Reg. Sess., which was approved on January 17, 2014 as P.L.2013, c.269).

12. In N.J. Att'y Gen. Op. No. 6-1983 (June 1, 1983), the New Jersey Attorney General interprets the statutory definition for something of value (*e.g.*, consideration) and seems to reject the viewpoint in *Lucky Calendar v. Cohen*, 117 A.2d 487 (N.J. 1955). In *Lucky Calendar*, the New Jersey Supreme Court ruled that there was consideration in a grocery store marketing promotion where the store inconvenienced participants by requiring them to drop off the entry resulting in the grocery store and its advertising company benefiting from increased business volume at the stores.

13. N.J. Stat. § 56:8-2.3 (2014).

14. N.J. Const. art. IV, § VII, paras. 2.A and 2.B.

15. *Id.*

16. N.J. Stat. §§ 5:8-25 and 5:8-51 (2014).

17. N.J. Stat. § 5:8-51-2.c (2014).

18. *See generally*, discussion of bingo and raffles in Section 9.2 of this Guide.

19. N.J. Stat. §§ 5:8-37 and 5:8-64 (2014).

20. N.J. Stat. §§ 5:8-25 and 5:8-51.1 (2014).

New Mexico

State Attorney General Office
Office of New Mexico Attorney General
408 Galisteo Street
Villagra Building
Santa Fe, New Mexico 87501
(505) 827-6000
Website: http://www.nmag.gov/

Selected State Laws, Regulations, and Constitutional Provisions

New Mexico's anti-gambling laws (Chapter 30, Article 19, Sections 30-19-1 to 30-19-15 of the New Mexico Statute), which are in its criminal offenses code, contain provisions related to promotions. In its consumer protection regulations, New Mexico includes prize promotion provisions (Title 12, Chapter 2, Section 12.2.2.1 *et seq.* of New Mexico Administrative Code). Specific New Mexico authorities frequently quoted in court cases and interpretive opinions related to promotions include the following:

Reference No.	Descriptive Name
N.M. Stat. § 30-19-1	Definitions (for anti-gambling laws including definitions for bet, consideration, and lottery)
N.M. Stat. § 30-19-2	Gambling (prohibited as petty misdemeanor)
N.M. Stat. § 30-19-3	Commercial Gambling (prohibited as fourth degree felony)

Summary of State Law

Prohibition of Lotteries and Gambling: New Mexico's statutory laws prohibit lotteries.[1] A promotion that combines a prize, chance, and consideration is a lottery in New Mexico.[2] New Mexico also has a general prohibition against gambling.[3] Exceptions to the lottery and gambling prohibitions include lotteries operated by the state and certain charitable lotteries.

New Mexico provides a statutory exemption that allows the common movie night promotion often referred to as bank night.[4] According to the movie night promotion law, anti-gambling laws do not "prohibit any bona fide motion picture theater from offering prizes of cash or merchandise for advertising purposes, in connection with such business or for the purpose of stimulating business, whether or not any consideration other than a monetary consideration in excess of the regular price of admission is exacted for participation in drawings for prizes".[5]

Contests: New Mexico permits contests as long as the contest does not conflict with anti-gambling laws. If the contest includes an element of consideration, the sponsor must award the contest prize based on skill and not on chance. Contests that charge consideration or whose primary purpose is the promotion of a product, service or business entity must comply with New Mexico's prize promotion laws discussed below.

The statutory definition of lottery implies that New Mexico applies the dominant factor doctrine[6] when evaluating whether or not chance determines the outcome of a promotion. The New Mexico statute defines lottery as an enterprise where in exchange for paying consideration, the participants receive an opportunity to win a prize and where chance determines the award of the prize even though chance may be accompanied by some skill.[7]

Sweepstakes: New Mexico permits sweepstakes as long as participants do not pay consideration and the sweepstakes does not violate anti-gambling laws. New Mexico regulations suggest the state takes a broad view of consideration.[8] The state's prize promotion law, referred to as the game promotion rule, defines consideration to mean "anything of pecuniary value" including "any business advantage to the sponsor, user or promoter of the game promotion".[9] Sweepstakes whose primary purpose is the promotion of a product, service or business entity must comply with New Mexico's prize promotion laws discussed below.

Prize Promotion Laws: New Mexico's version of a prize promotion law is referred to as the game promotion rule and is part of the consumer protection regulations.[10] The game promotion rule requirements are codified in Sections 12.2.2.6 to 12.2.2.14 of the Code of New Mexico Rules.

The game promotion rules are applicable to both sweepstakes and contests. New Mexico's statute defines a game promotion as any promotion in which entrants can win prizes based on chance or skill and whose primary purpose is promotion of a product, service or business entity, or the generation of money through the collection of entry fees or other consideration.[11] For purposes of the game promotion rule, New Mexico defines consideration broadly to include "anything of pecuniary value" including "any business advantage to the sponsor, user or promoter of the game promotion."[12]

Any game promotion, whether involving skill or chance, which requires consideration from entrants must include several specific disclosures.[13] The disclosure is not required for athletic competitions or other sports events, pari-mutuel betting, booths at fairs or competition whose entrants are judged on the results of their skilled efforts at raising animals, training dogs, growing flowers, baking cakes, creating arts and crafts or other endeavors.[14]

Gambling Exceptions for Non-Profits and Other Qualified Organizations

Raffles, Lotteries, and Bingo: New Mexico allows certain non-profit organizations to conduct raffles and bingo games as long as the organization uses the proceeds for educational, charitable, patriotic, religious or public-spirited purposes. Organizations eligible to offer raffles and lotteries include non-profit religious, charitable, environmental, fraternal, educational or veterans' organizations as well as voluntary firefighter organizations and labor organizations using the proceeds for scholarship or charitable purposes.[15]

Typically, in order to offer a raffle or bingo game, an organization needs a license from the New Mexico Gaming Control Board.[16] There is an exemption to the licensing requirement for an organization that holds no more than one raffle or one bingo session in every three consecutive months and no more than four bingo sessions in one calendar year.[17] However, if any single raffle prize has a value greater than $75,000, the organization must notify the Gaming Control Board at least ten days prior to selling raffle tickets or advertising the raffle and must also give the Gaming Control Board a post-raffle notice with a list of winner names, addresses, and phone numbers.[18]

The operation of raffles and bingo games must meet several statutory and regulatory requirements.[19] Licensees must file quarterly reports of their receipts, costs, and uses of the proceeds.[20]

The allowance is codified in the New Mexico Bingo and Raffle Act (Chapter 60, Article 2F, Sections 60-2F-1 to 60-2F-26 of the New Mexico Statute). Regulations for raffles and bingo games, issued by the New Mexico Gaming Control Board, are in Title 15, Chapter 4, Sections 15.4.1.1 *et seq.* of the New Mexico Administrative Code. Raffle and bingo registration and report forms as well as the regulations for raffles and bingo are available online from the New Mexico Gaming Control Board, 4900 Alameda Blvd NE, Albuquerque NM 87113, (505) 841-9700, website: http://www.nmgcb.org

Resources

New Mexico offers a searchable database for its attorney general opinions from the early 1980s through the present online at https://sites.google.com/a/nmag.gov/public-records-project/opinions

---

Endnotes

1. N.M. Stat. § § 30-19-1.E, 30-19-2 to 30-19-3 (2013).
2. N.M. Stat. § 30-19-1 (2013).
3. N.M. Stat. §§ 30-19-2 to 30-19-3 (2013).
4. N.M. Stat. § 30-19-6 (2013).
5. *Id.*
6. *See generally*, Section 3.4.3 of this Guide for a discussion of tests used when evaluating whether chance or skill prevails in a promotion combining elements of both.
7. N.M. Stat. § 30-19-1 (2013).

8. *See generally*, Section 4.3.1 of this Guide for a discussion of how consideration for a promotion can differ from consideration for a contract.
9. N.M. Code R. § 12.2.2.7 (2014).
10. N.M. Code R. §12.2.2 (2014).
11. N.M. Code R. § 12.2.2.7 (2014).
12. *Id.*
13. N.M. Code R. § 12.2.2.10. See generally, discussion of state prize promotion laws in Section 7.4.2 of this Guide.
14. N.M. Code R. § 12.2.2.10.J (2014).
15. N.M. Stat. § 60-2F-4.Y (2013).
16. N.M. Stat. § 60-2F-22.A (2013).
17. N.M. Stat. § 60-2F-26.A(2) (2013).
18. N.M. Stat. § 60-2F-26.B (2013).
19. N.M. Stat. § 60-2F-18 (2013). *See generally*, discussion of bingo and raffles in Section 9.2 of this Guide.
20. N.M. Stat. § 60-2F-19 (2013).

New York

State Attorney General Office
Office of the Attorney General
The Capitol
Albany, New York 12224
(800) 771-7755
Website: http://www.ag.ny.gov/

Selected State Laws, Regulations, and Constitutional Provisions

New York's anti-gambling laws (Part 3, Title M, Article 225, Sections 225.00 *et seq.* of the New York Penal Law) contain provisions related to promotions. New York also has prize promotion laws (Article 24A, Section 369-ee of New York General Business Laws). New York legal provisions frequently quoted in court cases and interpretive opinions related to promotions include the following:

Reference No.	Descriptive Name
N.Y. Const. art. I, § 9	Right to assemble and petition; divorce; lotteries; pool-selling and gambling; laws to prevent; pari-mutual betting on horse races permitted; games of chance, bingo or lotto authorized under certain restrictions
N.Y. Penal Law § 225.00	Gambling offenses; definitions of terms (definitions for anti-gambling laws including definitions for contest of chance, gambling, something of value, and lottery)
N.Y. Penal Law § 225.05	Promoting gambling in the second degree (prohibited as misdemeanor)

| N.Y. Penal Law
§ 225.10 | Promoting gambling in the first degree (prohibited as a felony) |
| N.Y. Gen. Bus.
§ 369-e | Use of games of chance in selling commodities |

Summary of State Law

Prohibition of Lotteries and Gambling: New York's Constitution prohibits lotteries.[1] A promotion that combines a prize, chance, and consideration is a lottery in New York.[2] New York also has a general prohibition against promoting gambling.[3] The anti-gambling laws refer to a lottery as an unlawful gambling scheme.[4] Exceptions to the lottery and gambling prohibitions include state-operated lotteries and certain charitable lotteries.

Contests: New York permits contests as long as the contest does not conflict with anti-gambling laws. If the contest includes an element of consideration, the sponsor must award the contest prize based on skill and not on chance.

The statutory definition of contest of chance suggests that New York applies the material element test[5] when evaluating whether or not chance determines the outcome of a promotion. The New York anti-gambling laws define a contest of chance as "any contest, game, gaming scheme or gaming device in which *the outcome depends in a material degree upon an element of chance*, notwithstanding that the skill of the contestants may also be a factor therein".[6]

Sweepstakes: New York permits sweepstakes as long as participants do not pay consideration and the sweepstakes does not otherwise violate anti-gambling laws. New York requires registration and bonding for sweepstakes offering prizes with an aggregate value over five thousand dollars.[7] The requirement applies to sweepstakes conducted in connection with the promotion, advertising or sale of consumer products or services. Sponsors must register with the New York Department of State at least thirty days prior to the start of the promotion.

The sweepstakes rules must be posted in any participating retail stores and must be included in all advertising copy. The sponsor must also open a trust account or provide a bond for an amount of money sufficient to pay or purchase the total value of prizes offered. Within ninety days after completion of the sweepstakes, the sponsor must file a report with the name and addresses of the winners, prizes awarded, and dates of prize awards.

The New York Department of State makes registration and report forms available through its website at http://www.dos.ny.gov/ within the portion of the website for the Division of Corporations, State Records and Uniform Commercial Code.

Prize Promotion Laws: New York's version of a prize promotion law is a statutory provision entitled Prize award schemes (Article 24, Section 369-ee of New York General Business Law). The provision applies to any person or company offering a prize in conjunction with the sale of a product or service.

A company must provide a written disclosure before offering a consumer a prize or opportunity to win a prize if obtaining the prize depends on chance and requires the consumer to take some type of affirmative action. That affirmative action could be traveling to a location to accept the prize, listening to a sales presentation, providing a credit card number, responding to the company verbally or in writing, or allowing a sales person into the consumer's home.

New York's prize promotion law includes prohibited practices as well as specific disclosures that must be included in the written disclosure.[8] New York's prize promotion law does not apply to and no disclosure is required for promotions offered by a retail store as long as the promotion is incidental to the retail store's business and any required consumer action to receive the prize is limited to traveling to the store.[9]

There is also a prize promotion component in New York's Telemarketing and Consumer Fraud and Abuse Prevention Act (Article 26, Section 399-pp of New York General Business Laws). If a telemarketing campaign includes a chance-based prize promotion, the telemarketer must comply with record keeping and disclosure requirements related directly to the prize promotion aspect of the campaign.[10]

Gambling Exceptions for Non-Profits and Other Qualified Organizations

Raffles and Lotteries: A constitutional provision allows municipalities to authorize non-profit organizations to operate raffles for charitable purposes.[11] Each municipality may authorize the conduct of games of chance by eligible organizations within its jurisdiction.[12] Raffles are included among the permissible games of chance.[13] Organizations eligible to offer charitable raffles and other games of chance consist of certain non-profit religious or charitable organizations, educational, fraternal or service organizations, veterans organizations, and volunteer firemen organizations. The organization must use the entire net raffle proceeds in a manner that is consistent with the organization's lawful purposes.

There are statutory and regulatory requirements for raffles.[14] An eligible organization does not need a license to offer raffles if it derives less than $5,000 in net proceeds from a single raffle and less than $20,000 from raffles conducted within one calendar year.[15] Eligible organizations with raffle net proceeds in excess of those amounts must make registration and raffle financial report filings with the New York State Gaming Commission as well as with the applicable municipal clerk.

New York codifies the constitutional allowance for raffles in the Games of Chance Licensing Law (Article 9A, Sections 185 *et seq.* of New York's General Municipal Code). The games of chance regulations (which include regulations for raffles) are issued by the New York State Gaming Commission and are codified in Title 9, Sections 4600.1 *et seq.* of the Official Compilation of Codes, Rules and Regulations of the State of New York.

The New York State Gaming Commission provides application forms, copies of the regulations, and additional information in the charitable gaming section of its website at http://www.gaming.ny.gov/

Bingo: A constitutional provision allows municipalities to authorize non-profit organizations to operate bingo games for charitable purposes.[16] Each municipality decides whether non-profit organizations may conduct bingo games within its jurisdiction.[17] Organizations eligible to offer bingo games consist of certain non-profit religious, charitable, educational, fraternal, civic, service, veterans, volunteer firefighters, and volunteer ambulance workers organizations. The organization must use all net bingo proceeds in a manner that is consistent with the organization's lawful purposes.

The operation of bingo games must satisfy several statutory and regulatory requirements.[18] Bingo operators must make registration and regular financial statement filings with the New York State Gaming Commission as well as with the clerk of the municipality in which the bingo games are offered.

The New York Bingo Licensing Law, which codifies the constitutional allowance, is at Article 14-H, Sections 475 *et seq.* of New York's General Municipal Code. Bingo regulations, issued by the New York State Gaming Commission, are codified in Title 9, Sections 4800.1 *et seq.* of the Official Compilation of Codes, Rules and Regulations of the State of New York.

The New York State Gaming Commission provides application forms, copies of the regulations, and additional information in the charitable gaming section of its website at http://www.gaming.ny.gov/

Resources

New York offers a searchable database for its attorney general opinions from 1995 through the present online in the resources section of the website of the Office of the Attorney General.

Endnotes

1. N.Y. Const. art. I, § 9.1.
2. N.Y. Penal Law § 225.00(10) (2014).
3. N.Y. Penal Law §§ 225.05 and 225.10 (2014).
4. N.Y. Penal Law § 225.00(10) (2014).
5. *See generally*, Section 3.4.3 of this Guide for a discussion of tests used when determining whether chance or skill prevails in a promotion combining elements of both.
6. N.Y. Penal Law § 225.00(1) (2014) (emphasis added).
7. N.Y. Gen. Bus. § 369-e (2014).
8. N.Y. Gen. Bus. § 369-ee(1) (2014). *See generally*, discussion of state prize promotion laws in Section 7.4.2 of this Guide.
9. N.Y. Gen. Bus. § 369-ee(3)(e) (2014).

10. N.Y. Gen. Bus. §§ 399-pp(2)(h) and (i), (6)b(3), and (8)a(2) (2014). *See generally*, discussion of state telemarketing laws in Section 7.5.2 of this Guide.
11. N.Y. Const. art. I, § 9.2.
12. N.Y. Gen. Mun. § 187 (2014).
13. N.Y. Gen. Mun. § 186.3 (2014).
14. *See generally*, discussion of bingo and raffles in Section 9.2 of this Guide.
15. N.Y. Gen. Mun. § 190-a (2014).
16. N.Y. Const. art. I, § 9.2.
17. N.Y. Gen. Mun. § 477 (2014).
18. *See generally*, discussion of bingo and raffles in Section 9.2 of this Guide.

North Carolina

State Attorney General Office
Department of Justice
Attorney General's Office
9001 Mail Service Center
Raleigh, North Carolina 27699
(919) 716-6400
Website: http://www.ncdoj.gov

Selected State Laws, Regulations, and Constitutional Provisions

North Carolina's anti-gambling laws (Chapter 14, Article 37, Sections 14-289 *et seq.* of the North Carolina General Statute), which are grouped with its criminal laws, contain provisions related to promotions. With its monopolies, trusts, and consumer protection laws, North Carolina includes prize promotion laws (Chapter 75, Article 1, Sections 75-32 – 75-35 of the North Carolina General Statute). Specific North Carolina authorities frequently quoted in court cases and interpretive opinions related to promotions include the following:

Reference No.	Descriptive Name
N.C. Gen. Stat. § 14-289	Advertising lotteries (prohibited as misdemeanor)
N.C. Gen. Stat. § 14-290	Dealing in Lotteries (prohibited as misdemeanor)
N.C. Gen. Stat. § 14-291	Selling lottery tickets and acting as agent for lotteries (prohibited as misdemeanor)
N.C. Gen. Stat. § 14-292	Gambling (prohibited as misdemeanor)

Summary of State Law

Prohibition of Lotteries and Gambling: North Carolina's anti-gambling laws prohibit advertising, dealing in, or making sales for lotteries.[1] North Carolina accepts that a lottery has the elements of a prize, chance, and consideration.[2] North Carolina also has a general prohibition against gambling.[3] Exceptions to the lottery and gambling prohibitions include state-operated lotteries and certain charitable lotteries.

Contests: North Carolina permits contests as long as the contest does not conflict with anti-gambling laws. If the contest includes an element of consideration, the sponsor must award the contest prize based on skill and not on chance.

Case law suggests that North Carolina applies the dominant factor doctrine[4] when evaluating whether or not chance determines the outcome of a promotion. In *Joker Club v. Hardin*, 643 S.E.2d 626 (N.C. Ct. App. 2007), while talking about gambling, a North Carolina court categorized poker as a game of chance rather than as a game of skill since chance predominated. The *Joker Club* court recognized that even though skills such as knowledge of human psychology, bluffing, and the ability to calculate and analyze odds weighed in favor of the skilled poker player, a novice player could still defeat the skilled player if luck supplied the novice with better cards.

Sweepstakes: North Carolina permits sweepstakes as long as participants do not pay consideration and the sweepstakes does not violate anti-gambling laws. An exception written into the prize promotion laws suggests that North Carolina would not view a promotion requiring participants to perform any of the following activities as a promotion with consideration:

- completing and mailing in an entry form obtainable locally or by mail
- visiting a local store to drop off an entry form obtainable locally or by mail
- calling in an entry by telephone[5]

Prize Promotion Laws: As part of its consumer protection laws, North Carolina has prize promotion laws (Chapter 75, Article 1, Sections 75-32 to 75-35 of the North Carolina General Statute). The law applies to giveaways and promotions offered as part of a campaign for the sale or lease of goods, services, or property. Requirements imposed by the prize promotions laws depend on the type of promotion.

REPRESENTATION THAT A PERSON HAS WON A PRIZE. If a company represents that a person has won a gift or a contest, the company must give the gift to the person without obligation within ten days of making the representation. The company cannot represent that a person has won a prize if the company gives the same prize to more than ten percent of the people considered for receiving the prize.[6]

REPRESENTATION THAT A PERSON IS ELIGIBLE TO WIN A PRIZE REQUIRES A DISCLOSURE. When a company offers a chance to win a prize in conjunction with its efforts to sell or lease any goods, property, or service, the company must make certain disclosures.[7] While the statute does not explicitly say the disclosure must be in writing, the statute does indicate that the disclosure must be displayed, clearly and conspicuously, adjacent to the description of the prize. The disclosure requirement applies broadly to any contest or sweepstakes offered as part of a sales campaign. However, the law is not applicable and there is no disclosure requirement if consumers wishing to compete for the prize can do so by submitting an entry by mail, phone, or at a local retail store, and are not required to listen to a sales presentation.[8]

PRIZE PROMOTION PROVISIONS OF TELEMARKETING LAWS. North Carolina's Telephonic Seller Registration and Bond Requirement laws (Chapter 66, Article 33, Sections 66-260 to 66-269 of the North Carolina General Statutes) include provisions related to prizes and giveaways incorporated into commercial telephone solicitations.[9] Telephone solicitation campaigns that include the offering of prizes or gifts with a value of $500 or more must submit to the state full details regarding the prize promotion, award all offered prizes, post a bond for the value of the prizes, and provide the state with proof that all prizes have been awarded.[10] Telephone sellers may not offer a prize if the consumer must call a pay-per-call number to further the transaction or pay money or make a donation in order to collect the prize.[11]

Gambling Exceptions for Non-Profits and Other Qualified Organizations

Raffles and Lotteries: Governmental agencies as well as tax-exempt, non-profit organizations may conduct two raffles per year.[12] No license is required. At least ninety percent of the net raffle proceeds must be used for charitable, religious, educational, civic, or other non-profit purposes.[13] North Carolina's statute explicitly states that non-profits may offer real property as a raffle prize.[14]

Bingo: North Carolina allows certain tax-exempt, non-profit charitable, civic, religious, fraternal, patriotic or veterans' organizations to operate bingo games.[15] Organizations qualified to conduct bingo also include non-profit volunteer fire departments, non-profit volunteer rescue squads, and homeowners' or property owners' associations. Bingo operators may use the proceeds only for related expenses; for religious, charitable, civic, scientific, testing, public safety, literary, or educational purposes; for acquisition and improvements to property owned by the organization; and other specific community purposes.[16]

Operation of the bingo games must meet several statutory requirements.[17] Eligible organizations wishing to offer bingo games need a license, issued by the North Carolina Department of Public Safety.[18] Organizations conducting bingo games must make annual filings with the North Carolina Department of Public Safety reporting the number of bingo games conducted, the receipts, the prizes awarded, and the use of proceeds.[19] No license or other filings are required for bingo games that do not offer prizes with a value over ten dollars—regardless of whether the bingo operator is a non-profit, charitable organization.[20]

Laws related to bingo are grouped with the criminal laws and codified in Chapter 14, Article 37, Sections 14-309.5 to 14-309.14 of the North Carolina General Statute. Bingo license and report forms are available in the Alcohol Law Enforcement/Bingo division of the North Carolina Department of Public Safety, 4201 Mail Service Center, Raleigh, NC 27699-4201 www.ncdps.gov

Resources

North Carolina offers a database for its attorney general opinions from 1977 through the present in the About DOJ/Legal Services portion of the website of the Department of Justice.

Endnotes

1. N.C. Gen. Stat. §§ 14-289, 14-290, and 14-291 (2013).
2. *See e.g., City of Winston v. Beeson,* 47 S.E. 457, 459 (N.C. 1904).
3. N.C. Gen. Stat. § 14-292 (2013).
4. *See generally,* Section 3.4.3 of this Guide for a discussion of tests used when evaluating whether chance or skill prevails in a promotion combining elements of both.
5. These are situations in which the prize promotion disclosure requirements do not apply. N.C. Gen. Stat. § 75-33(b) (2013). See further discussion about the prize promotion laws in this North Carolina State Summary in the paragraph titled Prize Promotion Laws.
6. N.C. Gen. Stat. § 75-32 (2013).
7. N.C. Gen. Stat. § 75-33 (2013). *See generally,* discussion of state prize notice laws in Section 7.4.2 of this Guide.
8. N.C. Gen. Stat. §75-33(b) (2013).
9. *See generally,* discussion of state telemarketing laws in Section 7.5.2 of this Guide.
10. N.C. Gen. Stat. §66-263 (2013).
11. N.C. Gen. Stat. §66-265 (2013). This prohibition is not intended to prevent a telephonic seller from offering a gift or prize in connection with the bona fide sale of a product or service. *Id.*
12. N.C. Gen. Stat. §14-309.15 (2013).
13. N.C. Gen. Stat. §14-309.15(f) (2013).
14. N.C. Gen. Stat. §14-309.15(g) (2013).
15. N.C. Gen. Stat. §14-309.5 (2013).
16. N.C. Gen. Stat. §14-309.11 (2013).
17. See generally, discussion of bingo and raffles in Section 9.2 of this Guide.
18. N.C. Gen. Stat. §§ 14-309.5 and 14-309.7 (2013).
19. N.C. Gen. Stat. §14-309.11(b) (2013).
20. N.C. Gen. Stat. §14-309.14 (2013). The statute refers to such bingo games as beach bingo.

North Dakota

State Attorney General Office
Office of Attorney General
600 E. Boulevard Avenue,
Bismarck, North Dakota 58505
(701) 328-2210
Website: www.ag.nd.gov

Selected State Laws, Regulations, and Constitutional Provisions

North Dakota's anti-gambling laws, which are in its criminal code (Title 12.1, Chapter 12.1-28, Sections 12.1-28-01 *et seq.* of the North Dakota Century Code) contain provisions related to promotions. In its sports and amusements code, North Dakota includes contest prize promotion laws (Title 53, Chapter 53-11, Sections 53-11-01 *et seq.* of the North Dakota Century Code). Specific North Dakota legal provisions frequently quoted in court cases and interpretive opinions related to promotions include the following:

Reference No.	Descriptive Name
N.D. Const. art. XI, § 25	(Prohibition on games of chance and lotteries)
N.D. Cent. Code § 12.1-28-01	Gambling—Definitions (including definition for gambling and lottery)
N.D. Cent. Code § 12.1-28-02	Gambling—Related offenses—Classification of offenses

Summary of State Law

Prohibition of Lotteries and Gambling: North Dakota's Constitution and its statutory laws prohibit lotteries.[1] In North Dakota, a promotion that combines a prize, chance, and consideration qualifies as a lottery, a gambling game, or both.[2] North Dakota also has a general prohibition against gambling.[3] Exceptions to the lottery and gambling prohibitions include state-operated lotteries and certain charitable lotteries.

Contests: North Dakota permits contests as long as the contest does not conflict with anti-gambling laws. If the contest includes an element of consideration, the sponsor must award the contest prize based on skill and not on chance.

The anti-gambling laws include an exemption from gambling for lawful contests of skill, speed, strength, or endurance in which awards are made only to entrants or to the owners of entries.[4] The statutory definition for gambling implies that North Dakota applies either the material element test or the dominant factor doctrine[5] when evaluating whether or not chance determines the outcome of a promotion. According to the state statute, gambling means "risking any money . . ., or other thing of value for gain, *contingent, wholly or partially, upon lot, chance, . .* [or other event], over which the person taking the risk has no control".[6]

It is unclear whether North Dakota permits contests that charge consideration. According to a 1998 North Dakota Attorney General Opinion, the state's gambling laws do not prohibit contests which require payment of an entry fee or purchase of a product to participate as long as the contest sponsor awards the prizes based on skill or achievement.[7] However, as discussed below, a literal reading of the state's prize promotion laws contradicts this attorney general statement and does prohibit contests with consideration.

Sweepstakes: North Dakota permits sweepstakes as long as participants do not pay consideration. As in most states, in an in-package sweepstakes or other sweepstakes where prize-playing opportunities are distributed with a purchase, the sponsor must offer a free alternative method of entry. Otherwise, the purchase of the product—even if at no increase in cost—is viewed as consideration and the sweepstakes violates North Dakota gambling laws.[8]

Prize Promotions Laws: With its sports and amusements laws, North Dakota has a contest prize promotion law (Title 53, Chapter 53-11, Sections 53-11-01 to 53-11-05 of North Dakota Century Code).

APPLICABILITY OF PRIZE PROMOTION LAWS TO CONTESTS CHARGING CONSIDERATION. The North Dakota prize promotions law is applicable to prizes awarded in any contest, sweepstakes, or similar competition. A portion of the law reads as follows:

> A sponsor may not require a person to pay the sponsor money as a condition of awarding the person a prize [in a contest, sweepstakes, or other competition], or as a condition of allowing the person to receive, use, compete for, or obtain information about a prize. A sponsor may not use a solicitation that creates the reasonable impression that a payment is required, unless the sponsor first has delivered to the person written prize notice containing [disclosures indicated in the statute][9]

On its face, the first sentence of this language prohibits charging any consideration to compete in a prize promotion in North Dakota. It is unclear how the first and second sentences fit together. One interpretation (based on the first sentence alone) is an absolute prohibition on contests and other promotions with consideration. An alternate interpretation (based on the second sentence qualifying the first sentence) is that a contest sponsor may charge monetary consideration as long as the sponsor provides a written disclosure to participants. Many contest sponsors and their advisors have adopted the former interpretation and operate with the presumption that North Dakota prohibits consideration for contests.

However, the North Dakota Attorney General has indicated that the latter interpretation reflects the true intent of the law. In a 1998 opinion, the North Dakota Attorney General noted that the North Dakota Contest Prize Notices law is based on laws in Iowa and Minnesota which do allow charging consideration in a contest as long as the sponsor provides a written disclaimer (*e.g.*, a prize notice).[10] The North Dakota Attorney

General suggested that if the legislature wishes to allow contest sponsors to charge consideration, the legislature should modify the statute to clarify that sponsors may require a person to purchase a product or pay money as a condition of being awarded a prize if a sufficient prize notice is given. As of the writing of this Guide, the statute has not been modified to make this clarification.

OBLIGATION TO AWARD PROMISED PRIZE. A company must actually deliver a prize if

- the company requires money from a person as a condition of awarding the person a prize or competing for or obtaining information about a prize[11] and
- the company represents to the person that the person has won a prize.[12]

Within thirty days of making a representation that the person has won a prize, the company must deliver one of the following to the person:

- the promised prize,
- a voucher for the promised prize,
- an alternate prize of equal or greater value, or
- a monetary payment equal to the retail value of the promised prize.[13]

Gambling Exceptions for Non-Profits and Other Qualified Organizations

Bingo, Raffles and Lotteries: The North Dakota Constitution allows the state legislature to authorize non-profit veterans', charitable, educational, religious, or fraternal organizations, civic and service clubs, or similar public-spirited organizations to offer bingo, raffles, and other games of chance.[14] There are a number of statutory and regulatory requirements for conducting bingos, raffles, and other games of chance.[15] The organizations must use the net proceeds of such games for educational, charitable, patriotic, fraternal, religious, or other public-spirited uses. To conduct games of chance, an eligible organization must obtain a site authorization from the governing body of the city or county in which the game is to take place as well as a license from the attorney general. Organizations must also file quarterly reports of their gaming activities.

The constitutional allowance for games of chance is codified with North Dakota's sports and amusements laws in Title 53, Sections 53-06.1-01 *et seq.* of the North Dakota Century Code. Relevant regulations issued by the North Dakota State Gaming Commission are at Sections 99-01.3-01 *et seq.* of the North Dakota Administrative Code. Report forms and copies of the regulations are available online from the Gaming Division of the North Dakota Attorney General, accessible through the Gaming link of the attorney general's website.

Resources

North Dakota offers a database for its attorney general opinions from 1942 through the present in the Legal Opinions portion of the website of the Office of the Attorney General. Earlier opinions may be requested from the Office of the Attorney General.

North Dakota publishes *The Gaming Update* newsletter on a quarterly basis. Current and previous issues are available for download at no charge at http://www.ag.nd. gov/Gaming/Gaming.htm

---

Endnotes

1. N.D. Const. art. XI, § 25; N.D. Cent. Code § 12.1-28-02 (2014).
2. N.D. Att'y Gen. Op. No. 98-L-132 (Sept. 3, 1998).
3. N.D. Cent. Code § 12.1-28-02 (2014).
4. N.D. Cent. Code § 12.1-28-01.1.a (2014).
5. *See generally*, Section 3.4.3 of this Guide for a discussion of tests used when evaluating whether chance or skill prevails in a promotion combining elements of both.
6. N.D. Cent. Code § 12.1-28-01.1 (2014) (emphasis added).
7. N.D. Att'y Gen. Op. No. 98-L-132 (Sept. 3, 1998).
8. N.D. Att'y Gen. Op. No. 93-L-98 (March 17, 1993). *See also*, discussion of in-package sweepstakes included with Section 3.6 of this Guide.
9. N.D. Cent. Code § 53-11-02 (2014). There is specific information to be included in the prize notice disclosures as well as specific fonts, wording,

and placement required for the disclosures. *See generally*, discussion of state prize promotion laws in Section 7.4.2 of this Guide.

10. N.D. Att'y Gen. Op. No. 98-L-132 (Sept. 3, 1998).
11. N.D. Cent. Code § 53-11-01.3 (2014).
12. N.D. Cent. Code § 53-11-03 (2014).
13. *Id.*
14. N.D. Const. art. XI, § 25.
15. *See generally*, discussion of bingos and raffles in Section 9.2 of this Guide.

Ohio

State Attorney General Office
Ohio Attorney General
30 E. Broad St., 14th Floor
Columbus, Ohio 43215
(614) 466-4986
Website: http://www.ohioattorneygeneral.gov

Selected State Laws, Regulations, and Constitutional Provisions

Ohio's anti-gambling laws (Title 29, Chapter 2915, Sections 2915-01 *et seq.* of Ohio Revised Code), which are in its crimes procedure code, contain provisions related to promotions. Specific Ohio authorities frequently quoted in court cases and interpretive opinions related to promotions include the following:

Reference No.	Descriptive Name
Ohio Const. art. XV, § 6	Lotteries, charitable bingo, casinos
Ohio Rev. Code § 2915.01	Definitions (for anti-gambling laws including definitions for scheme of chance, game of chance, gambling offense, and sweepstakes)
Ohio Rev. Code § 2915.02	Gambling (prohibited)

Summary of State Law

Prohibition of Lotteries and Gambling: Ohio's Constitution as well as its statutory laws prohibit lotteries.[1] A promotion that combines a prize, chance, and consideration is a lottery in Ohio.[2] Ohio also has a general prohibition against gambling.[3] Exceptions to the lottery and gambling prohibitions include state-operated lotteries and certain charitable lotteries.

Contests: Ohio permits contests as long as the contest does not conflict with anti-gambling laws. If the contest includes an element of consideration, the sponsor must award the contest prize based on skill and not on chance. Ohio Attorney General opinions suggest that Ohio applies the dominant factor doctrine[4] when evaluating whether or not chance determines the outcome of a promotion. In a 2004 opinion letter, while evaluating whether an amusement machine (*e.g.*, video or digital game) was a game of skill or game of chance, the Ohio Attorney General explained that a game was a chance-based game if ". . . the outcome of a game be determined more than fifty percent by chance . . . [or] . . . the element of chance predominates over skill in determining the outcome of a game".[5]

Sweepstakes: Ohio permits sweepstakes as long as participants do not pay consideration and the sweepstakes does not otherwise violate anti-gambling laws. Ohio sometimes evaluates intent when determining whether there is consideration involved in a sweepstakes. The element of price exists where there is evidence that an individual purchases a product or service with the intent to receive the chance to win a prize as opposed to the product or service.[6]

In October 2013, Ohio implemented changes to its anti-gambling laws in an effort to combat internet sweepstakes cafes.[7] One result of the revised law is more detail regarding the circumstances and activities that qualify as consideration in a promotion. Activities and circumstances that qualify as consideration are listed in Ohio's statutory definition for scheme of chance.[8] With the 2013 revisions, circumstances in which Ohio views a promotion as having consideration include the following:

- There is consideration if less than fifty percent of the goods or services sold by a sponsor in exchange for game entries are used or redeemed by participants at any one location.
- There is consideration if less than fifty percent of participants who purchase goods or services at any one location do not use or redeem the goods or services sold.

- There is consideration if a sponsor pays out in prize money more than twenty percent of the gross revenue received at one location.
- There is consideration if a participant pays more than fair market value for goods or services offered by the sponsor in order to receive one or more game entries.[9]

Prize Promotion Laws: Ohio incorporates some prize promotion protections into its telephone solicitors laws (Title 47, Chapter 4719, Sections 4719.01 to 4719.99 of Ohio Revised Code). A company is a telephone solicitor if the company uses the telephone to offer goods and services to consumers. Several categories of telephone solicitors are exempt from the Ohio telephone solicitor laws including companies that make telephone solicitations infrequently and companies that make telephone solicitations for religious, political or charitable purposes.[10]

If a company's actions place it under the telephone solicitors laws, the company must comply with the laws' registration, bonding, and disclosure requirements[11] including the requirements specific to giveaways and prize offers. If as part of the telephone solicitation, the solicitor tells consumers they might be eligible to receive a gift, award, or prize, the solicitor must disclose certain information about the prize offer. The disclosure must occur as part of the call to the consumer[12], in an information statement filed with the attorney general at least fourteen days prior to making the representation[13], and in the required written verification to the consumer following any sale.[14] The disclosure must include a description of the prize, its value, the terms and conditions the consumer must satisfy to receive the prize, and a statement that no purchase is necessary to compete for or receive the prize. Telephone solicitors are also prohibited from misrepresenting any aspects of the prize promotion.[15]

Gambling Exceptions for Non-Profits and Other Qualified Organizations

Raffles and Lotteries: Ohio allows certain non-profit, tax-exempt organizations to conduct raffles for fund-raising purposes. Ohio defines raffle as a form of bingo and incorporates the allowance for charitable raffles into the constitutional allowance for charitable bingo, discussed in the immediately following section of this Ohio State Summary.[16]

Nevertheless, Ohio raffle law differs from Ohio bingo law in some significant ways. Eligible organizations do not need a license to offer a raffle.[17] The category of organizations eligible to offer raffles is broader than that for organizations eligible to offer bingo. In addition to charitable organizations (definition provided in the Bingo paragraph below), eligible raffle sponsors include public schools, chartered nonpublic schools, community schools, veteran's organizations, fraternal organizations, and sporting organizations.[18] Even charitable organizations that do not meet the tax-exempt requirements of the raffle allowance may conduct a raffle provided that the organization uses fifty percent of the net profit for charitable purposes listed in the statute or distributes those proceeds to a government department or agency.[19]

Bingo: The Ohio State Constitution allows the state legislature to authorize and regulate the operation of charitable bingo.[20] The allowance authorizing charitable organizations to operate bingo games is codified with the anti-gambling laws.[21] The statute defines charitable organization as 501(c)(3) tax-exempt organizations as well as certain tax-exempt volunteer rescue service, volunteer firefighters', veterans', fraternal, and sporting organizations.[22]

Eligible organizations conducting bingo games must obtain a license from the attorney general's office.[23] Bingo operators must retain detailed records of the bingo operations and comply with operational rules.[24] The license and record retention requirements do not apply to bingo games operated for amusement, defined as games for which participants do not pay or pay a nominal amount and the prizes are non-monetary or of low monetary value.[25]

The Ohio Attorney General's Office regulates bingo and has issued a policy statement explaining its administration of bingo and other charitable gambling.[26] Additional information, application forms, and regulations for charitable gaming are available online in the Services for Bingo portion of the Ohio Attorney General's website.

Resources

Ohio offers a searchable database for its attorney general opinions from 1993 through the present available under the Legal portion of the Ohio Attorney General's website.

Endnotes

1. Ohio Const. art. XV, § 6; Ohio Rev. Code § 2915.02 (2014).
2. See e.g., *Kroger Co. v. Cook*, 244 N.E.2d 790, 795 (Ohio Ct. App. 1968).
3. Ohio Rev. Code § 2915.02 (2014).
4. *See generally*, Section 3.4.3 of this Guide for a discussion of tests used when evaluating whether chance or skill prevails in a promotion combining elements of both.
5. Ohio Att'y Gen. Op. No. 2004-029 (August 6, 2004) *citing Operators Group v. Dept. of Liquor Control*, No. 87AP-64 (Ohio Ct. App. 1987).
6. *See e.g.*, Ohio Att'y Gen. Op. No. 1985-013 (April, 9, 1985).
7. H.B. 7, 130th Gen. Assemb. (Ohio 2013) (amending Ohio Rev. Code §§ 109.32, 109.54, 2915.01, and 2915.02).
8. Ohio Rev. Code § 2915.01(C) (2014).
9. This is not the complete list of circumstances giving rise to consideration in a promotion. For the complete statutory list, see Ohio Rev. Code § 2915.01(C) (2014).
10. Ohio Rev. Code § 4719.01(B) (2014).
11. *See generally*, discussion of state telemarketing laws in Section 7.5.2 of this Guide.
12. Ohio Rev. Code § 4719.06(B)(5) (2014).
13. Ohio Rev. Code § 4719.05 (2014).
14. Ohio Rev. Code § 4719.07(F)(9) (2014).
15. Ohio Rev. Code § 4719.08(F)(5) (2014).
16. Ohio Rev. Code §§ 2915.01(O)(2), 2915.01(Q), 2915.01(CC) (2014).
17. Ohio Rev. Code § 2915.092 (2014).
18. Ohio Rev. Code § 2915.092(A)(1) (2014).
19. Ohio Rev. Code § 2915.092(A)(2) (2014).
20. Ohio Const. art. XV, § 6.
21. Ohio Rev. Code §§ 2915.07 to 2915.13 (2014).
22. Ohio Rev. Code § 2915.01(H) (2014).
23. Ohio Rev. Code § 2915.07 and 2915.08 (2014).

24. Ohio Rev. Code § 2915.10 (2014). *See generally*, discussion of bingo and raffles in Section 9.2 of this Guide.

25. Ohio Rev. Code § 2915.12 (2014).

26. Ohio Att'y Gen. Charitable Law Section, *Policy 201: Games of Chance*, http://www.ohioattorneygeneral.gov/Files/Publications/Publications-for-NonProfits/Bingo-Publications/Policy-201-Games-of-Chance (last visited Nov. 15, 2014).

Oklahoma

State Attorney General Office
Office of the Attorney General
313 NE 21st Street
Oklahoma City, Oklahoma 73105
(405) 521- 3921
Website: http://www.oag.state.ok.us/

Selected State Laws, Regulations, and Constitutional Provisions

Oklahoma's anti-gambling laws (Title 21, Chapter 38, Sections 21-941 *et seq.* of the Oklahoma Statute) and anti-lottery laws (Title 21, Chapter 41, Sections 21-1051 to 21-1068 of the Oklahoma Statute) contain provisions related to promotions. The Consumers Disclosure of Prizes and Gifts Act (Title 21, Chapter 38, Sections 21-996.1 to 21-996.3 of the Oklahoma Statute) provides protections to consumers offered giveaways. Specific Oklahoma authorities frequently quoted in court cases and interpretive opinions related to promotions include the following:

Reference No.	Descriptive Name
Okla. Stat. § 21-941	Opening, conducting or carrying on gambling game—Dealing for those engaged in game (prohibited)
Okla. Stat. § 21-942	Betting on or playing prohibited game—Punishment
Okla. Stat. § 21-965	"Thing of value" defined
Okla. Stat. § 21-981	Definitions (for anti-gambling laws including definitions for bet and consideration)
Okla. Stat. § 21-1051	Lottery defined—Consideration—Organizations permitted to issue tickets
Okla. Stat. § 21-1052	Lottery unlawful—Nuisance

Okla. Stat. § 21-1053   Preparing or drawing lottery—Punishment
(prohibited as felony)

Summary of State Law

Prohibition of Lotteries and Gambling: Oklahoma's statutory laws prohibit lotteries.[1] A promotion that combines a prize, chance, and consideration is a lottery in Oklahoma.[2] Oklahoma also has a general prohibition against gambling.[3] Exceptions to the lottery and gambling prohibitions include state-operated lotteries and certain charitable lotteries.

Contests: Oklahoma permits contests as long as the contest does not conflict with anti-gambling laws. If the contest includes an element of consideration, the sponsor must award the contest prize based on skill and not on chance. Oklahoma's anti-gambling laws suggest that Oklahoma applies the material element test[4] when evaluating whether or not chance determines the outcome of a promotion. The law prohibits betting on "any game of chance or [any game] in which *chance is a material element*".[5]

Sweepstakes: Oklahoma permits sweepstakes as long as participants do not pay consideration. Oklahoma court opinions from the 1940s and 1950s indicated that consideration could exist when a participant expended energy to enter a promotion—even if the participant paid no money for entry.[6] The Oklahoma legislature subsequently overruled this result by amending the state law to clarify that only money or goods of actual pecuniary value qualify as consideration for a lottery.[7] Similarly, Oklahoma clarified that for purposes of the anti-gambling laws, consideration was a commercial or financial advantage to the promoter or a disadvantage to any participant.[8] The anti-gambling laws also provide specific examples of activities which, by themselves, do not qualify as consideration:

- mere registration without purchase of goods or services
- personal attendance at places or events, without payment of an admission price or fee
- listening to or watching radio and television programs
- answering the telephone or making a telephone call[9]

Prize Promotion Laws: Oklahoma's version of prize promotion laws is the Consumers Disclosure of Prizes and Gifts Act, which is codified in Title 21, Sections 21-996.1 to 21-996.3 of the Oklahoma Statute. The prize notice law has the most impact on giveaways. The prize notice law makes it unlawful to use the term "prize", "gift", or similar term in a misleading manner.

REPRESENTATION THAT A PERSON HAS WON A PRIZE OR WILL RECEIVE A GIFT. It is unlawful to notify any person as part of an advertising campaign or program that the person has won a prize and that as a condition of receiving such prize the person must pay any money or rent any goods or services.[10] Similarly, it is unlawful to notify any person that the person will receive a gift and that as a condition of receiving the gift the person must pay any money, or purchase, lease or rent any goods or services, if certain circumstances exist.[11] Those circumstances include unreasonable shipping or handling charges and the availability of the goods or services at a lower price through the same marketing channels.

Oklahoma's Consumers Disclosure of Prizes and Gifts Act is stingy with its definitions and explanations. It does not provide a definition for advertising campaign or program. Also, while it contains one provision addressing prohibitions related to gifts and a separate provision addressing prohibitions related to prizes[12], it does not provide any explanations or clarifications regarding how a prize differs from a gift. One potential approach for sponsors is to treat prize as the result of a competition or drawing[13], gift as an item gratuitously given, and advertising campaign or program within its commonly understood meaning.

APPLICABILITY OF PRIZE PROMOTION LAWS TO CONTESTS CHARGING CONSIDERATION. The prohibitions in the Consumers Disclosure of Prizes and Gifts Act prevent a company from taking payment from a consumer when the company informs the consumer that the consumer has already won a prize. The prohibitions do not directly prevent a company from charging a consumer consideration for the opportunity to compete for a prize. Hence, in its literal wording, the Consumers Disclosure of Prizes and Gifts Act does not prohibit skill-based contests that charge consideration. Research for this Guide uncovered no Oklahoma authoritative opinions addressing the issue.

Prize Promotion Provisions of Telemarketing Laws. The Oklahoma Commercial Telephone Solicitation laws (Title 15, Chapter 20, Sections 775A.1 to Section 775A.5 of the Oklahoma Statute) include provisions related to prizes and giveaways incorporated into commercial telephone solicitations.[14] The required telemarketing registration with the attorney general includes submission of a description of the material terms for the award of any prizes or giveaways incorporated into the commercial telephone solicitation.[15] The state's telemarketing laws also explicitly prohibit misrepresentations that any person has won a contest, sweepstakes or drawing, or that the person will receive free goods, services or property.[16]

Gambling Exceptions for Non-Profits and Other Qualified Organizations

Raffles and Lotteries: Oklahoma allows certain organizations to conduct raffles. The allowance is written into the state's crimes and punishment's laws as an exception to the prohibition against lotteries and gambling.[17] Organizations eligible to offer raffles include churches, accredited schools and some of their affiliates, fire departments, police departments, and certain federally tax-exempt organizations.[18] Research for this Guide uncovered no legal provisions indicating that offering a raffle under this exception requires a license or permit.

While the raffle statute indicates that participants may provide a voluntary contribution in return for a raffle ticket, it offers no further instruction on when such a contribution qualifies as voluntary. The definition of consideration in the anti-gambling statute may shed some light on how non-profit raffle sponsors may solicit voluntary contributions. The anti-gambling statute indicates that the term consideration does not include sums of money paid in connection with games authorized by, or comparable to games authorized by, the Oklahoma Charity Games Act. Instead, Oklahoma presumes that any sums paid by participants in such charity games are paid for the benefit of the charitable organization.[19]

The Oklahoma Charity Games Act, which is codified with the state's amusements and sports code, does not mention raffles. Instead, the non-profit raffle allowance is part of the state's crimes and punishments laws. Hence, it is not clear that the exception allowing payments in connection with games authorized by the Charity Games Act also applies to and permits payments in connection with non-profit raffles. Nevertheless, one can reasonably argue that the non-profit fund-raising raffles are comparable to the games of chance allowed by the Charity Games Act. This arguably means that the consideration exception for games authorized under the Charity Games Act extends to a voluntary contribution paid in connection with a non-profit raffle.

Bingo: Organizations eligible to offer bingo games in Oklahoma include non-profit, federally tax-exempt religious, charitable, labor, fraternal, and educational organizations.[20] The eligible organization must have a bingo license issued by the Alcoholic Beverage Laws Enforcement Commission[21] and must maintain detailed records of the games.[22] There are exemptions from the licensing and reporting requirements available for organizations that conduct fewer than four games per year.[23] There are also licensing and reporting exemptions available for medical or senior citizen facilities.[24]

The bingo allowance is enacted by the Oklahoma Charity Games Act which is codified with Oklahoma's amusements and sports laws in (Title 3A, Sections 3A-401 to 3A-427 of the Oklahoma Code). Bingo regulations, issued by the Alcoholic Beverage Laws Enforcement Commission, are in Title 45, Chapter 50, Sections 45:50-1-1 to 45:50-1-12 of the Oklahoma Administrative Code. Additional information is available from the Alcoholic Beverage Laws Enforcement Commission, 3812 N. Santa Fe, Suite 200, Oklahoma City, Oklahoma 73118; website: http://www.ok.gov/able/; phone: (405) 521-3484.

Resources

The website of the Oklahoma Attorney General offers a limited number of recent attorney general opinions. Oklahoma attorney general opinions from 1948 through the present are available through a website maintained by the University of Oklahoma College of Law at http://www.oklegal.onenet.net/agopinions.basic.html

The Oklahoma Supreme Court Network also offers Oklahoma attorney general opinions from 1977 through the present at http://www.oscn.net/applications/oscn/index.asp?ftdb=STOKAG&level=1.

Endnotes

1. Okla. Stat. §§ 21-1051 to 21-1068 (2013).
2. *Draper v. Lynch*, 137 P.2d 949, 953 (Okla. 1943).
3. Okla. Stat. §§ 21-941 and 21-942 (2013).
4. *See generally*, Section 3.4.3 of this Guide for a discussion of tests used when evaluating whether chance or skill prevails in a promotion combining elements of both.
5. Okla. Stat. § 21-942 (2013) (emphasis added).
6. *See e.g., Knox Industries Corp. v. Oklahoma*, 258 P.2d 910 (Okla. 1953); *Draper v. Lynch*, 137 P.2d 949 (Okla. 1943). According to this line of cases, activities that require energy on the part of the participant sufficient to qualify as consideration include signing a register, waiting outside a theatre, or going into a store to ask for a lottery ticket.
7. Okla. Stat. § 21-1051.A (2013).
8. Okla. Stat. § 21-981.2 (2013).
9. *Id.*
10. Okla. Stat. § 21-996.3.B (2013).
11. Okla. Stat. § 21-996.3.C (2013).
12. Okla. Stat. § 21-996.3.B (2013) addresses prizes. Okla. Stat. § 21-996.3.C (2013) addresses gifts.
13. The regulations issued for the Oklahoma Charity Games Act define *prizes* to mean "cash or merchandise awarded to game winners". Okla. Admin. Code § 45:50-1-2 (2013).
14. *See generally*, discussion of state telemarketing laws in Section 7.5.2 of this Guide.
15. Okla. Stat. § 15-775A.3.E.7 (2013).
16. Okla. Stat. § 15-775A.4.A.5 (2013).
17. Okla. Stat. § 21-1051.A.4 (2013).
18. *Id.*
19. Okla. Stat. § 21-981.2 (2013).
20. Okla. Stat. §§ 3A-402.20 and 3A-408 (2013).
21. Okla. Stat. § 3A-408 (2013).
22. Okla. Stat. § 3A-414 (2013). *See generally*, discussion of bingo and raffles in Section 9.2 of this Guide.
23. Okla. Stat. § 3A-405.A and B (2013).
24. Okla. Stat. § 3A-405.C and D (2013).

Oregon

State Attorney General Office
Oregon Department of Justice
1162 Court Street NE
Salem, Oregon 97301
(503) 378-4400
Website: http://www.doj.state.or.us/

Selected State Laws, Regulations, and Constitutional Provisions

Oregon's anti-gambling laws, which are codified with its criminal laws (Volume 4, Chapter 167, Sections 167.108 to 167.167 of the Oregon Revised Statute), contain provisions related to promotions. With its trade practice laws, Oregon includes prize promotion provisions (Volume 14, Chapters 646 and 646A of the Oregon Revised Statute). The Oregon Department of Justice issues contest, sweepstakes, and prize notification rules (Sections 137-020-0410 to 137-020-0460 of the Oregon Administrative Rules). Specific Oregon authorities frequently quoted in court cases and interpretive opinions related to promotions include the following:

Reference No.	Descriptive Name
Or. Const. art. XV, § 4	Regulation of lotteries; state lottery; use of net proceeds from state lottery
Or. Rev. Stat. § 167.117	Definitions (for anti-gambling laws including definitions for contest of chance, gambling, lottery and something of value)
Or. Rev. Stat. § 167.122	Unlawful gambling in the second degree (prohibited as a misdemeanor)
Or. Rev. Stat. §167.127	Unlawful gambling in the first degree (prohibited as a felony)

Summary of State Law

Prohibition of Lotteries and Gambling: Oregon's Constitution prohibits lotteries.[1] A promotion that combines a prize, chance, and consideration is a lottery in Oregon.[2] Oregon also has a general prohibition against gambling.[3] Exceptions to the lottery and gambling prohibitions include state-operated lotteries and certain charitable lotteries.

Contests: Oregon permits contests as long as the contest does not conflict with anti-gambling laws. If the contest includes an element of consideration, the sponsor must award the contest prize based on skill and not on chance. Contest sponsors that charge consideration or solicit participation via direct mail must comply with Oregon's prize promotion laws discussed below in this Oregon State Summary.

The statutory definition of contest of chance in Oregon's anti-gambling laws suggests that Oregon applies the material element test[4] when evaluating whether or not chance determines the outcome of a promotion. The statute defines contest of chance as "any contest or game in which the outcome depends in a *material degree upon an element of chance*, notwithstanding that skill of the contestants may also be a factor".[5]

Sweepstakes: Oregon permits sweepstakes as long as participants do not pay consideration and the sweepstakes does not otherwise violate anti-gambling laws. Sweepstakes must comply with Oregon's prize promotion laws discussed below in this Oregon State Summary.

Oregon has explicitly stated that the consideration required for the finding of a lottery is greater than the consideration generally required to support a contract.[6] Consideration for a lottery or a gambling game must be something of value. The Oregon statute defines something of value as "any money or property, any token, object or article exchangeable for money or property, or any form of credit or promise directly or indirectly contemplating transfer of money or property. . ."[7]

The higher threshold for consideration in a promotion is illustrated in Oregon court opinions. In *Cudd v. Aschenbrenner*, 377 P.2d 150 (Or. 1962), the Oregon Supreme Court ruled that there is no consideration in a store drawing even if to be eligible to win a prize the participant must register in person at the store, visit the store to have his coupon validated each week he wanted to participate in the drawing, or be present on the store's premises at the time of the drawing. While requiring such activities would be sufficient consideration to form a contract, the Oregon Supreme Court concluded that a lottery requires greater consideration than is generally required to support a contract. Since no purchase or payment was necessary to participate in the *Cudd* grocery store drawing, there was no consideration and, thus, no lottery.

There is statutory authority to support the belief that Oregon does not consider any of the following activities to be consideration as long as the sponsor makes clear to participants that no purchase is necessary to enter the promotion:

- mailing or depositing a form or game piece with the sponsor,
- placing a call to a local or toll-free number, or,
- mailing a request or placing a call to a local or toll-free number to obtain a game piece or form which the entrant can then return by mail or deposit at a local retail establishment[8]

Prize Promotion Laws: Oregon has several laws with prize promotion provisions in its trade practices laws and regulations.

No False Statements. It is an unlawful business practice to make any false or misleading statement about a prize, contest or promotion used to publicize a product, business or service.[9]

Disclosure Requirements/Unfair Business Practices. Oregon contest, sweepstakes, and prize notifications rules, codified in Sections 137-020-0410 to 137-020-0460 of the Oregon Administrative Rules, add more specificity concerning requirements for assuring that a prize promotion will not be deemed to be an unfair or deceptive trade practice. When applicable, the regulations require that the sponsor provide specific disclosures and refrain from certain prohibited practices.[10]

The regulations are applicable to chance-based sweepstakes. The regulations also apply to contests that either require payment or a donation, or create the impression that payment or a donation is required. The regulations do not apply to sweepstakes, contests, or other promotions if the sole act required for entry, participation, or receipt of a prize is one of the following:

- mailing or depositing a form or game piece with the sponsor,
- placing a call to a local or toll-free number, or,
- mailing a request or placing a call to a local or toll-free number to obtain a game piece or form which the entrant can then return by mail or deposit at a local retail establishment[11]

Oregon requires that the disclosure be clear and conspicuous but does not explicitly state that the disclosure be in writing. It is, however, recommended that the disclosure be in writing. The prize notice regulations indicate that disclosures will be deemed to be clear and conspicuous if the disclosure is printed in a portion of the solicitation titled as "Consumer Disclosure," "Official Rules," or something similar; and the main text of the advertisement clearly and conspicuously refers to the disclosure near the same place the advertisement describes the prizes.[12]

USE OF DIRECT MAIL WITH PROMOTIONS. Another provision of Oregon law regulates how promotions are offered through direct mail. If a company uses United States mail to solicit participation in a sweepstakes or contest, the company must include certain disclosures in its mailing.[13]

PRIZE PROMOTION PROVISIONS OF TELEMARKETING LAWS. Oregon's Telephone Solicitation laws (Volume 14, Title 50, Chapter 646, Sections 646.551 to 646.578 of the Oregon Revised Statutes[14]) include provisions related to prizes and giveaways incorporated into commercial telephone solicitations. If a telephone solicitor offers a prize or gift to consumers as part of a telephone solicitation campaign, the telephone solicitor must disclose certain information to the consumer as part of the call and to the state as part of the required telemarketing registration.[15]

Exceptions for Non-Profits and Other Qualified Organizations

Bingo, Raffles, and Charitable Games: The Oregon Constitution provides an exception to the general prohibition on lotteries so that the state legislature may provide for the establishment, operation, and regulation of raffles and bingo by charitable, fraternal, or religious organizations.[16] Pursuant to this constitutional provision, Oregon allows federally tax-exempt organizations to offer raffles, bingo games, and other charitable gaming as a fund-raising mechanism.

Eligible organizations need a license to conduct bingo, raffle, or other charitable games. There are a few exceptions to the licensing requirement. No license is required for tax-exempt, non-profit organizations holding raffles with a cumulative gross sales of no more than $10,000 per calendar year.[17] No license is required for federally tax-exempt, non-profit organizations operating bingo games with gross sales of no more than $2,000 per bingo session and no more than $5,000 in gross sales per calendar year.[18]

There are additional statutory and regulatory requirements for bingo and raffle operators.[19] Laws related to charitable games are codified in Volume 11, Chapter 464, Sections 464.250 *et seq.* of the Oregon Revised Statute. Regulations issued by the Oregon Department of Justice are at Section 137-025-0020 *et seq.* of the Oregon Administrative Rules. Licensees are required to file annual reports and renewal applications and pay reporting fees based on gross sales and the class of license.

Additional information, registration and report forms are available from the Charitable Activities Section of the Oregon Department of Justice, 1515 SW Fifth Avenue, Suite 410, Portland, Oregon 97201, telephone (971) 673-1880, or http://www.doj.state.or.us/charigroup.

Resources

Oregon offers a searchable database for its attorney general opinions from at least 1997 through the present online in the Legal Resources portion of the website of the Oregon Department of Justice.

Endnotes

1. Or. Const. art. XV, § 4(1).
2. *Cudd v. Aschenbrenner*, 377 P.2d 150 (Or. 1962).
3. Or. Rev. Stat. §§ 167.122 and 167.127 (2013).
4. *See generally*, Section 3.4.3 of this Guide for a discussion of tests used when evaluating whether chance or skill prevails in a promotion combining elements of both.
5. Or. Rev. Stat. § 167.117(6) (2013)(emphasis added).

6. *Cudd. v. Aschenbrenner*, 377 P. 2d 150, 157 (Or. 1962). See also discussion of consideration for lottery versus consideration for contract in Section 4.3 of this Guide.
7. Or. Rev. Stat. §167.117(22) (2013).
8. These activities are listed in Or. Admin. R. 137-020-0410(3)(f) of Oregon's prize notice laws as types of contests, sweepstakes, and schemes not considered to be promotions under the rules.
9. Or. Rev. Stat. § 646.608(1)(p) (2013).
10. Or. Admin. R. 137-020-0430 to137-020-0440 (2013). *See generally*, discussion of state prize promotion laws in Section 7.4.2 of this Guide.
11. Or. Admin. R. 137-020-0410(3)(f) and (4) (2014).
12. Or. Admin. R. 137-020-0410(5) (2014).
13. Or. Rev. Stat. § 646A.803 (2013).
14. The accompanying regulations are codified in Sections 137-020-0200 to 137-020-0205 of the Oregon Administrative Rules.
15. Or. Rev. Stat. § 646.557(1) (2013); Or. Admin. R. 137-020-0202(14) and 137-020-0203(1) (2014). *See generally*, discussion of state telemarketing laws in Section 7.5.2 of this Guide.
16. Or. Const. art. XV, § 4(2).
17. Or. Rev. Stat. § 464.385 (2013); Or. Admin. R. 137-025-0040 (2014).
18. Or. Admin. R. 137-025-0040 (2014).
19. *See generally*, discussion of bingo and raffles in Section 9.2 of this Guide.

Pennsylvania

State Attorney General Office
Office of the Attorney General
16th Floor, Strawberry Square
Harrisburg, Pennsylvania 17120
(717) 787-3391
Website: http://www.attorneygeneral.gov

Selected State Laws, Regulations, and Constitutional Provisions

Pennsylvania's anti-gambling laws (Title 18, Chapter 55, Sections 5512 to 5514 of Pennsylvania Consolidated Statutes), which are in its crime and offenses code, contain provisions related to promotions. Specific authorities frequently quoted in court cases and interpretive opinions related to promotions include the following:

Reference No.	Descriptive Name
18 Pa. Cons. Stat. § 5512	Lotteries, etc.
18 Pa. Cons. Stat. § 5513	Gambling devices, gambling, etc.

Summary of State Law

Prohibition of Lotteries and Gambling: Pennsylvania prohibits lotteries.[1] A promotion that combines a prize, chance, and consideration is a lottery in Pennsylvania.[2] Pennsylvania also has a general prohibition against gambling.[3] Exceptions to the lottery and gambling prohibitions include state-operated lotteries and certain charitable lotteries.

Contests: Pennsylvania permits contests as long as the contest does not conflict with anti-gambling laws. If the contest includes an element of consideration, the sponsor must award the contest prize based on skill and not on chance. Court opinions indicate that Pennsylvania applies the dominant factor doctrine[4] when evaluating whether or not chance determines the outcome of a promotion. The court in *Pennsylvania v. Laniewski*, 98 A.2d 215 (Pa. Super. Ct. 1953), said that "chance need be only the dominant factor to turn a contest into a lottery, even though skill, judgment, or research enter into the matter in some degree . . ."

Sweepstakes: Pennsylvania permits sweepstakes as long as participants do not pay consideration and the sweepstakes does not otherwise violate anti-gambling laws.

Prize Promotion Laws: The Pennsylvania Telemarketer Registration Act (Title 73, Chapter 40, Section 2241 to 2249 of the Pennsylvania Unconsolidated Statutes) includes provisions related to prizes and giveaways incorporated into commercial telephone solicitations. The telemarketing disclosure requirements apply to an offer of a sweepstakes or other game of chance or to any oral or written representation that a person has won, has been selected to receive or may be eligible to receive a prize. With respect to such a prize promotion, prior to the customer's payment for any goods or services offered, the telemarketer must provide the odds of winning, advise the consumer that no purchase or payment is necessary to win, and identify any restrictions or conditions on obtaining a prize.

Other Pennsylvania consumer protection laws make it a deceptive or fraudulent business practice to attempt to obtain property from a person by making false or misleading representations by telephone about prizes the person has won or might be eligible to win. It is also an unfair or deceptive practice to solicit sales of goods or services over the telephone without first clearly, affirmatively and expressly stating that no purchase or payment is necessary to be able to win a prize or participate in a prize promotion if a prize promotion is offered.

Gambling Exceptions for Non-Profits and Other Qualified Organizations

Raffles and Games of Chance: Pennsylvania's Local Option Small Games of Chance Act allows eligible organizations to offer raffles and other games of chance for the purpose of raising funds for public interest purposes.

Each county or municipality may vote to allow eligible organizations to operate small games of chance within its jurisdiction.[5] Eligible organizations include non-profit charitable organizations, religious organizations, fraternal organizations, veterans organizations, club or civic and service associations.[6]

The operation of the raffle must meet several statutory and regulatory requirements.[7] To offer the raffles and other games of chance, the eligible organization must obtain a license from the county treasurer or other local government designee within the applicable municipality.[8] The Local Option Small Games of Chance Act is codified in Title 10, Chapter 7A, Section 328.101 *et seq.* of the Pennsylvania Unconsolidated Statutes. The accompanying regulations are with the state's revenue regulations, Title 61, Part VII, Chapter 901, Sections 901.1 *et seq.* of the Pennsylvania Code.

Bingo: Pennsylvania allows certain non-profit organizations to operate bingo games for charitable and civic purposes. Organizations eligible to offer bingo games include non-profit volunteer fire company, religious, charitable, fraternal, veterans, civic, county fair and agricultural associations.[9]

There are statutory requirements for the operation of the bingo games.[10] Eligible organizations wishing to offer bingo games must obtain a license from the county treasurer or other local government designee within the applicable municipality.[11] The Pennsylvania Bingo Law is codified in Title 10, Chapter 7, Sections 301 to 308.1 of the Pennsylvania Unconsolidated Statutes.

Resources

Pennsylvania offers a searchable database for its attorney general opinions from 1895 through the present online in the Opinions section of the website of the Office of the Attorney General.

Endnotes

1. 18 Pa. Cons. Stat. § 5512 (2012).
2. *Commonwealth v. Laniewski*, 98 A.2d 215 (Pa. Super. Ct. 1953).
3. 18 Pa. Cons. Stat. § 5513 (2012).

4. *See generally*, Section 3.4.3 of this Guide for a discussion of tests used when evaluating whether chance or skill prevails in a promotion combining elements of both.
5. 10 P. S. § 328.703.
6. 10 P. S. § 328.103.
7. *See generally*, discussion of bingo and raffles in Section 9.2 of this Guide.
8. 10 P. S. § 328.307.
9. 10 P.S. §§ 303 and 304.
10. *See generally*, discussion of bingo and raffles in Section 9.2 of this Guide.
11. 10 P.S. §§ 303 and 305(a).

Rhode Island

State Attorney General Office
Office of the Attorney General
150 South Main Street
Providence, Rhode Island 02903
(401) 274-4400
Website: http://www.riag.state.ri.us/

Selected State Laws, Regulations, and Constitutional Provisions

Rhode Island's anti-gambling laws (Title 11, Chapter 11-19, Sections 11-19-1 *et seq.* of the Rhode Island General Laws), which are codified with its criminal offenses laws, contain provisions related to promotions. Also, with its criminal offenses laws, Rhode Island has registration, posting, record-keeping and other requirements for sweepstakes that are offered at retail stores and that offer prizes over five hundred dollars (Title 11, Chapter 11-50, Sections 11-50-1 to 11-50-8 of the Rhode Island General Laws). Rhode Island also has prize promotion laws in its Prizes and Gift Act (Title 42, Chapter 42-61.1, Sections 42-61.1-1 to 42.61.1-9 of the Rhode Island General Laws). Specific Rhode Island authorities frequently quoted in court cases and interpretive opinions related to promotions include the following:

Reference No.	Descriptive Name
R.I. Const. art. VI, § 15	Lotteries
R.I. Gen. Laws § 11-19-1	Forms of gambling prohibited (promoting gambling prohibited as felony)
R.I. Gen. Laws § 11-50-1	Filing requirement (for sweepstakes offered at retail establishments with prizes valued over $500)

R.I. Gen. Laws § 11-50-2	Posting of available prizes—Rules and winners (for sweepstakes offered at retail establishments with prizes valued over $500)
R.I. Gen. Laws § 11-50-3	Records (retention and filing requirements for sweepstakes offered at retail establishments with prizes valued over $500)

Summary of State Law

Prohibition of Lotteries and Gambling: Rhode Island's Constitution prohibits lotteries.[1] A promotion that combines a prize, chance, and consideration is a lottery in Rhode Island.[2] Rhode Island also has a general prohibition against gambling which includes a prohibition against lotteries.[3] Exceptions to the lottery and gambling prohibitions include state-operated lotteries and certain charitable lotteries.

Contests: Rhode Island permits contests as long as the contest does not conflict with anti-gambling laws. If the contest includes an element of consideration, the sponsor must award the contest prize based on skill and not on chance. Rhode Island applies the dominant factor doctrine[4] when evaluating whether or not chance determines the outcome of a promotion.[5]

Sweepstakes: Rhode Island permits sweepstakes as long as participants do not pay consideration and the sweepstakes does not violate the anti-gambling laws. There is statutory authority to support the argument that Rhode Island does not consider any of the following activities to be consideration:

- completing and mailing or depositing at a local retail commercial establishment, an entry blank obtainable locally or by mail,
- calling in an entry by telephone[6]

If the sweepstakes offers prizes valued at over five hundred dollars and offers play opportunities through a Rhode Island-located retail store, Rhode Island imposes specific requirements on the sponsor. Most notably, the sponsor must register the sweepstakes with the Rhode Island Secretary of State.[7] In addition, the retail establishment offering sweepstakes-play opportunities must post the sweepstakes rules[8] and the sponsor must maintain records of winners and prizes awarded for at least six months and file that information with the secretary of state upon request.[9]

Prize Promotion Laws: Rhode Island's version of a prize promotion law is the Prizes and Gift Act, which is codified at Title 42, Chapter 42-61.1, Sections 42-61.1-1 to 42.61.1-9 of the Rhode Island General Laws. In addition to limitations on shipping/handling charges for gifts and give-aways[10] and other prohibited practices[11], Rhode Island's prize promotion protections include the following:

OBLIGATION TO AWARD PROMISED PRIZE. If in conjunction with a sales campaign, a company represents that a person has won a gift or a prize, the company must give the gift to the person without any obligation or expense to the person.[12]

REPRESENTATION THAT A PERSON IS ELIGIBLE TO WIN A PRIZE REQUIRES A DISCLOSURE. If in conjunction with a sales campaign, a company represents that a person has a chance to win a prize, the company must make certain disclosures.[13] The disclosure can be verbal for a verbal solicitation. There are requirements for font, placement, and wording for disclosures made in written solicitations.[14] The disclosure requirement does not apply if to be eligible to receive the prize the consumer can submit an entry by mail, phone, or at a local retail store, and is not required to listen to a sales presentation.[15]

PRIZE PROMOTION PROVISIONS OF TELEMARKETING LAWS. The Rhode Island Telephone Sales Solicitation Act (Title 5, Chapter 5-61, Sections 5-61-1 to 5-61-6 of the Rhode Island General Laws) includes provisions related to prizes and giveaways incorporated into commercial telephone solicitations.[16] The required registration with the attorney general for telephone solicitors includes submission of a description of the material terms for the award of any prizes or giveaways incorporated into the commercial telephone solicitation.[17]

Gambling Exceptions for Non-Profits and Other Qualified Organizations

Raffles, Lotteries, and Bingo: Charitable organizations may operate bingo games and other permitted games of chance authorized by the state police.[18] A raffle is one of the permitted games of chance.[19]

For purposes of charitable gaming, Rhode Island defines charitable organization to include any benevolent, educational, philanthropic, humane, patriotic, social service, civic, fraternal, police, labor, religious organization; as well as any other persons holding themselves out to be a charitable organization.[20] Net receipts from bingo games and raffles must be applied solely for the charitable purposes of the organization.[21]

Laws relevant to raffles, bingo, and other charitable games are codified with the state's criminal offenses laws in Title 11, Chapter 11-19, Sections 11-19-30 to 11-19-41 of the Rhode Island General Laws. The Rhode Island State Police issues regulations for raffles[22] and for bingo.[23] It offers regulations, licensing forms, and additional information on bingo and raffles in the Charitable Gaming section of its website, www.risp.ri.gov/

RAFFLES CONDUCTED BY CHARITABLE ORGANIZATIONS. There are statutory and regulatory requirements for the operation of the charitable organization's raffle.[24] To offer a raffle, the organization must complete a licensing process that involves submitting an application to the chief of police in the city or town where the raffle drawing will be held. Upon its approval of the application, the local chief of police forwards the application to the Rhode Island State Police Charitable Gaming Unit which makes the final licensing approval decision.[25] The organization conducting the raffle must complete a financial report and return it to the State Police Charitable Gaming Unit within sixty days after the drawing.

INCIDENTAL DOOR PRIZE FOR CHARITABLE CAUSE. A club, society, lodge, or association may offer a door prize at its annual or semiannual dinner or similar event even if the club, society, lodge, or association is not a charitable organization.[26] To qualify for the raffle exemption, the raffle must be purely incidental to the event[27] or the entire net proceeds of the event must be devoted to charity.[28] The organization must first obtain written permission from either the sergeant or police commissioner of the town in which the event is held.[29]

SENIOR CITIZEN RAFFLES; POLITICAL COMMITTEE RAFFLES. Housing communities for senior citizens may hold up to three raffles per year as long as the value of prizes for a single raffle does not exceed five hundred dollars.[30] Certain political committees and certified candidates may conduct a twenty week club or conduct a raffle once within a twelve-month period subsequent to notifying the Rhode Island Lottery Commission.[31]

BINGO. Operation of a charitable bingo game must meet statutory and regulatory requirements.[32] To offer bingo, the organization must submit an application to the Rhode Island State Police and receive a letter of approval. Bingo operators must also file annual financial reports with the Rhode Island Division of State Police. There are relaxed application requirements for recreational bingo games within senior citizen housing communities.[33]

Resources

Research for this Guide did not locate a free online database for Rhode Island Attorney General opinions. Opinions dating from 1981 to the present are available on the Westlaw research database.

Endnotes

1. R.I. Const. art. VI, § 15.
2. *Roberts v. Comm. Investment Club of Woonsocket*, 431 A.2d 1206, 1211 (R.I. 1981).
3. R.I. Gen. Laws § 11-19-1 (2013).
4. *See generally*, Section 3.4.3 of this Guide for a discussion of tests used when evaluating whether chance or skill prevails in a promotion combining elements of both.
5. *Roberts v. Comm. Investment Club of Woonsocket*, 431 A.2d 1206, 1211 (R.I. 1981).
6. These activities are listed in Rhode Island's Prizes and Gift Act (R.I. Gen. Laws § 42-61.1-3(d)). Normally when a company offers a person an opportunity to win a prize as part of a company sales campaign, the company must provide certain disclosures. There is no disclosure required if participating in the prize-winning opportunity only requires these simple acts.
7. R.I. Gen. Laws § 11-50-1 (2013).

8. R.I. Gen. Laws § 11-50-2 (2013).
9. R.I. Gen. Laws § 11-50-3 (2013).
10. R.I. Gen. Laws § 42-61.1-6 (2013).
11. *See generally*, discussion of state prize notice laws in Section 7.4.2 of this Guide.
12. R.I. Gen. Laws § 42-61.1-2 (2013).
13. R.I. Gen. Laws § 42-61.1-3 (2013).
14. *Id.*
15. R.I. Gen. Laws § 42-61.1-3(d) (2013).
16. *See generally*, discussion of state telemarketing laws in Section 7.5.2 of this Guide.
17. R.I. Gen. Laws § 5-61-4(11) (2013).
18. R.I. Gen. Laws §§ 11-19-32 and 11-19-36 (2013). The Rhode Island State Police have authority to license, regulate, supervise and exercise general control over bingo and permitted games of chance. R.I. Gen. Laws §11-19-41 (2013). *See also*, webpage of Rhode Island State Police Charitable Gaming Unit at http://www.risp.ri.gov/sectionsandunits/charitablegaming.php (last visited Oct. 9, 2014).
19. R.I. Gen. Laws § 11-19-30(e) (2013).
20. R.I. Gen. Laws § 11-19-30(a) (2013).
21. R.I. Gen. Laws §§ 11-19-32(3) and 11-19-36(3) (2013).
22. Rhode Island Division of State Police, Rules and Regulations Governing Raffles, available at http://www.risp.ri.gov/docs/GamesOfChance/RaffleRulesRegs.pdf (hereinafter R.I. Raffle Regulations).
23. Rhode Island Division of State Police, Rules and Regulations Governing Bingo, available at http://www.risp.ri.gov/docs/GamesOfChance/BingoRulesRegs.pdf.
24. *See generally*, discussion of bingo and raffles in Section 9.2 of this Guide.
25. R.I. Raffle Regulations, *supra* note 22, at ch.2, R. 2.1.
26. R.I. Gen. Laws § 11-19-13 (2013).
27. The statute does not provide details on what it means for a raffle to be incidental to the event. Some common sense practices might include not advertising the door prizes as part of the event marketing.
28. R.I. Gen. Laws § 11-19-13 (2013).
29. *Id.*
30. R.I. Gen. Laws § 11-19-34.1 (2013).
31. R.I. Gen. Laws § 11-19-1.1(a) (2013).
32. *See generally*, discussion of bingo and raffles in Section 9.2 of this Guide.
33. R.I. Gen. Laws §11-19-32.1 (2013).

South Carolina

State Attorney General Office
South Carolina Attorney General Office
Rembert Dennis Building
1000 Assembly Street, Room 519
Columbia, S.C. 29201
(803) 734-3970
Website: http://www.scag.gov

Selected State Laws, Regulations, and Constitutional Provisions

South Carolina's laws on gambling and lotteries (Title 16, Chapter 19, Sections 16-19-10 *et seq.* of the South Carolina Code), which are in the state's crimes and offenses code, has laws related to promotions. South Carolina's version of prize promotion laws is the Prizes and Gifts Act (Title 37, Chapter 15, Sections 37-15-10 *et seq.* of the South Carolina Code). Specific South Carolina authorities frequently quoted in court cases and interpretive opinions related to promotions include the following:

Reference No.	Descriptive Name
S.C. Const. art. XVII, § 7	Lotteries (prohibited)
S.C. Code § 16-19-10	Setting up lotteries (prohibited as misdemeanor)
S.C. Code § 16-19-20	Adventuring in lotteries (prohibited)
S.C. Code § 16-19-30	Selling lottery tickets (prohibited)
S.C. Code § 16-19-40	Unlawful games and betting
S.C. Code § 16-19-130	Betting, pool selling, bookmaking and the like are prohibited.

Summary of State Law

Prohibition of Lotteries and Gambling: South Carolina's Constitution and its statutory laws prohibit lotteries.[1] A promotion that combines a prize, chance, and consideration is a lottery in South Carolina.[2] South Carolina also has a general prohibition against gambling.[3] Exceptions to the lottery and gambling prohibitions include state-operated lotteries and certain charitable lotteries.

Contests: South Carolina permits contests as long as the contest does not conflict with anti-gambling laws. When the contest is offered in conjunction with a sales campaign effort, the contest sponsor must comply with the disclosure requirements in the South Carolina Prizes and Gift Act.

If the contest includes an element of consideration, the sponsor must award the contest prize based on skill and not on chance. It is unclear which test South Carolina uses when evaluating whether or not chance determines the outcome of a promotion.[4]

Opinions issued by the South Carolina Attorney General suggest that South Carolina might apply the dominant factor doctrine. When determining whether a game or promotion was actually an illegal lottery, the attorney general often evaluated whether chance or skill dominated in winner selection.[5]

However, the South Carolina courts have not judicially adopted the dominant factor doctrine, the pure chance doctrine, or any other specific test for determining whether a promotion is actually a lottery.[6] Furthermore, in *Town of Mt. Pleasant v. Chimento*, 737 S.E.2d 830 (S.C. 2012), the South Carolina Supreme Court rejected the dominant factor doctrine in a case where it evaluated whether a particular scheme violated anti-gambling laws. However, as the *Mt. Pleasant* court explained, South Carolina law distinguishes between a lottery and a gambling game. In the *Mt. Pleasant* case, the South Carolina Supreme Court did not explicitly address whether South Carolina should apply the dominant factor doctrine to lotteries. As a result, it is possible that the South Carolina Attorney General's preference for the dominant factor doctrine stands when determining the existence of a lottery.

Sweepstakes: South Carolina permits sweepstakes as long as participants do not pay consideration and the sweepstakes does not otherwise violate anti-gambling laws. When the sweepstakes is offered in conjunction with a sales campaign effort, the sweepstakes sponsor must comply with the disclosure requirements in the South Carolina Prizes and Gift Act.

The South Carolina Prizes and Gift Act suggests that South Carolina does not view a promotion that requires participants to perform one of the following activities as a promotion that has the element of consideration:

- completing and mailing an entry blank obtainable locally or by mail
- completing and depositing at a local retail commercial establishment, an entry blank obtainable locally or by mail
- calling in an entry by telephone[7]

The South Carolina Prizes and Gift Act requires certain disclosures when a company combines promotions with its efforts to sell other goods and service. The above activities are mentioned in the Prizes and Gift Act as activities that do not trigger disclosure requirements.[8]

Prize Promotion Laws: South Carolina's version of prize promotion laws is the Prizes and Gift Act which is codified in Title 37, Chapter 15, Sections 37-15-10 *et seq.* of the South Carolina Code. The Prizes and Gift Act applies to giveaways, sweepstakes, and contests that are combined with sales campaigns. The South Carolina prize promotion law prohibits practices that might deceive consumers such as use of simulated checks and charging excessive shipping and handling fees.[9]

OBLIGATION TO AWARD PROMISED PRIZE. If in conjunction with a sales campaign, a company represents that a person has won a prize or gift, the company must deliver the gift within ten days of the representation and without any expense or monetary obligation to the recipient.[10]

REPRESENTATION THAT A PERSON IS ELIGIBLE TO WIN A PRIZE REQUIRES A DISCLOSURE. There are disclosure requirements when, in conjunction with a sales campaign, a company represents that a consumer has a chance to win a prize or gift.[11] The disclosures can be given verbally. If given in writing, there are specific statutory requirements for placement, font, and wording.[12]

PRIZE PROMOTION PROVISIONS OF TELEMARKETING LAWS. In its laws regarding unsolicited consumer telephone calls (Title 16, Chapter 17, Article 7, Sections 16-17-445 of the South Carolina Code), South Carolina includes additional restrictions and disclaimer requirements for prize promotions offered as part of a telephone solicitation.[13]

Gambling Exceptions for Non-Profits and Other Qualified Organizations

Raffles and Lotteries: Codified with the laws related to alcohol and alcoholic beverages is a provision allowing any person or organization licensed to sell alcoholic beverages by the South Carolina Department of Revenue to hold bingo, raffles, and other similar activities for charitable fund-raising purposes.[14] However, on several occasions, the Attorney General's Office of South Carolina has expressed the viewpoint that this legislation is inconsistent with the South Carolina constitutional prohibition against lotteries since the constitutional prohibition makes no exceptions for charitable raffles.[15] To make charitable raffles legal, the attorney general indicates that a constitutional amendment is required. However, the South Carolina Attorney General has acknowledged that he has no power to declare the charitable raffle allowance unconstitutional and that this power rests with the South Carolina courts.

Bingo: The South Carolina State Constitution contains a provision allowing bingo to be conducted by certain federally tax-exempt, charitable, religious, or fraternal organizations.[16] The operation of the bingo game must meet several statutory requirements.[17] An eligible organization that wants to offer bingo must obtain a license issued by the South Carolina Department of Revenue. Most bingo licensees must file quarterly reports with information about the gross proceeds, expenses, use of proceeds, prizes awarded, and number of players at each bingo session.[18]

The Bingo Tax Act of 1996, which is codified in Title 12, Chapter 21, Article 24 Sections 12-21-3910 *et seq.* of the South Carolina Code, enacts the constitutional provision. Licensing information and forms are available from the bingo section of the South Carolina Department of Revenue's website, http://www.sctax.org.

Resources

Opinions from 1985 through the present are available in the Opinions portion of the website of the South Carolina Attorney General. South Carolina does not offer a free online searchable database for earlier attorney general opinions. Opinions dating from 1959 to the present are available on the Westlaw or Lexis research databases.

Endnotes

1. S.C. Const. art. XVII, § 7; S.C. Code § 16-19-10 (2014).
2. S.C. Atty. Gen Op. (May 4, 2005).
3. S.C. Code §§ 16-19-40 and 16-19-130 (2014).
4. *See generally*, Section 3.4.3 of this Guide for a discussion of tests used when evaluating whether chance or skill prevails in a promotion combining elements of both.
5. S.C. Atty. Gen Op. (Nov. 19, 2010); S.C. Atty. Gen Op. (July 31, 2006); S.C. Atty. Gen Op. (Sept. 5, 1995).
6. S.C. Law Enforcement Div. v. 1-Speedmaster, 723 S.E.2d 809 (S.C. Ct. App. 2011).
7. S.C. Code § 37-15-40(D) (2014).
8. *Id.*
9. S.C. Code §§ 37-15-60 and 37-15-70 (2014). *See generally*, discussion of state prize promotion laws in Section 7.4.2 of this Guide.
10. S.C. Code 37-15-30 (2014).
11. S.C. Code § 37-15-40 (2014).
12. *Id. See generally*, discussion of state prize promotion laws in Section 7.4.2 of this Guide.
13. *See generally*, discussion of state telemarketing laws in Section 7.5.2 of this Guide.
14. S.C. Code § 61-2-180 (2014).
15. S.C. Att'y Gen. Op. (Feb. 18, 2011); S.C. Att'y Gen. Op. (May 4, 2005); S.C. Att'y Gen. Op. (June 23, 2004).
16. S.C. Const. art. XVII, § 7.
17. S.C. Code § 12-21-4000 (2014). *See generally*, discussion of bingo and raffles in Section 9.2 of this Guide.
18. S.C. Code § 12-21-4100 (2014).

South Dakota

State Attorney General Office
Office of the Attorney General
1302 E Hwy 14, Suite 1
Pierre, South Dakota 57501-8501
(605) 773-3215
Website: http://atg.sd.gov

Selected State Laws, Regulations, and Constitutional Provisions

South Dakota groups its laws on gambling and lotteries (Title 22, Chapter 25, Sections 22-25-1 *et. seq.* of the South Dakota Codified Laws) with its criminal laws. As part of its trade regulation laws, South Dakota includes sweepstakes prize promotion laws (Title 37, Chapter 32, Sections 37-32-1 *et seq.* of South Dakota Codified Laws). Specific South Dakota legal provisions frequently quoted in court cases and interpretive opinions related to promotions include the following:

Reference No.	Descriptive Name
S.D. Const. art. III, § 25	Games of chance prohibited—Exception
S.D.C.L. § 22-25-1	Gambling defined—Keeping gambling establishment—Letting building for gambling—Misdemeanor
S.D.C.L. § 22-25-24	Lottery defined
S.D.C.L. § 22-25-26	Unauthorized bingo or lottery as misdemeanor

Summary of State Law

Prohibition of Lotteries and Gambling: South Dakota's Constitution as well as its statutory laws prohibits lotteries.[1] Under South Dakota law, a lottery combines a prize, chance, and consideration.[2] South Dakota also has a general prohibition against gambling.[3] Exceptions to the lottery and gambling prohibitions include lotteries operated by the state and certain charitable lotteries.

South Dakota's Constitution uses both the terms games of chance and lotteries. South Dakota courts have reasoned that the use of both terms means there is a constitutional distinction. Hence, South Dakota views the term game of chance as a broad term that includes most forms of gaming including lotteries. In contrast, it views the term lottery as a narrower sub-category of game of chance involving the sale of tokens or tickets to a large number of people for the chance to win a prize.[4]

Contests: South Dakota permits contests as long as the contest does not conflict with anti-gambling laws. If the contest includes an element of consideration, the sponsor must award the contest prize based on skill and not on chance.

Court opinions suggest that South Dakota applies the dominant factor doctrine[5] when evaluating whether or not chance determines the outcome of a promotion. When defining the state constitution's use of the term game of chance (which includes lotteries) in *Bayer v. Johnson*, 349 N.W.2d 447, 449 (S.D. 1984), the South Dakota Supreme Court defined a game of chance as "a contest wherein chance predominates over skill".

Sweepstakes: South Dakota permits sweepstakes as long as participants do not pay consideration and the sweepstakes does not otherwise violate anti-gambling laws. The state's attorney general has explained that South Dakota does allow the distribution of sweepstakes-playing opportunities along with a purchase as long as the sponsor clearly communicates to the public that no purchase is necessary and there is an easy way to enter without making a purchase.[6] In contrast, where the product for purchase is an artifice and there is no effective notification that no purchase is necessary for participation, a prize-promotion based on random selection will be deemed to have consideration and be characterized as a lottery.[7]

Prize Promotion Laws: South Dakota has prize promotion protections (Title 37, Chapter 32, Sections 37-32-1 *et seq.* of the South Dakota Codified Laws) with its trade regulation laws.

REQUIREMENTS FOR PRIZE-RELATED MATERIALS. South Dakota's prize promotion laws focus on the requirements for prize notices. A prize notice is material communicating that a person has won or will receive a prize and conditions receipt of the prize on payment to the sponsor.[8] A prize notice also includes material which requires or invites the individual to telephone or come for an in-person meeting to learn more about the prize opportunity.[9] A prize notice does not include a notice informing the individual that the individual has won a prize as a result of the person's actual prior entry in a game, drawing, sweepstakes or other contest.[10]

In its prize promotion laws, South Dakota indicates what information must be included in a prize notice[11]; specifies requirements for placement, font, and wording of the prize notice[12]; and prohibits practices that may mislead the recipients of a prize notice[13].[14]

REPRESENTATION THAT A PERSON HAS WON A PRIZE REQUIRES A PRIZE NOTICE. If a company tells a person that the person has won a prize, the company may not require any type of payment as a condition of receiving the prize before giving the person a written prize notice.[15]

REQUIREMENTS WHEN PRIZE NOTICE ENCOURAGES ATTENDANCE AT SALES PRESENTATION. When offering a prize as an inducement to view, hear, or attend a sales presentation, the sales presentation may not begin until the company offering the prize identifies the prize to be awarded and actually delivers the prize.[16]

EXCEPTIONS TO PRIZE NOTICE REQUIREMENTS. The prize notice requirement does not apply if all of the following conditions exist:

- No element of chance determines receipt of the prize;
- The recipient may review any merchandise or services purchased for at least seven days and may obtain a full refund or cancel within thirty days;
- The recipient may keep the prize offered in the promotion without obligation; and
- The recipient is not required to attend any sales presentation or spend any money in order to receive the item offered in the promotion.[17]

Gambling Exceptions for Non-Profits and Other Qualified Organizations

Lotteries, Raffles, and Bingo. An exception to the constitutional prohibition on lotteries allows the South Dakota legislature to authorize charitable and civic organizations to conduct games of chance.[18] The statute enacting the constitutional exemption allows charitable bingo games and lotteries.[19] South Dakota interprets the term lottery to include raffles[20] so the allowance for lotteries extends to raffles.

Organizations eligible for the exception are bona fide veterans, charitable, educational, religious or fraternal organizations, civic and service clubs, volunteer fire departments, and other public spirited organizations. The organization must devote the entire net proceeds of the games to educational, charitable, patriotic, religious, and other public spirited uses.[21]

Relative to other states, South Dakota has few rules regulating operators of raffles and bingo games. No license is required for eligible charitable organizations to conduct bingo games and lotteries. However, the organization conducting the bingo, lottery, or raffle must give thirty days' written notice of the time and place for the bingo game or raffle to the governing body of the county or municipality in which it intends to conduct the bingo game or lottery.[22] The county governing body has an opportunity to pass a resolution objecting to the game. If it is a statewide lottery, the sponsor need provide notice only to the secretary of state and to the governing body where the drawing for such lottery is held. In contrast to the relatively limited amount of operational procedures for qualified organizations offering games of chance, South Dakota does heavily regulate distributors and manufacturers of bingo and lottery equipment with license, record retention, and reporting requirements.[23]

Resources

South Dakota offers copies of its attorney general opinions from 1968 through the present in the Official Opinions portion of the website of the Office of the Attorney General.

Endnotes

1. S.D. Const. art. III, § 25; S.D.C.L. § 22-25-26 (2014).
2. S.D.C.L. § 22-25-24 (2014).
3. S.D.C.L. § 22-25-1 (2014).
4. *Poppen v. Walker*, 520 N.W.2d 238, 245 (S.D. 1994).
5. *See generally*, Section 3.4.3 of this Guide for a discussion of tests used when evaluating whether chance or skill prevails in a promotion combining elements of both.
6. S.D. Atty. Gen. Op. No. 86-07 (Mar. 27, 1986).
7. *Id.*
8. S.D.C.L. § 37-32-1(2) (2014).
9. *Id.*
10. *Id.*
11. S.D.C.L. § § 37-32-3 to 37-32-7 (2014).
12. S.D.C.L. §§ 37-32-3 and 37-32-6 (2014).
13. S.D.C.L. § 37-32-8 (2014).
14. See generally, discussion of state prize promotion laws in Section 7.4.2 of this Guide.
15. S.D.C.L. § 37-32-2 (2014).
16. S.D.C.L. § 37-32-9 (2014).
17. S.D.C.L. § 37-32-1(1) (2014).
18. S.D. Const. art. III, § 25.
19. S.D.C.L. § 22-25-25 (2014).
20. S.D. Att'y Gen. Op. No. 87-27, *2 (Aug. 10, 1987).
21. S.D. Const. art. III, § 25.
22. S.D.C.L. § 22-25-25(6) (2014).
23. S.D.C.L. §§ 22-25-28 to 22-25-51 (2014).

Tennessee

State Attorney General Office
Office of the Attorney General
312 Rosa L. Parks Avenue
8th Floor, Snodgrass Tower
Nashville, Tennessee 37243-1102
(615) 741-2078
Website: http://www.tn.gov/sos/

Selected State Laws, Regulations, and Constitutional Provisions

Tennessee's anti-gambling laws (Title 39, Chapter 17, Part 5, Sections 39-17-501 *et seq.* of the Tennessee Code), which are in its criminal offenses code, contain provisions related to promotions. As part of its Consumer Protection Act, Tennessee includes prize promotion laws (Title 47, Chapter 18, Sections 47-18-120 and 47-18-124 of the Tennessee Code). Specific provisions frequently quoted in court cases and interpretive opinions related to promotions include the following:

Reference No.	Descriptive Name
Tenn. Const. art. XI, § 5	(Prohibition of lotteries)
Tenn. Code § 39-17-501	Definitions (for anti-gambling laws including definitions for gambling and lottery)
Tenn. Code § 39-17-502	Gambling—Defenses (gambling prohibited as misdemeanor)
Tenn. Code § 39-17-503	Gambling promotion (prohibited as misdemeanor)
Tenn. Code § 39-17-504	Aggravated gambling promotion (prohibited as a felony)
Tenn. Code § 39-17-506	Lotteries, chain letters, and pyramid clubs

Summary of State Law

Prohibition of Lotteries and Gambling: Tennessee's Constitution and its statutory laws prohibit lotteries.[1] A promotion that combines a prize, chance, and consideration is a lottery in Tennessee.[2] Tennessee also has a general prohibition against gambling.[3] Exceptions to the lottery and gambling prohibitions include state-operated lotteries and certain charitable lotteries.

Contests: Tennessee permits contests as long as the contest does not conflict with anti-gambling laws. If the contest includes an element of consideration, the sponsor must award the contest prize based on skill and not on chance. Contests charging consideration must also comply with the disclosure requirements of Tennessee's prize promotion provisions discussed below.

It is unclear on which test[4] Tennessee relies when evaluating whether or not chance determines the outcome of a promotion. While some authority supports the argument that Tennessee follows the dominant factor doctrine, alternative authority supports the argument that Tennessee applies the any chance test.

When analyzing whether a pay-to-play poker tournament offering a jackpot prize constituted an illegal lottery, the Tennessee Attorney General cited opinions from other states and acknowledged that most states use the dominant factor doctrine. While the Tennessee Attorney General did not reject the dominant factor doctrine, he stopped short of saying that the dominant factor doctrine is the test applied by Tennessee.[5]

A literal reading of the Tennessee statute suggests that Tennessee might apply the any chance test when determining whether or not a promotion incorporates chance. The Tennessee statute defines gambling as "risking anything of value for a profit whose return is to *any degree contingent on chance*".[6] The reference to gambling can be interpreted to include a lottery since the Tennessee Supreme Court has accepted that a lottery is a form of gambling.[7]

TENNESSEE LAW GOVERNING BEAUTY PAGEANTS. Tennessee has laws that deal with beauty pageants. These beauty pageant laws are in Title 47, Chapter 18, Part 2, Sections 47-18-201 to 47-18-201 of the Tennessee Code. The law applies to beauty pageants that charge participants an entry fee. An entry fee includes any requirement for the beauty pageant participants to pay money, sell advertisements or tickets, or obtain sponsors. Every beauty pageant operator must register with the Consumer Affairs Division in the Tennessee Department of Commerce and Insurance. Along with the registration, the beauty pageant operator must file a bond in the amount of $10,000. The following groups are exempt from the registration and bond requirements:

- a bona fide civic club in existence for one year
- certain fairs including a community fair, a county fair, a district fair, and a regional fair
- a religious organization or church, or
- a local governmental entity and their auxiliary and affiliated organizations

The beauty pageant laws also do not apply to a non-profit corporation in operation for twenty years or more whose primary function is operating statewide beauty pageants and that is affiliated with annual nationwide pageants.

Sweepstakes: Tennessee permits sweepstakes as long as participants do not pay consideration and the sweepstakes does not otherwise violate anti-gambling laws. Citing Tennessee case law, the Tennessee Attorney General has indicated that any organization, charitable or otherwise, may lawfully conduct a cash or prize giveaway if all persons wishing to participate receive an opportunity to do so without being required to pay money, make a donation, or purchase any product or service.[8]

Prize Promotion Laws: Tennessee incorporates prize promotion protections into its Consumer Protection Act which is codified in Title 47, Chapter 18 of the Tennessee Code.

COMPANY OFFERING PRIZE GIVEAWAY AS INDUCEMENT FOR CONSUMER ACTION MUST PROVIDE DISCLOSURES. One provision of the prize promotion laws targets companies combining prizes or gift giveaways with their sales campaign efforts.[9] If a company tells a consumer that the consumer will or may receive a prize as an inducement for the consumer to take an action, the company must provide a disclosure. The action being induced can be purchasing a product or service, incurring a monetary obligation, visiting a business, attending a sales presentation, or contacting a salesperson.[10] Tennessee does not require that the disclosure be in writing unless the consumer asks for a written version.[11]

PUBLICITY RELEASE PROHIBITION. One somewhat unique aspect of Tennessee's prize promotion protections is a publicity release prohibition. A company may not make receipt of a prize contingent upon the recipient allowing the company to use his name for promotional purposes.[12] The provision also requires a company to obtain the express written or oral consent of a prize recipient before using the recipient's names for a promotional purpose in connection with a mailing to others.[13]

Many sponsors interpret this publicity prohibition as applying to any contest or sweepstakes promotion. A literal reading of the statute places doubt on that interpretation since the statutory section containing the publicity prohibition indicates that the statutory section applies to the following:

- a company that tells a consumer that the consumer will or may receive a prize as a way to induce the consumer to take some action (as discussed in the previous portion of this Tennessee State Outline)
- a company that sells travel services to consumers[14]

Hence, a literal reading of the statute seems to make the publicity prohibition inapplicable to a sponsor offering a contest or sweepstakes outside of a sales campaign.

PROMOTIONS CHARGING CONSIDERATION. Before a sponsor may require a person in Tennessee to pay the sponsor money as a condition of receiving, competing for, or obtaining information for a prize, the sponsor must provide a written disclaimer, referred to as a prize notice.[15] This provision is written sufficiently broadly to encompass any contest that charges consideration, regardless of whether the contest is offered in conjunction with a sales campaign. There are specific requirements for information the disclosure must include and how the disclosure is to appear.[16]

Gambling Exceptions for Non-Profits and Other Qualified Organizations

Raffle and Lotteries: The Tennessee Constitution does allow certain federally tax-exempt, non-profit organizations to offer an annual lottery.[17] Permissible games allowed under the non-profit annual lottery exemption include raffles, reverse raffles, cakewalks, and cakewheels. Bingo is not one of the games permitted. An eligible organization wishing to hold such an event must submit an annual event application to the Tennessee Secretary of State and must submit financial reports after the event.[18]

The Tennessee Charitable Gaming Implementation Law in Title 3, Chapter 17, Sections 3-17-101 *et seq.* of the Tennessee Code implements the constitutional raffle allowance. Regulations for charitable gaming events, issued by the Tennessee Department of State, are in Sections 1360-03-01 *et seq.* of the Official Compilation of Rules and Regulations of the State of Tennessee. Additional information is available in the Charity Games portion of the Tennessee Attorney General's website.

Bingo: There are no provisions allowing non-profits to conduct bingo games in Tennessee. In *Secretary of State v. St. Augustine Church/St. Augustine School,*766 S.W.2d 499 (Tenn. 1989), the Tennessee Supreme Court examined the legality of commercial for-fee bingo operations and concluded that constitutional provisions against lotteries prohibited the state legislature from authorizing the game of bingo.

Resources

Tennessee offers attorney general opinions from 2000 through the present online at the website of the Tennessee Attorney General. Opinions issued prior to 2000 can be obtained by requesting a copy through the opinion telephone line at (615) 741-2518.

Endnotes

1. Tenn. Const. art. XI, § 5; Tenn. Code § 39-17-506 (2013).
2. *Tennessee Secretary of State v. St. Augustine Church*, 766 S.W.2d 499, 501 (Tenn. 1989).

3. *See e.g.*, Tenn. Code §§ 39-17-502 to 39-17-504 (2013).

4. *See generally*, Section 3.4.3 of this Guide for a discussion of tests used when evaluating whether chance or skill prevails in a promotion combining elements of both.

5. Tenn. Att'y Gen. Op. No. 05-159 (Oct. 14, 2005).

6. Tenn. Code § 39-17-501 (2013) (emphasis added).

7. *See Tennessee Secretary of State v. St. Augustine Church*, 766 S.W.2d 499 (Tenn. 1989).

8. Tenn. Att'y Gen. Op. No. 89-72 (May 3, 1989) *citing Tennessee Secretary of State v. St. Augustine Church*, 766 S.W.2d 499 (1989) and superseding previous attorney general opinions with conflicting analysis including Tenn. Att'y Gen. Op. No. 84-272 (Sept. 27, 1984) (prize giveaway requiring participants to purchase a Knoxville Transit Authority ticket may be lawful) and Tenn. Att'y Gen. Op. No. 84-221 (July 18, 1984) (a reverse raffle requiring participants to purchase a ticket to a dinner or cocktail party may be lawful).

9. Tenn. Code § 47-18-120 (2013).

10. Tenn. Code § 47-18-120(b)(1) (2013).

11. Tenn. Code § 47-18-120(c)(2) (2013).

12. Tenn. Code § 47-18-120 (c)(3)(C) (2013).

13. *Id.*

14. Tenn. Code § 47-18-120(b) (2013).

15. Tenn. Code § 47-18-124(b) (2013).

16. Tenn. Code § 47-18-124 (c) & (d) (2013). *See generally*, discussion of state prize promotion laws in Section 7.4.2 of this Guide.

17. Tenn. Const. art. XI, § 5.

18. Tenn. Code §§ 3-17-103(a) and 3-17-106 (2013).

Texas

State Attorney General Office
Office of the Attorney General
300 W. 15th Street
Austin, Texas 78701
(512) 463-2100
Website: www.oag.state.tx.us

Selected State Laws, Regulations, and Constitutional Provisions

Texas' anti-gambling laws (Title 10, Chapter 47, Sections 47-01 *et seq.* of the Texas Penal Code) contain provisions related to promotions. Texas prize promotion laws, incorporated into the state's business and commerce code, include specific treatment for contests, gift giveaways, and sweepstakes (Title 13, Chapters 621 and 622 of the Texas Business and Commerce Code). Texas legal provisions frequently cited in court cases and interpretive opinions related to promotions include the following:

Reference No.	Descriptive Name
Tex. Const. art. III, § 47	Lotteries and Gift Enterprises; Bingo Games
Tex. Penal Code § 47.01	Definitions (for anti-gambling laws including definitions for bet, lottery and thing of value)
Tex. Penal Code § 47.02	Gambling (prohibited as a misdemeanor)
Tex. Penal Code § 47.03	Gambling Promotion (prohibited as a misdemeanor)
Tex. Penal Code § 32.42(b)(11)	Conducting a deceptive sales contest (prohibited as deceptive business practice)

Summary of State Law

Prohibition of Lotteries and Gambling: Texas' Constitution as well as its statutory laws prohibit lotteries.[1] A promotion that combines a prize, chance, and consideration is a lottery in Texas.[2] Texas also has a general prohibition against gambling.[3] Exceptions to the lottery and gambling prohibitions include state-operated lotteries and certain charitable lotteries.

Contests: Texas permits contests as long as the contest does not conflict with anti-gambling laws. If the contest includes an element of consideration, the sponsor must award the contest prize based on skill and not on chance. The anti-gambling laws specifically exempt from a gambling violation any offer of a prize to actual contestants (or to the owners of animals, vehicles, watercraft, or aircraft entered in a contest) where the prize is awarded based on skill, speed, strength, or endurance. Court opinions suggest that Texas applies the dominant factor doctrine[4] when evaluating whether or not chance determines the outcome of a promotion.[5]

Sweepstakes: Texas permits sweepstakes as long as participants do not pay consideration and the sweepstakes does not otherwise violate anti-gambling laws. Sweepstakes that use direct mail and offer prizes valued at $50,000 or more must comply with Texas prize promotion laws discussed below.

Texas law regulates sales contests which it defines as a contest in connection with the sale of a commodity or service by which the winner is determined based on a drawing, guessing, matching, or chance.[6] Although the statute uses the term contest, the description matches a chance-based sweepstakes. Adhering to the prohibition against deceptive sales contests requires that the sweepstakes sponsor disclose on a conspicuously displayed permanent poster (if the contest is conducted by or through a retail outlet) or on each card game piece, entry blank, or similar marketing material (if the contest is not conducted by or through a retail outlet) certain information including the geographical area or number of outlets in which the contest is to be conducted; an accurate description of each type of prize; the minimum number and minimum amount of cash prizes; and the minimum number of each other type of prize.[7]

Prize Promotion Laws: Texas has two categories of prize promotion laws in its business and commerce code.

OFFERING PRIZE AS INDUCEMENT TO ATTEND SALES PRESENTATION. The first category is the Contest and Gift Giveaway Act and is codified in Title 13, Chapter 621, Section 621.001 to 621.252 of the Texas Business and Commerce Code. It targets companies that use promotions as an incentive for consumer attendance at company sales presentations.[8] When a company offers a giveaway or a sweepstakes winning opportunity to those who attend the company's sales presentation, the company must provide in writing details about the sales presentation and about the prize.[9]

As the title implies, the Contest and Gift Giveaway Act is applicable to giveaways and to contests. However, for purposes of the Contest and Gift Giveaway Act, contest is defined in part as a promotional device in which the winner or recipient of a prize is *determined by random selection*.[10] That definition describes the characteristics of a sweepstakes but not the characteristics of a skill-based contest. Hence, the statute seems not to apply to skill-based contests.

In addition to written disclosure requirements, the Contest and Gift Giveaway Act lists other required actions and prohibited practices for companies using promotions to increase sales presentation attendance.[11] The company must maintain detailed records about the solicitations, prizes, and recipients of prizes and make those records available to members of the public or to the Texas Attorney General upon request.

The Contest and Gift Giveaway Act requirements do not apply to promotions that take place at trade shows and similar business conferences as long as the targeted participants are all attendees of the trade show.[12]

SWEEPSTAKES USING DIRECT MAIL. The second category of Texas prize promotion laws, codified in Title 13, Chapter 622, Sections 622.001 to 622.206 of the Texas Business and Commerce Code, applies to sweepstakes conducted through the mail and offering prizes valued at $50,000 or more.[13] It does not apply to those sweepstakes for which the only use of the mail is for a consumer to return an entry form.[14] There are a number of prohibited activities designed to disassociate the sweepstakes from the ordering or purchasing of a product and to prevent deception of consumers.

While this Texas law has similarities with other states' prize promotion laws[15], there are some unique prohibitions. For example, if the sponsor accepts entries via mail, the sponsor may not use that mailing address for any purpose other than accepting entries via mail.[16] Also, Texas essentially restricts sweepstakes sponsors to conducting only one promotion that uses the mail in every thirty-day period.[17]

PRIZE PROMOTION PROVISIONS OF TELEMARKETING LAWS. Texas also addresses prizes and giveaways incorporated into commercial telephone solicitations (Title 10 of the Texas Business and Commerce Code).[18] If a prize or gift offer is part of a telephone solicitation campaign, the telephone solicitor must disclose certain information to the consumer as part of the call[19] and to the state as part of the required telephone solicitation registration with the secretary of state[20].

Gambling Exceptions for Non-Profits and Other Qualified Organizations

Raffles and Lotteries: A constitutional provision allows the Texas legislature to pass laws permitting charitable raffles.[21] The Texas legislature has done so with the enactment of the Charitable Raffle Enabling Act, codified in Title 13, Chapter 2002, Sections 2002.001 to 2002.058 of the Texas Occupations Code.

Organizations eligible to offer raffles are certain religious societies, volunteer fire departments, volunteer emergency medical services, and other non-profit organizations.[22] Eligible organizations may hold up to two raffles per calendar year and must use all proceeds for the charitable purposes of the organization.

While eligible organizations do not need a license to hold a raffle, Texas law does impose several restrictions and requirements on raffles.[23] There are monetary limits on the value of the prize.[24] With the exception of money, any prize (including a house) may be offered as a raffle prize.[25] Sponsors may not advertise the raffle statewide or through paid television, radio, or newspaper advertisements.[26] No Texas court opinion nor attorney general opinion has yet defined or interpreted the term *statewide*. However, the Texas Attorney General website suggests that this restriction prohibits advertising the raffle on the internet.[27] More information about charitable raffles is available in the Charities & Nonprofits section of the Texas Attorney General's website.

Bingo. A constitutional provision allows the Texas legislature to authorize charitable bingo games.[28] Organizations eligible to offer bingo games include certain religious societies, fraternal organizations, veterans organizations, volunteer fire department, and other nonprofit organizations.[29]

The operation of the bingo game must meet several statutory and regulatory requirements.[30] Organizations conducting bingo games must obtain a license issued by the Texas Lottery Commission and must use all net proceeds in Texas for the charitable purposes of the organization.[31] Licensed bingo operators must submit quarterly reports to the Texas Lottery Commission.[32] No license or reporting is required for bingo games conducted solely for recreational purposes by medical facilities or by organizations serving senior citizens.[33]

The Bingo Enabling Act is codified in Title 13, Chapter 2001, Sections 2001.001 to 2001.657 of the Texas Occupations Code. The charitable bingo regulations are in Title 16, Sections 402.100 *et. seq.* of the Texas Administrative Code. The Texas Lottery Commission makes applications and regulations available in the charitable bingo portion of its website at www.txlottery.org.

Resources

Texas offers a searchable database for its attorney general opinions from 1939 through the present online in the Opinions section of the website of the Office of the Attorney General.

Endnotes

1. Tex. Const. art. III, § 47; Tex. Penal Code § 47.03 (2013).
2. *Brice v. State,* 242 S.W.2d 433, 434 (Tex. Crim. App. 1951).
3. Tex. Penal Code §§ 47.02 and 47.03 (2013).
4. *See generally,* Section 3.4.3 of this Guide for a discussion of tests used when evaluating whether chance or skill prevails in a promotion combining elements of both.
5. *Johnson v. Phinney,* 218 F.2d 303, 306 (5th Cir. 1955).
6. Tex. Penal Code § 32.42(a)(5) & (8) (2013).

7. Tex. Penal Code § 32.42(a)(5) (2013).
8. Tex. Bus. & Com. Code § 621.002 (2013).
9. Tex. Bus. & Com. Code §§ 621.052, 621.102, 621.104, 621.106 (2013). Note that Sections 621.104 (disclosure for matched contests (*i.e.*, scratch-off promotions)) and 621.106 (disclosure for drawings) require disclosure in writing. In contrast, Section 621.052 (disclosure for giveaways) requires only clear and conspicuous disclosure. The conservative sponsor whose promotions are governed by the Contest and Gift Giveaway Act might choose to put any required disclosures in writing.
10. Tex. Bus. & Com. Code § 621.003(a)(1) (2013).
11. Tex. Bus. & Com. Code §§ 621.053, 621.054, 621.103, 621.105, and 621.107 (2013). *See generally*, discussion of state prize promotion laws in Section 7.4.2 of this Guide.
12. Tex. Bus. & Com. Code § 621.004 (2013).
13. The statute does not define *mail*, or indicate whether the statute is applicable to sweepstakes offered via email.
14. Tex. Bus. & Com. Code § 622.051 (2013).
15. *See generally*, discussion of state prize promotion laws in Section 7.4.2 of this Guide.
16. Tex. Bus. & Com. Code § 622.102 (2013).
17. Tex. Bus. & Com. Code § 622.109 (2013).
18. *See generally*, discussion of state telemarketing laws in Section 7.5.2 of this Guide.
19. Tex. Bus. & Com. Code § 302.202(2) (2013).
20. Tex. Bus. & Com. Code § 302.153(b)(4) (2013).
21. Tex. Const. art. III, § 47(d).
22. Tex. Occ. Code § 2002.002(2) (2013).
23. See general discussion of bingo and raffles in Section 9.2 of this Guide.
24. Tex. Occ. Code § 2002.056 (2013).
25. *Id.*
26. Tex. Occ. Code § 2002.054 (2013).
27. Office of the Texas Attorney General, *Raffles and Casino/Poker Nights in Texas Frequently Asked Questions*, https://www.oag.state.tx.us/consumer/raffle_faq.shtml (last visited Oct. 13, 2014).
28. Tex. Const. art. III, § 47(b).
29. Tex. Occ. Code § 2001.101 (2013).
30. *See generally*, discussion of bingo and raffles in Section 9.2 of this Guide.
31. Tex. Occ. Code § 2001.551 (2013).
32. Tex. Occ. Code § 2001.505 (2013).
33. Tex. Occ. Code § 2001.551 (2013).

Utah

State Attorney General Office
Utah Office of the Attorney General
Utah State Capitol Complex
350 North State Street Suite 230
Salt Lake City, Utah 84114
(801) 366-0260
Website: http://attorneygeneral.utah.gov/

Selected State Laws, Regulations, and Constitutional Provisions

Utah's anti-gambling laws (Title 76, Chapter 10, Sections 76-10-1101 to 76-10-1109 of the Utah Code), which are with its criminal laws, contain provisions related to promotions. With its commerce and trade laws, Utah includes the Prize Notices Regulation Act (Title 13, Chapter 28, Sections 13-28-1 *et seq.* of the Utah Code). Specific Utah legal provisions frequently cited in court cases and interpretive opinions related to promotions include the following:

Reference No.	Descriptive Name
Utah Const. art. VI, § 27	Games of chance not authorized
Utah Code Ann. § 76-10-1101	Definitions (for anti-gambling laws including definitions for gambling and lottery)
Utah Code Ann. § 76-10-1102	Gambling (prohibited as a misdemeanor)
Utah Code Ann. § 76-10-1104	Gambling promotion (prohibited as a misdemeanor for first offense; felony for subsequent offense)
Utah Code Ann. § 76-10-1104.5	Advertisement or solicitation for participation in lotteries—Void in Utah

Summary of State Law

Prohibition of Lotteries and Gambling: Utah's Constitution and its statutory laws prohibit games of chance including lotteries and gambling.[1] A promotion that combines a prize, chance, and consideration is a lottery in Utah.[2]

Contests: Utah permits contests as long as the contest does not conflict with anti-gambling laws. If the contest includes an element of consideration, the sponsor must award the contest prize based on skill and not on chance.

A 1928 Utah court opinion suggests that Utah applies the dominant factor doctrine[3] when evaluating whether or not chance determines the outcome of a promotion.[4] Research for this Guide yielded no subsequent authorities either overturning or reiterating Utah's adoption of the dominant factor doctrine.

It is unclear to what extent Utah's prize promotion law, the Utah Prize Notices Regulation Act, applies to contests charging consideration. Hence, conservative sponsors might want to comply with the prize notice disclosure requirements in the Utah Prize Notices Regulation Act, discussed below in the Prize Promotions Law portion of this Utah State Summary.

Sweepstakes: Utah permits sweepstakes as long as participants do not pay consideration and the sweepstakes does not violate anti-gambling laws. In *Albertson's v. Hansen*, 600 P.2d 982 (Utah 1979), the Utah Supreme Court held that in order for there to be consideration in a lottery, the participant must pay something of value in exchange for the opportunity to win a prize. There is no consideration solely because the sponsor experiences an increase in sales as a direct result of the promotion.

In the *Albertson's* decision, a retail grocery chain's sales increased as a direct result of a promotion in which the chain distributed bingo-type boards to patrons and offered prizes to patrons whose boards had a winning bingo pattern. Since there was no purchase required for the game boards and patrons could obtain the boards for free at the store and via mail, the promotion was not an illegal lottery. In the same *Albertson's* decision, the Utah Supreme Court rejected the notion that participants' efforts to pick up or obtain one of the grocery store's game boards qualified as valuable consideration for purposes of a lottery.

Prize Promotion Laws: The Utah Prize Notices Regulation Act, Utah's version of a prize promotion law, is part of the state's commerce and trade laws and is codified in Title 13, Chapter 28, Sections 13-28-1 *et seq.* of the Utah Code. Utah's prize promotion laws focus on the requirements for a disclosure statement, referred to as a prize notice. As defined by the statute, a prize notice is a communication to an individual that does the following:

- represents that the individual has been selected or may be eligible to receive a prize and
- conditions receipt of the prize on a payment or donation from the individual or requires or invites the individual to contact the company to learn how to receive the prize or for more information related to the notice.[5]

When a prize notice is required, there is specific information that must be included and specific requirements for the placement, font, and wording of the required disclosures.[6]

REPRESENTATION THAT A PERSON HAS WON OR IS ELIGIBLE TO WIN A PRIZE REQUIRES A PRIZE NOTICE. If a company represents to an individual that the individual has been selected or may be eligible to receive a prize, the company may not request or accept a payment from the individual before giving the individual a written prize notice.[7]

REQUIREMENTS WHEN PRIZE NOTICE ENCOURAGES ATTENDANCE AT SALES PRESENTATION. If a company sends to an individual a prize notice offering a prize as an inducement to view, hear, or attend a sales presentation, the sales presentation may not begin until the company identifies the prize to be awarded and actually delivers the prize.[8]

APPLICABILITY OF PRIZE PROMOTION LAWS TO CONTESTS CHARGING CONSIDERATION. The Utah statute excludes from the definition of prize notice a notice informing an individual that the individual has won a prize as a result of the person's actual prior entry in a game, drawing, sweepstakes or other contest.[9] However, research for this Guide yielded no authorities addressing whether Utah's prize promotion laws generally apply to advertisements and promotional materials encouraging people to enter a contest with an entry fee. Hence, the conservative sponsor might choose to provide the same disclosures as part of its written official rules for any contest that charges consideration.

Gambling Exceptions for Non-Profits and Other Qualified Organizations

Raffles, Bingo, and Lotteries: Utah does not offer non-profit exceptions for the operation of raffles or bingo games.

Resources

Utah offers a searchable database for its attorney general opinions from 1990 through the present online at the website of the Utah Office of the Attorney General.

Endnotes

1. Utah Const. art. VI, § 27; Utah Code § 76-10-1102 (2014).
2. Utah Code § 76-10-1101(7) (2014).
3. *See generally*, Section 3.4.3 of this Guide for a discussion of tests used when evaluating whether chance or skill prevails in a promotion combining elements of both.
4. *D'Orio v. Startup Candy Co.*, 266 P. 1037, 1038 (Utah 1928).
5. Utah Code § 13-28-2(3) (2014).
6. Utah Code § 13-28-4 (2014). *See generally*, discussion of state prize promotion laws in Section 7.4.2 of this Guide.
7. Utah Code § 13-28-3 (2014).
8. Utah Code § 13-28-5 (2014).
9. Utah Code § 13-28-2(3) (2014).

Vermont

State Attorney General Office
Office of the Attorney General
109 State Street
Montpelier, Vermont 05609
(802) 828-3171
Website: http://www.atg.state.vt.us/

Selected State Laws, Regulations, and Constitutional Provisions

Vermont's gambling and lottery laws (Title 13, Chapter 51, Sections 2101 *et seq.* of the Vermont Statute) are with its crimes and criminal procedure laws. The consumer fraud division of the Vermont Attorney General Office issues a consumer fraud rule that offers protections in the context of promotions (06-031-003 Vt. Code R. § 109). Specific authorities frequently quoted in court cases and interpretive opinions related to promotions include the following:

Reference No.	Descriptive Name
Vt. Stat. tit. 13, § 2101	Setting up, promoting, or aiding (in lottery or other game of chance, prohibited and punishable by prison and/or fine)
Vt. Stat. tit. 13, § 2102	Disposing of property by way of chance (punishable by prison and/or fine)
Vt. Stat. tit. 13, § 2103	Lottery tickets (sale prohibited and punishable by fine)
Vt. Stat. tit. 13, § 2141	Winning or losing by gambling (punishable by fine)

Vt. Stat. tit. 13, § 2143b   Contests and sweepstakes (permissible; consideration allowed for skill contests but not for sweepstakes)

Vt. Stat. tit. 9, § 2507   Prize award services (disclosures required when offering prizes or awards as part of a pay-per-call service[1])

06-031-003   Contest and prizes
   Vt. Code R. § 109

Summary of State Law

Prohibition of Lotteries and Gambling: Vermont statutes include general prohibitions against gambling and lotteries.[2] A promotion that combines a prize, chance, and consideration is a lottery in Vermont.[3]

Contests: Vermont permits contests as long as the contest does not conflict with anti-gambling laws. If the contest includes an element of consideration, the sponsor must award the contest prize based on skill and not on chance. Research for this Guide did not uncover any authorities indicating which test Vermont applies when evaluating whether or not chance determines the outcome of a promotion.[4]

Vermont now allows sponsors of skill-based contests to charge participants a monetary entry fee or other consideration. Historically, Vermont was one of the few states that prohibited skill-based contests from requiring any kind of entry fee, service charge, purchase or similar consideration. This changed in 2013 when Vermont amended its laws to allow sponsors to charge consideration for skill-based contests.[5] Vermont accomplished this by adding a new provision to its Commerce and Trade Laws indicating that nothing in the Vermont consumer protection laws prohibits a sponsor from charging an entry fee, service charge, purchase, or similar consideration for entry into a game of skill or other promotion that is not based on chance.[6] The legislature also amended an anti-gambling statutory provision entitled Contests and Sweepstakes by adding the following sentence: "This [reference to section prohibiting sponsors from requiring consideration in a chance-based promotion] shall not be construed to prohibit a person from organizing, executing, or participating in a contest that is not a contest of chance".[7]

Sweepstakes: Vermont permits sweepstakes as long as participants do not pay consideration and the sweepstakes does not conflict with anti-gambling laws. The cost of mailing an entry is not deemed as consideration in Vermont.[8]

Gambling Exceptions for Non-Profits and Other Qualified Organizations

Bingo, Raffles and Lotteries: Vermont allows certain non-profit organizations to operate lotteries, raffles or other games of chance as long as the organizations use the net proceeds exclusively for charitable, religious, educational and civic undertakings.[9] Organizations eligible to offer bingo and raffles are federally tax-exempt non-profit corporations, churches, schools, fire departments, municipalities, fraternal organizations and agricultural fairs. Vermont also allows political parties organized under Vermont law to hold raffles as long as the political party uses the raffle proceeds for undertakings consistent with its purposes.[10]

The operation of the charitable games are subject to statutory requirements and restrictions.[11] However, there are no licensing requirements for eligible organizations to operate charitable bingo, raffles or lotteries in Vermont. Organizations operating games may be required to file annual financial reports with the Vermont Commissioner of Taxes which can provide forms for the required reports.

Resources

Vermont offers its attorney general opinions from 2000 through the present online in the Opinions section of the website of the Office of the Attorney General. The Office of the Attorney General provides copies of opinions from earlier years upon request.

Endnotes

1. *See generally*, discussion of disclosures required by state prize promotion laws and state telemarketing laws in Sections 7.4.2 and 7.5.2 of this Guide.
2. Vt. Stat. tit. 13, §§ 2101, 2102, and 2141 (2013).
3. *Vermont v. Wilson*, 196 A. 757, 758 (Vt. 1938).

4. *See generally,* Section 3.4.3 of this Guide for a discussion of tests used when evaluating whether chance or skill prevails in a promotion combining elements of both.

5. S.3 (Act 0009), 2013-2014 Gen. Assemb. (Vt. 2013).

6. Vt. Stat. tit. 09, § 2481x (2013).

7. Vt. Stat. tit. 13, §2143b (2013). The statute is using the term contest in a broad sense to refer to many types of promotions. It is not using the term contest as used in this Guide to refer exclusively to skill-based promotions.

8. Vt. Stat. tit. 13, §2143b (2013). Some commentators have stated that requiring entrants to provide return postage or a self-addressed envelope (*e.g.*, for receipt of an entry form) is deemed to be consideration by Vermont law. However, research for this Guide uncovered no authoritative sources either supporting or refuting this assertion.

9. Vt. Stat. tit. 13, §2143 (2013).

10. Vt. Stat. tit. 13, §2143(a) (2013).

11. Vt. Stat. tit. 13, §2143(e) (2013). *See generally,* discussion of bingo and raffles in Section 9.2 of this Guide.

Virginia

State Attorney General Office
Office of the Attorney General
900 East Main Street
Richmond, Virginia 23219
(804) 786-2071
Website: http://oag.state.va.us

Selected State Laws, Regulations, and Constitutional Provisions

Virginia's anti-gambling laws (Title 18.2, Chapter 8, Sections 18.2-325 *et seq.* of the Virginia Code), which are grouped with its crimes and offenses laws, contain provisions related to promotions. Virginia includes prize promotion laws (Title 59.1, Chapter 31, Sections 59.1-415 *et seq.* of the Virginia Code) as part of its trade and commerce laws. Specific Virginia legal provisions frequently cited in court cases and interpretive opinions related to promotions include the following:

Reference No.	Descriptive Name
Va. Code§ 18.2-325	Definitions (for anti-gambling laws including definitions for illegal gambling and interstate gambling)
Va. Code§ 18.2-326	Penalty for illegal gambling (punishable as misdemeanor)
Va. Code§ 18.2-328	Conducting illegal gambling operations; penalties (punishable as felony)

Summary of State Law

Prohibition of Lotteries and Gambling. The Virginia statute has a general prohibition against gambling.[1] While the statute does not clearly explain how Virginia characterizes lotteries, court opinions and attorney general opinions indicate that a promotion that combines a prize, chance, and consideration constitutes both a lottery and gambling in Virginia.[2] The Virginia Attorney General has described a lottery as "a generic term embracing 'all schemes for distribution of prizes by chance for consideration'".[3]

Contests: Virginia permits contests as long as the contest does not conflict with anti-gambling laws. If the contest includes an element of consideration, the sponsor must award the contest prize based on skill and not on chance. Virginia law explicitly exempts from the anti-gambling laws any contests of speed or skill between men, animals, fowl or vehicles.[4]

According to the Virginia Attorney General, Virginia applies the dominant factor doctrine[5] when evaluating whether or not chance determines the outcome of a promotion.[6] As an example, the Virginia Attorney General found that a talent contest was not illegal gambling. Even though the talent contest had the elements of a prize and consideration, it had no element of chance because the predominant factor for awarding the prize was the content of an essay submitted by participants.[7] Preparing the essay's content required skill on the part of the participants.

Sweepstakes: Virginia permits sweepstakes as long as participants do not pay consideration and the sweepstakes does not otherwise violate anti-gambling laws. The Virginia statute explicitly identifies specific activities that do not qualify as consideration under the gambling laws:

- going to a sponsor's premises
- completing, mailing or delivering an entry blank
- answering questions, whether verbally or in writing
- witnessing a demonstration or similar event[8]

In order for these activities not to be deemed consideration, the sponsor can not require the individual to make a payment or make a purchase in connection with the activity.

Prize Promotion Laws: Virginia's version of a prize promotion law is the Prizes and Gifts Act (Title 59.1, Chapter 31, Sections 59.1-415 *et seq.* of the Virginia Code). The law apples to any company offering contests and prizes in connection with the company's attempts to sell or lease goods, property, or services. In addition to prohibiting deceptive practices such as using simulated checks or invoices and charging excessive shipping and handling charges for giveaways and prizes[9], the Prizes and Gifts Act includes the following provisions:

REPRESENTATION THAT A PERSON HAS WON A PRIZE. If a company represents to a person that the person has won a prize, the company must actually award the prize within ten days of making the representation. Furthermore, award of the prize must impose no obligation or expense on the prize recipient.[10]

REPRESENTATION THAT A PERSON IS ELIGIBLE TO WIN A PRIZE. No company may tell a person that the person is eligible to win a prize without providing certain disclosures.[11] The disclosure can be verbal or written. If verbal, the disclosure must indicate the name of the sponsor; conditions to be satisfied to win the prize; any money the person must pay to receive the prize (including shipping and handling costs and the cost for purchase of another product); and any other material conditions. There are additional, more specific requirements for written disclosures including requirements for placement, font, and wording.[12] There is no disclosure requirement for the prize promotion if:

- to be eligible to win, the participant only has to complete and mail in, deliver to a local store, or call in the entry (exception is not applicable to pay-per-call telephone call), or
- the participant is not required to listen to a sales presentation or pay any sum of money for any merchandise, service or item of value

Gambling Exceptions for Non-Profits and Other Qualified Organizations

Raffles and Bingos: Virginia allows certain non-profit organizations to conduct charitable gaming which includes raffles and bingo. Organizations eligible to offer raffles and bingo games include volunteer fire departments; organizations operated exclusively for religious, charitable, community or educational purposes; athletic associations and booster clubs raising funds for school-sponsored activities; veterans associations; fraternal associations; local chambers of commerce; and other non-profit organizations.[13]

The operation of charitable gaming must meet several statutory and regulatory requirements.[14] The organization must use a minimum percentage (as set by regulation) of the gross charitable gaming receipts for activities that are consistent with the organization's stated purposes.[15] Eligible organizations that raise less than $40,000 during any twelve-month period from raffles, bingo, and other charitable gaming do not need a license and are exempt from other regulatory requirements.[16] Eligible organizations raising more than $40,000 during any twelve-month period from charitable gaming must obtain a charitable gaming license from the Virginia Department of Agriculture and Consumer Services, must file periodic financial reports of charitable gaming receipts and disbursements[17], and must comply with bingo and raffle regulations.

The laws enabling charitable gaming are grouped with the anti-gambling laws within the crimes and offenses laws in Title 18.2, Chapter 8, Sections 18.2-340.15 to 18.2-340.37 of the Virginia Code. The charitable gaming regulations, issued by the Virginia Department of Agriculture and Consumer Services, are codified in Title 11, Sections 15-40-10 *et seq.* of the Virginia Administrative Code. Licensing, report forms, and other information are available from the Office of Charitable and Regulatory Programs within the Virginia Department of Agriculture and Consumer Services, 102 Governor Street, Richmond, Virginia 23219, http://www.vdacs.virginia.gov.

Resources

Virginia offers a searchable database for its attorney general opinions from 1996 through the present from the Opinions and Resource portion of the website of the Office of the Attorney General.

Endnotes

1. Va. Code § 18.2-326 & 328 (2014).
2. *Rosenberg v. Virginia,* 181 S.E. 368, 370 (Va. 1935); Va. Att'y Gen. Op. (April 19, 1996).

3. Va. Att'y Gen. Op. (April 19, 1996).
4. Va. Code § 18.2-333 (2014).
5. *See generally*, Section 3.4.3 of this Guide for a discussion of tests used when evaluating whether chance or skill prevails in a promotion combining elements of both.
6. Va. Att'y Gen. Op. (Sept. 19, 1996).
7. *Id.*
8. Va. Code § 18.2-332 (2014).
9. Va. Code §§ 59.1-419 to 59.1-420 (2014).
10. Va. Code § 59.1-416 (2014).
11. Va. Code § 59.1-417 (2014).
12. *Id. See generally*, discussion of state prize promotion laws in Section 7.4.2 of this Guide.
13. Va. Code § 18.2-340.16 (2014).
14. *See generally*, the discussion of bingo and raffles in Section 9.2 of this Guide.
15. Va. Code § 18.2-340.19.A.1 (2014).
16. Va. Code § 18.2-340.23 (2014).
17. Va. Code §§ 18.2-340.23.A and 18.2-340.30 (2014).

Washington

State Attorney General Office
Office of the Attorney General
1125 Washington Street SE
PO Box 40100
Olympia, Washington 98504
(360) 753-6200
Website: http://www.atg.wa.gov

Selected State Laws, Regulations, and Constitutional Provisions

With its crimes and punishment laws, Washington has anti-gambling laws (Title 9, Chapter 9.46, Sections 9.46.010 *et seq.* of the Washington Revised Code) which contain provisions related to promotions. Washington also has prize promotion laws (Title 19, Chapter 19.170, Sections 19.170.010 *et seq.* of the Washington Revised Code) as part of its miscellaneous business regulations laws. Specific Washington legal provisions frequently cited in court cases and interpretive opinions related to promotions include the following:

Reference No.	Descriptive Name
Wash. Const. art. II, § 24	Lotteries and Divorce (lotteries prohibited)
Wash. Rev. Code § 9.46.0225	Contest of chance (defined)
Wash. Rev. Code § 9.46.0237	Gambling (defined)
Wash. Rev. Code § 9.46.0257	Lottery (defined)
Wash. Rev. Code § 9.46.0269	Professional gambling (defined)
Wash. Rev. Code § 9.46.160	Conducting (gambling) activity without license (prohibited as felony)
Wash. Rev. Code § 9.46.220	Professional gambling in the first degree (prohibited as felony)

Wash. Rev. Code § 9.46.221   Professional gambling in the second
degree (prohibited as felony)

Wash. Rev. Code § 9.46.222   Professional gambling in the third degree
(prohibited as misdemeanor)

Summary of State Law

Prohibition of Lotteries and Gambling: Washington's Constitution prohibits lotteries.[1] A promotion that combines a prize, chance, and consideration is a lottery in Washington.[2] Washington also has a general statutory prohibition against gambling[3] which includes prohibitions against lotteries.[4] Exceptions to the lottery and gambling prohibitions include state-operated lotteries and certain charitable lotteries.

Contests: Washington permits contests as long as the contest does not conflict with anti-gambling laws. If the contest includes an element of consideration, the sponsor must award the contest prize based on skill and not on chance. The definition for contest of chance in the anti-gambling laws implies that Washington uses the material element test[5] when evaluating whether or not chance determines the outcome of a promotion. The Washington statute defines contest of chance as a game in which the outcome depends in a *material degree* upon an element of chance, even though skill may also be a factor in the outcome.[6]

Sweepstakes: Washington permits sweepstakes as long as participants do not pay consideration and the sweepstakes does not conflict with anti-gambling laws. Sweepstakes must also comply with any applicable provisions of Washington's prize notice promotion laws[7] and Washington's unfair business practice laws[8].

PROMOTIONAL CONTESTS OF CHANCE. Washington law explicitly allows what it refers to as promotional contests of chance. Although the Washington statute refers to these promotions as promotional contests, these authorized promotional contests actually meet the definition of sweepstakes.[9] The promotional contest, which is designed to advertise the services or goods of a business, may include the elements of prize and chance but not the element of consideration.[10] If the sponsor combines a chance to win with the purchase of goods or services, the sponsor must also offer a free alternative method of entry.[11] The statute explicitly lists certain activities that do not qualify as consideration in such promotional contests of chance:

- visiting a business location,
- placing or answering a telephone call,
- completing an entry form or customer survey,
- furnishing a stamped, self-addressed envelope[12]

Prize Promotion Laws: Washington offers prize promotion protections in its laws for the promotional advertising of prizes.[13] The Washington prize promotion laws apply, if, as part of an effort to sell goods, services or other property, a company delivers written materials by hand, mail, or other print medium with a representation that the recipient has or will be awarded a prize. If the Washington promotion laws apply, there are specific disclosures the company must include in the written offer.[14] The prize promotion laws also list sponsor affirmative duties (such as actually awarding the promised prize) as well as prohibited activities designed to prevent sponsors from misleading consumers.[15]

The disclosure and prohibited practice requirements do not apply to a sweepstakes that qualifies as a promotional contest of chance[16], discussed above in the Sweepstakes portion of this Washington State Summary. The disclosure and prohibited practice requirements also do not apply to prize giveaways combined with sales campaigns when all of the following conditions apply:

- no element of chance determines whether the consumer will obtain the prize;
- the consumer may examine without obligation any merchandise offered and return any purchase within thirty days for a full refund;
- the consumer may keep the prize without obligation even if the consumer returns the merchandise; and
- the consumer is not required to attend a sales presentation or spend any money to obtain the prize.[17]

Gambling Exceptions for Non-Profits and Other Qualified Organizations

Raffles and Bingo: Washington allows certain charitable or non-profit organizations to conduct bingo games, raffles, and other games of chance.[18] Organizations eligible to offer raffles and bingo games in Washington include organizations existing for charitable, benevolent, eleemosynary, educational, civic, patriotic, political, social, fraternal, athletic or agricultural purposes.[19]

NO LICENSE REQUIRED FOR MEMBER-ONLY RAFFLES. Eligible organizations may hold raffles without a license provided that annual gross revenues from all such raffles do not exceed $5,000 and ticket buyers and eligible winners include only regular members of the organization.[20]

NOTICE, BUT NO LICENSE REQUIRED FOR LIMITED PUBLIC RAFFLES AND BINGO GAMES. There is a separate statutory provision that allows eligible organizations to offer bingo, raffle, and other amusement games to the public.[21] The organization may offer the public games no more than twice each calendar year. Bingo can be offered for no more than twelve consecutive days each time. Raffles can be offered for more than twelve days. After deducting its expenses, the organization must devote all proceeds from the raffle and bingo games to the charitable or non-profit purposes of the organization. These public games require no license; however, the organization must give notice to local police and maintain financial records for at least one year after the event.

LICENSE REQUIRED FOR OTHER RAFFLES AND BINGO GAMES. Qualified organizations wishing to offer bingo games and raffles falling outside the parameters discussed above must have a license issued by the Washington State Gambling Commission.

There are additional operational and record-keeping requirements for raffles and bingo games.[22] Washington's laws for charitable raffles and bingo are integrated into the state's anti-gambling laws (Title 9, Chapter 9.46 of the Washington Revised Code). Regulations for raffles are in Sections 230-11-001 *et seq.* of the Washington Administrative Code. Regulations for bingo are in Sections 230-10-001 *et seq.* of the Washington Administrative Code.

Additional information, license, and record-keeping forms are available through the Washington State Gambling Commission, 4565 7th Avenue S.E., Lacey, WA 98503, (360) 486-3440, http://www.wsgc.wa.gov/.

Resources

Washington offers a searchable database for its attorney general opinions on the website of the Office of the Attorney General.

Endnotes

1. Wash. Const. art. II, § 24.
2. Wash. Rev. Code § 9.46.0257 (2014).
3. Wash. Rev. Code §§ 9.46.160, 9.46.220 to 9.46.222 (2014).
4. Wash. Rev. Code § 9.46.0257 (2014).
5. *See generally*, Section 3.4.3 of this Guide for a discussion of tests used when evaluating whether chance or skill prevails in a promotion combining elements of both.
6. Wash. Rev. Code § 9.46.0225 (2014) (emphasis added).
7. Wash. Rev. Code § 19.170.010 *et. seq.* (2014).
8. Wash. Rev. Code § 19.86.010 *et seq.* (2014).
9. *See generally*, discussion of sweepstakes in Section 3.1.2 of this Guide.
10. Wash. Rev. Code § 9.46.0356 (2014).
11. Wash. Rev. Code § 9.46.0356(4)(b) (2014).
12. Wash. Rev. Code § 9.46.0356(6) (2014).
13. Wash. Rev. Code § 19.170.010 *et. seq.* (2014).
14. Wash. Rev. Code § 19.170.030 (2014). *See generally*, discussion of state prize promotion laws in Section 7.4.2 of this Guide.
15. Wash. Rev. Code § 19.170.040 (2014).
16. Wash. Rev. Code § 19.170.020(7) (2014).
17. Wash. Rev. Code § 19.170.020(5) (2014). There is a prohibited practice within the prize promotion laws that is applicable to all advertisers and companies. This is the prohibition on the use of simulated checks and continuing obligation checks. Wash. Rev. Code § 19.170.050.
18. Wash. Rev. Code § 9.46.0311 (2014).
19. Wash. Rev. Code § 9.46.0209 (2014).
20. Wash. Rev. Code § 9.46.0315 (2014).
21. Wash. Rev. Code § 9.46.0321 (2014).
22. *See generally*, discussion of bingo and raffles in Section 9.2 of this Guide.

West Virginia

State Attorney General Office
Office of the Attorney General
West Virginia State Capitol Building 1
Room 26-E
Charleston, West Virginia 25305
(304) 558-2021
Website: http://www.ago.wv.gov

Selected State Laws, Regulations, and Constitutional Provisions

West Virginia's anti-gambling laws (Chapter 61, Article 10, Sections 61-10-5 *et seq.* of West Virginia Code), located in the chapter of the state code entitled crimes and their punishment, contain provisions related to promotions. With its consumer credit and protection laws, West Virginia includes its prize promotion laws (Chapter 46A, Article 6D, Sections 46A-6D-1 to 46A-6D-10 of West Virginia Code). Specific West Virginia legal provisions frequently quoted in court cases and interpretive opinions related to promotions include the following:

Reference No.	Descriptive Name
W. Va. Const. art. VI, § 36	Lotteries; bingo; raffles; county option
W. Va. Code § 61-10-5	Betting on games of chance; furnishing money or thing of value therefor; penalty (prohibited as misdemeanor)
W. Va. Code § 61-10-11	Lotteries or raffles; penalty (promoting lottery prohibited as misdemeanor)

Summary of State Law

Prohibition of Lotteries and Gambling: West Virginia's Constitution and its statutory laws prohibit lotteries.[1] A promotion that combines a prize, chance, and consideration is a lottery in West Virginia.[2] West Virginia also has a general prohibition against gambling.[3] Exceptions to the lottery and gambling prohibitions include state-operated lotteries and certain charitable lotteries.

Contests: There are no provisions in its laws to indicate that West Virginia prohibits contests as long as the contest complies with anti-gambling laws. If the contest includes an element of consideration, the sponsor should award the contest prize based on skill and not on chance. Court opinions indicate that West Virginia applies the dominant factor doctrine[4] when evaluating whether or not chance determines the outcome of a promotion.[5]

Sweepstakes: West Virginia permits sweepstakes as long as participants do not pay consideration and the sweepstakes does not violate anti-gambling laws. An exception written into the prize promotion laws suggests that West Virginia would not view a promotion requiring participants to perform any of the following activities as a promotion with consideration:

- completing and mailing in an entry form
- visiting a local store to obtain or drop off an entry form
- making a toll-free or local phone call to enter[6]

Prize Promotion Laws: West Virginia's version of prize promotion laws is the Prizes and Gifts Act. The Prizes and Gift Act is grouped with West Virginia consumer credit laws and codified in Chapter 46A, Article 6D, Sections 46A-6D-1 to 46A-6D-10 of the West Virginia Code. Most of its provisions apply to companies holding promotions as part of a sales campaign for selling or leasing goods, property, or services. Broadly applicable provisions include a prohibition on using simulated checks in connection with a consumer transaction[7] and a prohibition on charging unreasonable shipping and handling charges in connection with a prize or gift giveaway.[8]

REPRESENTATION THAT A PERSON HAS WON A PRIZE. If, as part of a campaign to sell its goods or services, a company tells a consumer that the consumer has won a prize, the company must deliver the prize within ten days to the consumer without expense to the consumer and without further obligation on the part of the consumer.[9]

REPRESENTATION THAT A PERSON IS ELIGIBLE TO WIN A PRIZE REQUIRES A DISCLOSURE. If a company tells a consumer that the consumer is eligible or has a chance to win or receive a prize, the sponsor must disclose all material conditions for receipt of the prize.[10] The disclosure can be verbal or written. When in writing, there are specific requirements for information provided, placement, font, and wording.[11] There is no disclosure requirement for the prize offer promotion if

- to be eligible to win, the participant only has to complete and mail in, deliver to a local store, or call in the entry (provided that the call is a toll-free, local or free call), or
- the participant is not required to listen to a sales presentation or pay any sum of money for any merchandise, service or item of value.[12]

PRIZE PROMOTION PROVISIONS OF TELEMARKETING LAWS. West Virginia has telemarketing laws (Chapter 46A, Article 6F, Sections 46A-6F-101 to 46A-6F-703 of the West Virginia Code) which include disclosure requirements for sweepstakes and giveaways offered as part of a telephone solicitation.[13]

Gambling Exceptions for Non-Profits and Other Qualified Organizations

Generally: A constitutional provision allows charitable or public service organizations to offer bingo games and raffles for fund-raising purposes.[14] Each county has the power to disapprove the holding of bingo games and raffles within its jurisdiction. If bingo and raffles are allowed within the county, eligible organizations able to offer raffles and bingo games include non-profit, federally tax-exempt benevolent, educational, philanthropic, humane, patriotic, civic, religious, fraternal, or eleemosynary organizations; and volunteer fire departments, rescue unit and other similar volunteer community service organizations.[15] The organization must spend net bingo and raffle proceeds for charitable and public service purposes.[16]

Raffles and Lotteries: An eligible organization does not need a license to conduct a raffle if no single prize has a value over $4,000 and the organization does not derive annual revenue from raffles in excess of $15,000.[17] If the organization's raffle activities fall outside those limits, it must obtain a license from the West Virginia State Tax Department.

The charitable raffle law is codified in Chapter 47, Article 21, Sections §47-21-1 *et seq.* of the West Virginia Code. Raffle Regulations, issued by the West Virginia State Tax Department, are codified in Sections 110-37-1 to 110-37-28 of the West Virginia Code of State Rules.

Bingo: An eligible organization offering bingo needs a license, issued by the West Virginia State Tax Department. The charitable bingo law is codified in Chapter 47, Article 20, Sections 47-20-1 *et seq.* of the West Virginia Code. Bingo Regulations, issued by the West Virginia State Tax Department, are codified in Sections 110-16-1 to 110-16-31 of the West Virginia Code of State Rules.

Additional Information about Raffles and Bingo: Raffle and bingo licensees must file periodic financial reports with the West Virginia State Tax Department[18], which is the state administrator for West Virginia's charitable bingo games and raffles. Additional information and forms for applications and financial reports are available from the state tax department's website, www.wva.state.wv.us/wvtax/bingoraffletaxforms.aspx [19]

Resources

Copies of attorney general opinions issued during the current attorney general's tenure are available on the website of the Office of the Attorney General. All West Virginia attorney general opinions are published in the West Virginia State Register for which current and archived copies are available online at http://www.sos.wv.gov/administrative-law/register/Pages/default.aspx

Endnotes

1. W. Va. Const. Art. VI, § 36; W. Va. Code § 61-10-11 (2014).
2. *West Virginia. v. Wassick*, 191 S.E.2d 283, 288 (W. Va. 1972) *citing West Virginia v. Hudson*, 37 S.E.2d 553 (W. Va. 1946).
3. W. Va. Code § 61-10-5 (2014).
4. *See generally*, Section 3.4.3 of this Guide for a discussion of tests used when evaluating whether chance or skill prevails in a promotion combining elements of both.
5. *West Virginia v. Hudson*, 37 S.E.2d at 558.
6. These are situations in which the prize promotion disclosure requirements do not apply. W. Va. Code § 46A-6D-4(d)(1) (2014). See further discussion about the prize promotion laws in the Prize Promotion Laws portion of this West Virginia State Summary.
7. W. Va. Code § 46A-6D-6 (2014).
8. W. Va. Code § 46A-6D-7 (2014).
9. W. Va. Code § 46A-6D-3 (2014).
10. W. Va. Code § 46A-6D-4 (2014). *See generally*, discussion of state prize promotion laws in Section 7.4.2 of this Guide.
11. W. Va. Code § 46A-6D-4(a) & (b) (2014).
12. W. Va. Code § 46A-6D-4(d) (2014).
13. W. Va. Code §§ 46A-6F-111 and 46A-6F-401(b)(6) (2014). *See generally*, discussion of state telemarketing laws in Section 7.5.2 of this Guide.
14. W. Va. Const. art. VI, § 36.
15. W. Va. Code §§ 47-20-2(d) and 47-21-2(b) (2014).
16. W. Va. Code §§ 47-20-15(c) and 47-21-15(c) (2014).
17. W. Va. Code § 47-21-3 (2014).
18. W. Va. Code § 47-21-22 (2014).
19. *See generally*, discussion of bingo and raffles in Section 9.2 of this Guide.

Wisconsin

State Attorney General Office
Office of the Attorney General
Risser Justice Center
17 West Main Street
Madison, Wisconsin 53703
(608) 266-1221
Website: http://www.doj.state.wi.us/

Selected State Laws, Regulations, and Constitutional Provisions

Wisconsin's anti-gambling laws (Chapter 945, Sections 945.01 *et seq.* of the Wisconsin Statute), which are in its criminal code, contain provisions related to promotions. Wisconsin includes prize promotion laws (Chapter 100, Section 100.171 of the Wisconsin Statute) with its marketing and trade practices statutes. Specific Wisconsin legal provisions frequently quoted in court cases and interpretive opinions related to promotions include the following:

Reference No.	Descriptive Name
Wis. Const. art. IV, § 24	Gambling
Wis. Stat. § 100.16	Selling with pretense of prize; in-pack chance promotion exception
Wis. Stat. § 100.17	Guessing contests
Wis. Stat. § 945.01	Definitions (for anti-gambling laws including definition for lottery)
Wis. Stat. § 945.02	Gambling (prohibited as misdemeanor)
Wis. Stat. § 945.03	Commercial gambling (prohibited as felony)

Summary of State Law

Prohibition of Lotteries and Gambling: The Wisconsin Constitution includes an anti-gambling provision that precludes the legislature from authorizing most forms of gambling.[1] Wisconsin also has a general statutory prohibition against gambling.[2] The statutory gambling provision includes a prohibition against participating in or conducting a lottery.[3] A promotion that combines a prize, chance, and consideration is a lottery in Wisconsin.[4] Exceptions to the lottery and gambling prohibitions include state-operated lotteries and certain charitable lotteries.

Contests: Wisconsin permits contests as long as the contest does not conflict with anti-gambling laws. If the contest includes an element of consideration, the sponsor must award the contest prize based on skill and not on chance.

Court opinions indicate that Wisconsin applies the dominant factor doctrine[5] when evaluating whether or not chance determines the outcome of a promotion.[6] The anti-gambling laws exclude from gambling any competition in which the prize is awarded to a contestant based on skill, speed, strength, or endurance or to the owner of animals or vehicles entered in such contest.[7]

It is unclear to what extent Wisconsin's prize promotions laws apply to contests charging consideration. Hence, conservative sponsors might want to comply with the prize notice disclosure requirements in Wisconsin's Prize Notices statutory provision, discussed below.

Sweepstakes: Wisconsin permits sweepstakes as long as participants do not pay consideration and the sweepstakes does not conflict with anti-gambling laws.

WHAT IS CONSIDERATION UNDER WISCONSIN LAW? For purposes of the anti-gambling laws, Wisconsin views consideration as anything which is a commercial or financial advantage to the promoter or a disadvantage to any participant.[8] The Wisconsin anti-gambling laws carve out activities that are not to be deemed consideration for purposes of a lottery.[9] These activities include the following:

- listening to or watching a television or radio program;
- filling out and mailing in a coupon or entry blank that is received through the mail or published in a newspaper or magazine, pro-

vided that copies of the form or handwritten and other informal entries are acceptable or provided that no purchase is required;

- furnishing product packaging as proof of purchase
- mailing in an entry form or proof of purchase
- completing an entry form obtained at a trade fair or trade show provided that the facilities for obtaining and depositing the entry form are outside the area for which an admission fee is required
- visiting a retail store or other establishment as long as participants are not required to make a purchase or pay an admission fee; and
- participating in a promotion exempt under the in-pack chance promotion exception, discussed below.

IN-PACK CHANCE PROMOTION EXCEPTION. In Wisconsin, it is illegal to sell a product and represent that a sum of money or something of value, which is uncertain or concealed, is enclosed within, will be given to, or may be won or drawn by chance by reason of the sale.[10] The exception to this prohibition is the in-pack chance promotion exception. Such in-pack sweepstakes promotions are legal provided that a number of conditions are met including:

- there is a free method of entry available through the retailer, by toll-free phone call, or by mail;
- the label of the promotional packaging and any advertising clearly states the methods of play and the sweepstakes end date;
- the sponsor provides the retailer with an adequate number of free play forms;
- the sponsor does not misrepresent chances of winning;
- the sponsor randomly distributes all game pieces and retains records of the random distribution for at least one year;
- the sponsor randomly awards all prizes, if game pieces are not used; and
- the sponsor maintains name and address information for winners of prizes over $100 and makes those records available to a Wisconsin state agency upon request.[11]

The criteria—particularly the requirements for a free method of entry, clear communication of play rules, and no misrepresentation of odds—provide helpful guidance for all sweepstakes sponsors operating in Wisconsin, regardless of whether the sponsor is attempting to qualify for the in-pack chance promotion exception.

Prize Promotion Laws: Wisconsin has prize promotion protections within its trade practices laws. The statutory provision titled Prize Notices focuses on the requirements for a disclosure statement, referred to as a prize notice.[12] As defined by the statute, a prize notice is a communication to an individual that does the following:

- represents that the individual has been selected or may be eligible to receive a prize
- conditions receipt of the prize on a payment from the individual or requires or invites the individual to contact the company to learn how to receive the prize or for more information related to the notice.[13]

A prize notice does not include a communication given in conjunction with a promotion that satisfies the requirements for the in-pack chance promotion exception. When a prize notice is required, there is specific information that must be included in the disclosures and specific requirements for the placement, font, and wording of the required disclosures.[14]

REPRESENTATION THAT A PERSON HAS WON OR IS ELIGIBLE TO WIN A PRIZE REQUIRES A PRIZE NOTICE. If a company represents that an individual has been selected or may be eligible to receive a prize, the company may not request or accept a payment from the individual in any form before the individual receives a written prize notice.[15]

OFFERING PRIZE AS INDUCEMENT TO ATTEND SALES PRESENTATION REQUIRES A PRIZE NOTICE. If a company sends an individual a prize notice offering a prize as an inducement to view, hear, or attend a sales presentation, the sales presentation may not begin until the sponsor identifies the prize to be awarded and actually delivers the prize.[16]

APPLICABILITY OF PRIZE NOTICE DISCLOSURE REQUIREMENT TO CONTESTS CHARGING CONSIDERATION. The Wisconsin statute excludes from the definition of prize notice a notice informing an individual that the individual has won a prize as a result of the person's actual prior entry in a game, drawing, sweepstakes or other contest.[17] However, research for this Guide yielded no authorities confirming whether Wisconsin's prize notice requirement generally applies to advertisements and promotional materials encouraging people to enter a contest with an entry fee. Hence, the conservative sponsor might choose to provide the same disclosures required for a prize notice in the written official rules for any contest that charges consideration.

NO SELLING WITH PRETENSE OF PRIZE. When selling its goods or services, a company may not represent that a purchase will provide the buyer with an opportunity to win an item by chance.[18] This prohibition does not apply to a promotion that satisfies the requirements of the in-pack chance promotion exception, discussed above.

Gambling Exceptions for Non-Profits and Other Qualified Organizations

Raffles and Lotteries: The Wisconsin Constitution allows the legislature to authorize raffles conducted by religious, charitable, service, fraternal or veterans' organizations or by those organizations to which contributions are deductible for federal or state income tax purposes.[19] The organization must use all raffle profits to further the organization's purposes.[20] Eligible organizations wishing to conduct raffles must obtain a license from and file annual reports with the Wisconsin Department of Administration. Wisconsin imposes several requirements on the formatting and cost of raffle tickets and the conduct of the raffles.[21]

Bingo: The Wisconsin Constitution allows the legislature to authorize bingo games operated by religious, charitable, service, fraternal or veterans' organizations or by those organizations to which contributions are deductible for federal or state income tax purposes.[22] The organization must use bingo game profits exclusively for the organization's proper and legitimate organizational expenditures.[23] The organization must obtain a license from the Wisconsin Department of Administration, file periodic financial reports, and meet other statutory requirements. Licensed bingo organizations must pay an occupational tax on the gross receipts of one to two percent.[24] There are relaxed rules for bingo games operated in senior citizen facilities and certain medical facilities.[25]

Additional Information about Raffles and Bingo: The raffle and bingo exemptions are codified in Chapter 563 (Bingo and raffle control), Sections 563.02 *et seq.* of the Wisconsin Statute. Regulations for raffles, bingo, and other charitable gaming are located in Game 41.01 *et seq.* of the Wisconsin Administrative Code. Additional information, regulations, and report forms are available from the Charitable Gaming Division of the Wisconsin Department of Administration, 101 E Wilson Street Madison, Wisconsin, (608) 270-2530, http://www.doa.state.wi.us.[26]

Resources

Wisconsin makes attorney general opinions from 1982 through the present available online at http://docs.legis.wisconsin.gov/misc/oag.

Endnotes

1. Wis. Const. art. IV, § 24.
2. Wis. Stat. § 945.02 (2014).
3. Wis. Stat. § 945.02(2) and (3) (2014).
4. Wis. Stat. § 945.01(5) (2014); *Cowie v. La Crosse Theaters Co.*, 286 N.W. 707, 710 (Wis. 1939).
5. *See generally*, Section 3.4.3 of this Guide for a discussion of tests used when evaluating whether chance or skill prevails in a promotion combining elements of both.
6. *Wisconsin v. Dahlk*, 330 N.W.2d 611, 617 (Wis. Ct. App. 1983).
7. Wis. Stat. § 945.01(1)(b) (2014).
8. Wis. Stat. § 945.01(5)(b) (2014).
9. Wis. Stat. § 945.01(5)(b)2 (2014). The Wisconsin State Constitution lists some but not all of the same activities as activities that do not constitute consideration as an element of gambling. Wis. Const. art. iv, § 24(2).
10. Wis. Stat. § 100.16 (2014).
11. Wis. Stat. § 100.16(2) (2014); see also *Bohrer v. City of Milwaukee*, 635 N.W.2d 816 (Wis. Ct. App. 2001).
12. Wis. Stat. § 100.171 (2014).
13. *Id.*

14. Wis. Stat. § 100.171(3) (2014). *See generally*, discussion of state prize promotion laws in Section 7.4.2 of this Guide.
15. Wis. Stat. § 100.171(2) (2014).
16. Wis. Stat. §§ 100.171(1)(b) and 100.171(4) (2014).
17. Wis. Stat. § 100.171(1)(b).2.b (2014).
18. Wis. Stat. § 100.16(1) (2014).
19. Wis. Const. art. IV, § 24(4).
20. Wis. Stat. § 563.94 (2014).
21. Wis. Stat. §§ 563.93 and 563.935 (2014).
22. Wis. Const. art. IV, § 24(3).
23. Wis. Stat. § 563.51(8) (2014).
24. Wis. Stat. § 563.80 (2014).
25. Wis. Stat. § 563.69 (2014).
26. *See generally*, discussion of bingo and raffles in Section 9.2 of this Guide.

Wyoming

State Attorney General Office
Office of the Attorney General
123 Capitol Building
200 W. 24th Street
Cheyenne, Wyoming 82002
(307) 777-7841
Website: ag.wyo.gov

Selected State Laws, Regulations, and Constitutional Provisions

Wyoming's anti-gambling laws (Title 6, Chapter 7, Article 1, Section 6-7-101 *et seq.* of the Wyoming Statute), which are grouped with the state's crimes and offenses laws, contain provisions related to promotions. In its trade and commerce laws, Wyoming includes its prize promotion laws (Title 40, Chapter 12, Article 2, Section 40-12-201 *et seq.* of the Wyoming Statute). Specific Wyoming legal provisions frequently quoted in court cases and interpretive opinions related to promotions include the following:

Reference No.	Descriptive Name
Wyo. Stat. § 6-7-101	Definitions (for anti-gambling laws including definitions for gambling)
Wyo. Stat. § 6-7-102	Gambling; professional gambling; penalties (gambling prohibited as misdemeanor; professional gambling prohibited as felony)

Summary of State Law

Prohibition of Lotteries and Gambling: Wyoming has a general prohibition against gambling.[1] Court opinions indicate that Wyoming interprets its anti-gambling laws as making lotteries illegal.[2] A promotion that combines a prize, chance, and consideration is a lottery in Wyoming.[3] Exceptions to the lottery and gambling prohibitions include state-operated lotteries and certain charitable lotteries.

Contests: Wyoming permits contests as long as the contest does not conflict with anti-gambling laws. If the contest includes an element of consideration, the sponsor must award the contest prize based on skill and not on chance. Research for this Guide produced no clear indication of which test Wyoming uses when evaluating whether or not chance determines the outcome of a promotion.[4]

The anti-gambling laws exclude from the definition of gambling "bona fide contests of skill, speed, strength or endurance in which awards are made only to entrants or the owners of entries".[5] It is unclear to what extent Wyoming's prize promotion laws apply to contests charging consideration. Hence, conservative sponsors might want to comply with the prize notice disclosure requirements in Wyoming's laws addressing the Promotional Advertising of Prizes, discussed below.

Sweepstakes: Wyoming permits sweepstakes as long as participants do not pay consideration and the sweepstakes does not otherwise violate anti-gambling laws.

Prize Promotion Laws: Wyoming includes prize promotion provisions with its laws addressing the Promotional Advertising of Prizes, codified with the state's trade and commerce laws (Title 40, Chapter 12, Article 2, Sections 40-12-201 to 40-12-209). Wyoming's prize promotion laws focus on the requirements for a prize notice. As defined by the statute, a prize notice is a communication to an individual that does the following:

- represents that the individual has been selected or may be eligible to receive a prize and
- conditions receipt of the prize on a payment from the individual or requires or invites the individual to contact the company to learn

how to receive the prize or for more information related to the notice.[6]

When a prize notice is required, there is specific information that must be included as disclosures and specific requirements for the placement, font, and wording of the required disclosures.[7] The prize promotion laws also prohibit certain practices that might mislead consumers.[8]

REPRESENTATION THAT A PERSON HAS WON OR IS ELIGIBLE TO WIN A PRIZE REQUIRES A PRIZE NOTICE. If a sponsor represents to an individual that the individual has been selected or may be eligible to receive a prize, the sponsor cannot accept any form of payment or consideration from the individual without first giving the individual a written prize notice.[9]

REQUIREMENTS WHEN PRIZE NOTICE ENCOURAGES ATTENDANCE AT SALES PRESENTATION. If a sponsor sends to an individual a prize notice offering a prize as an inducement to view, hear, or attend a sales presentation, the sales presentation may not begin until the sponsor identifies the prize to be awarded and actually delivers the prize.[10]

APPLICABILITY OF PRIZE PROMOTION LAWS TO CONTESTS CHARGING CONSIDERATION. The Wyoming statute excludes from the definition of prize notice a notice informing an individual that the individual has won a prize as a result of the person's actual prior entry in a game, drawing, sweepstakes or other contest.[11] However, research for this Guide yielded no authorities confirming whether Wyoming's prize promotion laws generally apply to advertisements and promotional materials encouraging people to enter a contest with an entry fee. Hence, the conservative sponsor might choose to provide the same disclosures as part of its written official rules for any contest that charges consideration.

Gambling Exceptions for Non-Profits and Other Qualified Organizations

Raffles: In its anti-gambling laws, Wyoming exempts from the definition of gambling raffles held for charitable purposes.[12] While the exemption does not define charitable purposes, it does define "charitable or nonprofit organization" as an organization recognized as a charitable or nonprofit organization under Wyoming statutes and which is exempt from federal taxation as a 501(c) organization. It is unclear whether one must be a charitable or non-profit organization in order to hold a raffle for charitable purposes.

Wyoming does provide more guidelines for the organizations eligible to offer charitable bingo. It is possible that Wyoming might view eligibility for charitable raffles as broader than eligibility for charitable bingo. Nevertheless, a potential safe harbor for organizations wishing to offer a charitable raffle in Wyoming is to offer the raffle only if the organization also meets the criteria for organizations allowed to offer bingo games in Wyoming.

The exemption does not provide additional information on how such charitable raffles are to be implemented. Research for this Guide uncovered no legal provisions indicating that offering a charitable raffle requires a license or permit.

Bingo: Wyoming allows charitable bingo games. Organizations eligible to offer bingo are charitable or non-profit organizations which have been in existence in Wyoming for at least three years.[13] Wyoming provides less regulation for bingo games than other states.[14] The requirements for bingo operations are included with the definition for anti-gambling laws which exempt charitable bingo from the definition of gambling. Research for this Guide uncovered no legal provisions indicating that offering a charitable bingo game requires a license or permit. The statute does require that at least sixty-five percent of the bingo proceeds must be redeemed as winnings and at least seventy-five percent of the net proceeds remaining after payment of all costs and supplies be spent on a charitable or non-profit cause.

Resources

Wyoming makes some of its more recent attorney general opinions available on the website of the Office of the Attorney General.

Endnotes

1. Wyo. Stat. § 6-7-102 (2014).
2. *Williams v. Weber Mesa Ditch Extension Co.,* 572 P.2d 412 (Wyo. 1977); *Gambling Devices v. Wyoming,* 694 P.2d 711, 718 (Wyo. 1985).
3. *Gambling Devices,* 694 P.2d at 718.
4. *See generally,* Section 3.4.3 of this Guide for a discussion of tests used when evaluating whether chance or skill prevails in a promotion combining elements of both.
5. Wyo. Stat. § 6-7-101(a)(iii)(A) (2014).
6. Wyo. Stat. § 40-12-201(a)(ii) (2014).
7. Wyo. Stat. § 40-12-203 (2014). *See generally,* discussion of state prize promotion laws in Section 7.4.2 of this Guide.
8. Wyo. Stat. § 40-12-203(f) (2014).
9. Wyo. Stat. § 40-12-202 (2014).
10. Wyo. Stat. § 40-12-204 (2014).
11. Wyo. Stat. § 40-12-201(a)(iii)(B) (2014).
12. Wyo. Stat. § 6-7-101(a)(iii)(H) (2014).
13. Wyo. Stat. § 6-7-101(a)(iii)(D) (2014).
14. See general discussion of bingo and raffles in Section 9.2 of this Guide.

Appendices

The appendices include summary tables of state laws as well as a glossary of terms used in this Guide.

Appendices:

Appendix A
Tables of State Information

A.1. States with Registration and Bonding Requirements for Promotions

This table summarizes the registration and bonding requirements imposed on promotions by some states. Part Three of this Guide includes a detailed state-by-state discussion of such requirements for the relevant states.

A.1.1. Registration and Bonding Requirements for Contests and Sweepstakes

Arizona. Promotions that qualify as amusement gambling intellectual contests must be registered with the Arizona Attorney General's Office. Ariz. Rev. Stat. §13-3311 (2014).

Florida. There are registration, bonding, and other requirements for any sweepstakes offering prizes with an aggregate retail value over five thousand dollars. Fla. Stat . § 849.094 (2014).

New York. There are registration and bonding requirements for sweepstakes offering prizes with an aggregate value over five thousand dollars. N.Y. Gen. Bus. § 369-e (2014).

Rhode Island. Registration is required for sweepstakes offering prizes valued at over five hundred dollars and involving a Rhode Island retail store. R.I. Gen. Laws §11-50-1 *et seq.* (2013).

A.1.2. Registration Requirements for Prize Promotions Incorporated into Telemarketing Campaigns

In addition to the registration, bonding, and disclosure procedures commonly required of telemarketers, some states telemarketing laws impose additional requirements on telemarketing campaigns that incorporate prize promotions. These states include Alabama, California, Florida, Nevada, North Carolina, Ohio, Oklahoma, Oregon, Rhode Island, and Texas.

For most of these states, the telemarketer must submit to the state information related to the prize promotion component of the campaign. Information to be filed typically includes a statement about any prize or gift offered including a description, its value, odds of winning, and the terms and conditions for receiving the gift. North Carolina requires the posting of a bond for the value of the prizes if the telemarketing campaign offers prizes or gifts valued at five hundred dollars or more.

Section 7.5.2 of this Guide includes a general discussion of state telemarketing laws. The state summaries in Part Three of this Guide include brief information on the telemarketing laws of each state with telemarketing laws that include significant prize promotion provisions.

A.1.3. Registration and Bonding Requirements for Beauty Pageants

A few states require registration and/or the posting of a bond for beauty pageant contests that charge entry fees. These states include Arkansas, Georgia, and Tennessee. The state summary for each of these three states includes a discussion of the state's beauty pageant laws.

A.2. Summary of Tests Used by States for Chance-Skill Determinations

In some promotions, winning might be based on a combination of skill and chance. The tests used by states to determine whether such promotions are chance-based or skill-based include the dominant factor doctrine, the material element test, the any chance test, and the pure chance test. Most states use the dominant factor doctrine or the material element test.

Section 3.4.3 of this Guide describes each of these four tests. The approach used by each state is discussed further in the state summaries in Part Three of this Guide.

STATE	TEST	LEGAL AUTHORITY
Alabama	Material element test	Ala. Code §13A-12-20(3) (2013).
Alaska	Material element test	Alaska Stat. §11.66.280(1) (2014); Alaska Att'y Gen. Op. No. 663-01-0183 (May 22, 2001)
Arizona	Uncertain	
Arkansas	Dominant factor doctrine; some support for the pure chance test	*Longstreth v. Cook*, 220 S.W.2d 433, 438 (Ark. 1949).
California	Dominant factor doctrine	*Bell Gardens Bicycle Club v. Dept. of Justice*, 42 Cal. Rptr. 2d 730, 747-748 (Cal. Ct. App. 1995).
Colorado	Dominant factor doctrine	*Interrogatories of Governor Regarding Sweepstakes Races Act*, 585 P.2d 595, 598; Colo. Att'y Gen. Op. No. 93-05, *4 (April 21, 1993).
Connecticut	Dominant factor doctrine; some support for the material element test or any chance test	Conn. Att'y Gen. Op. (May 21, 2004). *But* Conn. Gen. Stat. § 53-278a(2) (2013) suggests support for material element or any chance test within broader context of gambling.
Delaware	Dominant factor doctrine	*National Football League v. Governor of the State of Delaware*, 435 F. Supp. 1372, 1384 (D. Del. 1977).
District of Columbia	Dominant factor doctrine	*Boosalis v. Crawford*, 99 F.2d 374 (1938).
Florida	Dominant factor doctrine	Fla. Att'y Gen. Op. No. 1990-58 (July 27, 1990).
Georgia	Uncertain; possibly any chance test or dominant factor doctrine	Ga. Code § 16-12-36 (2013) supports use of any chance test.
Hawaii	Material element test	Haw. Rev. Stat. § 712-1220(3).

STATE	TEST	LEGAL AUTHORITY
Idaho	Possibly pure chance test	Oneida County Fair Board v. Smylie, 386 P.2d 374, 391 (Idaho 1963).
Illinois	Uncertain	
Indiana	Dominant factor doctrine	*Lashbrook v. Indiana*, 550 N.E.2d 772, 775-776 (Ind. Ct. App. 1990).
Iowa	Material element test	Iowa Code § 725.12.3 (2014).
Kansas	Dominant factor doctrine	*Three Kings Holdings v. Six*, 255 P.3d 1218, 1223 (Kan. Ct. of App. 2011).
Kentucky	Uncertain; possibly pure chance test	Ky. Att'y Gen. Op. No. 05-003 (March 21, 2005) could be interpreted as supporting the pure chance test
Louisiana	Uncertain	
Maine	Uncertain; possibly dominant factor doctrine or material element test	Me. Rev. Stat. tit 17-A, § 952.3.C and Me. Rev. Stat. tit 17, § 1831.5 (2014) could be interpreted as supporting the dominant factor doctrine or material element test.
Maryland	Dominant factor doctrine or material element test	Md. Att'y. Gen. Op. No. 91-64, 65 (Mar. 2, 2006).
Massachusetts	Dominant factor doctrine	Office of Att'y Gen. of Mass., *Advisory on Poker Tournaments* (June 30, 2005), http://www. mass.gov/ago/doing-business-in-massachusetts/public-charities-or-not-for-profits/soliciting-funds/raffles-and-other-gaming-activity/poker-advisory.html (last visited Sept. 17, 2014), *citing Commonwealth v. Plissner, 295 Mass. 457, 463-64 (1936).*
Michigan	Dominant factor doctrine	In *Att'y Gen. v. Powerpick Club of Michigan*, 783 N.W.2d 515, 530-531 (Mich. Ct. App. 2010).
Minnesota	Dominant factor doctrine	Minn. Att'y Gen. Op. No. 510-C-3 (Sept. 24, 1947).

STATE	TEST	LEGAL AUTHORITY
Mississippi	Dominant factor doctrine	Miss. Code § 75-76-3(6)(b) (2013).
Missouri	Dominant factor doctrine or material element test	Some case law supports the dominant factor doctrine. *See e.g., Harris v. Missouri Gaming Commissioner*, 869 S.W.2d 58, 62 (1994). The Missouri statute suggests the material element test. Mo. Rev. Stat. § 572-010(3) (2013).
Montana	Dominant factor doctrine	*Montana v. Hahn*, 72 P.2d 459, 461 (Mont. 1937).
Nebraska	Dominant factor doctrine	*American Amusements Co. v. Neb. Dep't of Revenue*, 807 N.W.2d 492, 501-502 (Neb. 2011); *Indoor Recreation Enter. v. Douglas*, 235 N.W.2d 398, 400 (Neb. 1975).
Nevada	Dominant factor doctrine	*Las Vegas Hacienda v. Gibson*, 359 P.2d 85, 87 (Nev. 1961).
New Hampshire	Uncertain	
New Jersey	Material element test	N.J. Stat. § 2C:37-1.a (2014).
New Mexico	Dominant factor doctrine	N.M. Stat. § 30-19-1 (2013).
New York	Material element test	N.Y. Penal Law § 225.00(1) (2014).
North Carolina	Dominant factor doctrine	*Joker Club v. Hardin*, 643 S.E.2d 626 (N.C. Ct. App. 2007).
North Dakota	Uncertain; possibly the material element test or the dominant factor doctrine	N.D. Cent. Code § 12.1-28-01.1 (2014).
Ohio	Dominant factor doctrine	Ohio Att'y Gen. Op. No. 2004-029 (August 6, 2004).
Oklahoma	Material element test	Okla. Stat. § 21-942 (2013).
Oregon	Material element test	Or. Rev. Stat. §167.117(6) (2013).

STATE	TEST	LEGAL AUTHORITY
Pennsylvania	Dominant factor doctrine	*Pennsylvania v. Laniewski*, 98 A.2d 215 (Pa. Super. Ct. 1953).
Rhode Island	Dominant factor doctrine	*Roberts v. Comm. Investment Club of Woonsocket*, 431 A.2d 1206, 1211 (R.I. 1981).
South Carolina	Possibly dominant factor doctrine	Opinion letters, S.C. Atty. Gen Op. (Nov. 19, 2010), S.C. Atty. Gen Op. (July 31, 2006), and S.C. Atty. Gen Op. (Sept. 5, 1995), support the dominant factor doctrine. *But see, Town of Mt. Pleasant v. Chimento*, 737 S.E.2d 830 (S.C. 2012).
South Dakota	Dominant factor doctrine	*Bayer v. Johnson*, 349 N.W.2d 447, 449 (S.D. 1984).
Tennessee	Uncertain; possibly dominant factor doctrine or any chance test	Tenn. Att'y Gen. Op. No. 05-159 (Oct. 14, 2005) suggests dominant factor doctrine. Tenn. Code § 39-17-501 (2013) suggests the any chance test.
Texas	Dominant factor doctrine	*Johnson v. Phinney*, 218 F.2d 303, 306 (5th Cir. 1955).
Utah	Dominant factor doctrine	*D'Orio v. Startup Candy Co.*, 266 P. 1037, 1038 (Utah 1928).
Vermont	Uncertain	
Virginia	Dominant factor doctrine	Va. Att'y Gen. Op. (Sept. 19, 1996).
Washington	Material element test	Wash. Rev. Code § 9.46.0225 (2014).
West Virginia	Dominant factor doctrine	*West Virginia v. Hudson*, 37 S.E.2d 553, 558 (W. Va. 1946).
Wisconsin	Dominant factor doctrine	*Wisconsin v. Dahlk*, 330 N.W.2d 611, 617 (Wis. Ct. App. 1983).
Wyoming	Uncertain	

A.3. States that Prohibit or Restrict Consideration in Skill-Based Contests

This chart summarizes the laws of those states that prohibit or limit the ability of contest sponsors to charge consideration. The state summary of each state includes a more detailed discussion of each state's treatment of contests.

Arizona. Arizona's definition of gambling does not distinguish between skill-based games and chance-based games. Ariz. Rev. Stat. § 13-3301.4 (2014). This lack of distinction has led some to conclude that sponsors of skill-based contests may not charge consideration in Arizona unless the contest qualifies as an intellectual skill-based contest and has been registered with the state. Research for this Guide highlighted some doubts regarding this conclusion.

Arkansas. A literal reading of the Arkansas Prize Promotion Act could be interpreted as requiring the sponsor of a contest charging consideration to comply with certain disclosure and other requirements. Ark. Code §§ 4-102-102(3) and 4-102-106 (2013). The Arkansas Supreme Court has ruled in at least one case that the Arkansas Prize Promotion Act was not applicable in a skill-based contest where the participant paid an entry fee but was not required to purchase any of the sponsor's products.

California. If contest participants pay consideration, the contest sponsor must provide certain disclosures and comply with other requirements of California's prize promotion laws. Cal. Bus. & Prof. Code §§ 17539.1, 17539.2, 17539.35 (2014).

Colorado. Under the Colorado Consumer Protection Act, a contest implemented by direct mail solicitation may not include a requirement for the purchase of a product or payment of any fee. Colo. Rev. Stat. § 6-1-803(1) (2014).

Connecticut. There are advertising restrictions for contests that charge consideration and that offer a prize with a retail value over two hundred dollars. Conn. Gen. Stat. § 42-298 (2013).

Illinois. Some commentators interpret the Illinois Prizes and Gifts Act (Ill. Comp. Stat. Ch. 815, § 525/1 et. seq. (2014)) as prohibiting contests from charging consideration. As explained in the Illinois State Summary of this Guide, the applicability of the payment prohibition to skill-based contests has some ambiguity.

Iowa. Contests charging consideration must provide a written disclosure notice in compliance with the Iowa prize promotion laws. Iowa Code § 714B.2 (2014).

Maryland. As discussed in the Maryland State Summary of this Guide, it is unclear whether Maryland prize promotion laws prohibit consideration in a skill-based contest. Md. Code, Com. Law § 13-305 (2013). Accordingly, contest sponsors should exercise caution when charging consideration in Maryland.

Minnesota. Contests requiring payment of money must comply with the disclosure requirements of Minnesota's prize notice and solicitation laws. Minn. Stat. § 325F.755 (2014).

New Jersey. New Jersey passed legislation in 2014 to clarify that skill-based contests charging consideration are legal in New Jersey. N.J. Stat. § 5:19-1 (2014). However, as discussed in the New Jersey State Summary of this Guide, the 2014 legislation leaves ambiguities regarding whether all genres of skill-based contests may now charge consideration.

New Mexico. Contests that charge consideration or whose primary purpose is the promotion of a product, service or business entity must comply with New Mexico's prize promotion provision referred to as the game promotion rule. N.M. Code R. §12.2.2 (2014).

North Dakota. As discussed in the North Dakota State Summary of this Guide, it is unclear whether North Dakota permits contests that charge consideration. The North Dakota Attorney General has opined that a contest sponsor may charge monetary consideration as long as the sponsor provides a written disclosure to participants. N.D. Att'y Gen. Op. No. 98-L-132 (Sept. 3, 1998).

Oregon. Contest sponsors that charge consideration must comply with the disclosure and other requirements of Oregon's prize promotion laws and regulations. Or. Admin. R. 137-020-0430 to137-020-0410 to 137-020-0460 (2014).

Rhode Island. When a sponsor offers a contest in conjunction with a sales campaign effort, the contest sponsor must comply with the disclosure and other requirements in the Rhode Island Prizes and Gift Act. R.I. Gen. Laws § 42-61.1-3 (2013).

South Carolina. When a sponsor offers a contest in conjunction with a sales campaign effort, the contest sponsor must comply with the disclosure requirements in the South Carolina Prizes and Gift Act. S.C. Code § 37-15-40 (2014).

Tennessee. Contests charging consideration must comply with the disclosure requirements of Tennessee's prize promotion protections. Tenn. Code § 47-18-124 (2013).

Utah. As discussed in the Utah State Summary of this Guide, it is unclear to what extent Utah's prize promotion law applies to contests charging consideration. Hence, conservative sponsors might want to ensure that any contest with consideration complies with the prize notice disclosure requirements in the Utah Prize Notices Regulation Act. Utah Code § 13-28-1 *et seq.* (2014).

Vermont. Historically, Vermont was one of the few states that prohibited skill-based contests from requiring any kind of entry fee, service charge, purchase or similar consideration. In 2013, Vermont amended its laws to allow sponsors to charge consideration for skill-based contests. Vt. Stat. tit. 09, § 2481x (2013).

Wisconsin. As discussed in the Wisconsin State Summary of this Guide, it is unclear to what extent Wisconsin's prize promotions laws apply to contests charging consideration. Hence, conservative sponsors might want to ensure that any contest with consideration complies with the prize notice disclosure requirements in Wisconsin's Prize Notices statutory provision. Wis. Stat. § 100.171 (2014).

Wyoming. As discussed in the Wyoming State Summary of this Guide, it is unclear to what extent Wyoming's prize promotion laws apply to contests charging consideration. Hence, conservative sponsors might want to ensure that any contest with consideration complies with the prize notice disclosure requirements in Wyoming's laws addressing the Promotional Advertising of Prizes. Wyo. Stat. § 40-12-201 to 40-12-209 (2014).

A.4. Summary of the States' Raffle Laws

In a traditional raffle, the raffle sponsor sells tickets and selects a winning ticket via a random drawing. Hence, raffles have all the elements of a lottery or gambling game. Most states allow non-profit, charitable, and/or civic organizations to offer raffles for fundraising purposes. (Section 9.2 of this Guide)

Section 9.2 of this Guide provides a general discussion of raffles. The state summary of each state includes a more detailed discussion of each state's treatment of raffles.

STATE	ALLOWED	LEGAL AUTHORITY
Alabama	No	Alabama's Constitution as well as its statutory laws prohibit lotteries. Ala. Const. art. IV, § 65; Ala. Code §§ 13A-12-20—13A-12-22 (2013). There are no exceptions for non-profit raffles.
Alaska	Yes	Alaska Stat. § 05.15.010 *et seq.* (2014).
Arizona	Yes	Ariz. Rev. Stat. §13-3302 (2014).
Arkansas	Yes	Ark. Const., amend. no. 84; Ark. Code § 23-114-101 *et seq.* (2013).
California	Yes	Cal. Const., Art. IV § 19, subd. (f); Cal. Penal Code § 320.5 (2014).
Colorado	Yes	Colo. Const. art. XVIII, § 2; Colo. Rev. Stat. §12-9-101 *et seq.* (2013).
Connecticut	Yes	Each municipality decides whether non-profit raffles can be held within its jurisdiction. Conn. Gen. Stat. §§ 7-170 to 7-186 (2013).

STATE	ALLOWED	LEGAL AUTHORITY
Delaware	Yes	Del. Const. art. II, § 17B; Del. Code, tit. 28 § 1501 *et seq.* (2014).
District of Columbia	Yes	D.C. Code § 22-1717 (2013).
Florida	Yes	Fla. Stat . § 849.0935(2) (2013).
Georgia	Yes	Ga. Const. art. I, § II, para. VIII(b); Ga. Code § 16-12-22.1.
Hawaii	No	Gambling and promoting gambling are illegal in Hawaii. Haw. Rev. Stat. §§ 712-1221 to 712-1222, 712-1223 (2014). While there is no statutory exception for non-profit raffles, the Hawaii Attorney General has suggested an informal allowance for raffles offered as part of a charitable event.
Idaho	Yes	Idaho Const. art. III, § 20(1)c; Idaho Stat. § 67-7710(1) (2014).
Illinois	Yes	Ill. Comp. Stat. Ch. 230, § 15/0.01 *et seq.* (2014).
Indiana	Yes	Ind. Code §§ 4-32.2-1-2 and 4-32.2-2-2 (2014).
Iowa	Yes	Iowa Code § 99B.7 (2014).
Kansas	No	Both Kansas' Constitution and statutory laws prohibit lotteries. Kan. Const. art. XV, § 3; Kan. Stat. §§ 21-6403(b), 21-6404, 21-6406 (2013). There is no statutory allowance for non-profit raffles. However, the Sedgwick County District Attorney has suggested that raffles accepting voluntary donations may be permissible.
Kentucky	Yes	Ky. Rev. Stat. § 238.500 (2014).
Louisiana	Yes	LA. Rev. Stat. § 4:701 *et seq.* (2013).
Maine	Yes	Me. Rev. Stat. tit 17, §§ 1831 to 1846 (2014).
Maryland	Yes	Md. Code, Crim. Law. § 12-106 and Title 13 (2013).
Massachusetts	Yes	Mass. Gen. Laws ch. 271, §7A (2014).
Michigan	Yes	Mich. Comp. Laws §§ 432.101 to 432.120 (2014).

STATE	ALLOWED	LEGAL AUTHORITY
Minnesota	Yes	Minn. Stat. § 349.11 *et seq.* (2014).
Mississippi	Yes	Miss. Code § 97-33-51 (2013).
Missouri	Yes	Mo. Const. art. III, § 39(f).
Montana	Yes	Raffles are not restricted to non-profit and charitable organizations. Mont. Code §§ 23-5-112 and 23-5-413 (2014).
Nebraska	Yes	Neb. Rev. Stat. §§ 9-401 to 9-437, 9-501 to 9-513 (2013).
Nevada	Yes	Nev. Const. art. IV, § 24; Nev. Rev. Stat. § 462.015 *et seq.* (2014).
New Hampshire	Yes	N.H. Rev. Stat. § 287-A:2 (2014).
New Jersey	Yes	N.J. Const. art. IV, § VII, para. 2.B; N.J. Stat. §5:8-50 *et seq.* (2014).
New Mexico	Yes	N.M. Stat. Ann.§§ 60-2F-1 to 60-2F-26 (2014).
New York	Yes	Each municipality decides whether to allow raffles. N.Y. Const. art. I, §9.2; N.Y. Gen. Mun. § 185 *et seq.* (2014).
North Carolina	Yes	N.C. Gen. Stat. §14-309.15 (2013).
North Dakota	Yes	N.D. Const. art. XI, § 25; N.D. Cent. Code § 53-06.1-01 *et seq.* (2014).
Ohio	Yes	Ohio Rev. Code § 2915.092 (2014).
Oklahoma	Yes	Okla. Stat. § 21-1051.A.4 (2013).
Oregon	Yes	Or. Const. art. XV, § 4(2); Or. Rev. Stat. § 464.250 *et seq.* (2013).
Pennsylvania	Yes	10 P.S. § 328.101 *et seq.*
Rhode Island	Yes	R.I. Gen. Laws §11-19-30 *et seq.* (2013).
South Carolina	Yes	S.C. Code § 61-2-180 (2014). But constitutionality challenged by S.C. Att'y Gen. *See, e.g.,* S.C. Att'y Gen. Op. (Feb. 18, 2011).
South Dakota	Yes	S.D. Const. art. III, § 25; S.D.C.L. § 22-25-25 (2014).

STATE	ALLOWED	LEGAL AUTHORITY
Tennessee	Yes	Tenn. Const. art. XI, § 5; Tenn. Code § 39-17-101 *et seq.*(2013).
Texas	Yes	Tex. Const. art. III, § 47(d); Tex. Occ. Code §§ 2002.001 to 2002.058 (2013).
Utah	No	Utah Const. art. VI, § 27.
Vermont	Yes	Vt. Stat. tit. 13 , §2143 (2013).
Virginia	Yes	Va. Code § 18.2-340.15 to 18.2-340.37 (2014).
Washington	Yes	Wash. Rev. Code § 9.46.0311 (2014).
West Virginia	Yes	W. Va. Const. art. VI, § 36; W. Va. Code § 47-21-1 *et seq.* (2014).
Wisconsin	Yes	Wis. Const. art. iv, § 24(4); Wis. Stat. § 563.02 *et seq.* (2014).
Wyoming	Yes	Wyo. Stat. § 6-7-101(a)(iii)(H) (2014).

A.5. Summary of the States' Bingo Laws

When people pay to play bingo, the bingo game qualifies as a lottery and/ or as gambling. Many states offer an exception in their anti-gambling laws to allow non-profit organizations and other civic and charitable groups to offer bingo games for fundraising purposes.

Section 9.2 of this Guide provides a general discussion of bingo games. The state summary of each state includes a more detailed discussion of each state's treatment of bingo.

STATE	ALLOWED	LEGAL AUTHORITY
Alabama	Yes	Permitted in some towns and counties pursuant to constitutional amendments.
Alaska	Yes	Alaska Stat. § 05.15.010 *et seq.* (2014).
Arizona	Yes	Ariz. Rev. Stat. § 5-401 *et seq.* (2014).
Arkansas	Yes	Ark. Const., amend. no. 84; Ark. Code § 23-114-101 *et seq.* (2013).
California	Yes.	Cal. Const., art IV, § 19, subd. (c); Cal. Penal Code, § 326.5 (2014).
Colorado	Yes	Colo. Const. art. XVIII, § 2; Colo. Rev. Stat. §12-9-101 *et seq.* (2014).
Connecticut	Yes	Each municipality decides whether non-profit bingo games can be held within its jurisdiction. Conn. Gen. Stat. § 7-169a to 7-169g (2013).
Delaware	Yes	Del. Const. art. II, § 17A; Del. Code, tit. 28 § 1501 *et seq.* (2014).
District of Columbia	Yes	D.C. Code § 22-1717 (2013)
Florida	Yes	Fla. Stat. § 849.0931(2) (2014).
Georgia	Yes	Ga. Const. art. I, § II, para. VIII(b); Ga. Code § 16-12-50 to 16-12-62 (2013).
Hawaii	No	Gambling and promoting gambling are illegal in Hawaii. Haw. Rev. Stat. §§ 712-1221 to 712-1222, 712-1223 (2014). There is no statutory exception for non-profit bingo games.

STATE	ALLOWED	LEGAL AUTHORITY
Idaho	Yes	Idaho Const. art. III, § 20(1)c; Idaho Stat. § 67-7707 (2014).
Illinois	Yes	Ill. Comp. Stat. Ch. 230, § 25/1 *et seq.* (2014).
Indiana	Yes	Ind. Code §§ 4-32.2-1-2 and 4-32.2-2-2 (2014).
Iowa	Yes	Iowa Code § 99B.7 (2014).
Kansas	Yes	Kan. Const. art. XV, § 3a; Kan. Stat. § 79-4701 *et seq.* (2013).
Kentucky	Yes	Ky. Rev. Stat. § 238.500 (2014).
Louisiana	Yes	LA. Rev. Stat. § 4:701 *et seq.* (2013)
Maine	Yes	Me. Rev. Stat. tit 17, §§ 311 to 329 (2014).
Maryland	Yes	Md. Code, Crim. Law, Title 13 (2013).
Massachusetts	Yes	Mass. Gen. Laws ch. 10, §§ 38 to 39A (2014).
Michigan	Yes	Mich. Comp. Laws §§ 432.101 to 432.120 (2014).
Minnesota	Yes	Minn. Stat. § 349.11 *et seq.* (2014).
Mississippi	Yes	Miss. Code §§ 97-33-50 to 97-33-203 (2013).
Missouri	Yes	Mo. Const. art. III, § 39(a); Mo. Rev. Stat. §§ 313.005 to 313.085 (2013).
Montana	Yes	Bingo is not restricted to non-profit and charitable organizations. Mont. Code § 23-5-407 (2014).
Nebraska	Yes	Neb. Rev. Stat. 9-201 to 9-266 (2013).
Nevada	Yes	Nev. Rev. Stat. §§ 463.4091 to 463.40965 (2014).
New Hampshire	Yes	N.H. Rev. Stat. § 287-E:1 *et seq.* (2014).
New Jersey	Yes	N.J. Const. art. IV, § VII, para. 2.A; N.J. Stat. § 5:8-24 *et seq.* (2014).
New Mexico	Yes	N.M. Stat. §§ 60-2F-1 to 60-2F-26 (2014).
New York	Yes	Each municipality decides whether to allow bingo games. N.Y. Const., art. I, § 9.2; N.Y. Gen. Mun. § 475 *et seq.* (2014).
North Carolina	Yes	N.C. Gen. Stat. §§ 14-309.5 to 14-309.14 (2013).
North Dakota	Yes	N.D. Const. art. XI, § 25; N.D. Cent. Code § 53-06.1-01 *et seq.* (2014).

STATE	ALLOWED	LEGAL AUTHORITY
Ohio	Yes	Ohio Const. art. XV, § 6; scattered sections of Chapter 2915 of the Ohio Revised Code.
Oklahoma	Yes	Okla. Stat. §§ 3A-401 to 3A-427 (2013).
Oregon	Yes	Or. Const. art. XV, § 4(2); Or. Rev. Stat. § 464.250 *et seq.* (2013).
Pennsylvania	Yes	10 P.S. §301 *et seq.*
Rhode Island	Yes	R.I. Gen. Laws §11-19-30 *et seq.* (2013).
South Carolina	Yes	S.C. Const. art. XVII, § 7; S.C. Code §12-21-3910 *et seq.*
South Dakota	Yes	S.D. Const. art. III, § 25; S.D.C.L. § 22-25-25 (2014).
Tennessee	No	Tennessee prohibits lotteries and gambling. Tenn. Const. art. XI, § 5; Tenn. Code § 39-17-501 *et seq.* (2013). There is no statutory exception for non-profit bingo games.
Texas	Yes	Tex. Const. art. III, § 47(b); Tex. Occ. Code §§ 2001.001 to 2001.657 (2013).
Utah	No	Utah Const. art. VI, § 27.
Vermont	Yes	Vt. Stat. tit. 13 , §2143 (2013).
Virginia	Yes	Va. Code §§ 18.2-340.15 to 18.2-340.37 (2014).
Washington	Yes	Wash. Rev. Code § 9.46.0311 (2014).
West Virginia	Yes	W. Va. Const. art. VI, § 36; W. Va. Code § 47-20-1 *et seq.*
Wisconsin	Yes	Wis. Const. art. iv, § 24(4); Wis. Stat. § 563.02 *et seq.* (2014).
Wyoming	Yes	Wyo. Stat. § 6-7-101(a)(iii)(D) (2014).

Appendix B
Glossary of Terms

AMOE. *See* **free alternative method of entry**.

any chance test. When evaluating whether chance or skill prevails in a promotion combining elements of both, this test designates the promotion as a chance-based promotion if any element of chance influences the outcome.

best practice. A standard technique or procedure that is effective for achieving a desired result.

bet. Within the context of **gambling**, money or an item of value paid by a person to participate in a gambling game. Also called a stake or wager.

CAN-SPAM Act. For Controlling the Assault of Non-Solicited Pornography and Marketing Act. A federal law that regulates commercial email.

CAPTCHA. For Completely Automated Public Turing test to tell Computers and Humans Apart. A program that provides a challenge question (*e.g.*, a distorted word readable by people but not by computers) to verify that a human being—rather than an automated process—is submitting input to a website or other computer environment.

CDA. For Communications Decency Act. A federal law which includes provisions insulating operators of websites, blogs, and other interactive computer services from liability for defamatory statements posted by their online visitors.

chance. Within the context of promotions law, a method of awarding a prize by a random drawing or other form of random selection.

chance-based promotion. A prize promotion in which the sponsor selects a winner based on a random drawing or other form of random selection. *Contrast* **skill-based promotion**.

citation. A reference to a judicial opinion, statutory provision, or other source material containing information needed for locating such source material.

click-wrap agreement. An agreement presented online to which a person manifests his consent by clicking an 'accept' button, checking off a box, or taking a similar action while online.

commercial co-venture. A collaboration between a charitable organization and a for-profit business designed to benefit both the charitable organization and the business.

Communications Decency Act. *See* **CDA**.

compulsory license. Within the context of copyright law, authorization to use copyrighted material pursuant to terms and fees set forth in or pursuant to the Copyright Act. When a compulsory license is available, there is no need to acquire direct permission from or negotiate license terms with the owner of the material. Compulsory licenses offered through the Copyright Act include a **mechanical license** in a song. Also called statutory license.

consideration. Within the context of promotions, money, effort, or an item of value expended by a person for the opportunity to compete for a prize.

copyright. Legal rights in a literary or artistic work or other original work of authorship giving the creator of such work the exclusive right to reproduce, distribute, prepare a derivative work of, publicly perform and publicly display the work.

copyright fair use. A limited exception to a copyright owner's exclusive rights allowing a person other than the copyright owner to use a reasonable portion of the copyrighted work without the permission of the copyright owner.

counter notice. Within the context of the DMCA, a written document requesting the re-posting of material removed from a website as the result of an improper **takedown notice**.

Creative Commons license. Free documentation that copyright owners may use to grant others permission to use their works in a manner that relaxes many of the copyright exclusive rights without placing the work in the public domain.

defamation. The act of making a false statement about a person which statement damages the person's reputation.

Digital Millennium Copyright Act. *See* DMCA.

DMCA. For Digital Millennium Copyright Act. A federal law that amended the Copyright Act for the purposes of conforming United States law to various treaty obligations and addressing issues raised by emerging digital technologies. The law's provisions include safe harbors that insulate the operators of online sites from claims of copyright infringement for material posted by their customers and online visitors.

dominant factor doctrine. When evaluating whether chance or skill prevails in a promotion combining elements of both, this test designates the promotion as a chance-based promotion if chance dominates the selection of the winner, even though skill or judgment may impact winner selection to some degree.

Do Not Call Registry. A list, managed and enforced by the **Federal Trade Commission**, with the phone numbers of consumers who have indicated their preference not to receive telemarketing calls.

equal dignity rule. Within the context of a sweepstakes promotion, the requirement that persons who receive sweepstakes-playing opportunities without making a purchase have the same odds of winning a prize as persons who receive the sweepstakes-playing opportunity as part of a product or service purchase.

express license. A license which is granted in direct, explicit, and unambiguous terms. *Contrast* **implied license**.

fair use. *See* **copyright fair use** and **trademark fair use**.

fantasy prize. An award that has potential great value to a promotion winner even though the award has no specific quantifiable dollar value (*e.g.*, meeting a celebrity).

FCC. For Federal Communications Commission. A federal government agency that regulates interstate and international communications by radio, television, wire, satellite and cable.

Federal Communications Commission. *See* **FCC**.

Federal Trade Commission. See **FTC**.

Federal Trade Commission Act. See **FTC Act**.

forward to a friend. *See* **refer a friend promotion**.

free alternative method of entry. A means by which a person can participate in a sweepstakes without making a purchase. Typically required by federal and/or state law for a sweepstakes in which the sponsor distributes opportunities to play with the purchase of a product or service (*i.e.*, an **in-package sweepstakes**). Also called free alternate means of entry or AMOE.

friending. Within the context of a **social media network**, a method of connecting to another person's or organization's social media account or presence.

FTC. For Federal Trade Commission. A federal government agency that issues and enforces regulations designed to prevent business practices that are anticompetitive or deceptive or unfair to consumers.

FTC Act. For Federal Trade Commission Act. A federal law that created and empowers the Federal Trade Commission.

gambling. Making a **bet** for the opportunity to win money, a **reward**, or something of value where winning is dependent upon chance, upon the exercise of skill, or upon the transpiring of some unknown event. Also called gaming.

gaming. *See* **gambling**.

giveaway. A gift or something of value given to all individuals who take a specific action such as attending a sales presentation.

implied license. A license which is presumed to be granted as a result of the conduct of the person authorized to grant the license. *Contrast* **express license**.

indemnification. Responsibility to reimburse a person for loss or harm the person suffers.

in-package sweepstakes. A chance-based prize-winning opportunity that comes as an incidental component of a product or service purchase.

intellectual property. Creations of the mind such as literary and artistic works and inventions. Intellectual property is protected by copyright, trademark, patent, trade secret, and similar laws. Often abbreviated to ip.

Kraft clause. A provision commonly included in sweepstakes rules that provides the sponsor with solutions for resolving problems (*e.g.*, awarding too many prizes) caused by printing errors or other mistake.

like or liking. Within the context of a **social media network**, a method of connecting to, supporting, or showing approval of another person's or organization's social media account or presence.

like-gating. Restricting information, products, and promotion-partici-pating opportunities to those people who like or otherwise connect to the social media account of the organization offering the opportunities.

lottery. A game or scheme in which people pay money or something of value (*i.e.*, **consideration**) for the opportunity to win a prize that is distributed by **chance**.

master use license. Authorization from the copyright owner or his agent to use the sound recording of a song (typically within a motion picture, television program, or other audio-visual production).

material element test. When evaluating whether chance or skill prevails in a promotion combining elements of both, this test designates the promotion as a chance-based promotion if chance is an essential or important (*i.e.*, material) component in the selection of a winner—even if chance does not dominate the selection of the winner as in the **dominant factor doctrine**.

mechanical license. Authorization from the copyright owner or his agent or through a **compulsory license** to make and distribute recordings of a song.

non-exclusive. Within the context of licensing, a type of license that allows the grantor of the license to grant the same rights to other people.

patent. A property right for an invention that allows one to exclude others from making, using, offering for sale, selling, or importing the invention within the country issuing the patent.

privacy rights. A person's right to be left alone and right to have others stay out of his personal affairs.

prize notice. A written communication to a consumer informing the consumer that the consumer has won or is eligible to receive a prize or gift.

prize promotion laws. Federal and state laws that impose requirements and prohibitions on sponsors offering sweepstakes, contests, giveaways, and other prize-winning opportunities. Prize promotion laws often govern only those promotions that are offered by direct mail or telephone solicitation, that are offered in conjunction with a company sales campaign, and/or that require consumers to pay money or other consideration.

public performance license. Authorization from a copyright owner or his agent to perform a copyrighted work publicly.

publicity rights. The exclusive rights of every person to control and profit from the commercial use of his identity. A person's identity includes his unique characteristics including his name, likeness, and voice.

pure chance test. When evaluating whether chance or skill prevails in a promotion combining elements of both, this test designates the promotion as a chance-based promotion if chance completely controls selection of the winner and the participants' skill has no impact in the determination of the winner.

qualified organization. Term used by many state laws as reference to an organization eligible under the state's laws to offer non-profit raffles, bingo games, and gambling.

raffle. A type of **lottery** in which participants purchase numbered tickets, one or more of the tickets are drawn randomly, and the purchasers of the randomly selected tickets win a prize.

refer a friend promotion. A marketing method in which companies encourage consumers to share the company's messages and offers with the consumers' acquaintances. Also called forward to a friend and send to a friend.

release. Within the context of **rights clearance**, permission to incorporate a person (*i.e.*, the person's image, name, voice, *etc.*) or protected materials (*e.g.*, music, artwork) into a media production. Also called consent, clearance, license, or permission.

reward. Money or something of value awarded to the winner of a **gambling** game.

right of privacy. *See* **privacy rights**.

right of publicity. *See* **publicity rights**.

rights clearance. Within the context of entertainment, media, and advertising, the process of verifying that a media production contains no material that violates any laws or any persons' rights as well as the process of acquiring any necessary licenses or **releases**.

SAG-AFTRA. For Screen Actors Guild-American Federation of Television and Radio Artists. A labor union representing film, television, and radio performers.

send to a friend. See **refer a friend promotion**.

skill-based promotion. A promotion in which the sponsor selects a winner based on an evaluation of participants' knowledge, ability, and/or skills. *Contrast* **chance-based promotion**.

social media network. An online community of people who share common interests and activities. Also called social networking site.

sound recording. The recorded performance of a song.

sponsor. As used in this Guide, a company, organization, or person offering a contest, sweepstakes, or other promotion.

stake. *See* **bet**.

synchronization license. Authorization from a copyright owner or its agent to use a song within a motion picture, television program, or other audio-visual production. Also called synch license.

takedown notice. Within the context of the **DMCA**, a written request to remove from a website material that infringes the requestor's copyright.

TCPA. For Telephone Consumer Protection Act. A federal law designed to protect consumers from annoying and deceptive telemarketing practices.

Telephone Consumer Protection Act. *See* **TCPA**.

terms of service. The rules issued by a website, social media network, or other internet platform that govern one's use of the website, network, or platform. Also called terms of use.

terms of use. *See* **terms of service**.

trademark. A word, phrase, logo, graphic symbol, design, sound, shape, color, smell, or combinations thereof that identify and distinguish the source of a specific good or service.

trademark fair use. The right to use a trademark to refer to the trademark owner's goods or services as well as the right to use a trademark within its common English-language meaning (*e.g.*, even though Apple Computer owns a registered trademark for APPLE, one may still use the term "apple" to describe apple sauce, an apple orchard, or apple juice).

trade secret. A type of **intellectual property** consisting of the confidential information of a particular company that gives the company a competitive advantage over other companies.

user generated content. Content that is produced by everyday people as opposed to content produced by the mainstream, traditional media.

virtual currency. Digital money issued by and used within social media networks, online game environments, and other internet communities.

virtual goods. Images of objects used within social media networks, online game environments, and other internet communities.

wager. *See* **bet.**

work made for hire. In the context of copyright law, a work prepared by an employee as part of his job or a work prepared by a freelancer under certain conditions. Copyright law views the employer or the person commissioning the work as the author or creator of a work made for hire.

Index

(This index includes entries primarily from Part One, Introduction and Part Two, Overview. With some limited exceptions, this index does not include entries from Part Three, Summaries of State Laws or from the Appendices. Each separate state summary has a discussion of contests, sweepstakes, lotteries, gambling, registration and bonding requirements (where applicable), chance-skill determinations, consideration, prize notice laws, bingo, and raffles.)

About the Author

Joy R. Butler assists contests and sweepstakes sponsors as part of her transactional and advisory law firm practice. As a transactional business lawyer, Ms. Butler also works on matters involving commercial licensing, copyright, media productions, private equity financing, and company sales.

Other books she has authored include *The Permission Seeker's Guide Through the Legal Jungle: Clearing Copyrights, Trademarks and Other Rights for Entertainment and Media Productions* as well as *The Cyber Citizen's Guide Through the Legal Jungle: Internet Law for Your Professional Online Presence.*

Ms. Butler has a law degree from Harvard Law School and a B.A. degree in economics from Harvard College. She can be contacted through the website: www.joybutler.com

CPSIA information can be obtained
at www.ICGtesting.com
Printed in the USA
BVOW06*0914310317
479792BV00004B/11/P